# THE MAKING OF
# STAR TREK
# DEEP SPACE NINE®

# THE MAKING OF
# STAR TREK
# DEEP SPACE NINE®

## JUDITH & GARFIELD
## REEVES-STEVENS

POCKET BOOKS

New York   London   Toronto   Sydney   Tokyo   Singapore

An *Original* Publication of POCKET BOOKS

POCKET BOOKS, a division of Simon & Schuster Inc.
1230 Avenue of the Americas, New York, NY 10020

Copyright © 1994 by Paramount Pictures. All Rights Reserved.

STAR TREK is a Registered Trademark of
Paramount Pictures.

This book is published by Pocket Books, a division of Simon &
Schuster Inc., under exclusive license from Paramount Pictures.

All rights reserved, including the right to reproduce
this book or portions thereof in any form whatsoever.
For information address Pocket Books, 1230 Avenue
of the Americas, New York, NY 10020

Library of Congress Catalog Card Number: 94-68299
ISBN: 0-671-87430-6

*Book design by Richard Oriolo*

First Pocket Books trade paperback printing December 1994

10 9 8 7 6 5 4 3 2 1

POCKET and colophon are registered trademarks of
Simon & Schuster Inc.

Printed in the U.S.A.

*For*
*"Stephen E. Whitfield"*
*—who did it first,*
*and inspired a generation on his own.*

# Contents

# Introduction: How Dare We?

*It never hurts to suck up to the boss.*

—The 33rd Rule of Acquisition

**A**s an executive producer[1] and writer for three television series and a feature film, all in various stages of development and production, Rick Berman works more in a single day than most people do in a week. Which is why it's no surprise that he doesn't have a lot of use for small talk.

It's also why the first time we met with him to talk about *Deep Space Nine*, in February 1993, he got straight to the point. We had barely settled on the couch in his office, pens and yellow legal pads not even in our hands, when he said to us, "I've just spent a year and a half of my life bringing this show to life—how dare you come in here and ask me to talk about it in twenty minutes."

He wasn't joking, either. He was genuinely annoyed.

If we *had* been in his office for the reason he thought we were, he'd have every right to feel that way, too. But that wasn't why we were there, and we quickly tried to set the record straight.

That first meeting we had requested with Berman was not so much to talk about *Deep Space Nine* as to introduce ourselves and the project we had been assigned by our publisher. The twenty minutes of his time we had asked for and graciously been given were, we knew, pure gold in the life of a person whose days are scheduled minute by minute, often with millions of dollars riding on each decision he makes.[2] In fact, the most precious quantity in television production *is* time—there's never

[1] See Appendix I for a complete description of job titles and functions for everyone listed in the credits of the *Deep Space Nine* pilot episode.

[2] At the time, Berman was involved with up to eleven different episodes of *The Next Generation* and *Deep Space Nine* on any given day, in addition to developing *Voyager* and handling the preproduction of the seventh Star Trek feature, STAR TREK: GENERATIONS. As one of the illustrations for the Introduction, we asked Berman's assistant, Kristine Fernandes, if we could have a copy of his printed itinerary for a typical day to reproduce here. Fernandes explained that Berman's schedule changed so frequently that there was no point in ever having a printed version. Instead, it was recorded in pencil in his daybook, and on a dry-erase board outside his office, so it could be updated throughout the day.

**WELCOME TO REPLIMAT**

Replimat is well known for its wide varieties of exotic culinary delights

**WE'VE SEARCHED THE GALAXY**

From the blistering plains of Vulcan's Anvil to the cool and scintillating delicacies of exotic Risa

**REPLIMAT HAS WORKED HARD**

To delight your discriminating palate So relax and enjoy the pleasures of Replimat, The Restaurant at the End of the Galaxy

● **MAY WE SUGGEST** ●

*Wonderful Kohlanese stew simmered to perfection and served with steamed Azna*

*Ferengi Tube Grubs chilled just so, a wonderful complement to our famous Stardrifter*

*And an extra special dessert ... I' danian Spice Pudding*

enough of it, and what little there is is atrociously expensive. Yet here we were, two writers who had been foisted on him by Pocket Books, asking not only for his time, but for time from every single member of the *Deep Space Nine* crew, from stagehand to actor to visual-effects artist.

How dare we indeed.

But we had, we felt, a good reason for asking for all that we did—the book now in your hands: a chronicle not so much about the dry, technical end of television production, but about how and why creative decisions are made in the development and ongoing production of an hour-long, episodic dramatic television series.

Twenty-six years ago, Stephen E. Whitfield, working with Gene Roddenberry, wrote *The Making of Star Trek*—a journal of how the original STAR TREK series came to be. It is a true classic of its kind. Not just as a chronicle of the beginning of what was to become an unprecedented, *billion-dollar* entertainment franchise, and not just as a behind-the-scenes trove of trivia for die-hard STAR TREK fans, but as a fascinating account of the creative reality of weekly television series production in the 1960s.

Our brash presumption was not in asking for Rick Berman to reduce eighteen months of his trials and tribulations to twenty minutes, it was that we thought we could write such a book for the 1990s.

When we made that clear, Rick Berman relaxed, and we actually spoke with him for *thirty* minutes, not only about *Deep Space Nine,* but about Paramount, and the future of television, and actors, and executives, and the thirteen key months between November 1991 and December 1992, when a brand-new television series arose from a simple request from Paramount executives to become a ratings *and* a critical success.

When we walked out the door after that meeting, we went with Rick Berman's blessing. A week later we had his fellow executive producer and co-creator Michael Piller's as well.

For the next year, we had complete access to the entire *Deep Space Nine* production. We sat in on story-development sessions with the writing staff, took a 6 A.M. makeup call with Armin Shimerman, sat behind the camera in the Replimat as Odo and Quark were filmed at the next table, and wandered the Cardassian corridors of a space station to talk to the video technicians and sound engineers hiding behind the scenes.

We sat in Sisko's quarters and dodged quickly moving stagehands, watched dailies with the producers, talked with the actors in their trailers and on the sets, watched as phaser blasts were painstakingly added to a scene, frame by frame, on complex, multiscreened computer equipment that resembled what we'd expect to see on the *U.S.S. Enterprise*.

We watched props being made and repaired, heard music being scored, saw the real Deep Space Nine bolted to a motion-control rig as technicians programmed intricate camera moves around it.

We talked to programming executives, sat in on production meetings, read draft after draft of scripts to see how changes—both subtle and profound—were crafted into each week's story.

We watched potentially troublesome scenes transformed by a film editor's skill and artistry. We saw undetected flaws corrected by state-of-the-art computer graphics programs, and saw a rough Odo morphing sequence transformed into a smooth and haunting one, hours before the footage was to be shipped as a trailer for the next week's show.

And through it all, on set, in trailers, in offices on the Paramount lot or in those of outside suppliers, not one person refused to answer our questions, not one person didn't carve out a few precious moments to share with us his or her contributions to the series.

In fact, throughout the entire year we spent with the cast and crew of STAR TREK: DEEP SPACE NINE, the only complaint we heard was from supervising producer David Livingston, who told us we had more access to the postproduction of a particular episode he had directed than he had!

This kindness we were shown, the patience with which our often naïve questions were answered, the advice we were given to explore other aspects of the production we hadn't originally considered—this universal generosity with which we were treated will remain the high point of our visit to the world of *Deep Space Nine*.

At first we were puzzled that access was so easy—the few television productions we had seen before were usually grim races against the clock. But as the months went on and our interviews mounted, we began to see a pattern to the way we were treated.

The Hollywood sign as seen from the Paramount lot—the only major feature-film and television production facility still located in Hollywood.

There was pride, of course. Whether one is a STAR TREK or science-fiction fan or not, there is no doubt that *Deep Space Nine*, with STAR TREK: THE NEXT GENERATION, is among the best produced series on television, either network or syndicated. Quite rightly, all the people involved with the show are therefore pleased to see that their contributions are acknowledged.

But pride wasn't all of it. Neither was it a case of simply going along with a request from the executive producers to be nice to "the book writers."

Instead, at the core of the open reception we unfailingly received was what Rick Berman had said to us in the very first words of that very first meeting—"I just spent a year and a half of my life . . ."

The production of a one-hour dramatic television series like *Deep Space Nine* is not a nine-to-five job. It is an all-consuming mission, sometimes involving sixteen-hour days, sometimes twenty-four-hour days, and always demanding total dedication.

So the cast and crew of *Deep Space Nine* weren't just allowing us a glimpse of their jobs or a chance to watch them at work—they were inviting us to share their lives. When we went to their offices, or their cubicles, or their trailers, or their stages, we were entering their homes. When we were introduced to their coworkers, we were being introduced to their families and friends.

And when we, and millions of others, view the end result of their labors—thousands of hours and more than a million dollars' worth—distilled down to forty-two minutes and thirty seconds of *Deep Space Nine* each week, we're not looking at a product, we're sharing the lives of the almost two hundred people who have pushed themselves creatively and physically to make something more meaningful than just some pretty pictures designed to lull viewers into watching commercials.

The technical details of production you're about to read will hold true, more or less, for almost any one-hour dramatic series now being made for television. But the emotional details are, we think, unique to the team spirit that pervades the *Deep Space Nine* production.

It might be nice to think that this strong sense of family and common purpose is a reflection of the optimistic ideals Gene Roddenberry originally brought to STAR TREK in all its forms. Perhaps, in some way, it is.

But, as far as we can tell, the camaraderie, the drive for perfection, and the shared dedication of the *Deep Space Nine* production clearly derives from the two people who created the series and put the team together—Rick Berman and Michael Piller. The organization they have assembled is, like all great ventures, a reflection of their own personal styles, a mirror of the way they have approached their work—their life.

We thank them for allowing us to share that life with us. We hope the year we spent watching from the sidelines has resulted in a journal that does justice to their accomplishments and those of their team.

For a list of everyone we'd like to thank in addition to Berman and Piller, we invite everyone to read the credits on the next episode of *Deep Space Nine.* Whether it was a succinct answer to a quick question as we passed in the hall, or an informal conversation over lunch in the Paramount commissary, more people contributed to this book than we have room to list here, though many of their names will appear throughout these pages. There were a few people, though, whose ongoing work with us was truly above and beyond any help we had hoped for in even our most optimistic expectations. They are special-effects coordinator Laura Lang-Matz, who enthusiastically guided us through the labyrinth of postproduction; film editor Dick Rabjohn, who opened our eyes to an artistic process that few people realize they watch each week—we hope this book will open even more eyes; production designer Herman Zimmerman, who ransacked his files for the production art included here and provided many thoughtful insights on the underlying themes of Gene Roddenberry's Star Trek; longtime STAR TREK illustrator, designer, and technical consultant Rick Sternbach, for providing us with the richly detailed history of Cardassian space station design that appears in this book; STAR TREK mavens Mike Okuda and Denise Okuda, who showed us a world *behind* behind–the–scenes; the *Deep Space Nine* Art Department crew, including Jim Martin and Doug Drexler; story editor Robert Hewitt Wolfe, who bravely allowed his work to be scrutinized at far too many stages; script coordinator Lolita Fatjo, who opened all the episode files to us; and supervising producer David Livingston, for kindly donating his shooting-script sketches for "In the Hands of the Prophets," and for annotating the "earthquake" call sheet on page 4. Livingston's days are as tightly scheduled as Rick Berman's, and we greatly appreciate his patience, generosity, and good humor.

In addition, we have to thank Livingston's assistant, Cheryl Gluckstern, who took the set-construction photos long before she even knew about this book; STAR TREK

**TELEVISION CALL SHEET**

| | |
|---|---|
| Production Number 011-40511-721 | Day TUESDAY    Date AUGUST 18, 1992 |
| Production Name "STAR TREK: DEEP SPACE NINE" | 1  Day out of  22  Days |
| Producer BERMAN/PILLER | Crew Call 7A |
| Director DAVID CARSON | Shooting Call 7:30A |
| Episode "EMISSARY" | Rehearsal/Leave Call |
| | LUNCH: 1p-2p |
| PRODUCTION OFFICE: (213) 956-8818 | Location STAGE 4 |

**SCHEDULE**

| SET & SET | SCENES | CAST | D/N | PAGES | LOCATION |
|---|---|---|---|---|---|
| INT OPS | 30, 31pt | 1, 2, 3, Atmos | D-1 | 1 3/8 | STAGE 4 |
| INT BAJOR OFFICE | 31pt, 30pt | 9A | D-1 | 1/8 | |
| INT COMMANDERS OFFICE | 32pt | 1, 2, 3, Atmos | D-1 | 2 5/8 | |
| INT COMMANDERS OFFICE | 90pt | 1, 2 (V.O.), 23A, A | D-4 | 3/8 | |
| INT UNIVERSITY ON EARTH | 90pt | 23A | D-4 | 1/8 | |
| INT OPS | 91 | 1, 2, 3, 12 (V.O.), A | D-4 | 4/8 | ✓ |

✱ NOTE: VIDEO CREW: SHOOT VARIOUS ANGLES OF OPS F/ "SECURITY" MONITORS
NOTE:
POSSIBLE WATER BASE SMOKE ATMOS ON STAGE — LIGHT CRACK LEVEL

✓ = Minors over 18   ✱ = ND BREAKFAST   **TALENT**   TOTAL PAGES - 5 1/8

| CAST AND DAY PLAYERS | ROLE | MAKE-UP/LEAVE | SET CALL | REMARKS |
|---|---|---|---|---|
| 1. AVERY BROOKS (N) | SISKO | ✱ 6A | 7A | RPT TO MU |
| 2. NANA VISITOR (N) | KIRA | ✱ 4:45A | 7A | |
| 3. COLM MEANEY (N) | O'BRIEN | ✱ 6A | 7A | |
| 9A GENE ARMOR (W/F) | BAJORAN OFFICIAL | 5A | 7A | |
| 23A. JOHN CARTER (W/F) | CHANCELLOR | 11A | 2p | ✓ |

~~HAPPY LIFT-OFF!~~

GOOD LUCK!

NOTES:   (1)  ALL CALLS SUBJECT TO CHANGE BY A.D.   (2)  NO FORCED CALLS WITHOUT A.D./U.P.M.
APPROVAL.   (3)  CLOSED SET - NO VISITORS WITHOUT CLEARANCE FROM PRODUCTION OFFICE.
(4)  NO SMOKING, FOOD OR DRINKS ON SET, NO SMOKING ON STAGES.   (5)  DO NOT LEAN ON
OR TOUCH WALLS ON SET.

| ATMOSPHERE AND STANDINS | SPECIAL INSTRUCTIONS |
|---|---|
| 3 SI (JW. ANDREA PFLUG) RPT TO ST4 @ 7A | SFX: SMOKE, TURBO & DOORS WORK, VFX: MONITORS, BURN |
| ATMOS: 3 M STARFLEET              6:30A | IN (32pt), B.S. |
| NOB 1 F STARFLEET              6A | |
| ✱ 3 F BAJORANS IN 5AM BKKFST 6:30-7 RDY 7:30 | |
| ✱ 2 M BAJORANS IN 5:30 BKKFST 5:30-7 | |
| NOB 1 M BAJORAN IN 6A | |
| STANDINS?   SPECIAL INSTRUCTIONS | |
| GRIP/ELEC: ABRA CRANE? 2 SETS LIT F/ LIVE FEED, STARFIELD, B.S. | |
| CAMERA: LIVE FEED VIDEO (31pt, 90pt), BURN-IN, LOCK-OFF (32pt) | |

**ADVANCE SHOOTING NOTES**

| SHOOTING DATE | PAGE | SET NAME | LOC | CAST | D3R SCENE NUMBER |
|---|---|---|---|---|---|
| WEDNESDAY 8-19-92 | 5 1/8 | INT OPS / INT OPS / INT OPS | ST.4 | 1 (VO), 2, 3, 6, A / 3, A / 3, A | 108, 110, 113, 114, 118, 124, 128 / ✱ 189, 191, 195, 197 / 219pt, 220pt |
| | | | | ✱ NOTE ORDER CHANGE | |
| THURSDAY 8-20-92 | | INT AIRLOCK / INT SISKO'S QUARTERS / INT SISKO'S/JAKE'S QTRS / INT COMMANDER'S OFFICE | ST.4 | 1, 3, 8, A / 1, 3, 8 / 1, 2 (V.O.), 8 / 1, 12, A | 23 / 39 / 66, 67 / 94 |

| | | | |
|---|---|---|---|
| SPVR PROD:  D. LIVINGSTON | PHONE: 4879 | | OZOLS-GRAHAM / CAZANJIAN |
| UNIT PROD. MGR.:  B. DELLA SANTINA | PHONE: 8818 | ASST. DIR.: | BAXTER / MATLOVSKY |
| PROD. DESIGNER:  H. ZIMMERMAN | PHONE: 5606 | | |
| ART DIRECTOR:  R. McILVAIN | PHONE: 8547 | SET DECORATOR:  T. ROYSDEN | PHONE: 5250 |

Issued by: Operations Date          Time          Approved by

FORM NO. PP 820 Rev. '89

---

*It doesn't have a logo and the
stars' names are handwritten, but
this is the call sheet that
launched Deep Space Nine.
If you're wondering who
the Chancellor was, see
Chapter 13.*

set photographer Robbie Robinson, who stalked the sets on our behalf for many of the never-before-published pictures on these pages; Paula Block of Viacom Consumer Products, who kept the photos coming and always knew who we should call to obtain that "last" hard-to-get shot—all twenty of them; and, especially, Diane Castro, Loree McBride, and Jennifer Kissell of the public-relations firm Bender, Goldman & Helper, who we know made incredible sacrifices in their own impossible schedules to make sure we had access to the sets and stars of *Deep Space Nine*.

Off the Paramount lot, we're indebted to Tom Barron and the crew at his company, Image G, for the amazingly free access they granted us to their state-of-the-art motion-control studio. We're especially grateful to Tim Stell, who coordinated all our photography requests, and to Chris Schnitzer, who cheerfully opened up crates and rearranged models for us.

A final, heartfelt word of thanks is due Kevin Ryan, our editor at Pocket Books, for suggesting this project, and for his unwavering enthusiasm, support, and creativity. He has made an already great assignment a joy to work on.

In any chronicle of this nature, based on the recollections of so many people working under such intense time pressure, it was inevitable that we would come across certain interpretations of events for which different people shared different memories. In these cases, where we felt it was important to our narrative, we attempted to arrive at a consensus opinion among the people involved of how events unfolded and decisions were arrived at. In some cases, such a consensus was impossible, because some decisions that may have had a profound influence on the development of *Deep Space Nine* were made on the fly, as part of an endless series of sixteen-hour days, and at the time there was no special reason for noting when they were made or who made them. In other cases, we arrived at our own interpretation based on all the material available to us, sometimes at variance with other published accounts. Undoubtedly, we have made errors that arise solely from our own work and not the contributions of the many who helped us. We apologize for these in advance, hope that they are minor, and invite any comments that might lead to revisions in future editions of this book, especially where we might have failed to give proper credit where credit is due.

Twenty-six years ago, Stephen Whitfield wrote in his introduction to *The Making of Star Trek*, ". . . the STAR TREK group is indeed a truly unique group of people, perhaps like no other group in the world. This is as it should be. STAR TREK is a unique show, like no other in the world."

Despite all the technological change that has occurred in television production over the past quarter-century, that statement is still as true today about this latest incarnation of STAR TREK as it was about the first.

As for another of Stephen Whitfield's observations, "Anyone who wants to produce a television series (particularly one as complex as STAR TREK) has to be (1) a genius, and (2) completely out of his mind," we agree with (1) and make no comment about (2). After all, *Star Trek: Voyager* is in preproduction as we write this, and there's probably a book to be written about that series, too. . . .

J & G Reeves-Stevens
*June 1994*

# THE FUNNIEST

# JOKE IN THE

# UNIVERSE

*You will be assimilated.*
*Resistance is futile.*

—Picard/Locutus

T he quote with which this chapter begins was the first dialogue spoken in
"Emissary," the pilot episode of *Deep Space Nine*. In this story, Picard's
threat referred to the fate of those conquered by the Borg—an alien race in
which each individual was linked into a single collective consciousness. It's a good
science-fiction idea, but it's an even better metaphor for the collective effort required
in the making of a television series. As an example, let's turn to some other lines of
dialogue that were spoken for the camera during the filming of that pilot, words that
aren't quite as well known as Picard's threat, because they were never in the script.
In case you missed them, they told the funniest joke in the universe. It went like this:

**Biblism finger fink. Obligatory quotient joke fellow. Coconut concertina**
**cosmological argument. Banks fall fish story. Inculpate minuteman! Stress**
**certify lecithin? Hard-hearted dill, I domineer mindreader sextuple**
**garden fly honeysuckle garbage poultry rimfire?! GREENPEACE!! Change**
**is the ultimate solution.**

Well, perhaps it does lose something in the translation. But the story behind those
words—where they came from, who said them and why, and what happened to them
in the final version of the pilot episode—is in miniature the story of the making of the
*Deep Space Nine* television series, an intensely collaborative, relentlessly chaotic,
and exceptionally creative process involving close to two hundred people and more
than $30 million each season. And since that story is the purpose of this book, let's
begin by seeing how the funniest joke in the universe came to be.

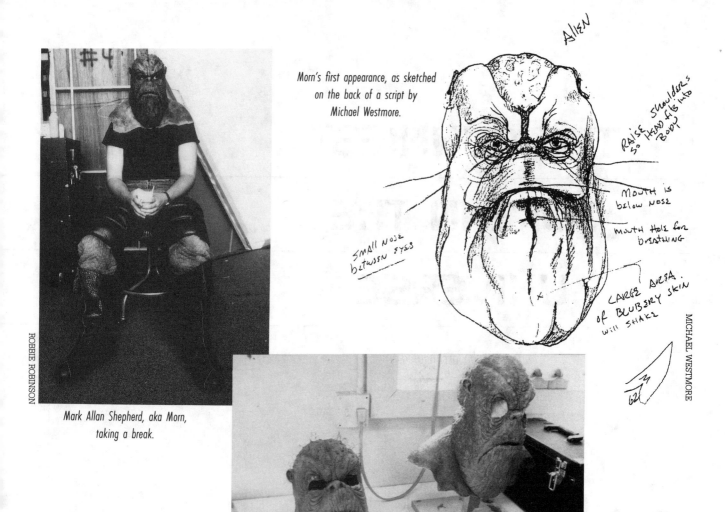

ROBBIE ROBINSON

Mark Allan Shepherd, aka Morn,
taking a break.

Morn's first appearance, as sketched
on the back of a script by
Michael Westmore.

ALIEN

RAISE SHOULDERS
SO HEAD FITS INTO
BODY

SMALL NOSE
BETWEEN EYES

MOUTH IS
BELOW NOSE

MOUTH HOLE FOR
BREATHING

LARGE AREA
OF BLUBBERY SKIN
WILL SHAKE

MICHAEL WESTMORE

New Morns under construction in
Michael Westmore's studio.

ROBBIE ROBINSON

First of all, the joke in question was told by a semiregular, though little-known, member of the *Deep Space Nine* ensemble cast. At the time the pilot was made—during August and September of 1992—the character had no name. On set, he was simply referred to as the "Grinch"—a big, bulky alien with a deeply lined, chinless face, intended to be one of the regulars seen hanging around the Promenade bar known as Quark's place in the pilot. But, after a few more episodes were shot and *Deep Space Nine* went from being the sole creation of its producers, writers, actors, and production team, and became a shared reality for millions of dedicated viewers, the alien acquired a name—Morn, the Lurian. According to some, the name was chosen in homage to another large, regular character who hung around another bar on the Paramount lot—Norm of *Cheers.*

The setting for Morn's joke was Quark's place itself, a permanent set on the multilevel Promenade of the *Deep Space Nine* space station, occupying Stage 17 of the Paramount lot. One of the first mentions of this important hub of life on board the station appears in an initial description of the series—called a "bible"—written by Rick Berman and Michael Piller, and dated April 8, 1992.

DEEP SPACE: "Emissary" REV. FINAL 8/10/92 - TEASER

DEEP SPACE NINE

"Emissary"

TEASER

FADE IN:

1    WHITE LETTERS ON BLACK:                                              1

On Stardate 43997, Captain Jean-
Luc Picard of the Federation
Starship Enterprise was kidnapped
for six days by an invading force
known as the Borg.  Surgically
altered, he was forced to lead
an assault on Starfleet at WOLF
359.                              FADE TO BLACK.

After a beat:
                    PICARD/LOCUTUS (V.O.)
You will be assimilated.
Resistance is futile.
                                  HARD CUT TO:
                                                                         2

2    CLOSE UP OF LOCUTUS (VIEWSCREEN) (OPTICAL)
                    PICARD/LOCUTUS
You will disarm all weapons and
escort us to sector zero zero one.
If you attempt to intervene, we
will destroy you.

3    REVERSE ANGLE - INT. BRIDGE - THE SARATOGA (OPTICALL)              3

A Battle Bridge... a male Vulcan Captain, a burly male
Bolian tactical officer (Lieutenant rank), female
humans at Con and Ops (Ensign rank)... our primary
attention is on Lieutenant Commander BENJAMIN SISKO,
the first officer, a rugged, charismatic man in his
late thirties... they react to the viewscreen
pronouncement... Sisko is monitoring signals on a
panel...
                    SISKO
Sir, Admiral Hanson has deployed
the Gage, the Kyushu and the
Melbourne...
                                  (CONTINUED)

*The first page of the first episode.*

*The music in Quark's place was eventually seen to be coming from this alien construction, originally described in an early draft of the pilot script as "a strange triple keyboard," now described only as "a strange instrument."*

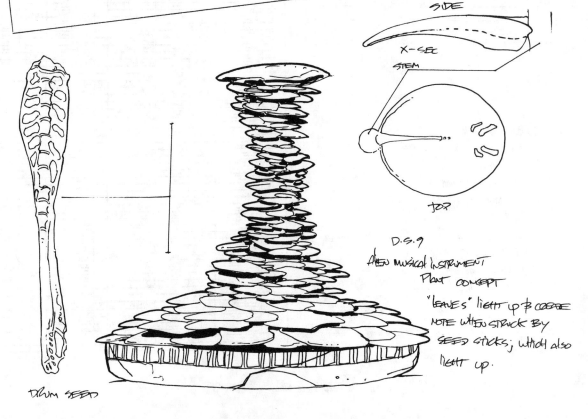

DRUM SEED

SIDE

X-SEC

STEM

TOP

D.S.9
ALIEN MUSICAL INSTRUMENT
PLANT CONCEPT
"LEAVES" LIGHT UP ‡ COERTE
NOTE WHEN STRUCK BY
SEED STICKS; WHICH ALSO
LIGHT UP.

RICARDO DELGADO

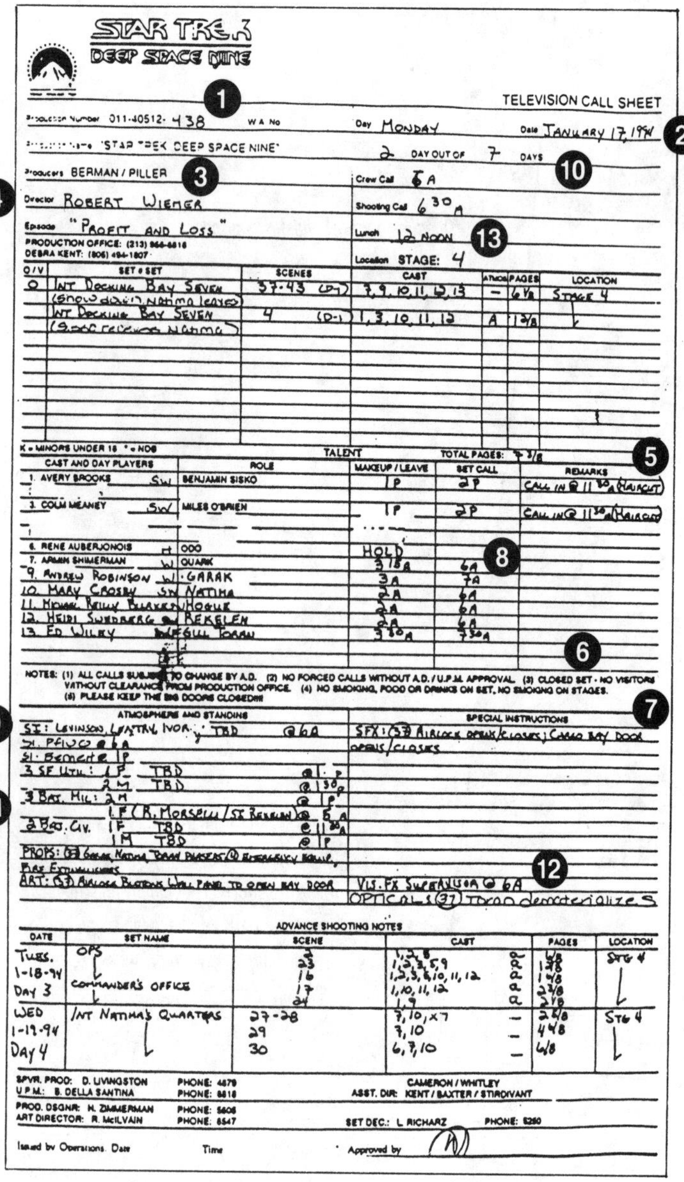

**TELEVISION CALL SHEET**

| | | |
|---|---|---|
| Production Number 011-40512-438 | W A No | Day MONDAY · Date JANUARY 17, 1994 |
| Production Name "STAR TREK: DEEP SPACE NINE" | 2 DAY OUT OF 7 DAYS | |
| Producers BERMAN / PILLER | Crew Call 6A | |
| Director ROBERT WIEMER | Shooting Call 6:30A | |
| Episode "PROFIT AND LOSS" | Lunch 12 NOON | |
| PRODUCTION OFFICE: (213) 956-8616 | Location STAGE: 4 | |
| DEBRA KENT: (805) 494-1807 | | |

| O/V | SET # SET | SCENES | CAST | ATMOS | PAGES | LOCATION |
|---|---|---|---|---|---|---|
| O | INT DOCKING BAY SEVEN (snow down Natima leaves) | 37-43 (D-7) | 9, 9, 10, 11, 12, 13 | — | 6⅔ | STAGE 4 |
| | INT DOCKING BAY SEVEN (goodbye to Natima) | 4 | (D-1) 1, 3, 10, 11, 12 | A | 1⅞ | |

**K = MINORS UNDER 18 · • = NOS · TALENT · TOTAL PAGES: 7 ⅝**

| CAST AND DAY PLAYERS | | ROLE | MAKEUP / LEAVE | SET CALL | REMARKS |
|---|---|---|---|---|---|
| 1. AVERY BROOKS | SW | BENJAMIN SISKO | 1P | 2P | CALL IN @ 11:30 (HAIRCUT) |
| 3. COLM MEANEY | SW | MILES O'BRIEN | 1P | 2P | CALL IN @ 11:30 (HAIRCUT) |
| 6. RENE AUBERJONOIS | H | ODO | HOLD | | |
| 7. ARMIN SHIMERMAN | W | QUARK | 3:15A | 6A | |
| 9. ANDREW ROBINSON | W | GARAK | 3A | 7A | |
| 10. MARY CROSBY | SW | NATIMA | 2A | 6A | |
| 11. MICHAEL REILLY BURKE | SW | HOGUE | 2A | 6A | |
| 12. HEIDI SWEDBERG | SW | REKELEN | 2A | 6A | |
| 13. ED WILEY | | GUL TORAN | 5:30A | 7:30A | |

NOTES: (1) ALL CALLS SUBJECT TO CHANGE BY A.D. (2) NO FORCED CALLS WITHOUT A.D./U.P.M. APPROVAL. (3) CLOSED SET - NO VISITORS WITHOUT CLEARANCE FROM PRODUCTION OFFICE. (4) NO SMOKING, FOOD OR DRINKS ON SET. NO SMOKING ON STAGES. (5) PLEASE KEEP THE BIG DOORS CLOSED!!!

| ATMOSPHERE AND STANDINS | SPECIAL INSTRUCTIONS |
|---|---|
| SI: Levinson, Lyttan, Ivory · TBD @6A | SFX: (37) Airlock opens/closes; Cargo bay door opens/closes |
| SI: Bernete 1P | |
| 3 SF Util: 1P TBD @1P | |
| 2M TBD @1:30 | |
| 3 Bat. Mil: 2M | |
| 1F (R. Morselli / SI Bernete) 6A | |
| 2 Bat. Civ 1F TBD @1P | |
| 1M TBD @1P | |
| PROPS: (37) Great Natima ready Hand phasers (4) emergency equip. | |
| Fire extinguishers | |
| ART: (37) Airlock buttons, wall panel to open bay door | VIS. FX: SuperNova @6A |
| OPTICALS: (37) Toran dematerializes | |

| DATE | SET NAME | SCENE | CAST | PAGES | LOCATION |
|---|---|---|---|---|---|
| TUES. 1-18-94 DAY 3 | OPS | 22 | 1,3,8,9 | 4/8 | STG 4 |
| | | 23 | 1,3,5,6,10,11,12 | 1⅞ | |
| | COMMANDER'S OFFICE | 16 | 1,10,11,12 | 1⅜ | |
| | | 17 | 1,9 | 2⅞ | |
| | | 24 | | 2 | |
| WED 1-19-94 DAY 4 | INT NATIMA'S QUARTERS | 27-28 | 9,10,×7 | 2⅝ | STG 4 |
| | | 29 | 9,10 | 4/8 | |
| | | 30 | 6,9,10 | 6/8 | |

| | | |
|---|---|---|
| SPVR. PROD: D. LIVINGSTON | PHONE: 4879 | CAMERON / WHITLEY |
| U.P.M: B. DELLA SANTINA | PHONE: 8818 | ASST. DIR: KENT / BAXTER / STIRDIVANT |
| PROD. DSGNR: H. ZIMMERMAN | PHONE: 5605 | |
| ART DIRECTOR: R. McILVAIN | PHONE: 8547 | SET DEC: L. RICHARZ PHONE: 5250 |

Issued by Operations Date ___ Time ___ Approved by ___

---

The call sheet for Morn's big day in Quark's, when the funniest joke in the universe was told. Since Morn had no name at this time, he's one of three "male hideous aliens" listed under "Atmosphere and Standins." This call sheet also notes the first appearance of "glop-on-a-stick."

---

**TELEVISION CALL SHEET**

| | | |
|---|---|---|
| Production Number 011-40512-438 | W A No | Day MONDAY · Date 1-17-94 |
| Production Name "STAR TREK: DEEP SPACE NINE" | | Crew Call 6A |

| PRODUCTION | | | | | MAKEUP / HAIR | | | |
|---|---|---|---|---|---|---|---|---|
| NO | ITEM | TIME | CHARGE | REMARKS | | | | |
| 1 | 1st Assistant Director | O.C. | 700-02 | WHITLEY / CAMERON | 1 Makeup Person | O.C. | 760-01 | WESTMORE |
| 1 | 2nd Assistant Director | 1.7 | 700-02 | BAXTER | 1 Makeup Person | 3.0 | 760-01 | WESTERFIELD Q |
| 1 | Script Supervisor | 6A | 705-08 | BROWN | 1 Makeup Person | 2.0 | 760-02 | CALVET NATIMA-F |
| 1 | DGA Trainee | 5:30A | 705-08 | STIRDIVANT | 1 Makeup Person | 2.9 | 760-02 | JONES GARAK |
| 1 | Asst'l 2nd 2nd | 6A | | LAURENCE | 1 Makeup Person | 3.0 | 760-02 | GATES TORAN/SS |
| | CAMERA | | | | 1 Hair Stylist | 1.7 | | NORMAND |
| 1 | Cinematographer | 6A | 710-01 | RUSH | 1 Hair Stylist | 4.2 | 760-06 | SMITH SISKO/O.B. |
| 1 | Operator | | 710-02 | CHESS | 1 Hair Stylist | 1.7 | 760-05 | SOLOMON |
| 1 | 1st Assistant | 5:17 | 710-07 | RAMIREZ | 1 Add'l Hair | 2.0 | | LEE |
| 1 | 2nd Assistant | 5:42A | 710-08 | STRADLING | 1 Add'l M.U. | 11.2 | | TINA (REKELEN) |
| | Camera PANA | TRK | 710-08 | | 1 Add'l M.U. | 13.0 | | TBD BAX |
| | Loop Operator | | 760-02 | | 1 Add'l M.U. | 2.0 | | TBD HOGUE |
| | Lens Assistant | | | | 2 Add'l Hair | 4.2 | | TBD |
| | Still Photographer | | 710 / 890 | | | | | |
| | ELECTRICAL | | | | | | | |
| 1 | Chief Lighting Tech | 6A | 730-01 | PEETS | | | | |
| 2 | A.C.I.T | | 730-01 | JACOBSON / BABER | | MISCELLANEOUS | | |
| 4 | Lamp Operators | | 730-02 | CHRISTENBERRY / SUZUKI | Wardrobe Check Room | | 725-23 | |
| | | | | FREDRICKSON / BOURSE | Donuts | | 725-25 | |
| X | EXTRA LAM. OPERATORS | 6A | | | Knock Down Set. Prep | | 725-23 | |
| X | Generator & Operator | 5.5 | 730 | | Knock Down Dr. Rmg. | | 725-23 | |
| | Air Cond (Head) | 5A | 725-02 | | 6 Portable Dressing Rooms | 3A | 725-23 | |
| X | Dressing Phone | | 725-21 | | X Hook-Up Dr. Rooms | | 725-24 | |
| X | Portable Telephone | 5:15 | 725-21 | | Schoolroom Trailers | | 725-24 | |
| X | Wig Wag | | 725-21 | | 8 Dressing Rm. Trailers | 5A | 725 / 775 | |
| X | Work Lights | | 725-21 | | Process Equipment | | 760-07 | |
| | SET OPERATIONS | | | | Process Camera Person | | 760-07 | |
| 1 | Key Grip | 6A | 725-01 | SORDAL | Process Asst. Cam. Per. | | 760-07 | |
| 1 | Best Boy | | 725-02 | BURGESS | Process Grip | | 760-04 | |
| 2 | Loco Grips | | 725-08 | WRIGHT / MOORE | Process Electrical | | 760-07 | |
| | Loco Grips | | 725-08 | | Visual EFX Supervisor | O.C. | | |
| 1 | Grip Daily Grip | 5:45A | 725-08 | KENNEY | Graphic Artist | | 715-08 | OKUDA |
| X | Crane Daily | TRK | | | | | | |
| X | Craft Service | 5:30A | 725-11 | AHERN | | POLICE AND FIRE | | |
| | Greensperson | | 725-13 | | 1 Fire Control Officer | 6A | 725 / 775 | |
| 1 | Standby Painter | 6A | 725-14 | GALVAN | 1 Fire Watchon Last | | 729 | |
| | Prop Makers | | 725-04 | | 2 Set Security Persons | 5:30A/6A | 725 / 775 | ENGLISH / ABNEY |
| 1 | Special Effects Person | 6A | 725-01 / 02 | PER MOHAK | Day Police | | 775-05 | |
| 2 | Special Effects Persons | | 725-02 | DEKEN-MOHMAN | Studio Police | | 775-05 | |
| 2 | Special Effects Persons | | 725-02 | SASGEN / FOSTER | Motorcycle Police | | 775-05 | |
| | SOUND | | | | First Aid | | 725 / 775 | |
| 1 | Sound Mixer | 6A | 760-01 | GOCKE | | | | |
| 1 | Mixel Operator | | 760-02 | OVERTON, M. | | MUSIC | | |
| | Sound Recorder | | 760-08 | | Piano | | 810-05 | |
| 1 | Cable Person | 6A | 760-08 | OVERTON, T. | 5 section Orchestra | | 810-05 | |
| | Lens Cable Person | | 760-08 | | Singers | | 810-05 | |
| | P.A. System | | 760-08 | | | | | |
| 2 | Playback Machine & Op | 2nd U. | 760-08 | UNSINN | | CATERER | | |
| | Sound Sysmam | | 760 | | Hot Lunches | | 775 / 780 | |
| 16 | Walkie Talkies | TRK | | | Box Lunches | | 775 / 780 | |
| X | Headsets | | | | Dinners | | 775 / 780 | |
| | PROPERTY | | | | X Gallons of Coffee | 5:30A | 775 / 780 | COMMISSARY |
| 1 | Property Person | O.C. | 750-01 | LONGO | X Dozen Doughnuts | | 775 / 780 | PER AHERN |
| 1 | Assort Prop Persons | 6A | 750-01 / 02 | MOUDAKIS / PEIFER | | | | |
| | Lone Asst Prop Person | | 750-02 | | | TRANSPORTATION | | |
| 1 | Set Dresser | O.C. | 745-01 | RICHARZ | 1 Transportation Coordinator | | 770 / 775 | SATTERFIELD |
| 1 | Lead Person | | 745-01 | VANNATTA | 1 Standby Car | | 770 / 775 | |
| 3 | Swing Gang Personnel | | 745-02 | FINKS / DiGIOVANNA / NEVILLE | 1 Camera Truck | | 770 / 775 | |
| | Wardrobe Racks | | 725-25 | | 1 Electric Truck | | 770 / 775 | |
| X | Makeup Tables | 4.0 | 725-25 | | 2 Minivans | | 770 / 775 | A., TRANS |
| X | Hair Dressing Tables | | 725-25 | | 1 Grip Truck | | 770 / 775 | CAL., DEC |
| | Armchairs | | 760-02 | STAGE 1 | 1 Property Truck | | 770 / 775 | SATTERFIELD |
| | Warmers | | 760-02 | | | | | |
| | A & B Representative | | 760-07 | | 1 Special Effects Truck | | | |
| | Hairdressers | | 760-03 | | 1 Wardrobe Set Truck | | | |
| | WARDROBE | | | | 1 Wardrobe Trailer | | | |
| 1 | Costume Designer | O.C. | 755-01 | | 1 Musical Trailer | | | |
| 1 | Costume Dept. Foreperson | | 755-01 | BLACKMAN | 1 Honeywagon | | 770 / 775 | |
| 1 | Costumer | | 755-07 | KUNZ | 1 Car | | 770 / 775 | |
| 1 | Costumer | | 755-11 | ARGUS | 1 Special Trailer | | 770 / 775 | |
| 1 | Costumer | | 755-11 | CORCORAN-WOODS | | | | |
| 1 | Costumer | | 755-07 | BOSCHE | | | | |
| 3 | Set Costumers | 5A | 755-07 | BOND CO. IN. | | | | |

**1** Our 38th DS9 episode.

**2** Day of the 6.7 Earthquake. The quake occurred at 4:31 A.M. Armin, five guest actors, 12 make-up and hair people (see back) and Michael Baxter, our intrepid 2nd 2nd assistant director were already at work. After the quake, everyone was released and shooting was canceled. Armin and Ed Wiley were well along in make-up but understandably anxious to get home -- so they left as a Ferengi and Cardassian respectively. Quite a surreal image -- two weird aliens driving the deserted dark and shaken streets of L.A..

**3** The reason the other names are on this list, the reason this call sheet exists, the reason I have my job. The deities of DS9. Our creators. (Ferengi Rule of Acquisition #33, "It never hurts to suck up to the boss.")

**4** His first "DS9" episode. A veteran of "TNG."

**5** Our cast usually gets a haircut before they start a new episode.

**6** You wouldn't believe how many people want a tour.

**7** SFX is special effects. Part of their job is to open and close doors -- they stand off camera and pull on a rope to do it, but don't tell anybody.

**8** These actors playing Cardassians have 4 hours of make-up, hair and wardrobe. Armin's lucky, he takes under 3 hours. Each Cardassian needs their own make-up person, sometimes two. (see #11)

**9** "SI" stands for stand-ins. When the shot is being lit, a person who matches the physical type of the actor "stands in" while the actor works on their lines, goes to make-up or, has a donut.

**10** The 2nd shooting day of the episode. Shows take 7 or 8 days to shoot. Shooting days run 13 hours or more including lunch.

**11** Extras with Bajoran noses cost about $200./day. Cardassians cost upwards of $1,500. Good thing Rick and Michael chose the Cardassians to leave the station and the Bajorans to stay instead of vice versa.

**12** Visual Effects Supervisors come to the set when we do a scene which they have to add an effect to in post production. (In this case "Toran" is being phasered out of existence.) They want to make sure we do our part right because to fix a mistake could cost thousands later.

**13** Lasts an hour except for the assistant directors who carry I.V. bottles of nutrients so they don't have to stop moving.

**14** Shooting crew runs approximately 60 persons. On a large production day, we could have over 100 on the stage including cast and extras.

**15** Coffee is to the crew what gas is to your car.

**16** We had to get extra space from the studio to accommodate all the extra make-up and hair people.

**17** Russ and Miles, our security officers, stop truck traffic when we're rolling (the sound comes through the stage walls), keep unwanted people out and keep the cast and crew in when they try to escape.

**18** Rush is Marvin Rush, A.S.C., our indefatigable Director of Photography. He doesn't get enough exercise running around the sets 12 to 14 hours a day, so he frequently rides his bike to work (36 miles round trip).

DAVID LIVINGSTON'S GUIDE TO CALL SHEETS

*As supervising producer for both Deep Space Nine and The Next Generation at the time we spoke with him, David Livingston had copious amounts of free time to lounge around in his office, gazing wistfully at the clouds, and filling his empty hours by helping us come up with material for this book. In between naps on an otherwise uneventful day, Livingston kindly annotated this call sheet for the day of production that never was—January 17, 1994—when a 6.7 earthquake hit the greater Los Angeles area, bringing an early end to a day that had begun at 2:00 AM.*

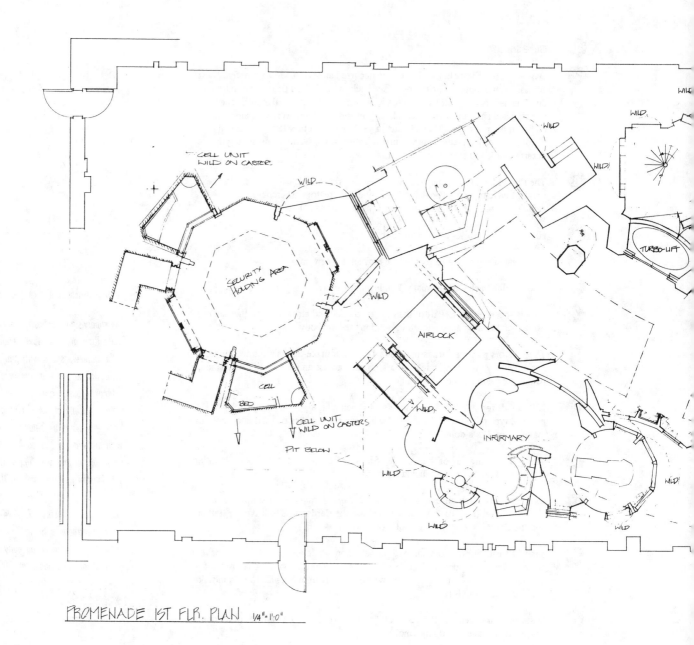

PROMENADE 1ST FLR. PLAN 1/4"=1'-0"

*Thirty-five years ago, Paramount's Stage 17 was the location of the Cartwright family ranch on Bonanza. Today, it is home to a section—the only section—of DS9's Promenade.*

**One aspect of life on the space station hasn't changed since the departure of the Cardassians. During their tenure, they sold commercial concessions to the highest bidder to provide services to the mining crews. The result is the Promenade . . . unlike any space interior ever seen on STAR TREK. It's somewhere between a free port and a flea market, bustling with aliens of all sorts when a ship's in . . . intriguing and unusual characters at every bend. There's gambling and smuggling . . . alien grifters at work here . . . bars with sexual holosuites upstairs . . . right next to traditional ship's stores, a Bajoran temple and a kiosk serving live food.**

Further on in the bible, under the character description of Quark, a bit more information is added.

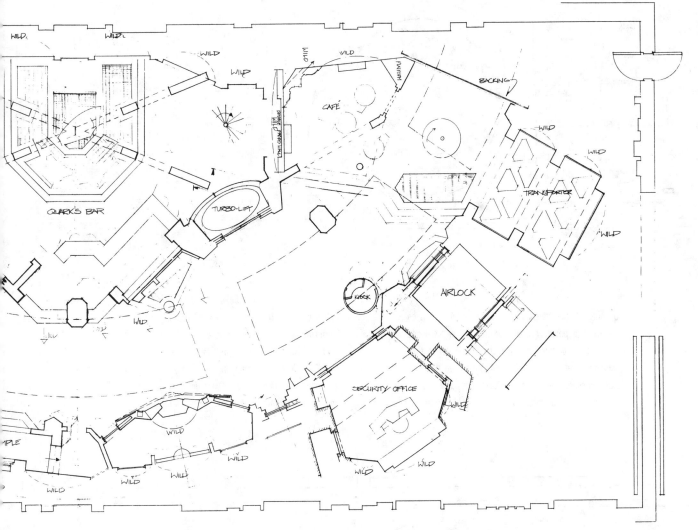

**Quark runs many of the entertainment concessions on DS9 including the bar/restaurant/gambling house and the holosuites upstairs (where your every fantasy can be played out).**

And that's all. Even in a revised version of the bible incorporating a Technical Primer, dated October 4, 1992, when the series was in full production, added little additional information.

*Quark's place.* **The interstellar place to meet and drink. A dramatic, three-story set featuring exotic beverages from around the galaxy, "honest" gambling, and the infamous sexual holosuites upstairs.[1]**

How the lean prose of the series' bible and scripts is brought to life as fully realized, fully detailed sets will be examined more closely in later chapters. But for now, to establish the setting for the telling of the funniest joke in the universe, that's all the information the writers provided in print.

The scene in which Morn told his joke, technically Scene 68 of the pilot episode, "Emissary," takes place approximately thirty minutes into the story when Com-

[1] The sexual holosuites became so infamous that publicists for the series routinely direct writers not to refer to them as *sexual* holosuites. Good thing we're just quoting the executive producers here.

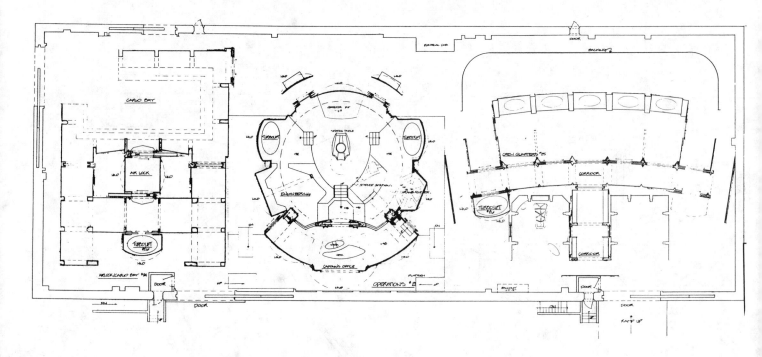

**Above:**

On Stage 4, the area marked "Crews Quarters" can be redressed as private quarters for Commander Sisko and his son, or for the O'Briens, or for any visitor to the station. When a scene calls for characters to enter or exit a runabout through a DS9 airlock, a portion of the runabout set is moved from Stage 18 to the Cargo Bay on Stage 4.

**Below:**

Most of Stage 18 is a "swing set," meaning it can be used for whatever special sets are needed for a single episode, such as a planet exterior, or alien spacecraft.

The Next Generation swing set acquired the affectionate nickname of "Planet Hell." So far, there's no such nickname for this Deep Space Nine equivalent.

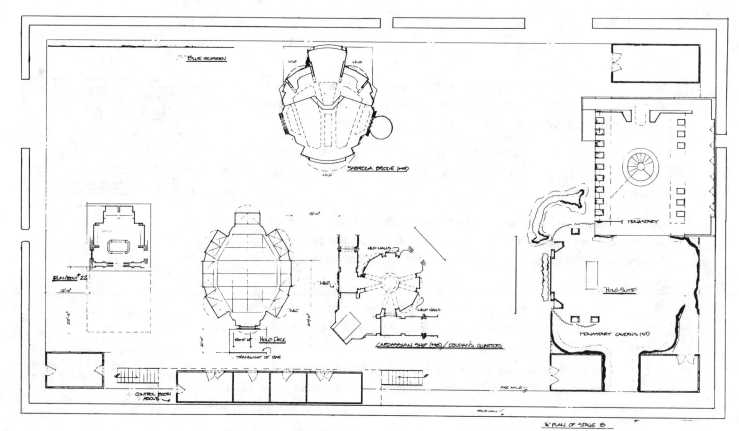

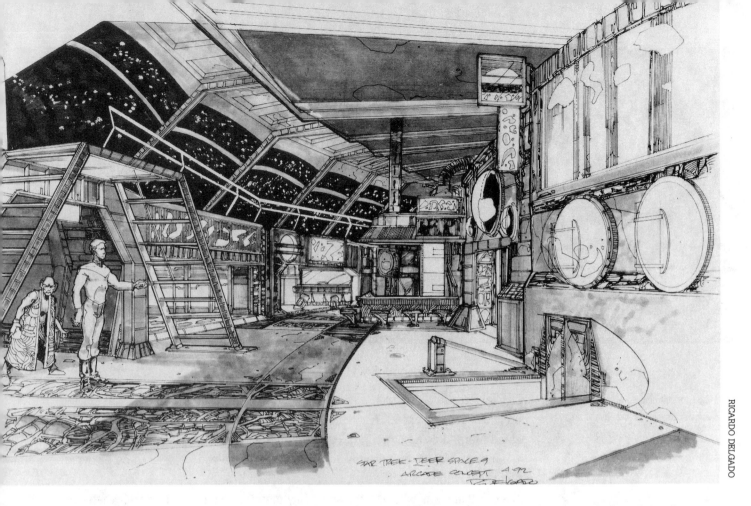

RICARDO DELGADO

mander Benjamin Sisko enters Quark's place for the first time. Here's how that scene was described on page 43 of the final draft of the shooting script, dated August 8, 1992.[2]

*An early concept drawing for DS9's Promenade, here called the "Arcade."*

68 INT. PROMENADE

> On a Turbolift as Sisko arrives . . . reacts to what we
> don't see yet . . . but we do hear alien music and as he
> leads us there, we reveal that Quark's is open for
> business . . . and it is a beacon for the otherwise
> unlighted thoroughfare . . . people are arriving . . . we can
> see smiling faces for the first time . . .

"We can see smiling faces for the first time . . ." After that simple line had been filtered through the production design of Herman Zimmerman, Michael Westmore's makeup department, director David Carson's imagination, and the combined input of at least a dozen other department heads in dozens of production meetings, the result is the atmospheric scene we see on television when Sisko arrives on a Promenade clouded with mist that softens the colored lights, and walks into a set jammed with forty actors, all in motion. Among those actors, regulars and extras alike, were Starfleet personnel, Bajorans, several Ferengi including Quark and his brother[3] (who was yet to be named Rom), and assorted other aliens including a musician playing

[2]For the record, this is also exactly how the scene was described in one of the earliest versions of the script, dated June 12, 1992, though it was then numbered as Scene 66. Other scenes, as we shall see, changed considerably.

[3]At the time the pilot was being filmed, Quark's brother—Rom, father of Nog—was not yet a character. Actor Max Grodénchik, who had portrayed other Ferengi on *The Next Generation*, had been in close contention for the role of Quark. But, when the final decision was made to cast Armin Shimerman, who had played a Ferengi in "The Last Outpost," the first *Next Generation* in which Ferengi had appeared, Grodénchik was given the role of FERENGI PIT BOSS in this scene. The later decision to make Nog Quark's nephew resulted in the need to have a brother or brother-in-law for Quark, and the producers were delighted when Grodénchik took the part because it gave them their two favorite Ferengi to pit against each other.

STAR TREK: DEEP SPACE NINE BAR CONCEPT
R. DELGADO 6·92

A later concept drawing for Quark's place,
coming close to the final design used
for the set's construction.

what appears to be a stack of slate chips on a spindle, and two Dabo girls—one humanoid, one a fishhead. Also among them was the alien who would eventually be named Morn, holding a group of Bajorans by the bar captivated with his version of the funniest joke of the universe—which his audience can be seen to be enjoying immensely.

Since there is nowhere in the script any mention of Morn or his joke, where did they come from? The deceptively simple answer is: From the collaborative television process.

To begin with, even as the pilot script was being written and rewritten and rewritten—the title page of the pilot script's revised final draft lists *twenty-one* revisions alone between August 12 and September 15, 1992—production meetings were being held to determine what the *Deep Space Nine* space station should look, sound, and feel like. As we shall see, production designer Herman Zimmerman and his coworkers were given responsibility for developing the Cardassian design aesthetic that distinguishes the unique architecture of DS9 from Federation starbases and Klingon warships. Rick Sternbach helped oversee the development of Cardassian technology, combined with a hodgepodge of devices from other cultures in the STAR TREK universe. Mike Okuda, well known for the distinctive and imaginative (and sometimes mischievously funny) graphics he's created for some of the STAR TREK movies and STAR TREK: THE NEXT GENERATION, led the effort to devise a completely different approach to Cardassian signage and control panels. Most importantly, throughout this entire process, no one person worked alone. Constant cross-fertilization was the rule, with executive producers and series co-creators Rick Berman and Michael Piller taking part at every stage.

One of the most crucial stages in this initial design process was coming up with a distinctive look for the inhabitants of and visitors to DS9—those characters we see in the background, known as extras or ''atmosphere.''

Extras on *Deep Space Nine* are generally grouped into categories reflecting their appearance: Starfleet civilians or utility officers in Starfleet uniforms; Bajorans (quaintly referred to as "nose-jobs" because of the makeup required for the bridges of their noses); and, humanoids and aliens.[4] Deciding how many of each category is required for any particular scene is a decision usually arrived at by consensus at a production meeting. Generally, the director asks for as many extras as can fit on the set in order to bring as much visual movement and life to a scene as possible. The production heads responsible for the extras' makeup and costumes, as well as for providing meals and direction, gamely outline the conditions under which they could handle so many extras—conditions which usually involve extra costs. (A fishhead Dabo girl, for example, can cost approximately $1,000 more than a humanoid Dabo girl, because of the expenses associated with the elaborate makeup and the technician required to apply it and maintain it throughout the shooting day.) Finally, Rick Berman and Michael Piller, who as executive producers share the ultimate responsibility for keeping the production of the series on time and on budget,[5] suggest that the director use a vastly smaller number of extras, sometimes causing the director to sputter and change colors in an entertaining fashion. After negotiations between all involved parties, a reasonable number of extras which serves the story's needs and with which everyone can be happy is agreed upon, in a speedy though sometimes spirited process surprisingly free of rancor.

It was in one of those initial pilot-episode production meetings that Morn was born, as just another alien created by makeup designer Michael Westmore to add exotic background atmosphere. But unlike many of the other aliens we see on a continuing basis in the series, Morn was on his way to acquiring a bit of life of his own.

Once Michael Westmore's sketches for the Morn alien had been approved, his face was sculpted, molds were made, and latex rubber castings were assembled to form Morn's familiar, prune-faced visage. The next stage was to find someone who would wear that rubber head and padded costume, which required a time-honored Hollywood tradition known as a "cattle call."

A cattle call is an open casting session. "Open" means that there are few if any restrictions placed on the qualities or qualifications of the actors who respond. For example, a casting call to find an actor to take the role of Commander Sisko's son, Jake, would of necessity be limited to teenage African-American males with the acting ability to carry an ongoing speaking role. In an open call for extras on *Deep Space Nine,* about the most important restriction placed on the actors is: Are you the right size to fit into a costume we already have? Costumes will, of course, be made or altered to fit any guest stars in an episode, but the financial realities of television production mean that money is seldom allocated for the alteration of costumes for nonessential characters.

On the day the role of Morn was to be cast, the open extras call for *Deep Space Nine* brought approximately three hundred actors of all ages, sexes, and sizes to the Paramount lot, photographs and résumés in hand. Casting assistants quickly divided the actors into groups based on the requirements of the day, among them: Bajorans and Hideous Aliens.

One of the actors in that group of three hundred was Mark Allan Shepherd, a young man just out of school with a major in music and additional studies in theater,

[4]The word "alien" has a special meaning in the STAR TREK universe. Beings like Bajorans and Vulcans and Klingons are called "humanoids" because they are much like humans. Aliens are those creatures who are completely *unlike* humans. On a practical level, these distinctions are used to establish the costs of creating nonhuman characters for an episode. Aliens such as Morn—who often require elaborate full-face or head prosthetics, and specially designed hands and feet and costuming—are generally far more expensive than humanoids, who might require nothing more than an odd nose and unusual skin color. Actors who are made up to be Bajorans are said to have been "nosed."

[5]As co-creators and executive producers of *Deep Space Nine,* both Rick Berman and Michael Piller are equal partners in all facets of the series' production. However, in day-to-day functions, they have split the workload so that Piller concentrates more on managing the writing and Berman more on managing the production. It must be noted, though, that Berman has extensive input on scripts, especially during the development stage, just as Piller has input on all aspects of the series' production.

## Michael Westmore: When the Script Says "Alien"

Michael Westmore is the third generation of a Hollywood makeup dynasty, beginning with his grandfather George Westmore, who started work in Hollywood features in the 1920s. Michael Westmore's father, Monty, ran the makeup department of Selznick International, and his uncles, Perc and Ern, who were twins, ran the same departments at Warner Bros. and 20th Century Fox respectively, with Ern later moving to RKO. Michael Westmore's other uncles included Wally, who ran Paramount's makeup department, Bud, who ran Universal's, and Frank, the youngest, who worked for both Wally and Bud at their respective studios.

Today, Michael Westmore has two brothers in the makeup business, as well as a nephew, a niece, and a cousin. In addition to the makeup artists in the family, his son, Michael Westmore II, was an assistant editor on *The Next Generation,* as well as the person who built all the interior electronics for scenes in which Data the android was opened up.

Winner of an Academy Award for his makeup in the feature *Mask,* as well seven Emmy Awards for makeup, of which two were for his *Next Generation* work and one for *Deep Space Nine,* Westmore is the combination artist and technician who has brought to life literally thousands of STAR TREK's aliens.

But for all his experience on *The Next Generation, Deep Space Nine* was and is his greatest challenge.

As supervisor of makeup for both STAR TREK series (as well as for the upcoming *Next Generation* feature and the newest series, *Star Trek: Voyager),* Westmore works with a regular staff of four makeup artists and four hairstylists, hiring additional technicians according to the changing demands of his daily workload. And Westmore starts planning that workload when he first receives a script and scans it for the magic word—"alien."

For the most part, that word is all Westmore has to go on. "Once in a while," he says, "about once in a blue moon, the script might say 'reptilian-type alien' or something, where the writer actually has a concept in mind for a specific reason."

The script for the first-season episode "Captive Pursuit" was one of those scripts. It told the story of Tosk—an alien visitor to DS9 who was bred to be the prey in a deadly hunt. When Westmore saw that the script mentioned "reptilian," he recalls thinking, "Jeez, we've done snakes and we've done lizards—and we've done everything else. But I happened to pick up a copy of *Smithsonian* magazine that had an alligator floating on the front of it. So, the skin texture for Tosk was, literally, based on the coloring and the design of an alligator. All the way from the belly skin down the front of the face to down the back. The same with his hands. Then we had contact lenses made, and I made new teeth for him, so we had all those little things that we don't normally have time to do.

"But, when the script says 'alien,' at that point I'll go ahead and I'll read the script further, to find out what the character of the person is."

Michael Westmore's studio.

Alien bumps being sculpted on a plaster cast of the back of an actor's head.

ROBBIE ROBINSON

Westmore had once planned on being an art teacher, so he has an extensive background in art and art history. "That gives me a pretty broad range of what was going on," he says, "even historically, in different races and times, with face-painting, tattooing, everything like that. So I'll bring all those elements into a character that I'm dealing with."

But there's even more in Westmore's background that he brings to his STAR TREK work, background that fits in perfectly with the dramatic requirements of his makeup designs. "When I was in the army, I was the cartoonist on the army newspaper. So I developed the feel for putting the look right into the sculpture. I mean, if it's a bad person, there are things you can do around the forehead, the eyebrows, nasal-labial folds, that make the person look like a bad person, all the time—like he's smelling something bad or he's wrinkling his forehead. Or, if it's a nice person, being able to put the little lines into the sculpture that create, you know, niceness and happiness, which is whether the lines go up or down, depending on the personality of the character." The result, Westmore points out, is that even if the character doesn't say a word, the audience can still know what his or her personality is, almost subliminally.

Regular viewers of both STAR TREK series early on noticed that *Deep*

Space Nine had more aliens than The Next Generation, as well as a greater range of alien types. Westmore says this is the direct result of Rick Berman's instruction to him: "More."

"Unlike The Next Generation," Westmore explains, "where we basically start the season and see what happens, for Deep Space Nine, we started off actually several weeks in advance, doing sketches and designs, getting a certain amount of them approved, and then going to work—sculpting them, and making the rubber." This preparatory work essentially gave the production a ready-made pool of aliens to draw upon, aliens that had been created with a slightly longer schedule than is possible in weekly production, giving Westmore and his team the chance to create more elaborate designs.

Another difference between the aliens of The Next Generation and those of Deep Space Nine, Westmore says, is that on The Next Generation, "after a character was over with, he was basically over with. But on Deep Space Nine, as aliens are created, they are, more or less, filtered into the Promenade and filtered into the bar, so when we see further episodes, it's not like a particular type of alien came in and disappeared on us—that alien is still there."

In keeping with the high standards evident throughout the production of both STAR TREK series, Westmore points out that there is no difference in quality or intricacy between the appliances made for actors in principal roles and for those who will merely appear as background extras. "Most of the heads that we have available, at least ninety percent of them, will permit the person to talk. There're only about eight heads that really can't talk. Their mouths can move, but the actors can't speak with them." Morn, however, is one of those masks in the ninety percent. "Morn could speak," Westmore says, "if they wanted him to. We could anchor those lips down tight enough for him so he could say a line."

The relative luxury of time that Westmore had during the beginning, preproduction, stages of Deep Space Nine quickly went by the boards as the series went into full production. In describing the process by which he moves from script to appliance, Westmore says, "I used to make sketches—when we had time to do sketches." In full production, Westmore is apt to have a sculptor begin work on a lifemask of an actor, building alien features in clay under Westmore's direction. Westmore has sometimes had to have full appliances sculpted, molded, poured, and ready to wear in six days. His wealth of experience is absolutely critical under these conditions, because, as he explains, "there's no time for making tests. There's no time for sketches. I have to take that face and go right to work with clay on it, and show the final clay to Rick Berman for approval." Westmore also points out that unless he's preparing a background head—that is, an appliance specifically designed so that a number of different extras can wear it—sketching can sometimes be a waste of effort if he doesn't know who has been cast for a role. The shape of an actor's face can have a significant influence on makeup design, especially for those designs where a great deal of the actor's face will remain visible.

Westmore smiles nostalgically as he thinks back to his work on feature films, which include Clan of the Cave Bear (Academy Award nomination, 1987), 2010 (Academy Award nomination, 1984), Blade Runner, Iceman, Masters of the Universe, Rocky I, II, III and V, Roxanne, and the superb though sadly neglected science-fiction film The Blood of Heroes, whose creative vision puts all the Mad Max films to shame. After describing the six-day accelerated design and fabrication schedule sometimes required for Deep Space Nine, Westmore says, "On Mask, I had three months to design one makeup. On Masters of the Universe, I had a month each to build the appliances for the principal characters and to change little things around and play with the designs by Bill Stout. Today, we have characters just as complex on Deep Space Nine, and I have to have them ready in a week. I don't have the luxury of a month's time."

Indeed, in a single month, Westmore might have to produce five to eight original designs, as well as adapt existing designs for guest stars. "On Next Generation alone," he says, "I poured out a ton's worth of molds in a single season. Between Next Generation and Deep Space Nine now, I probably have close to nine to ten tons of molds that are stored that I can grab and make copies of, to do things with."

Though he came to STAR TREK with impressive experience, Westmore says he has continued to learn just from the sheer volume of work he has had to produce. "I push things," he says. "I've pushed things on actors that didn't work. And then I'll say: 'Oh, that didn't work.' So, on the next show, we won't try that.

"But then you'll find something that does work. Like designing a movable eyelid or something. Or an air bladder [for making an appliance appear to pulse from inside] that goes somewhere. These shows have given me tremendous room to experiment and to create. I have probably—no, not probably—I have created more here in the seven years here than myself or any other makeup artist has done in their entire career. I mean, I have done thousands of aliens. And, if I survive the next seven years with Voyager, no one could come close to my output." If the last seven years are any example, the next seven should be spectacular indeed.

ROBBIE ROBINSON

Michael Westmore's studio, where the words "wall hanging" have a whole new meaning.

Each day of filming, Michael Westmore paints Trill spots onto Terry Farrell by hand. Since each application is unique, both Farrell and Westmore decided they were works of art. Thus Westmore informs us that he now signs and numbers each set of spots as he finishes them. We did not ask for specific location details.

A sampling of Michael Westmore's impressive and prodigious work for Deep Space Nine, ranging from a small variation on an ear, to a subtle touch of weirdness at a throat, to the hundred-percent coverage of an alien.

Salli Elise Richardson as Nidell, in "Second Sight."

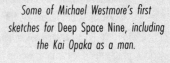

Randy Oglesby as Ah-Kel, in "Vortex."

Some of Michael Westmore's first sketches for Deep Space Nine, including the Kai Opaka as a man.

Scott MacDonald as Tosk, in "Captive Pursuit."

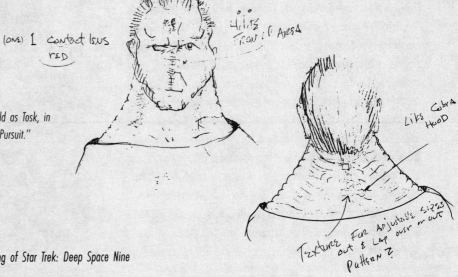

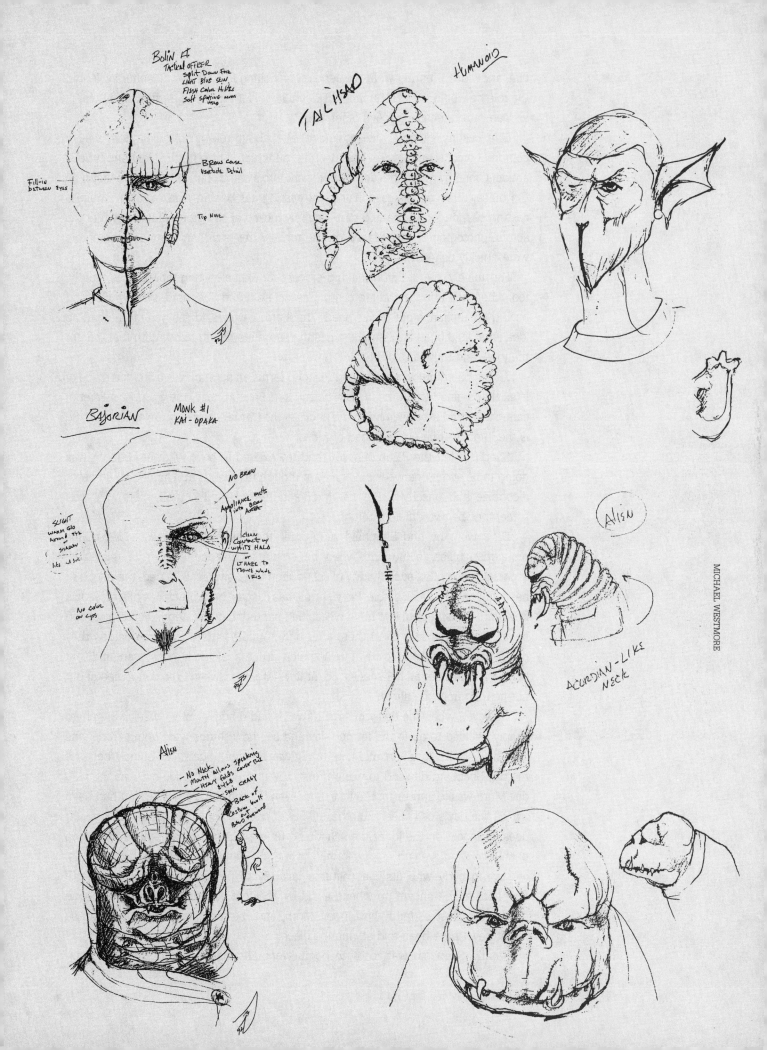

BOLIN 4
TACTICAL OFFICER
SPLIT DOWN FACE
LIGHT BLUE SKIN
FLESH COLOR HI-LITES
SOFT SPOTTING ARMS
HEAD

Fill-in
between eyes

BROW color
use etch Detail

TIP Nose

TAL'HEAD                    HUMANOID

BAJORIAN       MONK #1
               KAI-OPAKA

NO BROW

Appliance melts
into Brow Area

SLIGHT
WARM GLO
AROUND EYE
or
SHADOW
like WHITE

Clean Contact up
WHITE HALO
or
LT HAZE TO
BROWS white
IRIS

No color
on Lips

ALIEN                              ALIEN

ACCORDIAN-LIKE
NECK

MICHAEL WESTMORE

ALIEN

- No Neck Allows speaking
- MOUTH folds cover the
  HEAVY folds cover the
  EYES
  SKIN CRAZY
  BACK of
  costume built
  out BEND FORWARD

film, and video. Hearing what the series was looking for that day, Shepherd selected the role he would try for: Humanoid Doctor Type, for the scene in the pilot in which we see Jadzia receive her symbiont, Dax.

The casting process, like so much else about television production, was a combination of seemingly endless waiting, punctuated by a flurry of fast and furious action. Group by group, the actors were sent into a small office in lots of five to ten. In the office, three people responsible for casting sat behind a table and—unlike a casting session for a speaking part—simply looked at the group of actors while the actors' photographs were placed on the table. After less than a minute, the actors were quickly ushered out.

Fortunately, the decision-making process for extras casting moves more rapidly, too. About ten minutes later, a casting associate asked Shepherd if he would mind having an appliance put on his head. Shepherd bravely said yes, though he had no idea what kind of an appliance the casting associate had in mind. With that, he got the job—and the role—of Morn.

As Shepherd quickly learned, in makeup terms an appliance is a molded piece of latex that's glued to the body. The corrugated Bajoran nose, the enormous Ferengi ears, the corded exoskeletons on the necks of the Cardassians—all are appliances. So is the large, walrus-necked head of Morn.

Shepherd left the Paramount lot that day excited to have what he thought was going to be about one week's work, even though his friends and family would never recognize him onscreen. But being offered the job and actually getting it can sometimes be two different things.

Days went by and Shepherd didn't get the call from the *Deep Space Nine* production office telling him when he would be needed on set. In television, especially for a pilot, such fluidity of scheduling can be typical. Indeed, the pilot had been filming for a week before Terry Farrell was cast as the Trill science officer, Jadzia Dax, and it wasn't until two more weeks had passed that she stepped on the set and began filming her role. Even then, after only two days the producers decided they didn't want her makeup to cover up so much of her face, had it redesigned, and sent her back to reshoot all her scenes. So, at first, Shepherd wasn't too concerned about not hearing from the show.

However, when the delay in starting work had dragged on for weeks, Shepherd simply decided to go to the lot one day and see how things were going. Today, he calls his decision intuition, and it certainly was an enormous stroke of luck, because the day Shepherd decided to wander onto the lot to check things out was the very day Morn was to appear for the first time, even though the nameless alien had been left off the day's call sheet. Another reality of television production is that if a star doesn't appear on the lot at the scheduled time, production staff will start making phone calls and even go looking for him or her. But if an extra isn't on the lot on time, any warm body who fits the costume is likely to be dragooned into service. If Shepherd hadn't shown up when he did by accident or intuition or luck, someone else would most certainly have been Morn, and the funniest joke in the universe might never have been told at Quark's place.

Finally, Shepherd was ready to begin work. His mask—one of the least time-consuming of the *Deep Space Nine* aliens because it covers his head in one piece —was securely in place and his padded costume Velcroed shut. Then he was led into the cavernous white structure of Stage 17 and onto the Promenade, which was "dressed" by stagehands with piles of debris and damaged equipment to show how the departing Cardassians had left the station. Gaffers were adjusting the spotlights in Quark's place. Stagehands were crammed into narrow openings between the bulkheads to coordinate the opening of the turbolift doors through which Sisko would enter. Makeup artists trailed after their assigned actors with portable kits of makeup, brushes, and tissues on their belts, touching up imperceptible flaws. And at some time, for some reason, in that chaos of a set about to be filmed, the pilot episode's director, David Carson, decided that the Grinch-like alien should sit at the bar in Quark's place, right between two pillars where the camera could see him as it followed Sisko from the turbolift to Quark's front door—which was the action the script had called for.

But simply sitting is not enough. An extra's job is to bring life to a set and a scene, so it was necessary for Morn to be doing something as the camera came upon him. David Carson had his AD (assistant director) gather a few more extras around Morn, then gave Shepherd his direction: "Tell the funniest joke in the universe."

The special talent of actors is that when they're given that type of direction, they can create a role instead of freezing in a panic. Mark Allan Shepherd had come to the Paramount lot on a whim that day. He had been placed in a stifling costume with limited vision and hearing, and had been expecting to spend sixteen hours being shuffled from one place to another, never to open his mouth.[6] But the director had plunked him center stage and told him to come up with his own dialogue. Instantly the scene was set up for rehearsal. And in just the few brief minutes between the director's command and the first run-through of the scene, Shepherd had come up with the joke he would tell—the one related near the start of this chapter.

To be fair, Shepherd had delivered those words before. They were part of a performance piece he had developed in high school—a random assortment of words that *almost* made sense—and, drawing on his training as an actor, Shepherd was prepared to reuse any experience from his past to do his job. Which he did.

Spewing out his words forcefully enough to be heard beyond the muffling confines of his mask, Shepherd addressed his audience of fellow extras, gesturing grandly as he delivered his joke as only a Lurian can. In the end, his first appearance on camera lasted less than five seconds. But in true television tradition, those few seconds transformed the character, the actor, and, in a small way, even the series.

Shepherd had simply assumed that the role for which he had been hired was for the pilot episode only. A few days' work and commensurate pay were all he expected. The chance to be on the set of a major television production, observing and learning, was a fringe benefit. Then he would be off looking for another job on another production, his plan being that if he stayed at it, sometime, someday, he'd be on a set long enough for someone to notice something in him that made him stand out from the other extras.

But in Shepherd's case, he didn't have to wait long.

A few days into shooting, production staff told him that his character had caught

[6]The television production budget rears its head again—extras who speak individual lines get paid more, and earn residuals each time their episode is rerun. (See page 34 for an explanation of residual payments for performers.) This explains why so many times when Dr. Bashir gives an order to a medical technician, the technician just nods and hurries way, instead of responding, "Yes, Doctor," as any polite technician would. These two words uttered by an extra could end up costing the production thousands of dollars!

the eyes of the producers. They watched the printed film from each day's filming (called "dailies" for the obvious reason), and something about Morn did make him stand out from the start. It wasn't just the mask and costume—the producers were familiar with those long before Shepherd was cast. And it wasn't just Shepherd's onscreen presence, which, after all, was buried under several pounds of latex. But in some way, Shepherd had come up with a way of moving within an appliance created by Michael Westmore, wearing a costume designed by Robert Blackman, in accordance to the direction given by David Carson, on a set designed under Herman Zimmerman's direction, in a world created by Rick Berman and Michael Piller, in a universe first brought to life by Gene Roddenberry . . . and somehow from that complex creative stew, Shepherd had brought to life a new STAR TREK character.

"You might have a career here," a production staffer told Shepherd that first week, and though Shepherd thought it was a joke, the staffer was right.

Soon the nameless Grinch-like alien appeared in more episodes. He acquired a name in the episode "Progress," and a homeworld. He can be seen at Quark's when it's open, and sleeping it off on a bench or in Odo's security office when it's closed.

Behind-the-scenes, it's been hypothesized that Morn is a holophile, with an addictive love for Quark's holosuite fantasies. Some of the writers have even suggested that Morn and Odo might have a history, which one day might play a part in an episode yet to be written.

But the creative complexity of television doesn't end there, and Shepherd found himself making another small contribution to *Deep Space Nine*'s background that went beyond his role as a Hideous Alien extra. Off camera, during the sixteen-hour days that lead to five to eight minutes of usable film, there are many opportunities for the actors and production staff to talk. During one such conversation in the first season, Mickey Michaels, a first-season set dresser, heard about Shepherd's abstract/impressionistic paintings—another of his pursuits. In short order, those paintings ended up as part of the decor in Jake Sisko's bedroom, yet another example of the hard-to-predict collaborative process on which television thrives and survives.

But for all that television gladly uses the creative input of all involved with it, it is also a process without pity. Shepherd's "joke" was recorded that first day on the set, but it doesn't appear in the pilot episode, and neither does anything else Morn has said for the first two seasons.

Someday, perhaps we will be told Morn's story, learn what his relationship—if any—is to Odo, and discover what incident from his past might have driven him to become a holophile. But for now, Morn serves as an example of the best in television production—the unexpected result of an unplanned mixing of creative people, to create something unanticipated, yet entertaining.

Though this has been the story of just one of the background characters of *Deep Space Nine*, it's also the story of the series itself, and of all good television, as we're about to find out. But before we begin our in-depth look at this newest addition to the STAR TREK universe, let's take a quick trip back to where *Deep Space Nine* all began.

# THE

# FUTURE'S

# PAST

# TWO

*The television writer-producer faces an almost impossible task when he*
*attempts to create and produce a quality TV series. Assuming he conceived*
*a program of such meaning and importance that it could ultimately change*
*the face of America, he probably could not get it on the air or keep it there!*

—Gene Roddenberry[1]

S ome people divide the generations into those who can remember where
they were when President Kennedy was assassinated, and those who
weren't born at the time. Others draw a line between baby boomers and
the generation that followed based on those who appreciate the old joke about Paul
McCartney's first band, and those who say, "Paul who?"

In the world of STAR TREK, however, the demarcation between generations of
fans is whether or not one refers to "STAR TREK, and that new show," or "STAR
TREK, and that old show." For, unlike any other dramatic television series, even those
which have appealed to different generations through decades of reruns, STAR TREK
stands alone as the only show that has successfully found its audience in two
generations in two different incarnations—the original 1960s series, and *The Next
Generation* of the eighties and nineties. Even more remarkably, *Deep Space Nine* and
the unprecedented *fourth* STAR TREK series, *Voyager,* scheduled to debut in January
1995, seem poised to thrust STAR TREK into the consciousness of a third generation
and the new century. And all this from a poorly rated series from 1966 that barely
hung on for three full seasons.

The story of STAR TREK's unprecedented success is most of all a story of the
creative people behind it, especially Gene Roddenberry, who created *The Original
Series* and helped shape and hone the ongoing contributions made throughout the
ensuing years by the scores of writers, directors, actors, and production staff who
worked on STAR TREK in all its various forms. But it is also a story of network and
studio politics, conflicting and supportive personalities, money, changing audiences

[1]With this quote, Stephen E. Whitfield
began the first chapter of *The Making of
Star Trek*. Twenty-six years later, how
gratifying to know that Gene Roddenberry
*did* live to see that his creation, by giving
us a positive future to imagine, did change
at least a small part of the face of America
—and the world—and that as STAR
TREK: THE NEXT GENERATION it was
no longer under any threat of cancellation
for the foreseeable future.

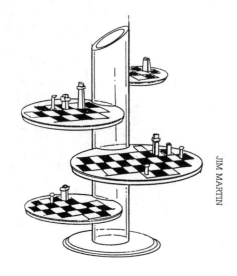

JIM MARTIN

ROBBIE ROBINSON

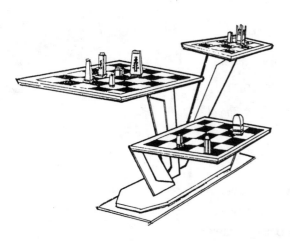

Other designs for 3-D games on DS9.

The spirit of the original series lives on in Sisko's quarters on DS9. This three-dimensional chess set can often be seen in the background—an homage to the set Kirk and Spock used to play with.

COURTESY OF DOUG DREXLER

*NBC's official response to the thousands who wrote to protest the cancellation of The Original Series. A copy of this letter hangs in the DS9 art department, where, presumably, everyone can gloat.*

and television technologies, and all the other volatile elements of a multimillion-dollar business venture in a highly, sometimes mercilessly competitive industry, each aspect of which could deserve a book of its own in order to be fully explored. Since our purpose is to get to *Deep Space Nine* as directly as possible, the following is a *brief* history of STAR TREK, free of politics, showing the simplest and most direct route from the first *U.S.S. Enterprise* to the Cardassian space station near the Bajoran wormhole that is our destination.

To begin, here's what the show-business journal *Variety* had to say about the first STAR TREK series after its debut on September 8, 1966. The review is dated September 14, 1966, and was written after viewing the first episode aired, "The Man Trap," known to fans as the Salt Vampire episode.

**"Star Trek" obviously solicits suspension of disbelief, but it won't work. Even within its sci-fi frame of reference it was an incredible and dreary mess of confusion and complexities from the kick-off. It's best suited to the Saturday morning kidvid bloc. The interplanetary spaceship trudged on for a long hour with hardly any relief from violence, killings, hypnotic stuff, and a distasteful, ugly monster. . . . By a generous stretch of the imagination, it could lure a small coterie of smallfry, though not happily time-slotted in that direction.**

So much for reviews.

In its first season, *The Original Series* received five Emmy nominations, but won none. Its ratings seldom brought it within even the top fifty television shows, and NBC correctly—given the time and circumstances—made the decision to cancel the show.[2]

But then the very first hint of what STAR TREK was to become made itself known. Dedicated fans began a letter-writing campaign that actually made the NBC

[2]Almost twenty other prime-time network series debuted when *Star Trek* did, and, as is usual in television, most were not renewed. Those series included *The Monroes, The Man Who Never Was, The Hero, Occasional Wife, Pistols 'n' Petticoats, Hey, Landlord,* and *The Road West.* Of all the debuting series that year, other than *Star Trek,* the one most often remembered is the half-season of the police drama, *Hawk,* primarily because it was the first major role for Burt Reynolds.

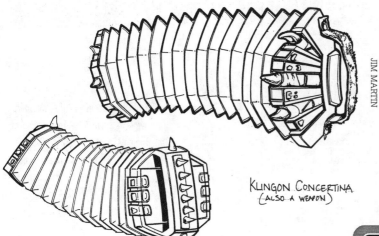

JIM MARTIN

KLINGON CONCERTINA
(ALSO A WEAPON)

Deep Space Nine *has revealed more about the nature of Klingons, first introduced in The Original Series. Note that this concertina, played by the proprietor of DS9's Klingon restaurant, can also be used as a weapon.*

*A DS9 shipping label shows that the Tantalus Colony from the original series is still in operation.*

*Another blast from the past. In the center of this Cardassian control panel is the distinctive silhouette of a DY-100 sleeper ship, just like the one that brought Khan into Kirk's time period.*

## PLANET 10 SHIPPING

**SHIP TO:**
CENTRAL BUREAU OF
REHABILITATION
ATTN: DR. TRISTAN ADAMS
RANDALL PFLUG PLAZA
STOCKHOLM, SWEDEN. EARTH.

**FROM:**
DR. SIMON VAN GELDER
TANTALUS COLONY
TANTALUS V

ROUTING CODE
-4975327 92 874598

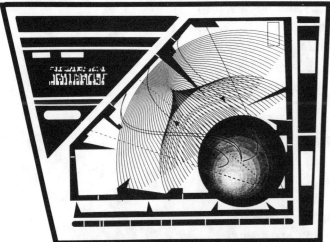

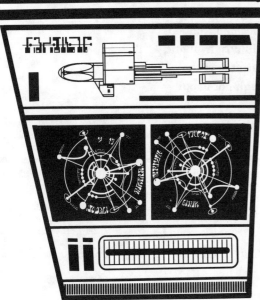

*The Vulcan IDIC, which made its first* STAR TREK *appearance as a medallion hanging from Mr. Spock's neck, has become the symbol of all things Vulcan on DS9. (IDIC is an acronym for Infinite Diversity in Infinite Combinations.)*

**ORNITHOID LIFE FORM**
PYRIS VIII

**HORTA - SILICON CYCLE LIFE FORM**

**CARBON CYCLE LIFE FORM**
EXCALBIA

**TRIBBLE - POLYGEMINUS GREX**
IOTA GEMINORIUM IV

**REGULAN BLOODWORM**
REGULUS II

**FLYING PARASITE - BLASTONEURON**
LARGE MAGELLANIC CLOUD ?

**DENEBIAN SLIME DEVIL - DENEBIA CARNIVORA**
DENEB IV

programming executives reverse their decision. Following an unprecedented, on-air announcement over the closing credits of the first season's last episode, STAR TREK was renewed for a second season.

However, the second season brought with it an unfortunate time slot—Friday at 10 P.M.—and STAR TREK once again languished at the bottom of the Neilsen ratings and once again was threatened with cancellation. Once again, a flood of protest letters inundated NBC.

STAR TREK returned for a second time, but only with an order for half a season's worth of episodes. Finally, despite the fans' best efforts, although they did last through the year, the show was cancelled in the spring of 1969. A few months later, Neil Armstrong and Buzz Aldrin stepped onto the moon. The era of real travel to other worlds had begun just as an era of fictional travels had come to an end.

But, of course, STAR TREK didn't end. That cancellation, after only seventy-nine episodes had been produced, was simply the beginning of its incredible growth.

Fittingly, the first reincarnation of STAR TREK was as a syndicated series. (Later we will look at the present-day syndicated-television market, which continues to erode the power of the traditional networks, and see how shows like *The Next Generation* and *Deep Space Nine* have helped create this new syndication era. Some might say this is fitting revenge on the network system that tried to kill STAR TREK.)

In 1970, Paramount[3] started to sell the series to the syndicated market. Soon STAR TREK was running in the afternoon and early evening on local stations across the United States, and throughout the world—bringing a whole new group of viewers under its spell.

*The alien life-forms encountered by Kirk and the original Enterprise are still being studied in Keiko's schoolroom on DS9, as this Federation learning chart shows.*

[3]Star Trek was originally produced by Desilu, the production company founded by Lucille Ball and Desi Arnaz, who were among the first to realize the substantial profits that could be made by selling rerun rights to old shows—specifically their own *I Love Lucy*—in the syndicated-television market. Paramount acquired all rights to STAR TREK when it bought Desilu in 1967. The building that housed the Desilu production offices still stands on the Paramount Lot.

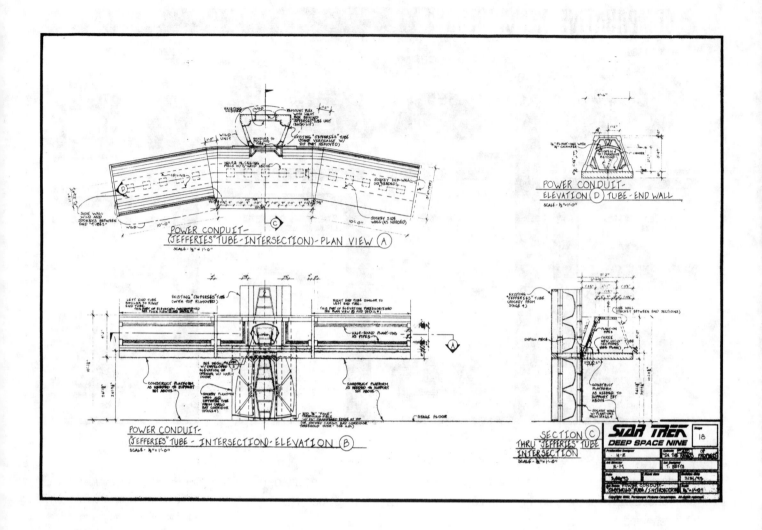

*Originally named for Matt Jefferies, art director on the original STAR TREK series, the Jefferies tube—from which much critical equipment can be accessed—has made its way to DS9.*

Two years later, in 1972, what is considered to be the first STAR TREK convention was held at the Statler-Hilton Hotel in New York City. STAR TREK fans had gathered together many times before, even while the series was still on NBC, often as part of a more wide-ranging science-fiction convention. But the Statler–Hilton convention was the first hotel convention to be dedicated completely to STAR TREK, and the first to have guest speakers from the show.

Instead of the few hundred fans who were expected, thousands turned up. Surprised by the growing legions of fans, and perhaps taking their cue from that first *Variety* review, Paramount brought back STAR TREK as an animated, Saturday morning series for the 1974-75 season. The twenty-two episodes that were produced, featuring the voices of the original cast, are once again in—what else?—syndication today.

STAR TREK was not the only science-fictional property enjoying growing success at this time. A fundamental shift in audience expectations was developing, and

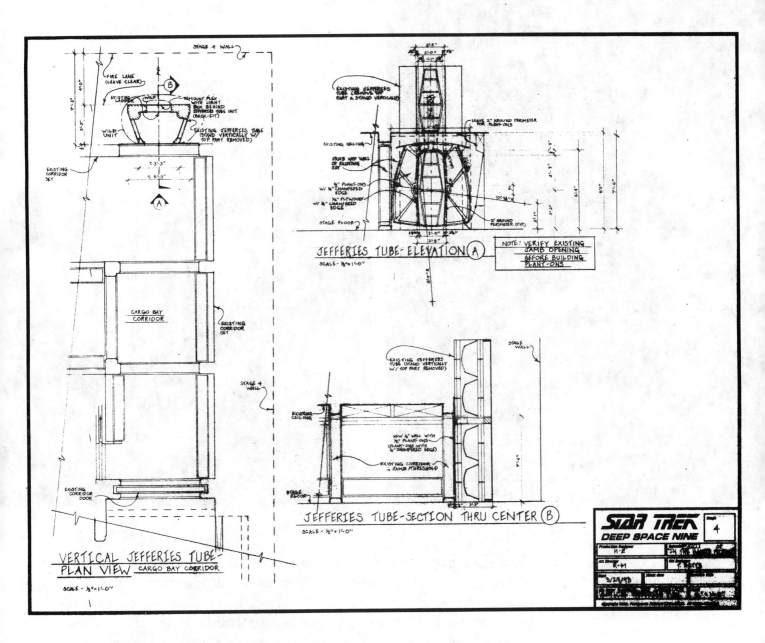

Paramount and Gene Roddenberry knew it. As the animated series was airing, Gene Roddenberry was back in his office at Paramount (now the office of Michael Piller), developing the motion picture STAR TREK II, to be released for Christmas 1975. Delays set in. The film was scheduled for release in the summer of 1976. But in January of that year, Paramount decided to make STAR TREK II as a television movie. By April 1976, it was to be a motion picture again and Paramount announced its plans as a tie-in to the publicity surrounding the naming of the first American space shuttle—four hundred thousand letter writers had convinced NASA to call it the *Enterprise*.[4] But more delays set in, and by June 1977, when the film was to have been released, STAR TREK was once again directed toward television, but not as an MOW (TV-speak for Movie of the Week, also known as a ''made-for''). Plans were finally under way for a second STAR TREK *series*—not STAR TREK: THE NEXT GENERATION, but STAR TREK: PHASE II.

Quickly renamed STAR TREK II, this new series was conceived as the ongoing

[4]This *Enterprise* wasn't destined to fly in space, though. Never outfitted with engines, it was used for atmospheric flight testing only, and is now on display at the Smithsonian Institution.

"THE FORSAKEN"
*In Michael Piller's earliest handwritten notes for the Deep Space Nine bible, he envisioned this meeting between the Next Generation's Lwaxana Troi (Majel Barrett) and DS9's shapeshifting chief of security. Odo (Rene Auberjonois): "Madam, at night I turn into a liquid." Lwaxana: "That's all right, I can swim."*

*Q and Vash (John DeLancie and Jennifer Hetrick), two favorite characters from The Next Generation, have also made the journey to DS9, helping weave all forms of STAR TREK together.*

adventures of the *Enterprise*'s second five-year mission, still under the command of Captain Kirk. (On the business side, Paramount was also hoping to use the series as a key element in its plans to establish PTS—Paramount Television Service, a fourth television network.) All the regulars except Leonard Nimoy as Mr. Spock were slated to return. New sets and a refitted *Enterprise* were designed. New scripts were commissioned and written. There were no more delays on the horizon. Everything seemed to be in place for STAR TREK to return to the television screen.

But then, as it so often does in the television industry, something unexpected happened.

# THE MO$T

# IMPORTANT CHAPTER

# IN THIS BOOK

# THREE

*Anything worth doing is worth
doing for money.*

—The 13th Rule of Acquisition

**W**hat was unexpected *this* time was that in 1977, a farmboy named Luke Skywalker took up arms against an evil galactic empire. And a giant alien spaceship landed at Devil's Tower in Wyoming.

As industry executives began toting up the phenomenal box-office grosses from *Star Wars* and *Close Encounters of the Third Kind,* it was astonishingly evident that science-fiction movies were no longer marginal productions designed to separate teenage boys from their allowances. Science fiction was box-office gold.

Thus, in November 1977, when Paramount changed course and gave up its plans to establish a fourth network, the second STAR TREK television series was canceled before it even went into production.[1] Instead, all the preproduction work that had been done was shifted from Paramount's Television division to Features, and STAR TREK: THE MOTION PICTURE was given the green light—movie jargon for a project being given authorization to begin production—and released in 1979, five years after the studio had decided to bring STAR TREK back to life.

Once again, history repeated itself. Initial reviews of this first movie were sometimes scathing. But the fans returned again and again, and in Hollywood's ultimate measurement of success, three years later, in 1982, the first sequel was released, STAR TREK II: THE WRATH OF KHAN. Succeeding years brought STAR TREK III: THE SEARCH FOR SPOCK (1984), STAR TREK IV: THE VOYAGE HOME (1986), STAR TREK V: THE FINAL FRONTIER (1989), and STAR TREK VI: THE UNDISCOVERED COUNTRY (1991).

[1] In 1993, Paramount once again announced its plans to form its own television network, though because of Fox, it would now be a fifth network. Created in conjunction with Chris Craft Broadcasting, Paramount's network is scheduled to begin operation in January 1995, by broadcasting on Monday and Tuesday nights. The flagship series for this new network is slated to be STAR TREK: VOYAGER.

*The Grand Nagus, leader of the greedy, profit-driven, often unscrupulous Ferengi race. Any similarity to Hollywood agents is purely co-incidental.*

Twenty-five years after it had said that STAR TREK "won't work," *Variety* acknowledged the first five STAR TREK movies as the most successful science-fiction movie series in film history, with combined box-office grosses of more than $400 million. STAR TREK VI has pushed that figure well over $500 million, and as this book goes to press, the first *Next Generation* movie—STAR TREK: GENERATIONS—is scheduled for a 1994 Thanksgiving Day release. Including revenue from all sources, STAR TREK is estimated to have grossed more than $1.3 *billion* for Paramount since 1966.

But the movies are only half the story. As Paramount executives assessed the earnings from the first three STAR TREK films[2] and listened to the requests from television stations eager to syndicate new episodes of *The Original Series*, they began to realize that STAR TREK might not have to be an either-or proposition as they had decided when they shut down the STAR TREK II television series to make STAR TREK: THE MOTION PICTURE. Perhaps the property *could* succeed in theaters and on television at the same time.

The only problem seemed to be that a new series involving the key cast members from *The Original Series* would be too expensive. With few exceptions, television productions can rarely afford the same salary levels that movie productions can. Also, some of the cast had moved on to new careers and might not be keen to return to the daily grind of a weekly series. So, though there were many other creative and business factors guiding them, Paramount and Gene Roddenberry decided to create a new STAR TREK series set many decades after the original—STAR TREK: THE NEXT GENERATION.

This time, the reception was mixed. Every network, including Fox, wanted the series. But no network would commit to ordering more than a pilot and thirteen episodes. That wasn't an acceptable number for Paramount for a fundamental dollars-and-cents reason. And dollars and cents are exactly why this is The Most Important Chapter in This Book. Allow us to digress.

No matter how thought-provoking and awe-inspiring and just plain entertaining STAR TREK stories are, no matter how fervently dedicated to quality the people who make them are, and no matter how passionately STAR TREK fans, appreciators, and ordinary weekly viewers feel about their show, the bottom line in the entertainment industry in general, and television in particular, is money.

Paramount spends millions of dollars each year to create STAR TREK stories and, as a publicly traded, for-profit company, the executives who authorize that expenditure must see to it that the company earns a profit on each dollar spent. When that profit disappears, so does the project. It's the same logic that led NBC to cancel *The Original Series,* and it's still in play today.

The people who make *The Next Generation* and *Deep Space Nine* are wonderfully creative, admirably motivated, and intensely driven to produce quality work they can be proud of, and that they hope will entertain generations beyond their own, just as the original STAR TREK series continues to do. But the harsh reality is that they are part of a business, and for there to be STAR TREK on television, in movie theaters, in whatever media are still to come, all aspects of STAR TREK must be run as a business. Some dedicated fans sometimes take exception to this dollars-and-cents attitude, which, they correctly perceive, shapes Paramount's thinking about STAR TREK. But what they must remember is that the STAR TREK they enjoy today has come about precisely because Paramount has so successfully nurtured it in a businesslike fashion over most of the past thirty years.

With money firmly established as the most basic and essential force in the ongoing production of STAR TREK, we return to the dollars-and-cents issue facing Paramount at the time it was eager to begin production of *The Next Generation.* At the same time, we'll take a quick look at the realities of present-day television finances.

In general, it costs more to produce an hour-long episode of a television series than a network will pay to show it. Thus, the production company covers the shortfall out of its own funds, hoping to recoup that money—and much more—when the

[2]In round numbers, STAR TREK: THE MOTION PICTURE cost $44 million and grossed $80 million at the domestic box office, STAR TREK II cost $12 million and grossed $70 million, and STAR TREK III cost $16 million and grossed $70 million. While a rule of thumb is that because of advertising and distribution expenses, including payments to theaters, a movie must gross at least three times its cost to "break even" (an extremely loose term in Hollywood), because of foreign box-office grosses, television broadcast fees, and, most importantly, home-video sales, the STAR TREK movies have brought Paramount a healthy return on investment.

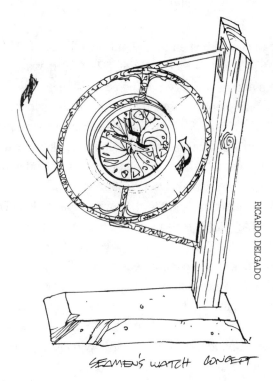

SEAMEN'S WATCH CONCEPT

Like all the STAR TREK productions before it, on Deep Space Nine money can be a driving force behind almost every production decision. An early draft of the first-season episode "Dramatis Personae" called for Sisko to become obsessed with building alien timepieces. Ricardo Delgado designed several, but each would have cost one to two thousand dollars to construct. In the end, the producers decided that Sisko's obsession could be presented just as effectively, and much less expensively, by having him build only one timepiece, as shown in the photograph.

TWO PENDULUMS

ALIEN PENDULUM TIMEPIECE.

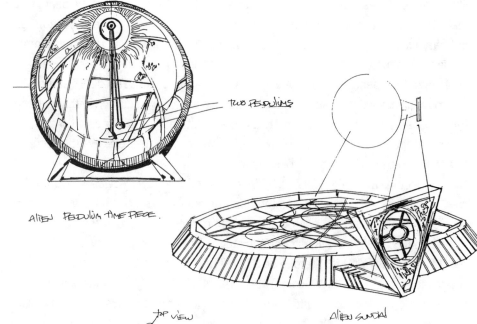

ALIEN SUNDIAL

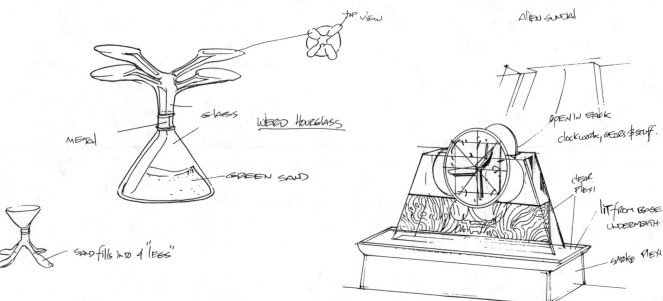

TOP VIEW

METAL

GLASS

WIERD HOURGLASS

GREEN SAND

SAND FILLS INTO 4 "LEGS"

OPEN IN BACK
clockwork, GEARS & STUFF.

CLEAR PLEXI

LIT FROM BASE UNDERNEATH

SMOKE PLEXI

series is eventually sold for syndication. Paramount had a good idea what an episode of a STAR TREK series was worth in syndication. *The Original Series'* episodes, which in the mid-sixties had cost from about $190,000 each to make in the first season to just under $180,000 in the third, had earned back more than $1 million per episode in syndication fees, and they were two decades old. New episodes would be considerably more valuable, even given that *The Next Generation*'s first-season budget was approximately $1.2 million an episode.[3]

But even though Paramount was willing to make up the difference between that $1.2 million per episode and the $400 to $500 thousand a network might pay as a licensing fee, a thirteen-episode order wasn't large enough. To be successful in syndication, a series generally needs sixty-five episodes available, which allows stations to "strip" a series—that is, show an episode each weekday for thirteen

Paramount wasn't looking for a sixty-five-episode commitment, because that would have been a completely unrealistic demand. But the company knew that it had to be able to make more than thirteen episodes to make any *Next Generation* syndication package attractive.

So Paramount took what, at the time, was considered a risky move. It turned the networks down and decided to produce *The Next Generation* for the direct-syndication market, bypassing the networks and their national broadcasts to sell the show station by station.

The direct-syndication market has been around since the 1950s. Series like ZIV's *Sea Hunt* and *Highway Patrol* had been lucrative syndicated successes. Some have even been groundbreaking, as in the case of ZIV's *Cisco Kid,* which in 1950 became the first American television series to be shot in color.

Direct-syndication television series remained quite common in 1986, though they tended to be half-hour game shows aimed at the early-evening, weekday Prime Access time slot in which networks were not allowed to broadcast,[4] or they were animated children's series or low-budget "reality" productions for earlier or much later time periods.

But Paramount gamely went ahead and offered a brand-new, sophisticated, one-hour drama with prime-time network-quality production values. And, quite fitting for the studio that produced the *Godfather* films, they made their offer one that stations couldn't refuse. The charge for showing that first season of twenty-six *Next Generation* episodes was . . . zero.

In the world of syndicated television sales, there are three basic ways to sell a program. The first is called "all cash," and requires each station to make a cash payment to the seller, based on the size of the local audience and the estimated ratings each episode of the series will earn, usually subdivided into demographic categories. For example, even if a show does not have high overall ratings, it might draw a large percentage of males between eighteen and twenty-five, which certain advertisers might pay a premium to reach. In terms of local audience size, when the hit series *Roseanne* was offered for syndication, KCOP–Los Angeles paid the syndicator, Viacom, approximately $75,000 to $80,000 per episode; WWOR–New York paid $60,000; and in St. Louis, the eighteenth largest broadcast market in the United States, the winning station paid $20,000.

[3]In truth, most television series don't hold themselves to a strict, episode-by-episode budget, which explains why so many different figures have been reported for the cost of a *The Next Generation* or *Deep Space Nine* episode. Usually, an overall budget is set for the whole season, and then individual episodes are targeted to come in either over or under the "pattern." Toward the end of a season, it's sometimes common to see episodes with fewer special effects, guest stars, and one-time-only sets, in order to make up for the "above pattern" costs of earlier, more expensive episodes.

[4]Technically, this provision—called PTAR for Prime Time Access Rule and enacted by the FCC in 1971—requires network affiliates in the top fifty markets to air non-network programming for the first hour of prime-time viewing from Monday to Saturday: 7:00 to 8:00 P.M. in the East and West, 6:00 to 7:00 P.M. in the Central and Mountain time zones. The rule also prohibits stations from airing reruns of shows originally broadcast on networks, with the intention being to limit the networks' control over the best time slots and encourage other production companies to supply shows.

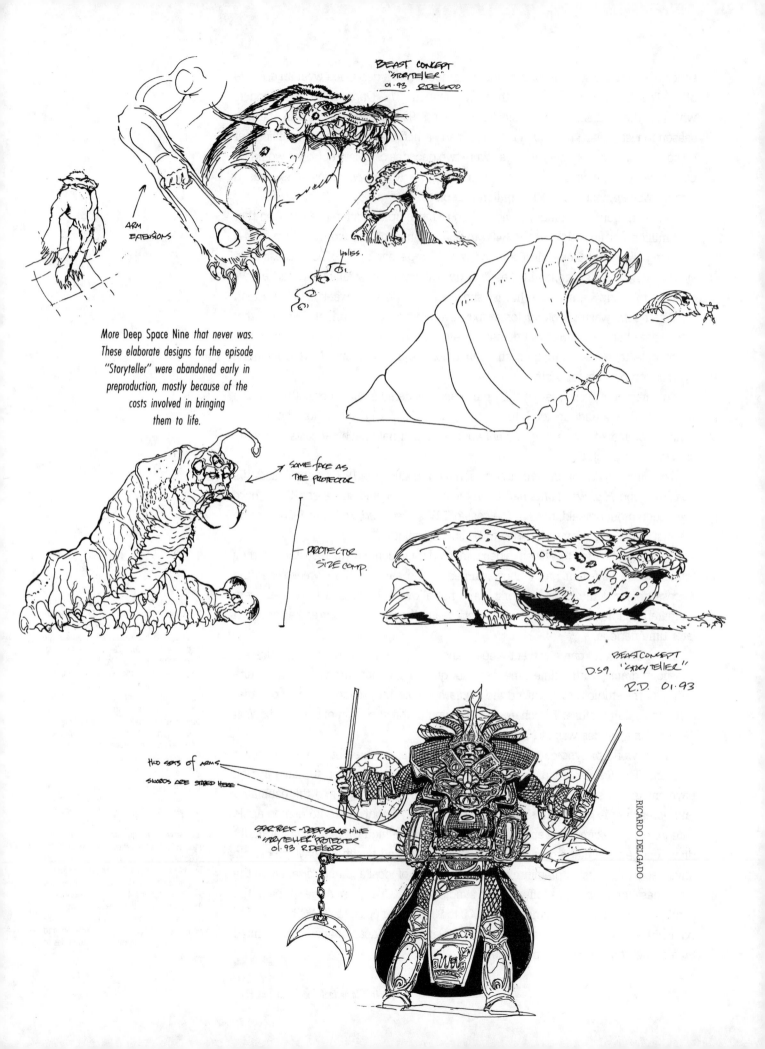

BEAST CONCEPT
"STORYTELLER"
01.93. R.DELGADO

ARM
EXTENSIONS

HOLES.

More Deep Space Nine *that never was.*
*These elaborate designs for the episode*
*"Storyteller" were abandoned early in*
*preproduction, mostly because of the*
*costs involved in bringing*
*them to life.*

SAME FACE AS
THE PROTECTOR

PROTECTOR
SIZE COMP.

BEAST CONCEPT
D.S9. "STORYTELLER"
R.D. 01.93

TWO SETS OF ARMS.

SWORDS ARE STORED HERE.

STAR TREK - DEEP SPACE NINE
"STORYTELLER" PROTECTOR
01.93 R.DELGADO

RICARDO DELGADO

Ideally under the all-cash system, the station then sells advertising time for the series which, it is hoped, will reimburse it for the up-front money and provide a profit.

The second sales method is called "cash plus barter." Under this plan, stations give the syndicator a smaller, up-front cash payment, and a certain number of minutes for advertising during each episode, which the syndicator can then sell to advertisers directly. This is the method that was used for subsequent seasons of *The Next Generation,* and is currently used for *Deep Space Nine.*

But for *The Next Generation*'s first season, Paramount offered the stations the third sales method for syndicated television—what is called an "all barter" deal. Under this plan, stations did not have to put up any money to obtain the series. Instead, Paramount would earn its money from selling about seven minutes of national advertising time in each episode. The station would earn money from selling the remaining time, about five minutes, to local advertisers, for what amounted to pure profit less the costs of selling that time. To sweeten the deal, Paramount also agreed that if the series was not successful enough to be picked up for a second season, the stations could add the first-season episodes to the original STAR TREK episodes they already stripped. The only party that could lose in such a situation was Paramount, which was committing more than $30 million of shareholder money with the expectation of earning back through advertising sales just over half that amount.[5]

But since Paramount was taking the big risk, it was only fair that they should also stand to be a big winner if the gamble paid off. And the gamble *did* pay off.

Despite what was by now a tradition for STAR TREK productions—some initial reviews weren't all-out raves—*The Next Generation* found its market and quickly became the most highly rated weekly dramatic series in syndication.[6] The syndication earnings of $1 million per episode that was reached by *The Original Series* over twenty years was achieved by *The Next Generation* in less than five. By its fifth season, the cost to advertise on *The Next Generation* was the highest of any syndicated series, reportedly $100,000 per thirty-second national spot. During 1991's two-part "Reunification" episode, which guest-starred Leonard Nimoy as Mr. Spock, thirty-second national spots went for a record-setting $200,000 each. And that record was astoundingly shattered by the cost for the same time on the series' final episode—*$700,000!*[7] Over its seven-year history, *The Next Generation* is estimated to have brought Paramount $511 million in revenue, of which $293 million has been profit.

Not only was STAR TREK now the most successful science-fiction film series of all time, it was the most successful dramatic syndicated series of all time, and, when the millions of dollars of additional revenue from books and toys and posters and dozens of other merchandising licenses were added in, perhaps the most successful entertainment franchise of all time, science fiction or not.

But, like any responsible business enjoying a spectacular run of success, in the midst of STAR TREK's phenomenal performance Paramount's executives faced a potentially depressing question: When would it all end?

The answer to that question involved three factors. The first was the audience's reaction: Was there any sign that moviegoers, video renters, and television viewers

[5]First-season revenues were estimated to be approximately $18 million from advertising sales, with a further guarantee of $6.5 million from presales of foreign home-video rights. In all, Paramount was on the line for almost seven million dollars' worth of red ink if *The Next Generation* didn't succeed. Studio executives regularly lose their jobs over much smaller losses.

[6]In its final seasons, *The Next Generation* usually appeared as the third- or fourth-highest-rated weekly syndicated series *of any kind* in the United States, generally coming in just behind shows such as *Oprah* and *Wheel of Fortune. Deep Space Nine* also currently ranks consistently in the top ten syndicated shows, usually only one or two places down from *The Next Generation,* even though it airs on about ten fewer stations. Ironically, the actual number of viewers who watched an average first-run episode of *The Next Generation* was about the same as the number who watched a first-run episode of *The Original Series*—about seventeen million. In the late sixties, that size audience was reason for cancellation, but in the nineties, it's a ratings triumph.

[7]This does not mean Paramount itself receives this full amount for each thirty-second advertising spot in a *Next Generation* episode. To begin with, the price per spot can be negotiated down by an advertiser who buys many spots at once over a specific time period. Next, any advertising agency that acts as the middleman between the advertiser and Paramount Television will take, on average, a ten-percent commission. On the other side of the transaction, the "cost of sale" for a syndicator—covering payroll and expenses—can take another ten to fifteen percent of the total, followed by the syndicator's commission of, again on average, thirty-five percent. (In Paramount's case, because it directly handles its own syndication sales, the syndicator's commission remains within the overall corporation rather than being paid out to a separate third party, which is a considerable benefit and source of extra revenue.)

Thus, speaking generally, Paramount might receive slightly less than half the total amount of money charged for advertising as direct revenue for the series. From that revenue, Paramount must then pay out all applicable residual payments to the producers, writers, directors, and actors. The rest is applied against the cost of making the series in the hopes that, with the addition of all other revenue, Paramount will have taken in more than it has spent. For *The Next Generation* and *Deep Space Nine* both, Paramount does so.

# Residuals: The Work That Keeps on Paying

When actors, writers, and directors in television are paid for their work on a particular episode, that payment typically gives the production company the right to broadcast the episode only once. Each time the episode is shown again, a residual payment based on the first payment must be made. Though we have made no attempt to research the individual contracts for key people on *Deep Space Nine,* the following are examples of the residual payments due performers under the minimum terms established by AFTRA, the American Federation of Television and Radio Artists, and SAG, the Screen Actors Guild, which is the actors' union with jurisdiction over television shows shot on film, such as the two STAR TREK series.

For the first two reruns on a network, each time, the performer receives seventy-five percent of the applicable minimum payment she or he originally received. (For example, under the SAG agreement current at the time this book is written, a performer in a nonstarring speaking role appearing in one episode of a prime-time network one-hour drama must be paid a minimum of approximately $600 a day for that work. Then, when that episode is rerun, the performer receives a residual payment of $450 times however many days she or he originally worked.) The third, fourth, and fifth reruns of a given episode pay fifty percent each. The sixth rerun pays ten percent, and the seventh *and each subsequent rerun* pay five percent. (For syndicated shows, which can be sold to more than two hundred stations across the country, the residual payment is based on the production company's licensing *national* rebroadcast rights for a particular episode, *not* for each time that episode is run on on a local station.)

While syndicated and cable reruns are paid at lesser percentages, individuals—especially those associated with a successful series.—are free to negotiate payments over these minimums. However, for a series such as *The Next Generation,* which undoubtedly will be syndicated well into the next century, even with minimum payments all those five-percents can and do add up. Additional residuals are also payable for videocassette and videodisc sales—currently 2.5 percent of the production company's gross receipts on the first $1 million, three percent thereafter, split between all principal players (i.e. the stars) and other performers on a two-to-one ratio. Also, foreign broadcasts of each episode have a separate residual scale. The first broadcast of an episode in the United Kingdom brings the performer a payment of twenty-five percent of her or his original fee. Most of the rest of Europe brings a residual of ten percent. And most rebroadcasts throughout the rest of the world result in an additional five percent per showing per region. Writers and directors have similar residual payment structures.

The basis for the residual payment system is, quite properly, that as long as the production company continues to make money from a given production, then those people most responsible for creating that production should share in the company's earnings. Ironically, the system in place at the time the original STAR TREK series was produced paid residuals to the key performers only for the first thirteen reruns of each episode. The incredible and unexpected longevity of that series—and, therefore, missed income for the actors—helped change the old system to the one in use today, in which there is no limit on the number of reruns for which residuals must be paid.

Clearly, actors in a successful series that will enjoy a healthy afterlife in reruns can soon find themselves in the position of working for reasons other than mere money.

were growing tired of STAR TREK? The answer then, as now, was no. If anything, the STAR TREK audience was—and still is—continuing to grow.

The second factor was creative. To be blunt, how many times could the crews of captains Kirk and Picard save the universe? Including both series and the movies, by 1991 more than two hundred STAR TREK stories had been filmed and, with only a handful of exceptions, the current writers strove never to repeat any earlier story. How much longer could they keep telling interesting stories that wouldn't disappoint the growing audience? For that matter, how much longer would the series' stars want to put in sixteen-hour days to portray characters that might no longer hold any acting challenge for them? Especially when residuals from the hard work they had already done gave them a firm base of financial security for the years ahead.

The third and most important factor governing the length of time *The Next*

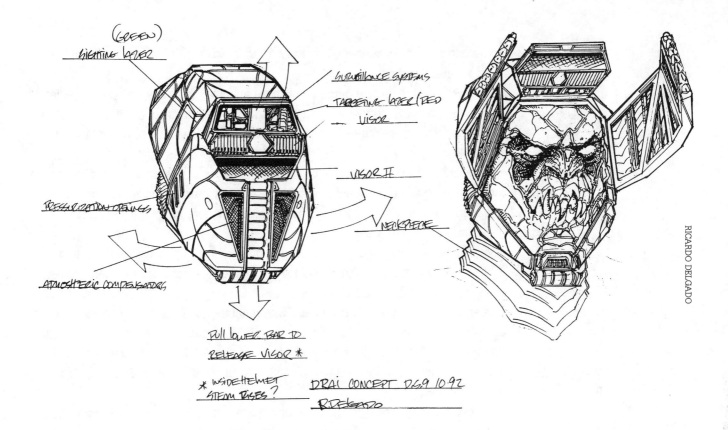

(GREEN)
SIGHTING LAZER

SURVEILLANCE SYSTEMS

TARGETING LAZER (RED)

VISOR

VISOR II

NECKPIECE

PRESSURIZATION OPENINGS

ATMOSPHERIC COMPENSATORS

PULL LOWER BAR TO
RELEASE VISOR *

* INSIDE HELMET
STEAM RISES?

DRAI CONCEPT DG9 10·92
R.DELGADO

RICARDO DELGADO

*Generation* would continue to run concerned the financial status of the show—a status that had two components. The first component was revenue. Syndicators now had seventy-nine episodes of *The Original Series*, and, with a fifth season of *The Next Generation* a certainty, could look forward to at least 125 episodes of that series as well; even more if it went to a sixth and seventh season. And like everything else in television, the price for running those shows went up each year, both in cost per episode and number of episodes. Brandon Tartikoff, chairman of Paramount Pictures during the period in which a third STAR TREK series was proposed, explained the situation this way: "After about seven years, the show, even as successful as it was, was probably going to have to be taken off the market, just because stations already had too many episodes." Kerry McCluggage, current chairman of Paramount TV Group, confirms that conclusion. "We didn't want stations to choke on all those episodes. The original episodes have been outstanding, but once they start repeating five days a week, we're usually looking at declining ratings over time."

The second financial component had to do with cost. Box-office grosses and the going rate for commercials are public knowledge. Everyone associated with STAR TREK movies and television knew how successful the productions were and, quite understandably, wanted to have their fair share of that success. Almost every movie brought a rise in salary and/or an increased shared percentage of gross earnings for the stars and producers, directors, and writers. Almost every television contract renegotiation upped the earnings for most of the equivalent people involved in *The Next Generation*. Furthermore, all the other television production costs mounted each season, not just because of expected inflation, but because of the ongoing creative need to show audiences new things—sets, props, spaceships, and elaborate aliens, with new, improved, and more expensive visual effects. By 1993, that

*This complex design for what would become the Hunters of "Captive Pursuit" was made more cost-effective simply by changing the description of the alien within the helmet to: "a rather mundane humanoid face, not far off human."*

first-season $1.2 million average cost per episode was reportedly close to $2 million, with no end in sight.

Plotted on a graph, the outcome of these financial pressures was quite predictable. At some point, no matter what the audience had to say about it, future STAR TREK productions threatened to become unprofitable. Or, for the cynical, not profitable enough.

Blessed with a growing audience, but also cursed with potential creative burnout, increasing costs, and the specter of falling revenue, it was inevitable that somewhere in Paramount the only, to coin a phrase, logical solution, be formally set forth—

A third STAR TREK series.

The beauty of the idea addressed each of the three factors that had led to it.

The fact that the audience for STAR TREK had easily embraced two different sets of characters indicated that it was the overall *context* of the STAR TREK universe that was appealing, not just the characters who inhabited it. Thus, it was reasonable to assume that the audience could accept a third ensemble cast as readily as it had accepted the first two, provided that many of the familiar touchstones of STAR TREK—Klingons, transporters, the Federation, phasers, Ferengi, Starfleet, and so on—were present.

Second, and this was, perhaps, the riskiest part of the equation, if the third series was *not* set on a Starship, perhaps yet another version of the *Enterprise* decades more into the future, a whole new creative window into the STAR TREK universe could be opened. Add in the new stories that would arise simply from having a new set of main characters with new lives to be recorded and explored, and many seasons more of new scripts set in a fresh arena could be written.[8]

From a financial point of view, the idea of creating a third STAR TREK series made the most sense of all. At the most basic level, new actors meant less—stratospheric salaries. Also, by setting a third series in the same time period as *The Next Generation*, there were seven years' worth of existing sets, props, and costumes to draw upon, further reducing production costs. Other savings could not be quantified as easily, but they seemed just as real: the look and feel of the STAR TREK universe was known, so the task of developing the look of the new series should be straightforward and thus less costly.[9] And, as further inducement, the *Next Generation* cast could be launched into a new series of movies.

Herman Zimmerman recalls Gene Roddenberry saying at the wrap of the pilot episode of *The Next Generation*, ''People say that you can't go home again. But we just proved that, under the right conditions, you can.''

Sadly, Gene Roddenberry died on October 26, 1991, before *Deep Space Nine* had been formally proposed, but his creation was growing stronger and more popular every day. Paramount was thus poised to go home for a third time, taking the twenty-six-year-old science-fiction idea that ''won't work'' into uncharted territory.

There was only one small detail to be finalized.

What was the third STAR TREK series going to be?

The past had finally caught up to the future, and that future was unknown.

But not for long.

[8]Michael Piller has pointed out that new characters and settings are not necessarily enough to insure fresh stories. The emotional and thematic underpinnings of a good STAR TREK story have a particular content, whether based on the crew of the original *Enterprise*, the new *Enterprise*, or *Deep Space Nine*. It is still a challenge for the writing staff to come up with compelling stories to explore STAR TREK's main theme—What does it mean to be human? —without treading too closely to what has gone before.

[9]Or so the executives thought. When the development process for *Deep Space Nine* began, Rick Berman firmly established that very little should be reused from the features or the *Next Generation*, so the new show would have a new identity all its own. Thus, for example, DS9 has runabouts, not shuttlecraft, and Starfleet personnel serving aboard the station have different uniforms from those who serve aboard Starships. Also, Herman Zimmerman's development of a Cardassian design ethic led to a completely new look for a STAR TREK production, not to mention a completely new approach to the design and construction of sets for television overall. Once again, what was planned and what actually came to pass were not necessarily related.

# SETTING

## THE STAGE

FOUR

*The trick is to take the situation that you have,*
*whether it's a science-fiction show like STAR TREK or an*
*action show like Simon and Simon, and bring humanity to it.*
*Use it as an opportunity to explore the human condition.*

—Michael Piller

*I t was to have been an exterior set, built about an hour away from Los Angeles,*
*somewhere up north. It would be a frontier outpost—a twenty-fourth-century*
*version of Fort Laramie on the edge of the frontier. Its alien structures had been*
*looted and burned by Cardassians—a twenty-fourth-century version of Los Angeles*
*itself, after the Rodney King trial riots.*

*In this outpost, somewhere in a trackless desert on the planet Bajor, each week*
*we would follow the adventures of such regular characters as Lieutenant Ro Laren*
*and Dr. Julian Amoros as Starfleet attempted to help the Bajorans bring order back to*
*their world.*

*Often conflicting with Starfleet's goals would be Kai Opaka—the man who was*
*spiritual leader of the Bajorans. Visitors who met with the Kai would have to disrobe*
*while the Kai probed their* pagh *through deep-tissue massage of their feet. . . .*

Huh? Does *any* of this sound familiar?

When last seen, Ro Laren was back on Picard's *Enterprise* (though she has since
gone AWOL from Starfleet to join the Maquis—a move that might have repercussions
for *Voyager*). Dr. Julian *Bashir* was assigned to a space station *near* Bajor and not an
outpost *on* it. The Kai Opaka is (or was) a woman. Her visitors *never* had to take off
their clothes. Bajoran religious leaders generally check people's *paghs* by grasping
their earlobes, not massaging their feet. And the permanent sets for *Deep Space Nine*
are all interiors, safely housed in three enormous soundstages on the Paramount lot
in LA.

*Jim Martin's preliminary designs for "Shadowplay," an episode in which all the world was a stage—holodeck technology taken to the ultimate extreme.*

No, the first few paragraphs weren't a parody or an incorrectly transcribed interview tape. They were a glimpse of what *Deep Space Nine might* have been—a sampling of some of the possibilities explored and cast away during the development and refinement of the series, long before a single actor was cast or design sketch was made. Thinking of these possibilities, like astronomers charting the galaxies rushing away from each other and imagining the distant time when they must all have been compressed together in a single point of space and time, inevitably the question comes to mind—*when* and from where did the first spark of *Deep Space Nine* flash into being?

For example, a well-known tale in Hollywood is that of Roy Huggins. In 1960, Huggins suddenly called to his wife to come and take his picture, which she did. Then, when she asked why, Huggins answered that he had just had a great idea for a television series and "I wanted to record the moment in history when I thought of it."

The photograph Huggins's wife took that day still hangs in his bedroom, thirty-four years later. It shows Huggins smiling smugly at the camera, and for good reason. The series he had just thought of came to be called *The Fugitive,* which, like STAR TREK, went on to become a successful feature film many years after its

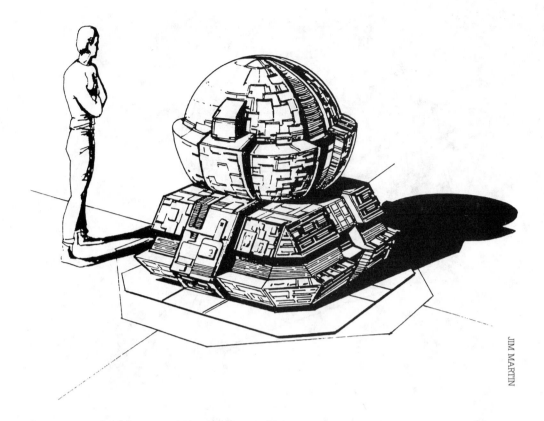

television run was over. (Of course, Roy Huggins knew a good television idea when he thought of it. He is also the creator of *Maverick, 77 Sunset Strip, Run For Your Life,* and, with Stephen J. Cannell, *The Rockford Files.*)

However, in the case of *Deep Space Nine,* there doesn't appear to be any *Fugitive*-like, precise moment of creation to look back upon, chiefly because the series is part of the ongoing continuum of STAR TREK. Given the staying power of that continuum, a third series was, in hindsight at least, inevitable, and the way it came about followed a fairly typical television-industry sequence of events. To understand that sequence, let's step next door and take a quick look at how things are done in the movie industry.

Among those who develop and produce motion pictures, one of the favorite phrases used to categorize a story is "high concept." A high-concept film is one with a story that can intrigue a potential audience member with just a single line of explanation. Dinosaurs are brought back to life through genetic engineering and go on a rampage in the theme park built to hold them . . . an obnoxious unemployed actor disguises himself as a woman to get work and becomes a better person as a woman than he was as a man . . . a young woman is hunted by an unstoppable cyborg from the future because she will someday give birth to the man who will defeat the machines in a future war. . . . All these ideas are succinct, appealing, and have been translated into highly successful movies.

But would they have worked just as well as television series? Let's think about it.

Millions of people loved seeing the incredibly lifelike dinosaurs created for *Jurassic Park,* but how interesting would those dinosaurs be if we could see them go on a rampage every week? After all, how many ways can a *T. Rex* eat a lawyer?[1] On a

[1]As of this writing, rumors continue to circulate that an animated *Jurassic Park* series for children is being developed, despite director Steven Spielberg's denials. Children's programming, however, can be different from adult series in that nonstop action, week after week, can succeed as the basis of a series. Witness the enormous success of *The Mighty Morphin' Power Rangers.*

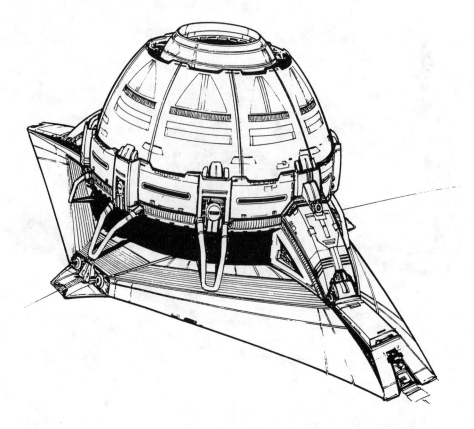

JIM MARTIN

less violent note, once "Tootsie" gets his job on the soap opera and learns his lesson about life, what more can he do—disguise himself as a woman to get a new job in a new industry every week, twenty-six weeks a year? And what about Sarah Connor being chased by the Terminator? Does that situation sound familiar? Could it work as a television series? The answer to that one is: Of course. Simply by stripping away the fact that her pursuer is a cyborg from the future and by changing the reason she's being chased from its science-fiction premise to one more instantly understandable to a larger number of people, you're on your way to a television success story as James Cameron's *Terminator* movie becomes Roy Huggins's *The Fugitive* television series.

Reduced to their most elemental premises, *Terminator* and *The Fugitive* are chase stories, in which the pursued—Sarah Connor and Dr. Richard Kimble—will lose their lives if captured by the pursuer—the Terminator robot and Lieutenant Gerard.

But what about the details that get added to those simple premises? What makes one suitable for a movie? What makes one suitable for television?

The movie, *Terminator*, was full of action, violence, hairsbreadth escapes, and incredible stakes—not only would Sarah Connor lose her life if the robot caught her, the future world would be ruled by machines dedicated to killing all humans. Wow.

But the television series *The Fugitive* didn't have a lot of action or violence, and the hairsbreadth escapes weren't played for exciting stunt work, but for the suspense of the chase. What the series focused on, instead, was the pursued himself, Dr. Richard Kimble, who, in Roy Huggins's words, was "a man who was in trouble the moment he got up from bed every morning."

The *Terminator* movie was about *the chase*. *The Fugitive* television series was about how Richard Kimble *coped* with the chase.

JIM MARTIN

The movie was about *action*. The television series was about the most important aspect of television storytelling—*character*.[2]

There's a story Michael Piller likes to tell that sheds some light on the importance of character in television stories. Years ago, when he had made the decision to become a writer but hadn't yet gathered the courage to quit his day job, he had dinner with his mother. "I was miserable," Piller said, "about a girl who had broken up with me. And, my mother said, 'Well, you'll never be a great writer if you aren't tortured.' And I said, 'Mom! What are you saying? Would you rather me be a great writer and be tortured—or be happy and be a mediocre writer?'" Piller's mother thought a second, then answered, "A great writer."

Piller continues the story by saying that "the truth is, age thirty to forty, perhaps even twenty-five to forty, were torturous years for me on a number of levels. It had to do with family, it had to do with relationships, and it had to do with massive opportunities to learn about myself and the people around me, and how I related to other people. I think when you get into therapy, you begin to start looking at character, and other people's characters, in more fundamental ways. You get below the surface of what you see on television as life—and you begin *living* life. And when you do collect experiences, and you go through the hard times, then you've learned to draw on those experiences, and feelings, and emotional contexts. Suddenly, all these conflicts and heartaches and tragedies begin to resonate as part of your life. You relate to them, and you have feelings that you share with them.

"When you're writing, the trick is to take the situation that you have, whether it's a science-fiction show like STAR TREK or an action show like *Simon and Simon*, and bring humanity to it, to use it as an opportunity to explore the human condition. You tell your plot, and take care of that, but the plot serves as an opportunity to talk about

[2]Of course, many excellent and successful movies have been made with a focus on character instead of action, such as *The Crying Game*, *Terms of Endearment*, and *The Big Chill*. In fact, some of the most popular films are those which combine over-the-top action with strong character work, such as the first *Lethal Weapon* film. But, with few exceptions, most notably among children's programs, television series that emphasize action over character seldom succeed, *The A-Team* notwithstanding.

character. And character is the way to deal with the window into the human soul.

"When I was in college, I couldn't figure out how to write character because I hadn't lived yet. So, now I feel like my strength is character. When I came in to meet Roddenberry for the first time on *The Next Generation,* I said, 'Look, I can't come in here with fifteen science-fiction stories. That's not what I know how to do. But I can write character. I can write relationships. I can help your characters grow.' And, essentially, that's what I set out to do.

"So the themes that have followed me around have basically been about the exploration of family and the interrelationships between people and exploring the human condition. And I think that that's ultimately the mark of superior television. Because you can tell a lot of good action stories, but it's when you begin to reach the audience on a level that touches them in their own lives, that it really becomes worthwhile."

Some people might take exception to the idea that the experiences of a group of space explorers and aliens centuries in the future could ever be relevant to a present-day audience, but to Piller, the STAR TREK context actually helps present the emotional content of the show. "You want to give the audience some distance, you want to give them some space. Other people call that 'escapism.' I don't. I think you want to take the audience away from the worst grittiness of their daily lives, but only far enough so that they have a perspective. Then you give it to them in a new and a different way, and they suddenly can have some objectivity and perhaps learn something by the experience. It's not an educational situation. It's not preaching. But it's an opportunity to examine the human condition with a little bit of distance from their daily lives."

To further reinforce this important distinction of character versus action in the two storytelling arenas of television and movies, remember how the story line of *The Fugitive* television series was altered for the successful, Academy Award–nominated 1993 movie version. First of all, action galore was added—the electrifying train wreck, the escape from the dam, and the helicopter attack on the hotel roof. Next, the stakes were raised—Kimble wasn't just the victim of circumstance, he was the victim of a conspiracy directed specifically against him and linked to a criminal drug company. And finally, Kimble was no longer just running away from the police as he tried to track the infamous one-armed man who killed his wife—he became an active investigator of the murder, and by that action increased the danger he was in. That's a fine story escalation for a two-hour movie, but we'd certainly lose patience with that situation if it were allowed to run over the four years *The Fugitive* television series ran.

Believe it or not, this discussion of the differences between movie and television story telling does bring us back to STAR TREK and *Deep Space Nine.*

STAR TREK II: THE WRATH OF KHAN is a perfect example of an action movie, full of exciting space battles and visual effects, heightened by high stakes, and driven by a clear-cut, high-concept story line of obsessive revenge. In fact, for the role of Khan, key parts of Ricardo Montalban's dialogue were lifted directly from one of the all-time great obsessive–revenge novels, *Moby Dick.* Plus, the character interactions are rich and varied (helped enormously by the fact that because of television, most of

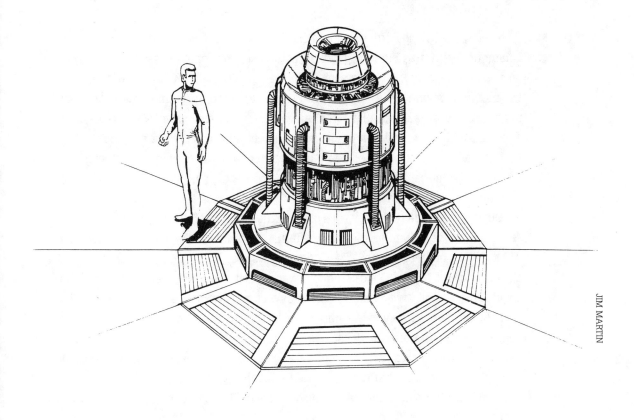

the audience was very familiar with the characters and their interactions long before they set foot in a movie theater—an advantage most movies don't share).

But the original STAR TREK *series* didn't have the luxury of state-of-the art visual effects and drawn-out space battles. Though the context of the stories it told was that of futuristic space exploration, that context was not the overriding point of the show. Instead, it was the story of how the *people* involved in futuristic space exploration *coped* with all they discovered and experienced. And—this should come as no great surprise—what the main characters discovered and explored, even though the story was played out against a fanciful, science-fiction backdrop, was no different from what those in the television audience encountered in their own lives.

Who hasn't been tempted to shuck off all their responsibilities and opt for a simpler, freer life—just as Mr. Spock did in "This Side of Paradise"? Who hasn't faced the specter of being replaced on the job by a more efficient system—just as Captain Kirk was in "The Ultimate Computer"? And who hasn't been forced to take on the persona of a 1920s gangster in order to bring peace to warring gangs—well, all right, in television as in everything else, there are always exceptions to every rule.

But overall, the most important aspect of any television series is character—accessible, understandable, and entertaining people we can identify with, and want to see again and again and again.

With this as a starting point, most often creating a television series does not necessarily mean waiting for a burst of sudden inspiration to hit. Instead, it is more often a slow and careful process of logical thinking, applying all the rules of television storytelling, to make something that is sufficiently different from all that has come before, yet comfortably the same as everything that has been successful in the past.

That's what Rick Berman and Michael Piller were faced with in 1991, when Paramount executives Brandon Tartikoff, John Pike, and John Symes, with eyes fixed on the bottom line and anxious to maintain the STAR TREK franchise as one of Paramount's crown jewels, asked Rick Berman to come up with a new series that might be able to take the place of the soon-to-be-too-expensive *Next Generation:* Take all that had worked before, make it different, but make it just as good.

Tartikoff, especially, had some initial ideas for what direction a new show might take, and in the early summer of 1991, he discussed them with other Paramount executives and Rick Berman.

Drawing on Gene Roddenberry's succinct description of the original STAR TREK series as "*Wagon Train* to the stars," Tartikoff originally suggested that the new STAR TREK series might be "*The Rifleman* in space."[3] He proposed that the lead character could be like Chuck Connors was in that classic Western series, and he could have his child with him—perhaps as a stowaway or as an official part of the ship. *Deep Space Nine* viewers might see in this idea the genesis of Commander Benjamin Sisko and his son, Jake.

Tartikoff goes on to say, "I pitched that idea to Berman and he said he'd think about it. And then, right after that, Gene Roddenberry passed away and his widow, Majel,[4] was very open to the idea of having this deal happen and happen quickly. I suppose that somewhere in that idea, *Deep Space Nine* has its roots, though obviously it became its own thing."

Fortunately, Berman, as creative people are wont to do, had for the last year been talking over with Piller just such a project as Tartikoff had suggested, as part of an ongoing series of discussions relating to other television projects they might possibly want to pursue in the future. Up to Berman's meeting with the Paramount execs, those discussions had just been unhurried brainstorming sessions. But now that they had a mandate, it was time to go to work in earnest, and after thinking over Paramount's request, Rick Berman gave Michael Piller a call and asked him if he would like to become involved in creating the new series. Piller, as we know, said yes.

But before we take a look at how Berman and Piller came up with *Deep Space Nine,* let's take a look at Berman and Piller.

[3]Until he attended a rough-cut screening of STAR TREK VI: THE UNDISCOVERED COUNTRY in his role as chairman of Paramount Pictures, at the age of forty-three, Brandon Tartikoff had never seen a complete episode of either STAR TREK series. This is not all that surprising, though, because it is quite common that those people who work in television watch it far less than does almost any other segment of the audience, probably for the same reason that cabdrivers don't take drives in the country on their days off.

[4]Majel Barrett has the distinction of being in every incarnation of STAR TREK. She played "Number One," Captain Pike's female first officer in the first pilot of *The Original Series,* Nurse Christine Chapel in the original series (later Dr. Chapel in the movies), and Lwaxana Troi—the "Auntie Mame of space"—in *The Next Generation* and *Deep Space Nine.* She also has provided the voice for Federation computers in all three series.

# THE

# STAGEMAKERS

*There's a good chance that when I'm gone, others will*
*come along and do so well that people will say, "Oh,*
*that Roddenberry. He was never this good."*
*But I will be pleased with*
*that statement.*

—Gene Roddenberry[1]

**R**ick Berman is a tall, imposing man with a deceptively calm demeanor. Deceptive because no person should be able to executive-produce two of the most expensive and complex television series ever made, while helping to develop a third, *and* produce a feature film at the same time. But somehow, Rick Berman does, without ever looking as if he's on the verge of a nervous breakdown.

He's the first to say that the secret to handling so much work is to have an exceptional group of people working for him, and that's certainly true. But more than that, Rick Berman shares what all great television producers have—an incredibly discerning eye for detail and a computerlike mind that can keep track of it all, effortlessly shifting from dealing with the editing of an action sequence on *Deep Space Nine,* to making comments on a new script for *The Next Generation,* to helping plan the alien makeup effects required for the *Next Generation* movie. And all this intense, creative activity is coupled with what he feels is the enormous responsibility to keep all that he does, all that appears onscreen in the various projects he oversees, true to the vision of STAR TREK's original creator, Gene Roddenberry.

Rick Berman never forgets that obligation. A handsome bust of Roddenberry sits on his desk to help him remember. It is true that the bust has been known to sport a red blindfold from time to time, but only in the spirit of affectionate fun. The most-often-asked question in the offices housing the production staff and writers for

[1]As reported in the *Los Angeles TV Times.* Jan. 3–9, 1993. "Star Trek's New Frontier" by Daniel Cerone.

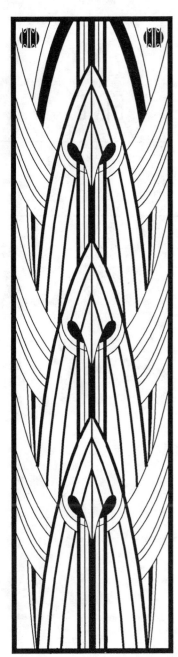

*This is the giant backlit mural that dominates the gambling action at Quark's—a fitting design to introduce the two people to whom Paramount entrusted its "crown jewel," STAR TREK.*

*The Next Generation* and *Deep Space Nine* is: Is this in keeping with Gene's STAR TREK? The deep respect with which Roddenberry and his creation are viewed is truly in evidence, though always with a sense of down-to-earth good humor, which Roddenberry himself encouraged while he was alive and would certainly approve of today.

In addition to admiring his talents and skills, some people also consider Rick Berman one of the luckiest people in television as well. Just as Mark Allan Shepherd happened to wander onto the Paramount lot at exactly the right time to secure his job as a *Deep Space Nine* extra, and then ended up, through an unforeseen chain of events, making his own small ongoing contribution to STAR TREK's rich background texture, so, too, did Rick Berman find himself on the Paramount lot at exactly the right time to do the same, though at a very different level.

Berman had come to Paramount from Warner Bros. in 1984. At Warners, he had been Director of Dramatic Development for the studio's television division. Earlier, from 1982 to 1984, his production credits included HBO's *What on Earth?* and the PBS special *The Primal Mind*. Previous to that, he had been senior producer of ABC's *The Big Blue Marble*, for which he had received an Emmy Award for Outstanding Children's Series.

Even before those notable accomplishments, Berman had experienced bits and pieces of many of the job functions he would later come to supervise as an executive producer for *The Next Generation* and *Deep Space Nine*. Working for a variety of production companies after leaving college (which in true Hollywood tradition he had entered hoping to become an actor), Berman tried his hand at everything from writing to recording sound to being an assistant cameraman. He even spent seven years traveling all over the world with different film crews for the United Nations, making documentaries for the organization that had served as one of the inspirations for STAR TREK's United Federation of Planets.

Though other industries might frown on such a mixed background, a varied production record is actually a good thing to have in Hollywood, because it prevents one from being pigeonholed as ''a children's-show producer only,'' or ''a documentary producer only.'' By having produced a wide range of projects, Rick Berman was known as a *producer*, period, with the positive implication being that he could produce anything. Which he could.

The question then arises: What, exactly, *is* a producer? We all know people who as children said, ''I want to write,'' or ''I want to act,'' but what child announces, ''I want to produce''? Part of the reason for this lack of understanding about a producer's role is, as Berman himself says, because '' 'producer' is a very misunderstood word. And I think one of the reasons for that is that a producer is quite different in different media.

''In the motion-picture world, a producer is much more of a packager and an overseer. But in television, a producer has responsibilities that are more like those of a movie's director.'' In other words, a television producer, especially at Berman's executive level, is the one who is ultimately responsible for everything we see and hear on the screen.

Berman puts it succinctly when he says, ''I'm involved in *everything*.'' The

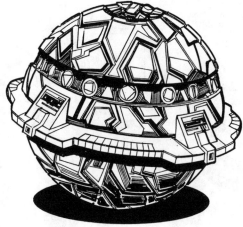

JIM MARTIN

LARGE 4 PERSON GAMBLING ORB

PERSONAL SIZE

*Whether it's the permanent floating poker game on the Enterprise-D or the many games of chance at Quark's, including these Causal Orbs from "Rivals," gambling seems to be an undercurrent in many aspects of STAR TREK—perhaps an indication of what the producers feel they're doing when they try to create shows that millions will continue to enjoy.*

amount of his involvement varies from one area to another, but when asked to elaborate, Berman does so in detail. To begin: "I am very involved in the scripts. I get involved conceptually in the stories, and then, when the stories go to the various drafts, I sit down with Michael and the writer and I give notes, usually copious. I also get involved with the final dialogue polishing of the script, though I'm not anywhere near as involved with the structural work on the scripts as Michael is.

"Then, I'm in charge of all the production meetings, and all the elements of design, whether it be set design, or costume design, or makeup design, or hair design—all of these things come through me. During the course of filming, I view the dailies, and discuss them with the directors and with supervising producer David Livingston. Then I get very involved in the postproduction, including the opticals[2] as they come in in various stages. I sit for two or three days with each episode, working with the editor and the supervising editor on the final cut.

"*Then*, I get involved with the spotting[3] of the sound effects and the music, and finally I review each one of the dubs.[4] As well, I'm the final voice when problems occur with the actors or with the crew or with anything that has to do with the studio. I tend to be the person who has to work those things out."

No wonder the best producers, like Berman, have wide-ranging work experience.

When Berman came to Paramount in 1984, his position was Director of Current Programming, in which he was responsible for overseeing the hit Paramount sitcoms *Cheers, Family Ties*, and *Webster*. Before a year had passed, he had been upped to Executive Director of Dramatic Programming, overseeing the production of the ABC miniseries *Space*,[5] *Wallenberg: A Hero's Story*, and the top-rated, one-hour dramatic adventure series *MacGyver*. True to his beginnings, Berman's talents and skills were the equal of any type of television production, from documentary to miniseries to drama.

[2]An "optical" is any special-effect shot involving the manipulation of an image after it has been photographed. This can include phaser beams, model shots, view-screen mattes, Odo morphing, or any one of a number of computer-aided techniques used to improve a shot, which viewers never realize they're seeing. More on this in Chapter 14.

[3]A spotting session is a meeting in which the producers meet with the composer or, in the case of sound effects, the sound editors, in order to determine where music or sound effects should be added, and what both components should sound like. In the case of music, a videotape of the final cut is literally "spotted" with dots and lines that show the composer exactly where the music should begin and end, and which key actions should be emphasized with a musical flourish.

[4]Here, "dub" refers to versions of a particular episode at various stages in the postproduction process, e.g. one with opticals, one with sound effects, one with scoring, one with second-unit inserts, etc.

[5]Based on James Michener's fictionalized history of the United States space program, *Space* can be considered borderline science fiction because one of its climactic scenes involves the fictional Apollo 18 lunar mission (which in real life was canceled because of budget constraints), in which the astronauts do not survive their mission. Other than this, Rick Berman had no special background in science fiction when he joined the STAR TREK family.

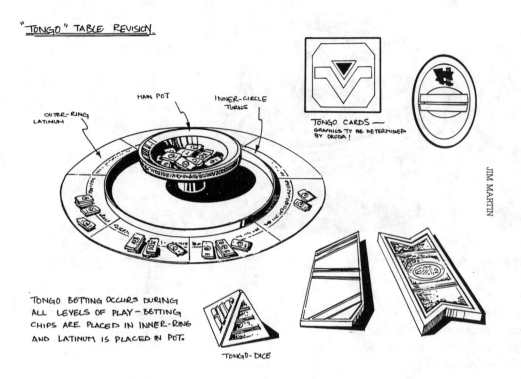

"TONGO" TABLE REVISION

OUTER-RING LATINUM

MAIN POT

INNER-CIRCLE TURNS

TONGO CARDS —
GRAPHICS TO BE DETERMINED
BY OKUDA!

JIM MARTIN

TONGO BETTING OCCURS DURING
ALL LEVELS OF PLAY — BETTING
CHIPS ARE PLACED IN INNER-RING
AND LATINUM IS PLACED IN POT.

TONGO-DICE

1) DICE IS ROLLED IN CENTER
2) CARDS ARE DEALT
3) BETS ARE PLACED WITHIN OUTER CIRCLE

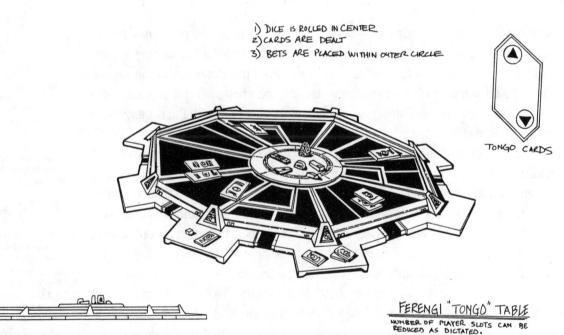

TONGO CARDS

FERENGI "TONGO" TABLE
NUMBER OF PLAYER SLOTS CAN BE
REDUCED AS DICTATED.

*Preliminary designs for Tongo—a
backroom game of chance popular
at Quark's.*

TONGO CARDS

Another promotion was quick in coming and he became Vice President, Longform[6] and Special Projects, in May 1986, which was, by a coincidence no television writer would *ever* be allowed to get away with, the same month Paramount announced the cast of its new syndicated television series, *Star Trek: The Next Generation,* scheduled to debut that fall.

As it turned out, the words "Special Projects" were the operative term in Berman's new title, because at just about the same time he took on his new position Paramount came to the decision that there was no money to be made in longform television production and decided to exit that end of the business. Berman's superior was suddenly without a job, and if Berman's only responsibility had been longform, he might have been facing the prospect of a very empty desk. *Except,* there was this one very special project starting up on the lot that was in the throes of preproduction and suffering from some understandable growing pains—*Star Trek: The Next Generation.* Since, as he says, he was the "lowest-tenured" executive on the lot, Berman was asked by the studio to be the studio's liaison on the series, acting as observer, offering advice where and when necessary, and generally keeping an eye on how everything was progressing for the company that was putting up the money for the venture. Berman himself defines the job as being "the studio guy."

But being the *Next Generation* studio guy was somewhat equivalent to Mark Allan Shepherd being asked to put on the Morn suit for the first time—no one was prepared for what would happen next.

After about two weeks in his new role, Berman was asked to lunch by Gene Roddenberry. So well did the two men get on that Berman characterizes the meeting as "love at first sight." Roddenberry's response was more to the point—the next day he asked Paramount if Berman could come work on the show as a producer. Berman recalls that "over the first three-month period, I went from producer, to supervising producer, to co-executive producer, and by the middle of the first season I was running the show with Gene." Though none could know it at the time, Gene Roddenberry had taken the first step in preparing to pass the torch of STAR TREK's stewardship.

Several years later, at a STAR TREK convention in Los Angeles, about a year before his death, Gene Roddenberry spoke to the gathered fans about the future of STAR TREK. He had seen his creation span generations of viewers, he had heard the fans of both *The Original Series* and the new debate the pros and cons of both, and though there had been no formal talks of a third series at this time, he spoke of how he perceived STAR TREK's future, after he was gone.

With a charm and sincerity that clearly came from a person who was used to studying human behavior from the perspective of one who looked into the future, Roddenberry said that he expected—indeed, he hoped—that in the years to come, new generations of fans would look at the new forms of STAR TREK being produced and say, "This is *real* STAR TREK. Those other people back there at the beginning, they didn't do it half as well."

Clearly Roddenberry, then sixty-nine, saw the success his creation was enjoying and understood that STAR TREK would endure without him. By this time, with *The Next Generation* going into its fourth season more popular than ever, and with Rick

[6]"Longform" is an industry term referring to television projects longer than an hour. It includes MOWs and miniseries, which are essentially MOWs shown on more than one night.

SISKO   KIRA   BASHIR.   DAX

DS.9 SORE LOSERS CHULA GAME PIECES R.DELGADO 11.92

*Preliminary designs for the game pieces in the episode that would be called "Move Along Home."*

Berman's name joining Roddenberry's in the closing credits as the series' executive producer, it was quite evident to insiders to whom Roddenberry wished the torch to be passed. Equally clear from the warmth and graciousness of Roddenberry's remarks that day was the confidence he felt in Rick Berman as the one to take over his creation and guide it through its continuing growth.

The meeting in which Berman was asked to come up with a third STAR TREK series took place shortly before Gene Roddenberry's death, and Berman did have a chance to sound out Roddenberry on how he felt about the idea of a third STAR TREK series. Roddenberry, Berman reports, thought that it would be great, and that they should talk about it soon.

Unfortunately, that talk never took place. But no one connected with STAR TREK doubts that Gene Roddenberry would have had anything but confidence and enthusiasm for the way in which Rick Berman has kept his creation alive, relevant, and vital, including the creation of *Deep Space Nine*.

But just as Gene Roddenberry brought together scores of talented individuals to make ongoing contributions to his creation, Rick Berman did not create *Deep Space Nine* alone. When Paramount asked him for a new series, Berman went to the person who was responsible for the acclaimed scripts that had brought *The Next Generation* its highest ratings and critical praise—Michael Piller.

The 1994 Members Directory of the Writers Guild of America lists Michael Piller's credits as follows:

The Chula "gameboard" from "Move Along Home."

**TV:** *Cagney & Lacey*, Orion; *Hard Time on Planet Earth*, Touchstone (3 eps.[episodes]); *Legmen*, UTV [Universal Television]; *Miami Vice*, UTV; *Sidekicks*, Disney; *Simon & Simon*, UTV (11 eps.); *Star Trek: The Next Generation*, Paramount (12 eps.); *Star Trek: Deep Space 9*, Paramount; *The Dukes of Hazzard*, WB [Warner Bros.].

It's typical of Piller that the list is so short, not because those are his only writing credits—which they aren't—but because he's made no effort to correct the directory's omissions. First and foremost, Michael Piller is a writer, and everything else—with the exception of his family—is not quite as important. The same intense and critical attention to detail that Rick Berman brings to the production end of *Deep Space Nine*, Piller brings to the creation of its scripts. Theirs is a perfect television partnership.

Anyone familiar with the television industry in Los Angeles could peg Piller as a writer from twenty paces. That's because he often wears the television writer's "uniform" of slightly faded jeans, white sneakers, and a baseball cap. One aspect typical of a television writer that he lacks, however, is the haunted, slightly pallid look of desperation that usually comes from too many late nights chasing too many short deadlines. Like Rick Berman, there's an unexpected air of calm around Piller, and a quick and genuine readiness to smile, as if the fate of tens of millions of dollars' worth of television production were not resting on his shoulders twenty-four hours a day.

In short, Michael Piller has the look of success about him—a quality that comes to those who work hard and are rewarded by having that work awarded both respect and wide appreciation. As might be expected, it's an attitude that's shared by many of the people who work on *Deep Space Nine,* and helps contribute to the remarkably calm atmosphere that pervades almost all stages of the show's production.

Unlike Rick Berman, though, Michael Piller came into contact with STAR TREK by choice. Though what he intended to do and what he ended up doing were two incredibly different things.

Piller had always been drawn to becoming a writer, and with that goal in mind, he enrolled in a creative-writing course when he was in college. This was the beginning of the torturous route he alluded to in Chapter 4. As Piller puts it, "I had a very, very bad experience."

He continues, "The creative-writing teacher was a fairly renowned writer, at least at that time, and he opened his class by telling all the students, 'There are enough bad writers out there, and if I think you can't write, I'm going to do everything in my power to discourage you.' I happened to be one of those people whom he decided should not be a writer."

Piller recalls that the teacher would read his work in class, tear it apart, and the class would laugh. "It was horrible. By the time it was over, I couldn't go near a typewriter. I didn't want to write anymore." Piller decided he would, by default, go into journalism. That way he could still put words on paper, but it would be different from creative writing. He didn't write another word of fiction for five years.

"Then one night in New York, I went to see a very early performance of *Chorus Line,*" Piller explains. "One of the kids in the chorus tells the story of the acting teacher who has the students in his class pretend to go down a hill on a toboggan. And he basically says if you don't have talent, you won't feel the snow and the wind in your face. And if you don't start feeling the wind in your face, you're going to get transferred and you're never going to make it. In the song the kid in the chorus sings, she confesses that she feels 'Nothing.'

"Now, I'm sitting on the edge of my seat saying, This is my story! I know this teacher. And the kid in the chorus goes to her church and prays to Santa Maria for guidance. And I'm saying to myself, What's the answer to this?, because I never could find the answer. And, of course, the voice of Santa Maria comes down and tells her: 'This class is *nothing.* This man is *nothing.* Go out and find a better class.' And I said: Why didn't I think of that?

"So, I had a very religious experience watching *Chorus Line.* It was a big night for me, and I started writing again from that time on."

But, it must be said that during the five years he hadn't been writing fiction, Piller had been working hard. True to his revised goals, he began his career writing local television news for CBS in New York. That led to positions as managing editor of the WBTV-TV News in Charlotte, North Carolina, and senior news producer at WBBM-TV, the CBS affiliate in Chicago. While at WBBM-TV, Piller became the senior producer on the 5 and 10 o'clock news, and produced two Emmy-winning news specials. One was a series of minidocumentaries about living with cancer, and the other an annual wrap-up of the year's events. His newscast also won the Associated Press Award for Best Newscast in the state.

But television journalism was not where Piller wanted to spend the rest of his life and despite his success he was unhappy. He wanted to get into entertainment, and an opportunity eventually came along at which he jumped.

He was offered a job at CBS in Los Angeles as part of the network's department of broadcast standards and practices, specializing in docudramas. In plain English, Piller came to LA to become a censor for television movies. It was to be an educational experience.

"As a censor, I was reading a script every day, and I happened to be in a department that worked with some of the best writers: David Rintels,[7] Stanley Greenberg,[8] and just a whole variety of wonderful television writers. So I started reading some very good scripts, and I also read some very bad scripts. And I found myself saying: I can do this. And I started writing.

"Frankly, the first couple of scripts were not great. It took me two years of writing to write a good script. By that time, I'd been promoted to the Entertainment Division of CBS and was working at prime-time shows,[9] and I started writing speculative material.[10] I got some of the people I was working with to read them, and they encouraged me a little bit more until, finally, because my career at CBS didn't seem to be going anywhere, I decided that I was going to quit and become a writer. My father said I shouldn't do it—he'd had a bad experience as a writer out here—but I went ahead and got my first two assignments as favors. One from Barney Rosenzweig at *Cagney and Lacey*, and one from Richard Chapman and Phil De Guere at *Simon and Simon*. Both of those scripts were shot, and later I was hired by *Simon and Simon* and was there for three years, eventually becoming a producer."

After his stint on *Simon & Simon*, Piller went on to work on a variety of other shows, in addition to co-creating and co-producing the syndicated series *Code One Medical*.

But it was while he was working at Disney on the short-lived series *Hard Time on Planet Earth* that Piller had his unexpected first contact with STAR TREK.

"I had called Maurice Hurley[11] to ask him about a writer that we were considering, who had worked for STAR TREK. I wanted to know what he thought of that writer and, during the course of our conversation, I told Maurice how much I enjoyed *The Next Generation*. I had been watching it with my family for two years and I thought it was a wonderful show.

"Then he said, 'Hey, if you're interested in the show, I'm leaving. You should meet Roddenberry.' So he set me up with a lunch with Rick Berman, Gene Roddenberry, and himself, to just get acquainted. We had a very nice lunch at Le Chardonnay, and the week before, I believe, 'Measure of a Man' had been on for the first time, and I told them what a remarkable show I thought that was.[12] We got along quite well."

Since Hurley's decision to leave the show had been made before the lunch, it was no surprise that a replacement had already been found—Michael Wagner, who had been a story editor on the acclaimed *Hill Street Blues*.

[7]Rintels's credits include the television movies *Andersonville* and *Execution*, the Hallmark Hall of Fame presentation of *Gideon's Trumpet*, and the motion picture *Not Without My Daughter*.

[8]Greenberg's credits include the television movies *Blind Ambition*, *Huey Long*, *Missiles of October*, and the motion pictures *Soylent Green* and *Skyjacked*.

[9]Among them, *The Incredible Hulk*, *The Dukes of Hazzard*, and *Cagney & Lacey*.

[10]See Appendix III for the importance of "spec" scripts in starting a career in television writing.

[11]At the time, Hurley was a co-executive producer of *The Next Generation*. He and Piller had worked together on *Simon & Simon*.

[12]"Measure of a Man" aired the week of February 13, 1989. It was the first produced television script by Melinda M. Snodgrass and told the story of the Starfleet hearing in which the android Data has his rights as a sentient being called into question. The script was nominated for a Writers Guild award and was a perfect example of Gene Roddenberry's goal for STAR TREK—to explore the question: What does it mean to be human? Piller couldn't have chosen a better episode to praise.

"As so often happens in this town," Piller recalls, "Michael and I were old friends. He had been the co-creator of a show called *Probe*[13] and I had been one of the producers on the show. So I said, 'Maybe I can do an episode for you,' and a few weeks later, after Michael came on board, he called me up and said, 'I've got an idea [for a script]. Would you like to come in and do it?' I said, 'Sure.' "

"But then I called my agent and told him I wanted to write a freelance script for *Star Trek: The Next Generation*. He said, 'Don't do it! You will be pigeonholed as a freelance writer. You will never work on staff again!' "

Needless to say, Piller did not take his agent's advice and wrote the third-season episode entitled "Evolution," sharing story credit with Wagner. The story's plot was a solid if somewhat dry science-fiction concept in which Wesley's science project—an interaction between two microscopic medical devices called "nanites"—threatens the *Enterprise*. But Piller was able to bring to it the personal edge that distinguishes his scripts and the direction *Next Generation* took under his guidance, and with which *Deep Space Nine* began.

"I remember sitting down saying, What is going to make this a personal story? And since this happens to be one of the first shows where Beverly Crusher is back from her second-season hiatus, why don't I use this as an opportunity to reacquaint the audience with her, and with the relationship between her and her son? She's been away for at least a year, and there's going to be a lot of stuff going on between them.

"Ultimately, if you look at that episode, it became a story about Wesley and the relationship he has, not only with his mother who's come back, but with the scientist who is consumed by his work, by his profession, by his need for success, and for solving the problem that will give him his one shot at fame.

"I thought that the key—the breakthrough—for that show that made it work was that I wrote the scientist to be the adult personification of Wesley Crusher, so that the audience could see, and, ultimately, Wesley could see, that if he stayed on his present course he would grow up to be this sort of a lonely, unhappy, obsessed kind of adult. And he chooses during the course of the episode not to follow that trend. That's what made it an episode that was worth writing from my standpoint. It really got to the core of a man's obsession and a young man's decision about what kind of life he wanted to lead."

But the irony of Piller wanting to write one episode of one of his favorite television series for an old friend was that Michael Wagner had decided that he didn't wish to remain with the production, and he left the series.

"That's when they called me up," Piller remembers, "and said, 'Look, you're the only one who's written a script we can use this year. Come on the writing staff.' And I said yes."

This staff position—which his agent said he would never get again—brought with it Piller's first co-executive producer title in dramatic television, and even though Hollywood has the reputation for being an unforgiving town, Piller still has the same agent today who told him not to write for *The Next Generation*. Of course, Piller says, his agent now takes all the credit for getting Piller on the show.

[13]The show's other creator was celebrated science-fiction author Isaac Asimov. The series—about a crime-solving scientist—ran from March to June, 1988.

Michael Piller's tenure at *The Next Generation* brought a fresh perspective and new depth of storytelling, which was greatly appreciated by viewers—ratings kept climbing, and although the series was being shown on more stations than any other syndicated dramatic show, even more stations signed up to carry it. In the fourth season, the series achieved record-high syndicated ratings, and in the fifth season, coinciding with STAR TREK's twenty-fifth anniversary, key demographic ratings among men age eighteen to forty-nine actually climbed high enough to eclipse even network-television fare, including *Cheers, Roseanne, 60 Minutes,* and, astoundingly, *Monday Night Football!*

Over those years, Michael Piller's contributions to STAR TREK were considerable. His ongoing success brought with it a continuity of thought and attracted a group of regular writers, which gave the series a welcome consistency so vital in maintaining the ongoing interest of viewers. Piller was clearly helping to make a twenty-five-year-old franchise even more appealing to its new generation of viewers.

Even if one wished to debate the importance of character in television script writing, the success of *The Next Generation* and now *Deep Space Nine* proves Piller's perspective without doubt. And that observation takes us back to *Star Trek: Deep Space Nine,* or, as it was known for a few brief moments in its initial stages, *The Final Frontier.*

# SIX

# IN THE BEGINNING

*Nobody knows anything.*

—William Goldman

To be creative is to take part in a process in which the end result is unknown. Only *after* the act of creation is it sometimes possible to trace back through the initial unexpected steps that led from the starting conditions to the final result. In mathematics, this type of process is termed "chaotic." This does not imply that a process is messy or out of control. It simply means that the process is so mind-bendingly complex that its outcome can't be predicted, and only by approximation can it be mapped out and understood after the fact.

The initial steps in creating *Deep Space Nine* are no exception. To be sure, the origin points of certain names, certain situations, and certain characters can be identified with precision. But faced with the complexity of the creative process—the way a writer's mind can create an entire character, fully detailed, in a sudden burst of inspiration that perfectly answers a troubling story point, but later struggles for days to come up with the most obvious of ideas—there is no way to proceed for this part of the making of *Deep Space Nine,* except by approximation.

In this chapter, we try to re-create the process by which Rick Berman and Michael Piller created the rich interweaving of character, setting, and story for their series. Some of the stages we describe took place in an instant. Some took place over months. And very little took place in the clear and logical order we describe, though that is the order in which, in hindsight, it makes most sense.

As you read this orderly breakdown of the creative construction of the series, also

A preliminary study of Bajor after the Cardassian occupation.

keep in mind that most stages happened all at once. The development meetings between Berman and Piller constantly jumped back and forth between pilot plot points and character back story[1] and space-station design, all in a jumble. At best, this is a simplified account of how Berman and Piller brought their talent and experience to bear on the task before them, and why they chose the directions they did. As for *how* the human mind comes up with such things, that's probably a matter best suited for a few hundred psychology texts.

To begin with, the task Berman and Piller were facing in the summer of 1991 was apparently quite simple: Come up with a premise for a third STAR TREK series. But the conditions that applied to that seemingly simple direction were horrendously complex.

First of all, the series had to be the same as what had gone before. At the most basic level, that meant a one-hour dramatic science-fiction series, *probably* with the name "STAR TREK" somewhere in the title.

We say "probably" because different recollections of this pivotal decision abound. Rick Berman recalls that in his initial conversations with Paramount executives, specifically Brandon Tarktikoff, he was simply asked to come up with a science-fiction series that Paramount could promote as being produced by the person who had been bringing the world STAR TREK for the past five years. Michael Piller recalls that once he was brought on board by Berman, both he and Berman had to convince the studio executives that making the new series a STAR TREK spin-off[2] was the best way to go.

Brandon Tartikoff, however, believes that the decision to make the new series part of STAR TREK was never really in question, primarily because of those familiar dollars-and-cents considerations. "At Paramount," Tartikoff explains, "it was seen as a slam dunk from the beginning. When you looked at the books you saw that STAR TREK: THE NEXT GENERATION was a twenty-five-million-dollar goody, every year.

[1] "Back story" refers to the fictional background created for characters (and premises) that is not directly connected to a specific story, but serves to define the character. For example, part of Benjamin Sisko's back story is that he has several brothers, a personal note from his past that is yet to become part of any *Deep Space Nine* story, except for being mentioned in passing, as in the second-season episode "Paradise."

[2] Technically, *The Next Generation* is a sequel to the original series, because it comes after the original. *Deep Space Nine* is a spin-off because it takes place concurrently with the already existing series.

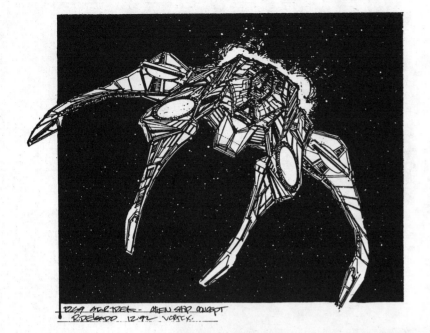

DS.9 STAR TREK - ALIEN SHIP CONCEPT
R.DELGADO 12.92 VORTEX

New starship possibilities for the
new series.

RAPTOR
DS.9 STAR TREK - ALIEN SHIP CONCEPT
R.DELGADO 01.93

RICARDO DELGADO

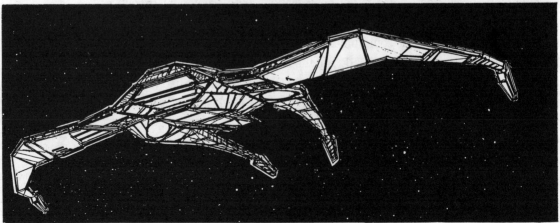

STAR TREK D.S. NINE
RAPTOR - REAR VIEW
R.DELGADO 01.92

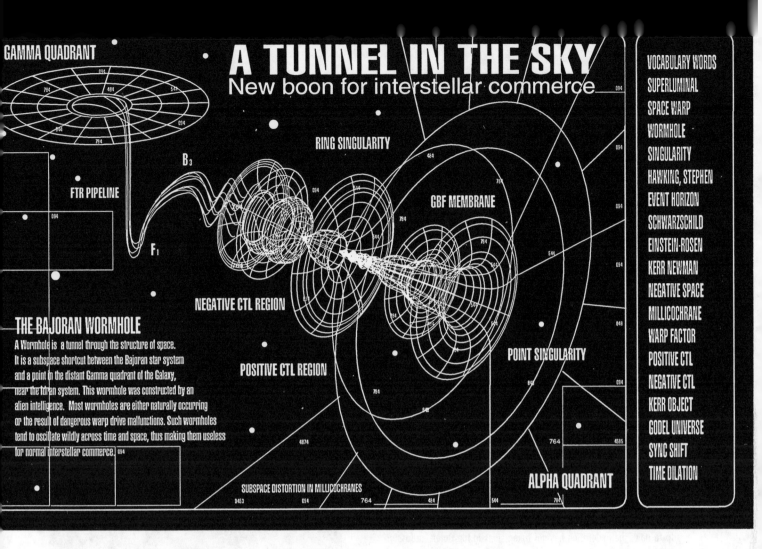

# A TUNNEL IN THE SKY
## New boon for interstellar commerce

**GAMMA QUADRANT**

RING SINGULARITY

$B_3$

FTR PIPELINE

$F_1$

GBF MEMBRANE

**THE BAJORAN WORMHOLE**

A Wormhole is a tunnel through the structure of space. It is a subspace shortcut between the Bajoran star system and a point in the distant Gamma quadrant of the Galaxy, near the Idran system. This wormhole was constructed by an alien intelligence. Most wormholes are either naturally occurring or the result of dangerous warp drive malfunctions. Such wormholes tend to oscillate wildly across time and space, thus making them useless for normal interstellar commerce.

NEGATIVE CTL REGION

POSITIVE CTL REGION

POINT SINGULARITY

SUBSPACE DISTORTION IN MILLICOCHRANES

**ALPHA QUADRANT**

**VOCABULARY WORDS**
SUPERLUMINAL
SPACE WARP
WORMHOLE
SINGULARITY
HAWKING, STEPHEN
EVENT HORIZON
SCHWARZSCHILD
EINSTEIN-ROSEN
KERR NEWMAN
NEGATIVE SPACE
MILLICOCHRANE
WARP FACTOR
POSITIVE CTL
NEGATIVE CTL
KERR OBJECT
GODEL UNIVERSE
SYNC SHIFT
TIME DILATION

*A wormhole—STAR TREK style.*

That's the profit it would generate for Paramount. So, it was like willing into existence another twenty-five-million-dollar property. Potentially, it was like a two-for-one stock split.''

No doubt all parties have differing recollections over this point for the simple reason that because so many executives took part in the discussions over so many months, at any given time the parameters of the project were different as well. But however the decision was made, by the time Berman and Piller sat down to polish their final presentation, ''STAR TREK'' would definitely be part of the new series' title, with all the thematic content those words evoked.

Second, in classic television doublethink, while remaining the same as what had gone before, the new series had to be sufficiently different to be fresh and new. Since the new show would most likely appear on television while *The Next Generation* was still running, that ruled out a Starship-based show, which left only a few other options.

As Michael Piller says, ''if you're going to have a show set in space, you basically have three options—on a ship, on an alien planet, or on a space station.''

With the ship option ruled out for the moment,[3] Berman and Piller decided to set the series in another common STAR TREK setting—a starbase, and they briefly thought about selecting a starbase on an alien planet. The alien planet that came to mind was Bajor—a world that they had created in their *Next Generation* script ''Ensign Ro.''

[3]But not forever. The third series, 1995's *Star Trek: Voyager*, is also ship-based, though with a significant difference from *The Original Series* and *The Next Generation*. In *Voyager*'s case, the ship has been accidentally transported to the other side of the galaxy, where it is out of contact with Starfleet and the Federation, and the crew—composed of factions on two different sides of a political conflict—are forced to deal with their situation completely on their own.

## The Missing Bajoran: "Ensign Ro"

"Ensign Ro" was the third episode of *The Next Generation*'s fifth season. Story by Rick Berman and Michael Piller. Teleplay by Michael Piller. Directed by Les Landau.

The intent of the story was to add a sharp-edged female character to the crew, someone with the strength and dignity of a Starfleet officer, but with a troubled past to give her personality an edge that some felt was lacking in the other regulars.

In the story as it was aired, Bajor is revealed to have been occupied by the Cardassians for the past forty years. Starfleet Ensign Ro Laren (played by Michelle Forbes) is a Bajoran who at the age of seven saw her father tortured to death by the Cardassians. The episode begins with Ro being assigned to the *Enterprise*, after she has been pardoned by an admiral for disobeying orders while part of an away-team mission undertaken by the crew of the *Wellington*. As a result of her disobeying those orders, eight people died, and some of the *Enterprise* crew, including Picard and Riker, resent her presence on their ship.

Ro's assignment to the *Enterprise* is connected to political machinations involving the fate of Bajor, the Cardassians, and the admiral who pardoned her. As the price of her freedom, Ro is to lure a Bajoran resistance leader into a Cardassian trap, to help convince the Federation that it should aid the Cardassians in subduing the Bajorans. Up to now, the Federation has not taken sides in the Bajor-Cardassian conflict because of the restrictions of the Prime Directive of noninterference. When Picard learns of the plot, he changes the situation so the Cardassians' true intentions are exposed, and the episode ends with Picard offering and Ro accepting a permanent transfer to the *Enterprise*, provided she can wear the emblem of her heritage—her Bajoran earring.

At the time, no one knew what would grow from this single, well-received episode.

Michelle Forbes as Ensign Ro, from the episode "Ensign Ro."

---

[4] A first-unit crew is the production staff responsible for filming the main scenes involving the key actors and is led by the director. A second-unit crew, with its own director, is in effect a backup operation. On *Deep Space Nine*, the second-unit director is most often visual-effects producer Dan Curry, who also filled the same role on *The Next Generation*. Curry explains that on *Deep Space Nine*, second-unit work consists of, "close-ups, hands operating things, monitors, big bluescreen shots, sometimes involving the principal actors and sound recording."

That episode had briefly featured a makeshift Bajoran refugee encampment on the planet's surface, and Berman and Piller thought equally briefly of expanding on that idea as the new series' setting—envisioning it as an alien version of a Hong Kong colony, built as a live set north of Los Angeles.

But with the cost of a full, first-unit[4] production crew running at about five to six thousand dollars per hour, and thinking about those charges totaling up each week for the two half-days it would take to move production of the series from the interior sets on the Paramount lot to the hypothetical live sets in some undetermined location and back again, both Berman and Piller gave up the idea of that kind of setting very

The realistic re-creation of natural lighting on a set is one of the impressive technical details that set STAR TREK productions apart from most other television shows. In this scene—shot indoors—from "The Alternate," Dr. Weld Ram (Matt McKenzie) shows Dr. Mora Pol (James Sloyan) and Odo a tiny life-form that might be related to Odo.

A call sheet for the DS9 second unit. On this day, the second unit was supposed to shoot footage for four different episodes—434, 435, 436, and 437—all on Stage 18. IF you wonder why we say "supposed to," check the date on the sheet, then refer back to David Livingston's annotated call sheet in Chapter 1.

A preliminary design for the obelisk in "The Alternate."

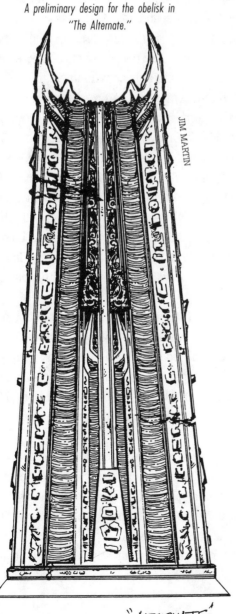

JIM MARTIN

"ALTERNATE"
MARTIN

The smaller second unit is also used when there is a complex shot that is too time-consuming to tie up all the actors with the first unit. "Say if we have a complex Odo morph," Curry says, "or shots of little skittering beasties—stuff that, for either time or technical considerations, is more convenient to shoot without a full crew. Sometimes, something that may be on the screen for only a couple of seconds may require hours and hours to set up because it requires some precise thing happening, and they just don't want to deal with that in the first unit."

[5]Though it must be noted that *The Next Generation*'s technical team had made impressive strides in creating an outdoor look on an indoor set, which continue on *Deep Space Nine* today. Notice how often other series—especially the original STAR TREK—shot supposedly outdoor scenes indoors, with lighting designs that gave people three or four shadows. That's a production shortfall which is seldom seen on either current STAR TREK show today.

[6]In the real world, travel through a wormhole could result in information traveling faster than the speed of light, which is considered to be forbidden in modern physics, though recent tantalizing experiments hint that it might not be *absolutely* forbidden. However, STAR TREK's Starships have routinely been moving faster than light since *The Original Series'* first pilot, so strict scientific accuracy was not a consideration here.

[7]What STAR TREK does to science has not been ignored by the scientific community, who by and large enjoy the results. In Vol. 38 No. 3 of *The Journal of Irreproducible Results*, a humor magazine in which scientists let off steam by writing spoofs of serious scientific papers, the following footnote appeared in an article about novel uses for a common technique to illustrate the nature of space-time—"The Use of Feynman Diagrams to Model Macroscopic Phenomena," by Martin Phipps of McGill University:

1. There is some hope that loop diagrams could be used to model processes that occur without the constraint of linear time. See R. Berman and M. Piller, "Wormholes and Non-linear Time," *Federation Journal of Physics*, Vol. 1 No. 1, 1993.

A second note made reference to science-fiction writer Harlan Ellison, putting the date of his contribution to the *Federation Journal*, "Time Loops," as 1967, the year he wrote *The Original Series* episode "City on the Edge of Forever."

quickly. And since outdoor settings are difficult to realistically achieve on an indoor set,[5] that propelled them toward the third option: a space station.

In addition to simplifying the production requirements of the new series, a space-station setting provided many story advantages as well. Since the station couldn't move to new worlds like the *Enterprise*, new worlds would have to come to it. And what better way to ensure that aliens from thousands of new worlds—both known and unknown—would be interested in coming to an occupied planet than by putting the space station next to another familiar concept from the STAR TREK universe—a wormhole.

"Wormhole" is a term coined by Albert Einstein to describe a theoretical offshoot of his General Theory of Relativity. It refers to a pathway connecting two distant points in such a way that the distance through the wormhole is less than the distance separating the two points in normal space-time.

Today, wormholes are a generally accepted—though never-observed—part of modern physics, assumed to be prevalent at incredibly small dimensions and existing for equally incredibly short periods of time. The end result of these postulated conditions is that we never notice them, and they don't allow for anything to pass through them that could upset the universe's observed pattern of cause and effect.[6] In STAR TREK's universe, wormholes are familiar to anyone who remembers STAR TREK: THE MOTION PICTURE, in which the first test of the *Enterprise*'s new warp engines creates an unstable version which almost destroys the ship.[7] A wormhole also played an important part in the third-season *Next Generation* episode "The Price," written by Hannah Louise Shearer. This story contained several key concepts that underlie some of the premises of *Deep Space Nine*. In "The Price," the inhabitants of the planet Barzan attempt to sell rights to use the wormhole discovered in their solar system, hoping for a commercial windfall. The Barzan wormhole extended seventy thousand light-years to the Delta Quadrant, just as the Bajoran wormhole was later discovered to extend seventy thousand light-years to the Gamma Quadrant. Unfortunately, the Barzan wormhole was discovered to be unstable, making it useless for regular travel.

But what if, Berman and Piller thought, their Bajoran space station just happened to be near one end of a *stable* wormhole that was always open? A wormhole that provided a quick shortcut between two distant regions of space, like an interstellar Panama Canal. In that case, ships would constantly be passing the space station, including a fair number from planets and races that had never been seen before. With a setting agreed upon, *Deep Space Nine* edged closer to liftoff, though it was still without a name.

Another key element of any successful television series is conflict. Conflict is the wellspring of stories. Detectives are in conflict with criminals. Doctors are in conflict with death and disease. Young people at a high school are in conflict with each other over romance. Where was the source of conflict in the unnamed space station by the Bajoran wormhole?

The most obvious conflict was the one that had already been established between the Bajorans and the Cardassians. But the idea of a science-fiction series set

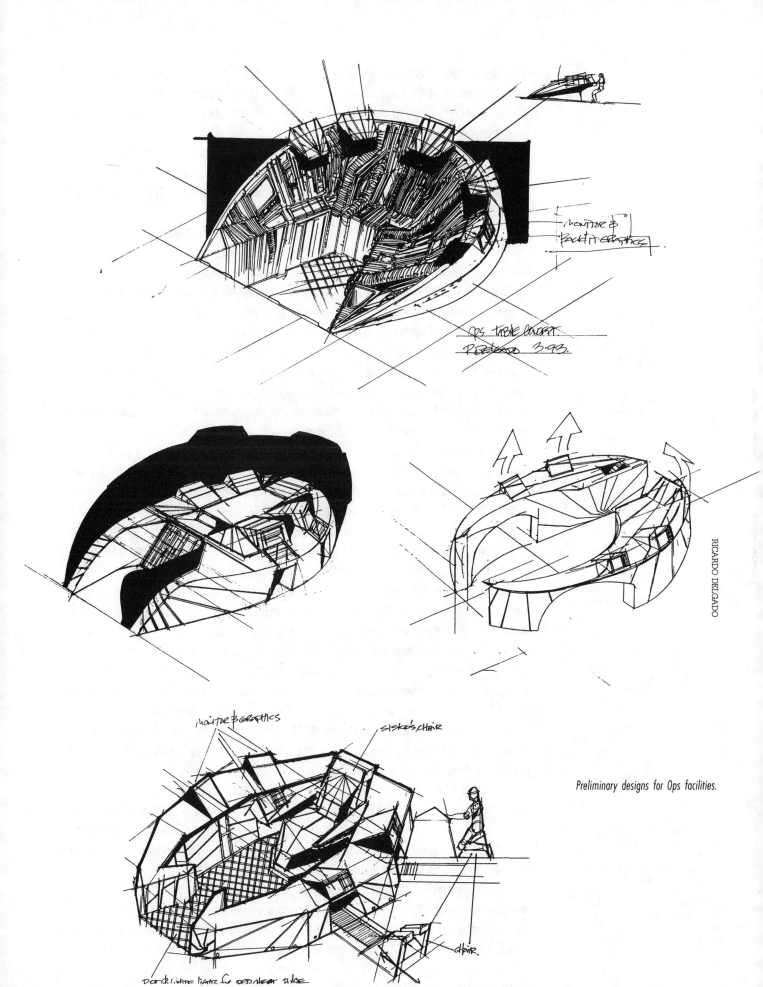

monitor &
backlit graphics.

Ops table concept
R. Delgado 3-93

RICARDO DELGADO

monitor & graphics                    sisko's chair

Preliminary designs for Ops facilities.

chair.

monitor & graphics

among an ongoing interplanetary war is not a STAR TREK idea. STAR TREK themes focus on peace and cooperation. Any STAR TREK episode that has used an interplanetary conflict in its plot has usually focused on *ending* that conflict, not taking part in it.

Once again, a logical answer moved the series forward a step—the series would open with the Cardassians *leaving* Bajor. Instead of being about war, the series would be about a society recovering from war, rebuilding itself. *Those* were STAR TREK themes.

In this development phase, each solution to a dramatic question brought more questions. Sometimes they would be agonized over during long meetings. Sometimes they would be solved as quickly as Berman and Piller could write them down.

Questions: Why did the Cardassians leave Bajor? Why would anyone abandon a stable wormhole? Answer: The Cardassians didn't know about the wormhole. Therefore, the first episode could be about its discovery.

Question: How to make the show different from *The Next Generation?* Answer: Lose the hotel-like comfort of a Federation facility and make the space station an alien design never intended for humans. Heighten the discomfort level by establishing that the space station has been sabotaged and gutted, removing the reliability and predictability of Starfleet equipment.

Rick Berman explained the appeal of this premise by comparing it to what we would think about a person who visits Los Angeles's fashionable Beverly Center shopping mall and decides to stay, in contrast to what we would think about a person visiting South Central Los Angeles after the 1992 riots making the same decision. A city torn apart is a much more interesting setting than a shopping center, and a person who would stay to rebuild a torn-apart city is much more interesting than one who has not faced such a complex and potentially troublesome dilemma.[8]

So the process went on. Like dominoes falling in a chain reaction, the creation of a television series owes more to a series of logical steps than the sudden flash of inspiration that starts the process.

Berman provides another metaphor to describe the process he and Piller went through—the building of a house. He explains that after having lived in one house for a number of years, when it comes time to build a new one, there are certain features you know you can't live without, and others that you'd definitely like to change. As he saw it, the chance to create a new STAR TREK series was the chance to take all the elements that had worked so well in the past, while leaving behind those that had proved troublesome.

The most important change of all that Berman and Piller came up with for a new series that was intended to bring a fresh rush of creativity to the STAR TREK universe was to leave behind the most troublesome aspect of *The Next Generation* and do the one thing that was absolutely forbidden on that show—create the opportunities for interpersonal conflict among the regular characters.

Think of popular television series and you will almost always find some of the characters in conflict with each other: the constant scheming and backbiting on *LA Law;* the romantic attraction disguised by bickering between the title characters in *Lois & Clark;* any one of a dozen lone cops going after criminals on his or her own

[8]The decision to change the condition of the space station was made after Piller had written an initial draft of the script that incorporated an opening shot that Paramount had requested—showing the Promenade in all its glory, including people gambling. Piller did not find that a compelling dramatic situation, and in the next draft the Promenade has been gutted and Sisko must immediately begin to restore it.

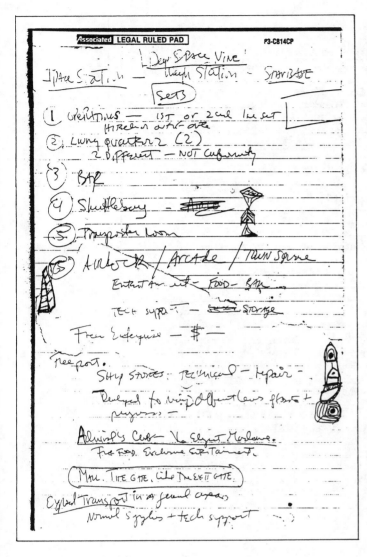

COURTESY OF MICHAEL PILLER

Perhaps Michael Piller's most unusual talent is the ability to read his own handwriting. In these pages, dating from early 1992, we see the first thoughts he and Rick Berman had for the new series, including one of the first references to Deep Space Nine as the name of the station.

The boxed section in the middle shows the early importance Berman and Piller put on dealing with security on board the station. Here, the Promenade is called the Arcade, a note is made to have a character who operates the station's main computer, and a final note states that the security force is already in place, with the person in charge "Mr. Inside"—the first glimmer of Odo.

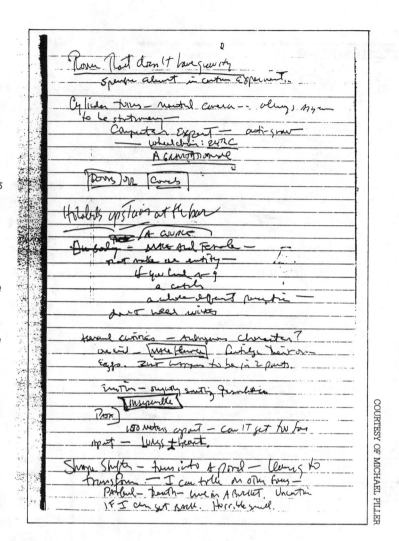

*The first note on this page calls for a room without gravity, perhaps for the computer expert who will require a wheelchair in normal gravity. Though this idea was dropped for a continuing character, it returned in the form of the guest character, Melora. This page also calls for a being composed of two individuals who can't move apart from each other without losing sentience—the first step toward having an already established Trill on board. The final note mentions a shapeshifter character for the first time, pointing out that he or she would turn into a pool and have to live in a bucket. It also notes the shapeshifter would have a horrible smell. Fortunately, that aspect of Odo has been dropped.*

terms, against the wishes of her or his commander; and, of course, the perpetual arguing of STAR TREK's own Mr. Spock and Dr. McCoy.

Without a doubt, the absence of interpersonal conflict had been the hardest obstacle for writers to overcome on *The Next Generation*. In laying down the framework for life in the twenty-fourth century, Gene Roddenberry had made it clear that he expected humans to have learned to be above petty personal conflicts, especially the select few who made it into Starfleet. Thus, from the very first episode, the regular characters aboard the *Enterprise* 1701-D could not fight or argue among themselves as the command crew of the original *Enterprise* had done. With conflict so necessary for the development of stories, by forbidding it Roddenberry had shut off an important source of story premises, and Berman and Piller were eager to reopen it for the new series.

However, because this was a STAR TREK series, both felt a strong obligation to remain true to Roddenberry's hopeful vision of the future. Thus, they concluded, some of the characters in the new series would be Starfleet officers, by nature and training in accord with one another, *but* . . . some of the regulars could be non-Starfleet personnel, so that Roddenberry's restrictions would not necessarily apply to them. Once again, the characters in a STAR TREK series could argue and

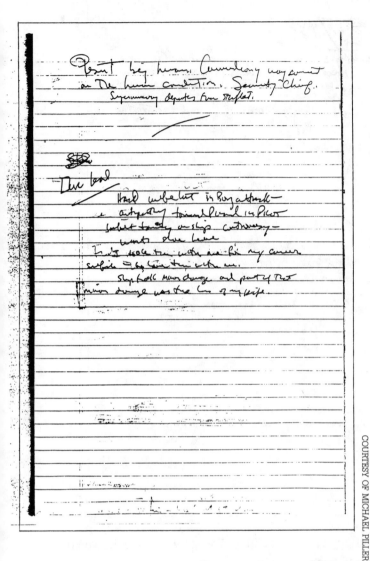

Continuing with early thoughts on Odo—who still didn't have a name—these notes suggest that his character would be a good way to comment on the human condition, an important part of STAR TREK from the beginning. Though the middle section of the page is difficult to make out, even for Michael Piller's assistant, it appears to be the first notes on the character who would become Commander Sisko, mentioning his involvement in the Borg attack, and ending with the bitter line, "Ship took minor damage, and part of that minor damage was the loss of my wife."

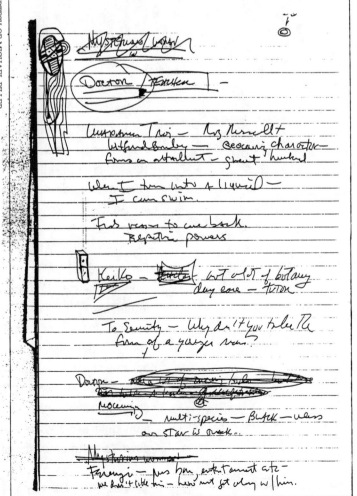

More thoughts on possible characters, including having Lwaxana Troi form an attachment with the shapeshifter. "I turn into a liquid—I can swim." Chief O'Brien's wife, Keiko, is also mentioned with the note that she could be in charge of day care, or be a tutor. The role of the doctor is noted as being multispecies, perhaps black unless our star (lead actor) is black. The bottom of the page has the first mention of the character who would become Quark: "Ferengi—his bar, entertainment, etc.—we don't like him—hero doesn't get along with him." Except for the part about not liking him, that's Quark.

*More early thoughts on the development of Odo.*

bicker and perhaps even outright dislike each other. The story possibilities would be endless—or at least enough to last another seven seasons.

But now that the setting and tone had been broadly established, the most critical part of the series needed to be addressed: Who were the people who would populate the setting—the all-important main characters who would entice viewers to tune in each week, season after season?

Again, the logic of television and the context of STAR TREK shaped the decisions to be made.

First of all, STAR TREK tradition required a commander. For all that fans of the first two series had complained that viewers never saw enough of the lesser-ranked crew on the two *Enterprises*,[9] it made good story sense to focus on the command level. That's where the ultimate decisions were made. That's where the stakes were highest. So the space station would have a commander, too. Human, so the audience could relate to him or her. And most likely a Starfleet officer, so he or she would be out of place and—you guessed it—in conflict with the setting.

Perhaps drawing on Brandon Tartikoff's "*Rifleman* in space" suggestion, the commander was given a child, but not a wife or husband. Thus, in addition to rebuilding a devastated alien planet, the commander would also face the more down-to-earth problems of being a single parent.

[9]Kirk commanded a crew of 430. Picard had responsibility for 1,012 crew and civilians.

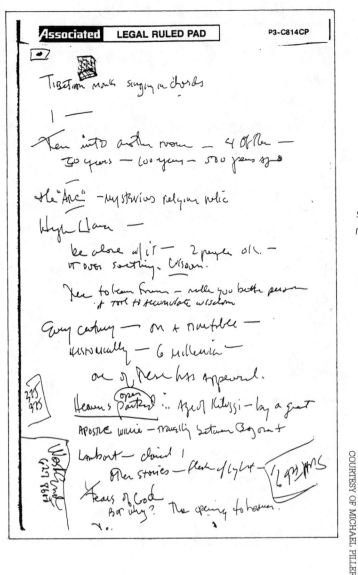

More pages from Michael Piller's notepads show the development of several central ideas. Here we see first mention of the "Tears of the Prophets" and the way they appear on Bajor.

The seeds of the character Garak appear at the top of this page with the note "Cardassian spy on space station." We also see some of the names being considered for the regular characters.

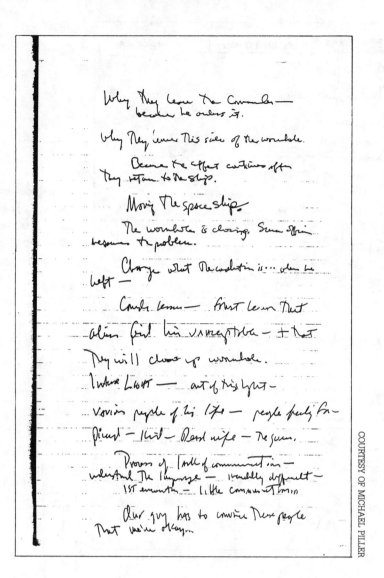

*Here we see the process of story building in action, with the writer asking himself questions and then trying to answer them. We see the first references to the need for moving the space station, and the note that because the entities in the wormhole find Sisko unreceptive, they will close the wormhole. The very last line clearly states Sisko's task in traditional STAR TREK terms—"Our guy has to convince these people that we're okay . . ."*

Since the regulars could be in conflict, what better than to have a second character of almost equal stature to the commander, who had a different agenda for Bajor's reconstruction? That role called out for a Bajoran, and *The Next Generation* already had one who had proved popular with viewers—Ensign Ro Laren. She was strong-willed with a combative personality and would find herself the Bajoran liaison officer on the space station. With a woman in such a strong position, the commander could therefore be a man and, just like Lucas McCain, he would have a teenage son.

Now the search for characters broadened. STAR TREK tradition and story logic had demonstrated that for a science-fiction series, a science officer, a physician, and an engineer[10] were good characters to have around to help stories move quickly along.

On the original *Enterprise,* Dr. McCoy had been an older man, wise in many ways, always a measured voice of experience. Why not turn that character upside down and have a doctor fresh from medical school, brash and inexperienced? Such a character fit the pattern of being the same and different at the same time.

For a science officer, an alien had worked well in the first series; perhaps another could work again. But what kind of alien? Something already known to viewers, like a Vulcan or a Ferengi? Or something completely unknown, like a shapeshifter or a

[10]*The Next Generation* had begun without an engineer among its regular cast, but in the second season, Navigator La Forge was promoted to Chief Engineer, ending the joke of the *Enterprise* being piloted by a blind man, but adding to the ease with which technical plot elements could be handled in scripts.

More of Michael Piller's character notes arising from discussions with Rick Berman over a preliminary draft of the bible. The shapeshifter will no longer feel pain when he changes shape. The human doctor was the top of Starfleet, knows everything, sees his posting to DS9 as a short stay, and needs seasoning. Near the bottom of the page is reference to the science officer working well in weightlessness outside the space station, showing that the idea of a science officer from a low-gravity world hadn't been dropped. But directly beneath that is mention of a character who would be a 500-year-old officer in a symbiotic relationship with a superior physical specimen—the continuing development of Jadzia Dax.

— LOSE PAIN OF SHAPE SHIFT

— MOVE KID TO RECURRING

— Don't call ☐ Security Officer

► New Human

— 2 or 3d Episode — 30-50 Male SF Humans.

→ HUMAN DOCTOR — AFRICAN ACCENT IF BLACK. or West Indian

— Top of Starfleet,
— Knows everything
— Sees this as a short stay — moving on soon to Starfleet Medical — They all get field service waiting for him. Spanner. Cocked. Needs seasoning. (Dudley?)

Character

ADD SENTENCE — Starship at The Station — more activity — one ship in... Other ships — involved last to go — waiting for transport.

OUTSIDE — works well in weightlessness — outside space station...

OLD 500 year old Officer in a symbiotic relationship ...the astronomical specimen

Centuries ago — symbiotic — creature lived underground — humanoid dying because of unclear winters — joined up one another — As centuries went on — now physically join.

Two individuals become one.

I hear her thoughts...

A unique joining. Part of him is a young woman — part him — unusual, wise... Late, fit, great sense of humor. (The body lives in prior to times.) When my worm was in the previous body.

Athletic — aerobic — not superhuman.

That will be best first (the head sits on a woman

SYMBIOT (or symbiant
Picard Resolution — Tear up The Resignation.

Temple — gutted. Desecrated. Stunned by desecration — monks with limbs cut off — statue cut in a half — Cardassian revenge for terrorism — several earth period — left behind ruins —

More character notes on the symbiont. See how a writer creates an impression of a character by writing down dialogue the character might say—"I hear her thoughts. . . . When my worm was in the previous body. . . ." Then, in the midst of character notes, is a story point—"Picard resolution—tear up the resignation"—referring to the end of "Emissary" and Sisko's decision to remain as Commander. The final notes on this page refer to the state of the Bajoran Temple Sisko visits in the pilot episode. "Temple—gutted. Desecrated. Stunned by desecration—monks with limbs cut off, statue cut in half, Cardassian revenge for terrorism."

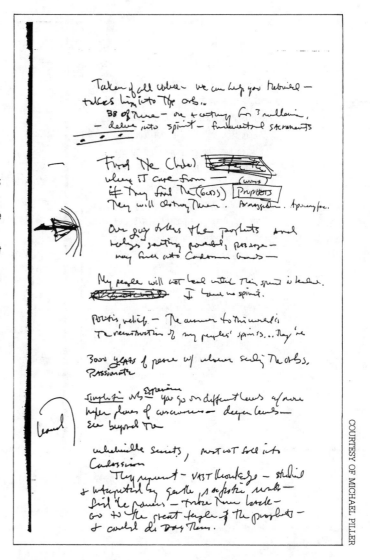

Here we see the starting points of the complex politics of Deep Space Nine, as Sisko is taken to the Orb and told their story. What isn't complex, though, is the final entry, which states that the Orbs have "unbelievable secrets and must not fall into Cardassian hands." All part of the growing texture of the new series.

creature composed of two bodies whose consciousness could exist only when they were close together? Or instead of an alien, what about a human who had grown up under different conditions? The idea of a woman from a low-gravity world who could only function in a wheelchair on the space station was appealing. And to make her character even more science-fictional, when she was off duty she could turn off the gravity in her quarters and fly!

As for an engineer, someone who would have to deal with broken-down, alien equipment and a shortage of tools and parts, who better than Miles O'Brien, the *Enterprise*'s transporter chief, who also came with a wife and baby?

And those characters were just the command contingent—what about the other aspects of life on the space station? Conceptually, it was to be a community for travelers, and smugglers, as well as for explorers—a "Casablanca in space."[11] Was there going to be a "Rick's" on board? And who would police the civilian sections of the station if the smugglers and other ne'er-do-wells got out of hand? The task of creating a television series was momentarily eclipsed by the problem of planning a community in space.

But eventually, by establishing these broad strokes of setting and establishing at least the *types* of characters who would serve the series, if not exact individuals,

[11]This phrase was also used to describe the successful Warner Bros. syndicated science-fiction series *Babylon 5*, which is also set on a space station situated near a faster-than-light "jump point." Much was made of the fact that *Babylon 5* and *Deep Space Nine* were announced by their respective studios within days of each other and shared many common elements, especially since *Babylon 5*'s creator, J. Michael Straczynski, originally pitched the series to Paramount executives. The executives, Straczynski reports, declined the series because they felt it would interfere with the studio's STAR TREK franchise. However, *Babylon 5*'s initial ratings success and renewal for a second season show that there is room for more than one version of the future in today's television market.

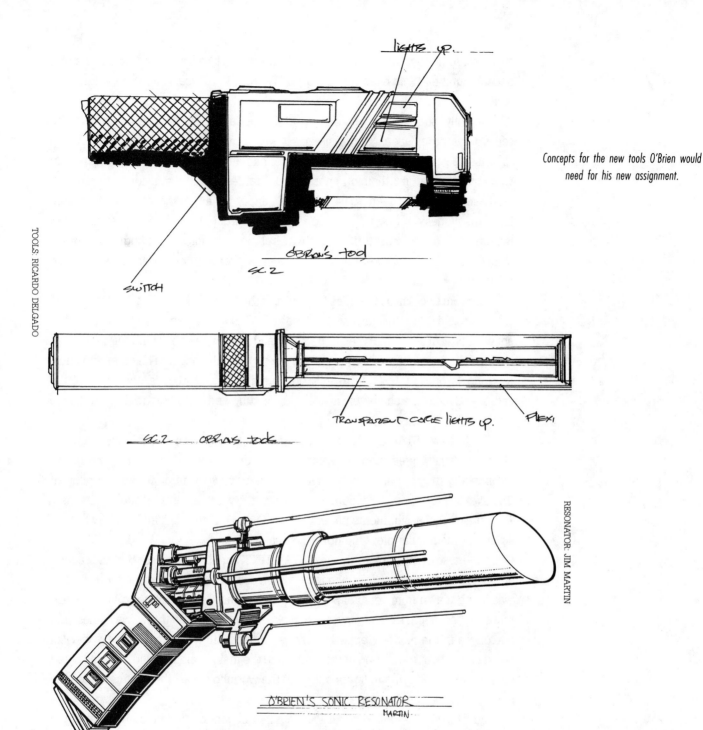

lights up...

O'BRIEN'S tool
sc. 2

switch

sc.2 — O'BRIAN'S tools

TRANSPARENT CORE lights up.    FLEXI

O'BRIEN'S SONIC RESONATOR
MARTIN

*Concepts for the new tools O'Brien would
need for his new assignment.*

enough of the pieces of the puzzle were now on Berman's and Piller's figurative table. With all the story possibilities they had brought into being, it was time to find the one story that would crystallize the series. In other words, drawing on the terminology of basic journalism, now that they knew the *who, when,* and *where,* Berman and Piller had to find the answers to the *why* and the *how.* It was time to think about the pilot—and a title.

The title part was easy because it was so hard. Hard enough that Berman and Piller couldn't come up with anything they liked. One way or another, according to Brandon Tartikoff, STAR TREK was going to be part of it. *The Final Frontier* was an evocative term from the opening preamble of the first two series, and it had a certain appeal. But it had also been the title of STAR TREK V, the least successful of the film series.

Logically, the station would have a Cardassian or Bajoran name, and in the second-season episode "Cardassians," it was established that *Deep Space Nine*'s Cardassian name is Terek Nor. But both Berman and Piller wanted to avoid an alien word in the title. Yet their original, bland, Starfleet designation for the station—Starbase 362—didn't seem to work as a title either. Finally, almost from desperation, Berman suggested *Deep Space Nine* for no particular reason that anyone can remember. No one was thrilled with it, but no one hated it enough to suggest something else. There were more important concerns to consider. Especially the pilot.

There are two basic strategies for devising the pilot episode of a television series. One way, said to be the method of choice at CBS, is to come up with an episode that shows a typical series story, as if the show had already been running for a month or two and the audience was familiar with its setup and characters. The other approach, a strong favorite at NBC, is to tell the "premise" story, that is, the story of the setup—how did the characters arrive at the setting and first begin to do what they'll be doing each episode?

The first two STAR TREK series had used both approaches. Both pilots for *The Original Series*[12] presented a typical adventure for the crew of the *Enterprise*, establishing the ship as already engaged in her five-year mission. But the pilot for *The Next Generation*, "Encounter at Farpoint," was set during one of the new *Enterprise*'s first assignments under Captain Picard's command, and dealt with how several of the regular crew members first came aboard.

In the case of the pilot for the next STAR TREK series, it was clear that the second approach would be better, for one important reason. Since the premise for the series was being drawn from years of STAR TREK continuity, it was going to be complex, probably too complex for viewers to pick up by means of throwaway lines and references in the first few episodes. By beginning with a "premise" story, viewers could learn about the setting at the same time the main characters did. And, as noted earlier, instead of trying to figure out what the wormhole was, the pilot could tell the story of how it was discovered.

Thus, the simple logic of what was required began to build up a checklist of the story points that had to be included in the first episode:

- The Cardassians leave Bajor, abandoning and trashing a space station in the process.
- Starfleet personnel arrive to help Bajor recover from the Cardassian occupation, although some Bajorans don't want them there.
- During the events of the story, the following regular characters will arrive and/or be introduced: a Starfleet commander and his son; Miles O'Brien and his family; Ro Laren; a brash young doctor; a science officer confined to a wheelchair; the owner of a "Rick's"-type bar; and a civilian law-enforcement officer.

[12]The first pilot, "The Cage," starred Jeffrey Hunter as Captain Christopher Pike. NBC rejected the pilot but found the premise intriguing enough to put up the money for an unprecedented second pilot, "Where No Man Has Gone Before," this time with William Shatner as Captain Kirk. Portions of "The Cage" were then reused in the two-part episode "Menagerie." "The Cage" is also now available in its original form on video.

A preliminary sketch of Bajor rebuilt.

- After the Cardassians leave, a stable wormhole will be discovered, making the space station an interplanetary crossroads.

There was also one, final, major story point for the pilot which was never in doubt—

- The *Enterprise* and several members of her crew must take part in the story.

This was essential not only to establish the lineage of the new series but to ensure that a sizable portion of the audience for *The Next Generation* would tune in for the pilot as well. At the end of the day, no one forgot *why* they were engaged in this creative process.

The pattern of creation that had been followed here, a pattern common to the development of almost every television series, had reached its next stage.

The process had begun with a single creative idea: setting a new STAR TREK series in a space station. The process had then moved into a largely mechanical stage—asking a series of questions for which the creative and financial needs of television guided the answers. Now that the basic building blocks had been gathered together, it was time to start assembling them, which necessitated a return to the creative process of writing.

By weaving together the key story points to arise out of the initial development discussions, the pilot story was, on the surface, simple and straightforward: A Starfleet commander arrives with his personnel to take charge of an abandoned Cardassian space station near Bajor, and faces opposition in trying to help Bajor while becoming involved in the discovery of a stable wormhole.

Using all of the story elements they had assembled in the bible, Berman and Piller went to work, creating the ''beats''[13] of the all-important premise story, and by April 8, 1992, everything had come together. The co-creators of *Deep Space Nine* turned in to the Paramount executives an initial bible and story treatment for the two-hour pilot episode, ''The Ninth Orb.''

This is what Berman and Piller's presentation looked like when, in Michael Piller's words, ''the studio was poised to approve our bible and premiere story.''

[13]Writing jargon for key story developments, akin to and possibly derived from beats in music. The listing of an episode's story beats from start to finish is called a ''beat outline.'' The process of creating that outline is sometimes called ''beating out the story.'' And a particularly intense story conference will often leave writers feeling beaten. More about this in Appendix III.

# SEVEN

# THE

# ORIGINAL

# PRESENTATION

*It's time for some cheap chicken.*

—Rick Berman[1]

[1]This is a Rick Berman call to action. As Berman explains it, "Michael and I do all of our work over lunch. When you order lunch from the [Studio] Commissary and you want chicken, there are two kinds of chicken you can get. One is from the sit-down side of the commissary, which is a kind of fancy chicken with the skin on. The other is from the cafeteria side of the commissary, which is skinless chicken that comes with sliced raw vegetables. The latter we prefer, and we refer to it as 'cheap chicken.' So, 'It's time to sit down and eat some cheap chicken' means, 'It's time to start having our lunches and get down to writing.'"

[2]A television "act" is the portion of an episode that runs between commercial breaks. On most one-hour dramatic series, an episode is written with four acts, more or less of equal length. Sometimes the four-act structure includes a short introductory segment up front—called a "teaser"—and/or a short wrap-up scene at the end, called an epilogue.

However, *The Next Generation* broke this tradition by moving to a five-act structure, with a teaser. The reason for this was that a five-act episode has room for an additional commercial break—five breaks for four acts, six for five acts, which includes a break between the teaser and Act One, and between the end of the show and the closing credits.

In television, a "bible" is a blueprint for a series yet to be made. It presents brief descriptions of the characters and any special settings in which they might appear on a regular basis. Most importantly, it describes the *interactions* between the characters—who gets along with whom, and who doesn't; and it describes the mood or flavor of the stories to be told—lighthearted, gritty, tongue-in-cheek, and so on. Often it will include a few lines of sample dialogue to help define a character, or refer to several story premises that are intended to become the basis of future scripts.

The purpose of the series bible is twofold. First, it is a critical sales tool designed to present the series concept to the executives who have the power to say yes or no to its production. No matter how good a pilot script is, the first question any executive will ask is, Where do the rest of the stories come from? If the premise can't sustain a never-ending set of episodes—or at the very least, sixty-five, the magic number for stripping in syndication—it's not meant for television.

The second purpose of the bible is to serve as a guidebook for other writers, usually with additions describing the length of scripts, the act-break structure,[2] set descriptions and/or drawings, and other technical matters that have evolved from the process of producing the pilot episode. At this stage, the bible is usually called a writer's guide.

Generally, the bible is developed at the same time as the pilot story, if not the pilot script, which is what happened in the case of *Deep Space Nine*. It is not by any

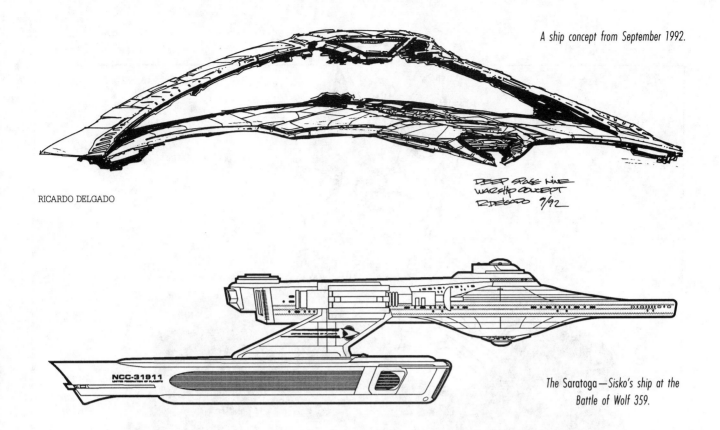

RICARDO DELGADO

DEEP SPACE NINE
WARSHIP CONCEPT
R DELGADO 7/92

NCC-31911
UNITED FEDERATION OF PLANETS

The Saratoga—Sisko's ship at the
Battle of Wolf 359.

means a final document, any more than a first-draft script is a final script. But it *is* a road map with signs pointing to a variety of pathways. In the event a series is approved for production, some of those pathways are bypassed, some are followed then abandoned, and some become the solid structure of a new arena for storytelling.

Just as a bible is a road map for a series, a treatment is a road map for a script. The final script for the *Deep Space Nine* pilot ran 124 pages. The first treatment describing that story was 29 pages.

Usually, a treatment makes no attempt to break a story into acts, and simply recounts a continuous narrative in the present tense. A few key lines of dialogue might be included, but for the most part it is a condensed version of the structure of a script yet to be written. The key advantage of a treatment is that it's faster to write and make major revisions to a 29-page story than it is to write and revise a 124-page script.

The pages that follow are excerpts from the original bible and pilot treatment written by Rick Berman and Michael Piller, dated April 8, 1992. There was nothing fancy about this presentation. The bible was nineteen pages of double-spaced computer printout that looked no different from typewritten pages. The treatment, at twenty-nine pages, looked the same. In writing for television, fancy presentations count for nothing; content is everything.

These versions ultimately went to the executives who had told Berman that they wanted him to create new STAR TREK series.

This is what helped convince them that they had made the right decision.

Though the FCC's restrictions on the amount of advertising that can be shown on television were repealed in 1984, the major networks generally limit the amount of commercial time in prime-time broadcasts to between eight to ten minutes per hour, resulting in one-hour prime-time dramas actually having about forty-eight minutes of air time to tell a story, not including the time for credits. *The Next Generation* and *Deep Space Nine*, however, have an average length of 42.5 minutes, so that more commercial time can be sold.

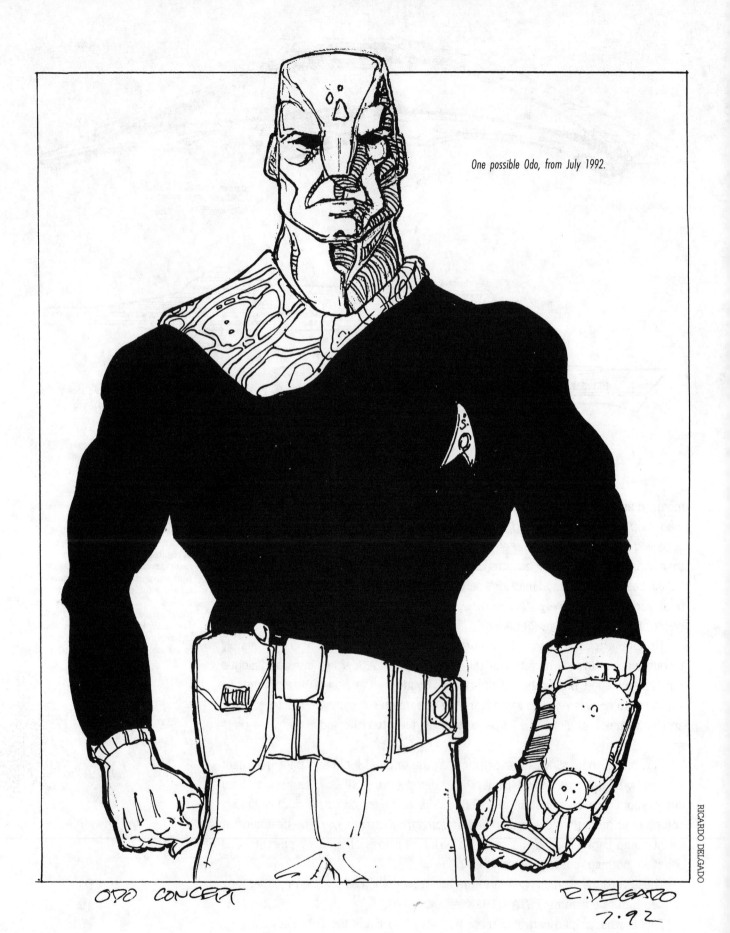

One possible Odo, from July 1992.

ODO CONCEPT

R. DELGADO
7·92

RICARDO DELGADO

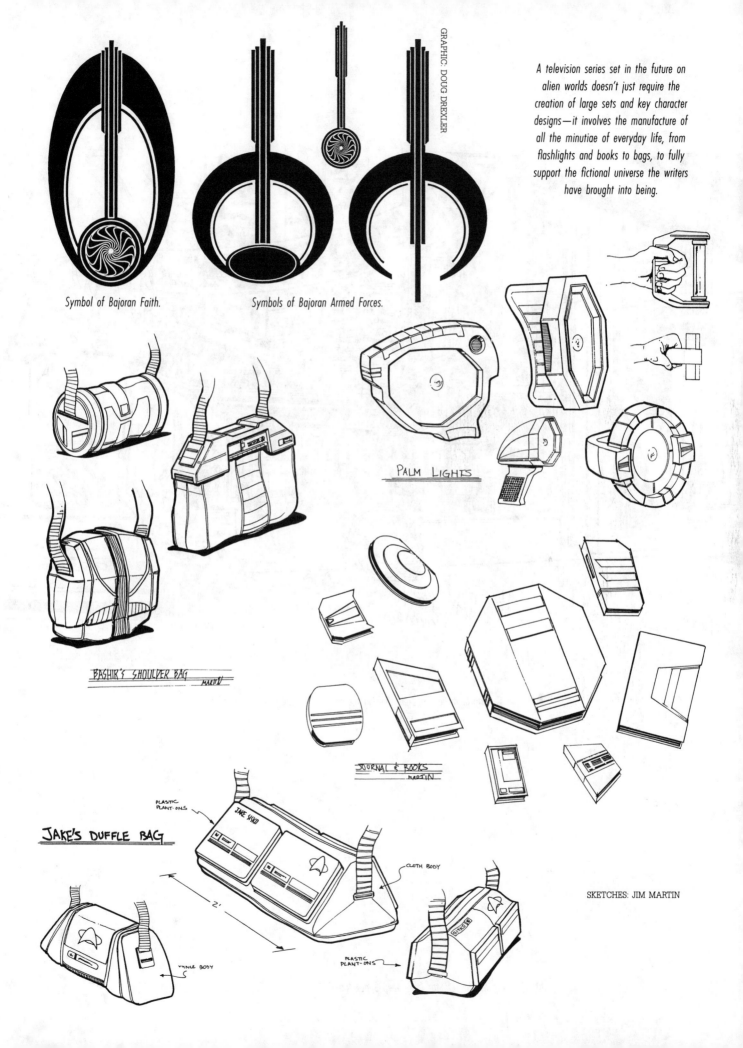

GRAPHIC: DOUG DREXLER

Symbol of Bajoran Faith.

Symbols of Bajoran Armed Forces.

A television series set in the future on alien worlds doesn't just require the creation of large sets and key character designs—it involves the manufacture of all the minutiae of everyday life, from flashlights and books to bags, to fully support the fictional universe the writers have brought into being.

PALM LIGHTS

BASHIR'S SHOULDER BAG
MARTIN

JOURNAL & BOOKS
MARTIN

JAKE'S DUFFLE BAG

PLASTIC PLANT-ONS

JAKE SISKO

CLOTH BODY

2'

VYNLE BODY

PLASTIC PLANT-ONS

SKETCHES: JIM MARTIN

Early Promenade designs showing the evolution of the multistory approach.

RICARDO DELGADO

D.S. NINE ARCADE CONCEPT          R. DELGADO

**STAR TREK: DEEP SPACE NINE, a series set in the ''Next Generation'' of Star Trek Lore, follows a team of Starfleet officers who take command of an alien space station situated near the Bajoran wormhole, one of the most strategic locations in the galaxy.**

In Hollywood, much is made of the process by which the most complex story lines are reduced to a one-sentence premise, and the words above are exactly how Berman and Piller introduced their new series at the beginning of their bible.

The series is, without question, far more than any single sentence could ever hope to describe, but with those forty-four introductory words, especially with the invocation of *The Next Generation,* the reader can immediately grasp the setting, the style, and the main characters. Everything else that follows in the bible is expansion of detail. Here's how they did it.

The first topic included in the bible focuses on the broad physical setting, THE BAJORAN WORMHOLE, and includes details about the distance it traverses, the visual effects seen while traveling through in both directions, the revelation that it is an artifically constructed wormhole, and the story point that the entities who created it are encountered within during the pilot episode, when we will discover that they are responsible for sending mysterious Orbs to the people of Bajor. Only one detail in this brief, one-page description of that wormhole changed by the time the pilot episode was produced: orginally, the wormhole was to have been situated in the ''Denorios asteroid field.'' Why that minor detail was changed is something we'll address in the next chapter, because it illustrates exactly the type of production response a bible is designed to elicit.

After the wormhole is described, the physical setting is expanded upon by placing it in *context* with a brief, page-and-a-half description of the history of Bajor and its interaction with the Cardassians. This section is titled THE BACK STORY, and is essentially a history lesson. We learn that the Cardassian occupation of Bajor began one hundred years earlier, that now their mining operations have been completed and the planet stripped bare, that they have decided to unilaterally withdraw, and that in revenge for Bajoran terrorism, they have enacted a ''scorched earth'' policy and ravaged the planet.

On the Bajoran side, Berman and Piller reveal that Bajor has asked for admission into the Federation, but because of the confused political situation it is not considered safe to set up a Federation outpost on the planet itself. Thus the provisional government requests that Starfleet take over an abandoned space station, becoming, as the bible states, ''in contemporary terms, a United Nations base located within the territory of a sovereign nation.''

With the broad strokes in place, Berman and Piller then turn their attention to the *specifics* of the setting, DEEP SPACE NINE itself. As we shall see in Chapter 10, there were many possibilities put forth over the preceding months as to what, exactly, the fictional origin of the Cardassian space station should be, including whether or not it should be Cardassian at all. But in April of 1992, this is what the bible had to say.

> The station designated *DS9* by Starfleet was assembled haphazardly over several years by Cardassian and Bajoran work teams and anybody else who happened to offer services at a premium. It was used by the Cardassians primarily to monitor mining operations on Bajor, and to service incoming and outgoing crews. About two hundred people, mostly Bajorans, still live there. By episode three, there will be about fifty Starfleet officers and crew stationed there.
>
> When the Cardassians abandoned Bajor, they stripped the station of all advanced technology and defense capabilities . . . and the Starfleet team has a huge job of making it operational again. In fact, it will never work up to our requirements and will always be causing the engineering crew a lot of headaches.

The bible then goes on to describe key elements of the station, including Ops, shuttlebays, and the Promenade. The bible also makes reference to a key function of the station that, as we shall see, was dropped from the series before the pilot went into production. After describing the types of visitors who might come to DS9, the bible says:

> All of their ships need to stop at DS9 to be outfitted and tuned with special impulse energy buffers to travel safely through the wormhole. (In the first episode, we learn that ships' power sources are destructive to the ionic field that is home to the aliens who created the wormhole, and live within it on a different time plane. During that experience, we are told how to travel through without harming them.)

More on what happened to this story element later.

Next comes a short description of the RUNABOUTS, which are given special importance because they are "the symbol of the Federation presence in this sector . . . the only Starfleet hardware in this eclectic environment." In the bible, their top speed is given as warp 4.7, though they have not been held to this in the actual series.

The final section of the bible to deal with setting is a half-page on BAJOR, which sets up an ongoing source of contention for the series by stating that Bajorans "are devoted to a non-secular philosphy that goes against the Federation's logical, scientific way of life."

With setting established, in only six pages, the bible then concentrates on the heart of any televison series—its characters.

BENJAMIN SISKO is introduced first, as a Starfleet Commander with a twelve-year-old son, and a "gentle, strong, soft-spoken demeanor that belies a temper he's constantly trying to control." Key elements of Sisko's character are his love of baseball—a dead sport in the twenty-fourth century—the loss of his wife in the Battle of Wolf 359 at the hands of the "Borgified" Captain Picard, and his objection to being placed in command of DS9. Explaining that Sisko's encounter with the aliens in the wormhole will allow him to move on with his life, Sisko's first character description ends by saying, "His important work on DS9 gives him a new direction, but his is still very much a life framed by tragedy."

The next character described never made it to the series—RO LAREN.

**Established on ST:TNG. She is properly addressed as Lieutenant *Ro* since Bajorans put their family name first. (Note: She will receive a promotion from Ensign to Lieutenant on an episode of ST:TNG before this series begins.) As a Bajoran, Ro cares passionately about her people's independence. That's why she volunteered for duty on the space station. Sisko originally refused to accept her transfer . . . he didn't want anything to do with someone with her undistinguished service record and reputation. But during the first episode, she proves her value to him and becomes his first officer.**

**As noted, Ro is a woman with a troubled past; she does not trust authority and does not follow orders well. In one situation, her failure to do so apparently led to the deaths of an away team. She was court-martialled and imprisoned. Picard invited her to join his crew after she performed beyond the call of duty on a mission to uncover Bajoran terrorists. (ST:TNG episode: "Ensign Ro")**

**She loathes the Cardassians. She was forced as a child to witness the Cardassians torture her father until he died. When she tells Picard about the incident in "Ensign Ro," she says: "I remember feeling so ashamed as my father begged for mercy . . . I was ashamed of him for being so weak. I was ashamed of being Bajoran. Later, I began to understand how misguided those feelings were. And yet, somehow they have remained a part of me. I do not want to be ashamed of my heritage any longer."**

**She has also appeared in the following ST:TNG episodes: "Disaster," "Conundrum," "Power Play," "Cause and Effect," and "The Next Phase."**

**She has a reputation as a loose cannon . . . a reputation she uses to her advantage whenever she can.**

**There is conflict at every turn between Ro and by-the-book Starfleet officers.**

More on the fate of Ensign Ro later.

MILES O'BRIEN is next, introduced as "one of the primary officers frequently in conflict with Ro." His character description includes mentions of his wife, Keiko, and his three-year-old daughter, Molly.

Adding to the conflict that O'Brien can bring to the show, his section also looks back on details about his past to come out of a *Next Generation* episode. In "The Wounded," we learned that O'Brien had been involved in bitter fighting with the Cardassians while serving aboard the *U.S.S. Rutledge.* He witnessed Cardassian atrocities, he lost close friends at the infamous massacre at Setlik III, and the first person he ever killed was a Cardassian who ambushed him while O'Brien was on patrol. Part of O'Brien's conversation with a Cardassian in "The Wounded" is quoted: "I'd never killed anything before. When I was a kid, I would worry about having to swat a mosquito. It's not you I hate, Cardassian. I hate what I became . . . because of you."

Next is JADZIA DAX, science officer. A short background of her "joined" species, the Trill, is given based on what was established in *The Next Generation* episode "The Host." Essentially, she is an attractive, twenty-eight-year-old woman, Jadzia, who shares her consciousness with a three-hundred-year-old worm, Dax, which lives within her body.

Like certain details about the DS9 station, some of Jadzia Dax's back-story details changed between this version of the bible and the production of the pilot.

**As we see in the first episode, when a host dies (in Dax's case, her last host was an elderly man), doctors surgically remove the symbiont. The worm then burrows itself into the new host. Dax's host was joined with her when she was six years old.**

**Ro, who forms a very close relationship with Dax, often tells her to loosen up. Dax admires Ro for her youthful energy, her purpose and her drive and becomes something of a mentor to her.**

**Dax and Ben Sisko have a back story. They worked together on Mars not long before coming to DS9. A potential romance between them never materialized because of his inability to move forward with his life. He would deny it—he would joke that he couldn't get used to the fact that she is a three-hundred-year-old worm . . . and one who used to be a man . . . or part of a man anyway. There is a sexual tension between them which they both resist. But he does not hide the respect and affection he has for her.**

ODO is next, and his natural state is described as "a gelatinous liquid." His back story includes the details that he was the Bajoran law-enforcement officer for DS9 under Cardassian rule, and because of his familiarity with the Promenade and its regular customers, Starfleet has retained him in that position. It's also revealed that he was discovered in the Denorios Asteroid Belt fifty years earlier in a mysterious spacecraft, with no memory of who he was or where he came from. In the beginning, he was treated as an "elephant man," doing tricks such as shifting into a chair or a pencil, until he realized he would have to take on a humanoid form in order to function in Bajoran society. But, the bible adds, he resents it.

**As a result, Odo performs a uniquely important role in the ensemble—he is the character who explores and comments on human values . . . and**

because he is forced to pass as one of us, his point of view usually comes with a cynical and critical edge.

The way he figures it: laws change, justice is justice. This puts him into conflict with Commander who tells him he can't take the law into his own hands if he wants to stay on DS9. Ro finds his negative attitude toward authority delightful and they have a Bajoran fellowship.

Once every day he must return to his gelatinous form.

The Ferengi bartender, QUARK, is next, with the introductory note that the Ferengi race has been part of ST:TNG since the beginning. But after a short description of Ferengi greed and Quark's many business interests on the station, the bible goes on to say that Quark . . .

. . . forges an interesting relationship with Sisko. They actually enjoy sparring together and now and then the Ferengi lends a hand to solve a problem for the Commander . . . as long as there's something in it for him. His effete sexist attitudes make Ro an obvious adversary. He is consumed with passion for Dax.

As an indication of how things change in television, that part about Quark's relationship with Sisko seems to describe Quark's relationship with Odo now that the series is in production.

The half-familiar DR. JULIAN AMOROS comes next, described as a human male in his mid-twenties, with the note: "May have an accent depending on casting."

The Julian Amoros described is quite similar to the Julian Bashir who's in the series, but once again a key character interaction started out a different way from what actually occurs onscreen.

O'Brien becomes Amoros's confidant . . . as a man who has seen combat, a decorated veteran of Starfleet duty, O'Brien represents an ideal to the young doctor. He'll ask O'Brien's advice before doing something to make sure he's not out of line. He likes to go to the phaser firing range to practice with O'Brien.

As O'Brien might say today, not bloody likely.

With the original seven lead characters introduced, the bible then devoted its final three-and-a-half pages to RECURRING CHARACTERS.

These include JAKE SISKO, described as an army brat who doesn't remember life on Earth, and who harbors a suppressed bitterness over living in space because he knows his mother would still be alive if his family had lived somewhere else.

Jake is also said to have no technical expertise, and struggles with his homework, certainly a change from the traditional child geniuses so popular on television series, including *The Next Generation*'s own Wesley Crusher.

KEIKO O'BRIEN is also presented as a recurring character. She's described as not being happy with her husband's assignment to DS9. The bible points out,

"There's an interesting contemporary conflict echoed here . . . of how one side of a couple must sacrifice for the good of the other's career." However, Keiko is shown to make the best of a bad situation when, "In an early episode, she will perceive serious shortcomings in the educational facilities and volunteeer to be the station tutor."

The next recurring character, who in the first two seasons has appeared only once, is LWAXANA TROI, the mother of *The Next Generation*'s Deanna Troi. Her romantic attachment to Odo is set forth, along with a memorable exchange of sample dialogue that would appear in the first-season episode "The Forsaken": "He tries to discourage her: Ma'am, I turn into a liquid form at night. Lwaxana: I can swim."

The teenage Ferengi, NOG, comes next, Jake Sisko's best friend on the station, even though, the bible notes, he's "the kind of kid our parents didn't want us to associate with." Because the character of Quark's brother, Rom, had not been established, Nog is identified as the teenage son of one of the Ferengi who work for Quark, and not as Quark's nephew.

GUL DUKAT receives a paragraph, identifying him as the previous "landlord" of DS9 under Cardassian rule, in his role as Prefect of the Bajoran province. He "represents the continuing threat to our people."

The final recurring character underwent a sex change before appearing on the series—KAI OPAKA. *He* is described as "the spritual leader of Bajor who provides sharp counterpoint to the secular nature of Starfleet." In this version of the bible, the Kai is also said to require his guests to disrobe, and to explore their *pagh* through deep-tissue foot massage.

With the recurring characters introduced, the final element of the bible is a simple summation of the preceding nineteen pages:

> **STAR TREK: DEEP SPACE NINE brings into the Star Trek universe an original set of characters as diverse and memorable as the crews of the first two series. It also provides far more interpersonal conflict than we've seen before in the 24th century. If, as Gene Roddenberry always said, *Star Trek* is *Wagon Train* in space, think of *Deep Space Nine* as Fort Laramie on the edge of the frontier.**

But the bible was only a description of the *pieces* Berman and Piller had created for their series. For a series to be successful, those pieces must be assembled into the reason we watch dramatic television—a story.

As of April 8, 1992, the pilot story as written in treatment form was titled "The Ninth Orb," and in it the solid beginnings of *Deep Space Nine* can clearly be seen.

Rick Berman & Michael Piller

4-8-92

STAR TREK: DEEP SPACE NINE

Two Hour Treatment

"The Ninth Orb"

Over black, super: WOLF 359, STARDATE 44002.3. We hear the voice of
Picard/Locutus: "You will be assimilated. Resistance is futile."

The face of Picard, mutilated by the Borg, is the first image we see . . . and it
is on a viewscreen of a Starfleet ship . . . the bridge crew moves into action,
led by their Captain and First Officer, Commander Benjamin Sisko, a
charismatic man in his late thirties who is giving orders to the crew . . .

History has recorded the battle that follows as the bloodiest in Federation
annals. For the first time, Star Trek viewers will see how the single Borg
vessel, under the leadership of Picard, destroyed the Starfleet armada.

Our focus is on Sisko who takes command as his Captain is fatally
injured . . . instead of retreating, he moves to aide another Starfleet vessel
under attack by the Borg. Sisko's ship takes a massive hit on the deck where
the officers' quarters are located. He knows his family is down there. His ship
disabled and finally forced to withdraw . . . Sisko moves to coordinate rescue
efforts . . . finds his quarters in flames . . . he is able to rescue his nine year
old son . . . but his wife is dead, buried under the wreckage. Evacuation is
ordered because an explosion is imminent . . . Sisko refuses to leave and the
security chief has to pull him out of the room. They climb into an escape pod
with several other people and as it is launched to a safe distance, he holds the
boy in his arms . . . watching the ship carrying his wife explode . . . and on
his face, we fade to black.

Super: Stardate xxxxxx. Three years later.

Fade in to a peaceful, spectacular setting . . . a creek in the Colorado
mountains . . . two figures fishing . . .

Sisko and his son, Jake, now twelve, are having an uneasy conversation.
Jake isn't happy about his father's new posting. You promised we'd stay on
shore duty, the boy says. It'll be just like shore duty, says Sisko. It's a space
station. Orbiting a planet called Bajor which is a beautiful world with an
ancient culture. Jake asks why they can't live on the planet. And Sisko briefly
explains the turmoil that has existed on Bajor since the withdrawal of the
Cardassians. Starfleet has decided the best and safest place for us is on the
space station. Jake remains unconvinced, will there be kids there?
Absolutely, says Sisko, hoping that he's telling the truth.

Their conversation is interrupted by a com voice: an officer informs Sisko
they have reached Deep Space Nine . . . Sisko tells the computer to end the
program and the holodeck walls replace the vistas of Colorado and they exit

into a ship's corridor (not the Enterprise) . . . they move to an observation window . . . to see the space station . . . a strange, intriguing object in orbit of Bajor . . .

When they arrive . . . the Enterprise is already docked at the station on an emergency relief mission for the Bajorans that we'll learn about later. When Sisko and Jake enter the Ops center, O'Brien is already at work . . . he introduces himself to Sisko, 'I'm your Chief Operations Officer, sir' . . . (we'll either take care of the promotion on an earlier 'Next Generation' episode or write so it took place off camera before we arrived.) A Bajoran takes Jake to his quarters.

O'Brien tells Sisko the Cardassians stripped away any advanced technology when they abandoned the space station . . . there are missing components, non-functioning stations, virtually no defense systems, the replicators can only make Felogian wafers, the environmental controls are stuck at 91 degrees (F). A dozen problems need immediate attention.

Sisko asks about the status of the science and medical officers and O'Brien says they are en route, a day away. He tells Sisko that Captain Picard has asked to see him as soon as possible. Sisko reacts with an edge to the name, ignores the urgency of the request . . . wants to take a look around first . . .

As Sisko walks along the Promenade, we see a dozen or so crew members of various species, some in Starfleet uniforms who are part of the relief effort, involved in the activities this extraordinary setting has to offer . . . some are getting supplies at one of the ship's stores, others are on leave simply looking around . . . there's a kiosk serving live food . . . an odd looking alien grifter (RULOD) tries to sell smuggled goods to pedestrians, retreats as he watches the new Starfleet commander pass by. Sisko glances his way, moves toward the saloon.

Music and laughter fill the room as Sisko enters, looks around, sees Starfleet crewmen and aliens gambling at gaming tables run by Ferengi . . . customers wait for openings at the sexual holosuites up the stairs . . . Sisko moves to the bar.

At the far end, a Ferengi bartender (QUARK) chats with an odd looking alien humanoid (ODO) who looks sort of 'unfinished' without distinct features on his face. Quark comes over, takes his order, asks if Sisko is the new Commander they've been expecting. Sisko acknowledges. Quark pumps him for inside information about his mission that he might use to his economic advantage. During the conversation, we learn that Bajor has been granted provisional acceptance into the Federation and that Sisko's orders are to spearhead the arduous diplomatic and scientific efforts that accompany the entry procedure. At the request of the Bajoran provisional government, Starfleet has established a Federation presence by taking command of the space station.

Suddenly a fight breaks out at the gaming table . . . two aliens are clearly sore losers, accuse the Ferengi of cheating them, one pulls out a sharp weapon. Customers move out of the way as Odo moves quickly to intervene, throws the alien holding the weapon across the room with tremendous strength and as the other one comes at him, slugs him . . . the one with the weapon throws it across the room at Odo . . . and as he reacts, his entire midsection *twists into a new shape* . . . and the weapon flies harmlessly by . . . but Odo is mad now and he charges at the man who threw it . . . but a phaser blast over their heads stops them.

That's enough, says Sisko, who is holding the phaser. And he tells the two aliens to get off the station. Odo, angry at Sisko's interference, identifies himself to the Commander as the Chief Bajoran Security Officer. And says he doesn't allow weapons on the promenade and that includes phasers. Sisko says it may be better to have phasers than to have public brawls. And Odo says he doesn't need a Starfleet officer coming in and telling him how to handle this job. And exits.

Sisko glances at Quark . . . who tells the Commander that Odo's something of a curmudgeon but a good man to have on your side. Sisko says, maybe. Curious, he asks Quark about the shape shifting . . . no Bajoran I ever knew could do that. Quark acknowledges. They found him as a newborn in a spacecraft . . . seemed to appear out of nowhere, near the Denorios Asteroid Belt. Only one of him inside. Only one of his kind anyone's ever seen.

They are interrupted by a call from O'Brien . . . The Enterprise called again . . . Captain Picard is waiting to see Sisko. He acknowledges and leaves to meet the man he blames for the death of his wife.

The Enterprise. When Sisko beams aboard, he is met by Lieutenant Ro . . . and she insists on talking to him. He politely tells her he gave serious consideration to her request for transfer to DS9 but ultimately decided he needed someone with different qualifications for his first officer. Ro knows he's blowing her off but she won't accept it . . . she follows him into the turbolift, arguing a case for herself (reminding us of her Bajoran heritage and backstory). It falls on deaf ears. Although he doesn't tell her, he doesn't want to have anything to do with someone with her undistinguished service record and reputation.

He enters the Obs Lounge . . . and already there's tension. "It's been a long time, Captain."

"Have we met before?"

"Yessir, we met in battle. I was on the Saratoga at Wolf 359."

Picard blinks an acknowledgment, moves on. He briefly tells Sisko anything else we have to know about the political situation on Bajor. The Enterprise has been overseeing the relief operation . . . coordinating the convoys of medical supplies and technological aide to help these people rebuild. Sisko asks about the status of the Bajoran terrorists that plagued the Cardassians. Uncertain, Picard answers. They are keeping a low profile.

It becomes clear during this discussion that Sisko objected to being assigned to this remote outpost . . . that he has a son to raise, he's been asking for an Earth assignment, not this. Picard has been made aware of Sisko's dissatisfaction by Starfleet Command . . . and answers that they need him here . . . that qualified officers of his rank are still in short supply. Sisko even hints that he's considering resigning from Starfleet.

Picard infuriates Sisko even more by asking Lieutenant Ro to speak with them . . . Picard says she has valuable insights about the Bajoran situation that you need to hear. Sisko reluctantly agrees to listen.

Ro says that Bajor is on the verge of civil war. Factions that had been unified in opposition to Cardassian rule have resumed age old conflicts. It is impossible to determine what the legitimate government is . . . let alone coordinate efforts for their entry into the Federation.

The only force that holds these people together are their religious beliefs, says Ro. The one man they all respect and heed is their spiritual leader Opaka, a mystical figure known as the Kai. If Kai Opaka would step forward and call for unity, they would listen. She recommends that Sisko go to Bajor to see him. She emphasizes there is not much time before the provisional government will collapse.

During the conversation, Sisko is impressed with Ro's grasp of The Bajoran situation and her passion about her people.

Bajor. The capitol city. Mystical looking with rounded domes and spherical shapes. Striking ancient architecture marks the landscape.

Close-up of a monk who is chanting mournfully in *chords* . . . a three note voice . . . and find Sisko arriving at the Kai's monastery, reacting with shock as he sees it has been literally torn apart by the Cardassians before they withdrew. Statues are beheaded, windows are broken, walls have been blown out . . . the desecration is appalling.

Kai Opaka will see him but Sisko is told that he will have to disrobe. He is given a monk's sheath to wear and led into a chamber where Opaka, a strange looking, elderly Bajoran sits on the floor . . . his ears being massaged by a monk.

The Kai seems to have an awareness on a higher plane of consciousness, knows things he cannot possibly know. Although our people do not accept his 'powers' at face value, we cannot always explain them either. He speaks in vague, mystical and indirect language, forcing the listener to seek his meaning.

Opaka immediately puts Sisko back on his heels by asking if he's aware that the space station is being used as a base in the black market traffic of medical supplies to his people. Sisko calmly responds that it won't be after today.

Opaka dismisses the monk, dons a robe and apologizes to his guest for the condition of the temple. It is the Cardassians' final atrocity . . . revenge for the years of terrorism conducted by the Bajoran underground. Four monks were tortured to death. Although controlled, the Kai obviously feels the pain of the Bajoran people . . . and he suffers for them.

Sisko is sympathetic and asks Opaka to step forward to unite his people, end the political turmoil that is threatening to erupt in civil war. But the Kai responds that the Bajoran *spiritual* life is in great jeopardy and that is much more important than political strife or entry into the Federation. Sisko is compassionate, but as a practical 24th century human, his priorities are significantly different. Their discussion threatens to become a frustrating confrontation . . . until the Kai softly asks Sisko to sit. Sisko politely complies . . . and is surprised as Kai Opaka begins to massage his feet . . . and as their conversation continues, the Kai explores the Commander's 'pagh' (rough translation: energy meridian) with slow moving strokes of his hands across one foot and then the other, moving deep into the tissue. When he finds a painful point, he shakes his head sadly as though the foot is talking to him about the man. He inquires about Sisko's life . . . and suggests that perhaps this is not just another mission but the beginning of a personal journey for him. And when he is finished, he looks at Sisko with a new appreciation. I have misjudged you, says Opaka. You have been sent to us to find the celestial temple of the prophets. And Sisko doesn't believe in celestial temples and tries to talk politics . . . but Kai Opaka ignores that as he leads him deep below the monastery . . . under ground to a chamber and opens a cabinet . . . inside, there is a strange, floating orb, shaped like an hourglass— glowing green, transparent.

'What is it?,' Sisko asks.

'The tear of the prophet' is Kai Opaka's vague reply . . . and as Sisko hears the door close behind, he turns and the Kai is gone. And suddenly something strange is happening to the orb . . . and to Sisko . . . as he finds himself transported to the best day of his life . . . to the wonderful moment when he met his wife . . . and he gets to meet her all over again . . . with the full knowledge of the miracle that is occurring . . . and he tries to explain to her how much she means to him but she thinks he's crazy because she hasn't even met him yet, but she does find him kind of cute . . . and it is almost too much for him to bear as the vision ends . . . and he is back alone in the Kai's chamber . . . and Opaka has returned.

Sisko attempts to disguise the emotional impact of the event as he quietly asks the Kai if the orb is some kind of holographic device. No, says Opaka, it has been studied and documented since it appeared from the skies a millennium ago . . . what you have experienced is not an illusion. Not an illusion?, asks Sisko. Opaka: It is one step into your soul.

He says what Sisko has experienced barely begins to reveal the orb's powers. He explains that over the last thousand years, nine orbs have been discovered. They have been studied for generations by the monks, who have used their powers for spiritual guidance. But now, the other eight orbs are in the hands of the Cardassians who stole them during the desecration of the monastery. They will stop at nothing to unleash the orbs' powers . . . including trying to find their source. If they are successful, the Cardassians may destroy the prophets themselves. The repercussions would be devastating. The Kai tells Sisko he must find the prophets and warn them. He offers the last orb to the Commander as a symbol of his trust.

Sisko does not expect to find a celestial temple, but he wonders where these powerful alien devices came from . . . and he knows the Cardassians must be wondering the same thing. He asks the Kai: If I do as you ask, will you help me accomplish my mission? Opaka smiles gently, nods, but adds, my help will be meaningless unless you warn the prophets.

Sisko returns to find the chaos of the OPS center . . . with O'Brien having everything pulled apart and trying to put it back together properly . . . complaining about the short cuts he has to take to make this stuff operational. And now the Enterprise is about to leave and he won't have the technical support he needs any longer. He asks the Commander's permission to return to the Enterprise to help his wife finish with their moving. Sisko approves, asks O'Brien to have Lieutenant Ro report to him . . .

In the meantime, he goes to the saloon and confronts Quark about the black market business that Opaka told him about. Quark is happy to admit that if there's gold to be made in the black market, he's not above it . . . but there is a Ferengi code of honor . . . a short one . . . but nevertheless, a code—he wouldn't exploit people in desperate need of medical supplies. He might, however, know someone who would. And directs Sisko's attention to Rulod at a corner table.

Sisko moves to Rulod, and in a controlled voice, tells him that he's no longer welcome on DS9 . . . and when Rulod refuses to leave, Sisko's temper gets the better of him . . . and he kicks the chair out from under Rulod and lifts him up bodily by the collar. If you're here tomorrow, says Sisko, I'll confiscate your ship and throw you in the brig. He exits with Rulod looking bitterly after him . . .

As Sisko moves along the Promenade, Ro finds him . . . Sisko: I've approved your transfer, Lieutenant. After getting my feet rubbed, I've decided I'm going to need all the help I can get in understanding your people. Ro is delighted. They discuss the first priority of investigating the orb. They are interrupted by a com voice . . . the Gannetian transport has arrived, Lt. Dax, the science officer, and Doctor Amoros are ready to come aboard. Ro and Sisko go to greet them . . . Sisko, who worked with Dax not long ago on Mars, takes the opportunity on the way to briefly explain what a Trill is to Lieutenant Ro . . .

Dax and Amoros come out of the airlock . . . and are met by Ro and Sisko. We might notice a sexual tension between Dax and Sisko.

Ro offers to show them to their quarters, but Sisko wants Dax to see the orb immediately and he accompanies her while Ro escorts the Doctor away. En route, Dax and Sisko play a personal beat that hints at their backstory. On Mars, a potential romance between them never materialized because of his inability to move forward with his life. He would deny it—he would joke he couldn't get used to the fact that she is a three hundred year old worm . . . and one who used to be a man . . . or part of a man anyway.

Meanwhile Amoros goes with Ro to his quarters . . . and in an amusing scene tells her about his gung-ho expectations about adventures in Starfleet. He's naive and charming and cocky all at the same time . . . a know-it-all. He's chosen this remote outpost instead of the cushy job he was offered at Starfleet Medical because this is where the action is, where heroes are made, in the wilderness . . . and Ro keeps her tongue planted firmly in her cheek as she says this wilderness is my home world . . . and he tries to regroup as she tells him to start thinking about the adventure of trying to control the dysentery being caused by the faulty food replicators . . .

On the Enterprise, O'Brien goes to his quarters and finds Keiko crying (the first time we've seen her in this story).

He comforts her . . . and there's an interesting contemporary conflict echoed here . . . of how one side of a couple must sacrifice for the good of the other's career. She wonders what a botanist will do on the space station. She's been happy on the Enterprise. It's not for long, says O'Brien, and we agreed the promotion is an incredible opportunity. She nods, smiles, but her unhappiness will come up again in later episodes. Three year old Molly is certainly happy. He sends them along to transport aboard DS9 as he takes one last sentimental tour around the Enterprise . . . and has a final, important moment with Picard in his old transporter room . . . Picard salutes him and grants permission for him to leave the ship. He climbs aboard the transporter padd . . . and Picard operates the controls. O'Brien dematerializes.

The Enterprise warps away.

Dax studies the orb which is housed within a forcefield in a laboratory. Her scientific curiosity gets the better of her . . . and she releases the forcefield. Suddenly she is six years old . . . looking into the eyes of a very old man who is sick . . . and he's lying down in a medical facility . . . he takes her hand and smiles at her. She is lifted by an unseen doctor onto a surgical bed beside the old man . . . and as she lies there, fully aware of what is going to happen . . . we see the hands of the doctor make an incision on the chest of the old man and lift out a dripping wet worm-like symbiont . . . and place it on the little girl's abdomen. And as it burrows its way into her, there is a joining, an enlightment, a wonder that crosses the girl's face. And then it is over and Dax is alone in the lab with the orb. She reacts to the extraordinary experience . . .

Jake is wandering through the promenade looking quite lonely . . . when an off camera voice says, hi . . . and Jake turns to see a Ferengi teenager, NOG . . . and after a beat of introduction, Nog asks Jake if he wants to have some fun . . . shows Jake something in his pocket . . . a 'match' box with tiny colorful alien critters inside. What are they?, asks Jake. Garanian Bolites, says Nog. With a conspiratorial wink: C'mon, I'll show you. As they go off . . .

O'Brien calls Sisko to the Ops center . . . on the viewscreen: a huge Cardassian warship is approaching. Their commandant has announced that he and some of his officers are coming aboard to greet us. Sisko reacts and . . .

Jake is hiding, watching as Nog casually opens the box and leaves it by a bench where a man and woman are talking . . . then Nog joins Jake to watch from their hiding place . . . as the couple suddenly starts scratching like dogs with fleas and react with panic as their skin turns GREEN AND PURPLE. They scream for help until they return to normal a few seconds later. Jake and Nog's brief frivolity is interrupted by the dramatic gestapo-like arrival of dozens of Cardassians who head for the saloon to gamble.

The Cardassian Commandant, GUL DUKAT, goes to introduce himself to Sisko. Dukat is overly cordial, as classic bullies can be . . . reveals that he is the former Prefect of the Bajoran Province . . . thus the former landlord of the space station. He knows it well . . . complains he could never get the replicators working properly either. He wasn't happy about leaving, he says, and adds sarcastically that the Cardassian Central Committee obviously understands the needs of the Empire . . . far more than a lowly Prefect does. It becomes obvious that Dukat would like nothing more than to be back in charge.

Sisko asks him what he wants. And Dukat smiles and says, only to be helpful, Commander. You're far from the Federation fleet, alone in this remote outpost, with poor defense systems. Your Cardassian neighbors will be quick to respond to any problems you might have.

Dukat is suspicious of our motives for coming to Bajor. He tells Sisko that he knows the Commander went to the surface to see the Kai (terrible what happened to their temple, he sighs, terrible). He knows Sisko brought back one of the orbs. He says, we thought we had them all. Sisko says he doesn't know what Dukat is talking about. Dukat ignores the denial, continues, saying our scientists are working hard deciphering the mystery of their powers as I'm sure yours are. Perhaps, he suggests, we could have an exchange of information, pool our resources. Sisko still denies any knowledge of the orb. Dukat shrugs, says he will stay in close proximity should Sisko change his mind. And it will give his men the opportunity to enjoy the hospitality of the promenade.

The Cardassians move their ship a kilometer off the station . . . an ominous presence as Dax and Sisko work on the mystery of the orb. Sisko wonders how the Cardassians found out about the ninth orb . . . is concerned there are spies everywhere.

Dax has contacted Opaka's historians and they have begun to analyze two thousand years of Bajoran lore . . . working like archaeologists to comb through bits and pieces of information that might provide some clues to the origin of the orbs. With her genius, she has taken completely disparate pieces of information and deciphered a pattern of events that suggest a relationship between the appearances of the orbs and a remote part of the Bajoran system near the Denorios Asteroid Belt.

They know they cannot go to investigate the area with the Cardassians sitting on their back porch. Somehow, they need to disable the warship long enough to get a runabout past them undetected.

Down in the bar, a group of Cardassian foot soldiers have been on a lucky streak at the gaming tables . . . and have won a lot of gold. Suddenly, Ro appears with O'Brien and announces the place is being closed by order of Starfleet. Quark is outraged and they get into a shouting match but Ro prevails and the Cardassians are unhappy as they pack their gold away in a knapsack that Quark provides. As the last Cardassian exits, our final shot is on Quark's face as he exchanges an odd smile with Ro and O'Brien . . .

On the Cardassian warship, the soldier puts the knapsack in a locker and goes back on duty . . . a beat later, an odd substance oozes out of the cracks of the locker . . . forms on the floor and then turns into Odo . . .

He moves into the engine room . . . turning into a computer monitor to avoid being detected . . . when one of the Cardassians tries to use it and it doesn't operate, he leaves. Odo reshapes and manages to quickly sabotage the Cardassian ship . . . making all systems go haywire . . . engines and sensors are not functional . . . and as the Cardassian crew is in chaos . . . Sisko and Dax leave the station in a runabout undetected . . . and O'Brien is able to beam Odo out through the non-functioning shields.

Sisko and Dax go to the asteroid belt . . . pick up some vague sensor readings that are difficult to define. As they move to the coordinates of these readings, suddenly they find themselves enveloped in a thrill ride with an incredible light show of brilliant colors surrounding them . . . visually distorting them as they tear through the space-time continuum. Finally, it ends. Wondering what the hell it was, they take readings that reveal they are in the Gamma Quadrant . . . a distance that would usually take over sixty years to travel at warp nine.

They realize they have passed through a wormhole . . . and not an ordinary one. All other known wormholes have been unstable . . . but none of the usual fluctuations in energy readings were evident in this one. They speculate that if the orbs have been coming through this wormhole . . . and coming for a thousand years . . . this could very well be a stable wormhole, the first one known to exist. It is a discovery that would change the face of the quadrant . . . with a permanent shortcut through space in their territory, Bajor will become the leading center of commerce and scientific exploration in the sector. Sisko smiles ironically—comments that maybe old Opaka knew what he was doing when he sent us looking for the celestial temple.

They take the ship back into the wormhole . . . (and there is a different optical effect going through the opposite direction) . . . but they don't make it back to the other side . . . their readings are incomprehensible . . . and suddenly they find they have stopped . . . Somehow they have landed, trapped somewhere within the wormhole . . .

Blinding light pours through the windows . . . but the sensors identify a life supporting environment . . . so they open the hatch and get out to investigate. When they do, Sisko perceives a brutal terrain, rock cliffs, dark, surrounded by strange electrical storms, winds swirling around them. And yet as we intercut with Dax's perception, the same locale is idyllic, a garden, calm . . . how is it possible they can see this world in such different ways?

They are confronted by an alien that Sisko perceives as an old humanoid man . . . and Dax perceives as a young female child. To both Dax and Sisko, the alien is yelling fragments of sentences that don't make sense . . . it is agitated, unhappy . . . and after a minute of failed communication attempts . . . there is an extraordinary optical effect . . . as Sisko and Dax's universes are literally torn apart in front of our eyes . . . and Sisko is sinking into a pool of white light like quicksand . . . and Dax tries to reach him . . . but she is enveloped by threads of spinning light . . . taking on the shape of an orb . . . as Sisko sinks into the light, she is suddenly flung into space . . .

We see the wormhole illuminate into view as the orb containing Dax returns to the asteroid belt (wormholes only appear when something goes in or comes out).

A cut to a distant angle . . . and we're on the surface of an asteroid . . . where the alien smuggler, Rulod, has the 'warehouse' for his black market operation . . . he reacts as he sees the wormhole. After a beat of thought, he opens a channel and hails Gul Dukat.

On the space station, O'Brien has been monitoring the asteroid belt with long range sensors since the runabout disappeared . . . he detects the object, checks sensors and tells Ro the readings are configured like human life signs. They beam it aboard. As it appears on the transporter pad, the spinning light disintegrates revealing Dax. She begins to tell them what happened . . .

Meanwhile, on the promenade Quark finds Odo and tells him that a wormhole has been discovered in the asteroid belt . . . how does he know? Rulod the smuggler saw it with his own eyes . . . Odo reacts . . .

In Ops, Dax is beginning to plan a rescue operation with Ro, O'Brien and Amoros . . . when Odo arrives to ask about the wormhole. Our people react to the news that the word is out . . . just as O'Brien notices the Cardassian ship is leaving its position heading straight for the coordinates of the wormhole. Ro realizes that if the Cardassians figure out the potential of this wormhole, their whole damned fleet will be on its way.

Ro asks O'Brien what it would take to move the space station to that part of the system. O'Brien says it's impossible . . . the way this place is built, it wouldn't hold together under the torsional stress. Ro tells him to start reinforcing it. The Bajorans have to stake a claim to that wormhole and there has to be a Federation presence to make that claim stick. If the Cardassians or anyone else try to take the wormhole, they'll have to run over a Federation base in the process and not many will choose to do that. They also put in a call to Starfleet command asking for support but help is several days away.

Ro and Dax will lead the rescue attempt and Ro tells Amoros it's time to be a hero, Doc, you're with us . . . Dax goes to collect some techno gear that will assist with the rescue. On the move to the runabout, Odo asks Ro to go along on the rescue mission. This is a Starfleet operation, Constable, she says. I can't ask you to risk your life.

He explains to her that he was found in the Danorios asteroid belt. He has no idea where he came from, no idea if there are others like him . . . how he has been forced to fit in as a humanoid . . . always wondering who he really is. 'The answers to a lot of questions in my life may be somewhere on the other side of that wormhole, Commander.' It is a touching and bonding scene for these two characters. And she decides to bring him along.

Meanwhile, Sisko finds himself in a white environment without detail . . . and in a sequence of intercutting scenes with the action back at the space station, he attempts to bridge the communications gap with their aliens. They fade in and out of the whiteness, appearing to him as people from his own life . . . apparently being drawn from his mind . . . the first he sees is his wife . . . and there is Picard and the Kai and more. As the sequence continues, they will learn more about human nature by examining Sisko's life . . . and on another level, he must examine his own life as well . . . and deal with questions and pain he has not wanted to confront. He will eventually experience an emotional passage that will allow him to move beyond the grief of his wife's death.

The away team launches the runabout . . . and O'Brien gives the orders to begin the tow. Towing the space station is complicated and is a tremendously dramatic piece of space business with detailed opticals intercut with O'Brien coordinating the effort like Toscanini conducting an orchestra.

In the runabout, the away team is monitoring Dukat's ship . . . it's heading straight for the wormhole . . . at their current speed, the Cardassians will enter it in less than two minutes. Ro has no love for Cardassians, but she finally decides she must warn them. She hails Dukat, tells him they've already lost Sisko . . . don't go in there, you may never get back. Dukat believes the warning is a ploy to fool him while Sisko negotiates with the aliens to learn the secret of the orbs. He takes the ship in.

Intercutting: as the Cardassians go through the wormhole, the aliens with Sisko react with rage . . . almost as though they are in pain . . . the Cardassian ship's power sources are disrupting the ionic fields in which they exist. Continuing the intercuts, we see fascinated reactions from the Cardassians as their ship exits the wormhole into the Gamma Quadrant. Sisko begins to understand that these beings, who live in several time frames simultaneously, see us as incredibly primitive and unsophisticated . . . not at all what they expected other lifeforms to be . . . not what they hoped would respond to their probes. We cannot even recognize what damage our arrival has already done to their existence. Our nature as three dimensional humanoids, living in linear time is incredibly threatening to them. The aliens groan again as we intercut with . . .

The runabout as it enters the wormhole . . . Dax intense, taking readings . . . reaching an incredible conclusion—based on the evidence we have, I believe this wormhole is not a natural phenomenon. Not natural?, says Ro. You're saying it was constructed? Dax: I'd say whoever made the orb, also created this wormhole.

Suddenly, they are rocked by an incredible wave of energy . . . Dax reacts, saying this didn't happen the last time . . . and they are tumbling backwards, end over end, as the wormhole goes through terrible contortions . . . and as they are expelled back to the asteroid belt where the space station is being towed into position, the wormhole shatters in an incredible optical display of fireworks. It has collapsed. Sisko is gone. The Cardassians are trapped a hundred years away.

The aliens reflect this event by telling Sisko that the wormhole has been terminated, no more of his kind will ever threaten them. Sisko, understanding now that we must seem to these aliens like Godzilla would to humans, begins the process of trying to explain that we are not their enemy. If our engines disrupt their environment, we can make technological adjustments, even shut them down during the passage. The aliens are not convinced.

At the space station, Ro has the sad duty of telling Jake that his father is lost . . . they are interrupted by O'Brien who calls all officers to the OPS center . . .

As she arrives, she sees on the viewscreen the approach of six Cardassian warships. The Cardassian commander, Gul Jasad, hails them. Ro, as First Officer, steps forward and responds to the hail. The Cardassian asks to speak to the Starfleet Commander in charge. She says he's not available. Gul Jasad says he's not used to talking to Lieutenants. I'm all you've got, she answers. Where is our warship?, he wants to know. On the other side of the wormhole, she answers. Our sensors don't show any indication of a wormhole, says the Cardassian. That's because it just collapsed. He doesn't buy it. O'Brien reports they are powering up their forward phasers. Shields up, says Ro. What shields?, says O'Brien.

Meanwhile, within the wormhole . . . by taking on the form of Sisko's human memories, the aliens are inadvertently grasping the first definitions of humanity . . . but it is a minefield of confusing observations and misunderstandings that Sisko must guide them through.

On the space station, O'Brien gives Ro a depressing report. The Enterprise is en route but still a day away. Ro says, somehow they have to hold out until it gets here. Suggestions? He can transfer some power to the shields but if they happen to hit any of the lower decks, we'll sustain heavy damage. As far as offensive weapons, only half the phaser arrays are working, we have torpedo launchers operational but only a handful of photon torpedoes. Ro tells Odo to move everyone to the upper decks.

The Cardassian Gul hails Ro, after conferring with his ship's commanders, says they must assume that the missing warship was destroyed by Starfleet . . . he demands the surrender of the space station. Starfleet officers will be taken to Cardassia for trial. Ro and O'Brien know the Cardassians well; both have back stories with reason for great bitterness toward them. They know the Cardassians torture their prisoners . . . and they have no intention of surrendering a Federation outpost to these bastards. She tells Gul Jasad that she needs a day to prepare for the surrender. The Cardassian replies: You have an hour. Ro turns to a very nervous looking Amoros. Ro: Did I mention that heroes often die young, Doc?

Within the wormhole, the last personification the alien takes is Sisko's son,

Jake, representing the future. As Sisko reaches a sense of peace within himself, he inadvertently provides the key to an understanding between the two species. As 'Jake' touches his hand to his father's hand . . . the boy suddenly turns into blinding light . . . and Sisko finds himself back in the cockpit of the runabout . . . the light pouring in from the windows as before . . .

At DS9, the hour is up and Gul Jasad demands an answer . . . Ro proceeds to give it by firing all four of her photons off their starboard bow as warning shots . . .

You don't think Starfleet put us on this space station without the ability to defend it, do you?, she tells the Cardassian Gul, bluffing to the hilt. The Cardassian tells her she's crazy. There's no way the space station can defend itself against an assault by even one Cardassian warship.

"You're probably right" says Ro. "If you were dealing with a Starfleet officer who had any common sense, they'd see we've got a hopeless cause here. But I have a reputation as a loose cannon. So if you want a war, I'll give you one." And she signs off.

The Cardassian Gul wonders if it is a bluff . . . after a beat of musing, he issues a short demand: destroy the space station. The Cardassian ships fire several times . . . shields are weakening . . . an outlying fuel depot is blown up . . .

As the shields fail and the situation looks hopeless, the wormhole suddenly reappears, igniting the heavens and the tiny Starfleet vessel comes through, followed seconds later by the huge Cardassian warship.

Sisko returns to the space station, has an emotional reunion with his 'real' son . . . then hails Dukat. He tells him that he has brought back with him the secret for safe passage through the wormhole. Anyone who wishes to pass through the wormhole will have to be outfitted at DS9 with the necessary modifications. Or they will find themselves lost between here and the Gamma quadrant. The wormhole will be used in peace and in cooperation with the entities who created it or it will not be used at all. If you care to test their resolve, I suggest you fly back into the wormhole. The Cardassians have little choice but to agree. Who are these entities?, asks Dukat. Sisko smiles . . . The prophets of the celestial temple.

Opaka greets Sisko at the monastery, everything has occurred exactly as it was prophesized, he says . . . you have performed a great service for my people. Sisko! I have a lot to tell you about your prophets. But Opaka does not care to hear about the prophets . . . tell me about *you*, he tells Sisko. You were right about this being a different kind of journey for me, says Sisko, quoting the Kai's foot massaging prediction. The Kai looks at him and smiles mysteriously. Opaka: It is only the beginning of your journey, Commander.

Time cut to:

The return of the Enterprise.

Picard and Sisko have another scene in which Picard offers his admiration for the way Sisko handled the crisis and Sisko graciously accepts the compliment without animosity. He is somehow different than the last time they spoke, suggests Picard. Perhaps, agrees Sisko. The encounter in the wormhole has given him a lot to think about . . . but one thing he's quite sure of . . . he has no doubts any longer about his Starfleet career. And, he has it on good authority, that this is where he was meant to be. He intends to stay. Picard leaves, wishing him well . . .

And as Sisko returns to OPs, O'Brien reports that three Frunalian exploration vessels are four hours away, requesting permission to dock . . . and O'Brien complains all the air locks were damaged during the tow . . . and Amoros asks O'Brien where he can practice with his phaser . . . and as we pull back and our people go to work . . .

Cut to DS9 in space . . . as the ships arrive and . . .

FADE OUT

*THE END*

# EIGHT

# THE

# FIRST

# REVISIONS

*The situation may be nothing that I've ever seen
or anyone has ever seen, but you can understand it,
relate to it, if you can believe the people in it.*

—Morris Chapnick[1]

[1]Chapnick was a Paramount studio executive, originally hired to be Gene Roddenberry's assistant for the first pilot of *The Original Series*. His comments about his initial reaction to the first series' bible are still true today.

[2]By some accounts, the two-hour pilot had an initial budget of approximately $10 million, with about an additional $2 million spent on reshooting scenes and other unanticipated production requirements. This estimated $12 million total was considerably more than double the cost of producing two hours of *The Next Generation*, though still far less than the cost of making a feature film. However, because the series was essentially starting from scratch, a number of start-up costs were involved, including $2 million just for permanent sets. Various sources peg the average per-episode budget at between $1.2 and $1.7 million. Understandably, these figures are closely guarded in order to keep confidential the specific amounts paid to key personnel and outside suppliers. The $1.7 million figure does seem high, though, given that the show is estimated to bring in approximately forty million dollars' worth of advertising revenue each season.

**A**fter receiving and considering this bible and treatment—and participating in dozens of earlier meetings—Paramount executives gave the approval for *Deep Space Nine* to proceed to pilot, with an order for eighteen additional episodes to follow for the first season. The projected cost outlay for the shows—anywhere between $32 to $40 million[2] depending on which source one accepts—was more than the initial outlay for the first season of *The Next Generation*, but virtually no one on the business end of the decision felt that Paramount faced anywhere near as much risk as it had in 1987.

But the confidence the executives felt was not immediately shared by Berman and Piller. More than anyone, they knew that the decision to make a series was not the end of the development process—it was just the beginning. Thus far, they had been working on ideas. Now it was time to face the hard facts of making those ideas concrete. And as anyone familiar with the show will know after reading that first presentation bible and treatment, there were many changes to come.

Let's take a look at some of them, first by comparing parts of the April 4 bible with the corresponding parts of the September 10 version, which was completed about halfway through the filming of the pilot episode, no longer called ''The Ninth Orb.''

First of all, there was the little matter of the ''Denorios asteroid field.'' To be blunt, asteroids cost money. Each chunk of space rock would require construction of a model (though in practice, a single model can be photographed from several different

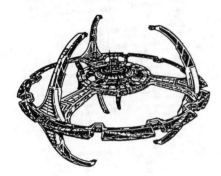

# STAR TREK
## DEEP SPACE NINE

"Emissary"

REV. FINAL DRAFT
AUGUST 10, 1992

*Paramount Pictures*

To:   MICHAEL PILLER

From:  RICK BERMAN

Date:   FEBRUARY 20, 1992

Subject:  DEEP SPACE NINE

Copies:

Michael,

I find myself troubled about the direction our story is going. I remain confident about our bible and its series potential, but I feel the pilot story has become bogged-down. Before anything else, we can't forget that this is STAR TREK. It has to soar. It has to resonate with a powerful and positive vision of the human spirit. It has to stimulate ideas (and God knows how we'll do it) with new and tantalizing elements of science fiction. I believe that with the story we've begun to put together, the critics will have a turkey shoot. "Without Roddenberry, they turned it into a thoughtless shoot 'em up."

In our first pilot, Roddenberry concocted two thought-provoking storylines; an enslaved creature (the shape-shifting space station) forced to serve a sadistic master, and an enigmatic Q who forced Picard to defend mankind.

Although I feel our story is headed in the right direction, it can't simply rely on a Cardassian/Federation stand-off. I believe the missing key is whatever lies on the other side of the wormhole. We need to find something on the other side. Something new, something inexplicable, something tied to a millennia of Bajoran secrets. I'm not saying we need to figure it all out in this episode, or even in the first season for that matter, but it's got to become an integral element of our showdown. The Cardassians are thugs, which is what they should be. But they can't be the exclusive antagonist here. They're boring. I believe they have to be part of a more complex threat. If we can pull it off, I think the other enemy (on the other side  of the wormhole) will be far more interesting and satisfying.

It's time for some cheap chicken.

*Rick*

*A Paramount Communications Company*

angles to create the illusion of several different rocks). Each model would have to be mounted on a motion-control rig[3] and photographed at least three times to account for its various lighting sources and to allow it to be added to a background starfield. A simple shot of a runabout traveling into the Denorios Belt with, let us say, about fifteen asteroids tumbling across the screen would require forty-five separate images to be photographed and combined for each frame, in addition to the four or five elements required for the runabout itself and the background field of stars. *The Next Generation* had often required much more complicated shots, and *Deep Space Nine* would go on to set new records for number of exposures in a single shot, so no one was worried that an asteroid belt *couldn't* be realistically created. However, by setting the wormhole in an asteroid belt, it appeared that asteroids would have to be shot for almost every episode in which the wormhole appeared—which was almost all of them. Since the asteroids weren't an important story point—already established STAR TREK deflector shields kept them from being a danger to ships and the station—they were simply written out, replaced by a "charged plasma field" that served the back-story purpose of disguising the wormhole's presence over the centuries, and which could be created much less expensively as a reusable piece of

*Above left:*
*The cover for the script that started it all. By August 10, 1992, the pilot script had a new title, the DS9 station had a design, but there was still no series logo. The script would continue to be revised into September as filming was under way.*

*Above right:*
*Memo from Rick Berman to Michael Piller, dated February 20, 1992. Berman is referring to an initial pilot treatment, not a script. In this memo the seeds are sown for what waits in the wormhole—the emotional heart of the pilot story's final incarnation.*

[3] See Chapter 14 for details on *Deep Space Nine*'s model photography.

4/27

Re: DS9 first three acts (en route)

Rick ---

Here's what we may want to do.

1. Start act one with Picard and Jake arriving at the promenade instead of Ops...using the gags from scenes 30-32. This showcases our hot set right off the bat and playing it with the kid could be funnier.

2. Then go to OPs for scene 27. Have Picard summon him immediately.

3. Lose all of Odo & Quark intro & barfight. Some general exposition will have to be resituated. I realize I haven't been writing logs.

4. Go to Ro (?)/Picard sequence, play through to the end of act one. This pushes the story up sooner, makes for better pace.

5. Play act two through the whole Opaka/fantasy sequence to end.

6. Open act three with Ops sequence as written. Then add a short scene at the security office where Sisko and we meet Odo for the first time...Sisko starts to tell him about the black market...

7. Go to the saloon where we meet Quark for the first time...he fingers Rulod...make Rulod more dangerous with a gang...the fight breaks out here, we see Odo do his shape shifter gag...

8. Outside the bar, Odo gives a little of his own backstory to Sisko before Ro shows up.

This will yield a savings of about four and a half pages, significantly improve the storytelling pace. I can trim another 2 pages with line cuts. It ain't 20 pages but it's a start.

Off the issue question: to give this a different look, do we want to put video monitors in the set for internal comm..or would the additional opticals kill us?

No notes yet...I make changes every day.

Michael

1

---

Paramount Pictures

To:        RICK
From:      MICHAEL                        Date:    MAY 18, 1992
Subject:   DS9 1ST DRAFT                  Copies:

I haven't made this work yet.

It's not that there hasn't been progress, because there has. It's not that what's here isn't interesting, because it is. But as I try to get a feeling for the whole thing, I am plagued by fundamental questions that I cannot easily answer. In many ways, they are the same note.

1. So what? Truly, the success of this script depends on Sisko's personal journey but what is it? It starts with: I'm not going to stay long because I'm unhappy (which is a petulant, whiny kind of thing to say anyway) and ends with: okay, I'll stay. Not a very high arch to our arc. I've already made changes to make his crisis more pronounced when we meet him. But it seems to build to nowhere and ends with a psychobabbling climax that I fear will be disappointing. I've tried to make it work with mirrors. Maybe I'm too close to it. I understand why he feels the way he does, but as an audience, I have no doubt from the first frame that he'll see the light...and I am not attached emotionally to the struggle.

2. Once the hero meets the aliens, he isn't very heroic. Sisko is generally passive while the aliens dissect his life. (You will see rewrite attempts by me to make him seem less passive and they may seem like band-aides in context.) Yes, it is his essence as a man that saves the day, but that isn't slaying a dragon. In a sense, we kind of cooked our goose when we said the aliens "inadvertently" understand through the process of exploring Sisko's life...because it may not allow Sisko to be active enough.

Some minor things that I haven't quite fixed yet -- the aliens are rather convenient in their knowledge - knowing some things like fear and hate and not knowing others like pleasure and pain. As I've made them more threatening, in my attempts to make Sisko more active, the question is raised why did they so easily allow Dax to leave if they are so concerned about what Sisko represents.

Michael

1

A Paramount Communications Company

---

Above left:
Memo from Michael Piller to Rick Berman, dated April 27, 1992. Rulod is still a character. Ro might not be.

Above right:
Memo from Michael Piller to Rick Berman, dated May 18, 1992. Here we see Michael Piller homing in on Sisko's encounter with the Entities in the wormhole—the emotional core of the story.

background animation. The money saved could thus go to creating different special effects each week to serve specific stories.

Thus the September 10 bible includes the following description of the renamed Denorios asteroid field, added as a final paragraph to the *Back Story* section.

**The wormhole is located in the Denorios Belt which is located within Bajoran space. It contains a "charged plasma field." The region is almost invisible to the naked eye, except for the presence of light blue streaks of space dust. The electromagnetic characteristics of the region have made it a major navigational hazard for centuries. Modern equipment and special shielding now makes it possible to transverse the area. This explains why the wormhole has not been discovered until now.**

Since conflict in television storytelling is a good thing, a great deal of conflict is even better, so the September 10 bible also includes the following addition to the original description of the Cardassians and their reason for unilaterally leaving Bajor.

**(And although the Cardassians would not admit it, another reason for their withdrawal are power shifts and discord at home that require more attention than their distant colonies.)**

That simple line set the stage for all manner of stories featuring Cardassians fighting among themselves, at the same time that it increased their motivation to leave Bajor.

Some character changes were made in the revised bible as well, most notably, the replacement of Ensign Ro Laren. There was no dramatic or technical reason for this change. Quite simply, Michelle Forbes, the actor who portrayed Ro, did not want to commit to a series. She liked the character. She liked appearing on occasional episodes of *The Next Generation,* but given the success of that show, it was quite reasonable to expect that becoming a main character on *Deep Space Nine* would be at least a five- to six-year-long career commitment. Forbes had other acting goals to pursue, and so declined Berman's and Piller's impassioned entreaties to sign aboard.

However, there was an unexpected upside to the loss of Ensign Ro. From the beginning, Berman and Piller had wanted to insure that there would interpersonal conflict among the regulars, and, in hindsight, how much conflict could there be between Ro and Sisko when both were Starfleet officers? But if Sisko's Bajoran liaison officer was *not* Starfleet, if she was *not* under any obligation to follow his orders or even like him, a whole new character dynamic came into play.

Using the character of Ro as a starting point, Berman and Piller came up with her replacement—Major Kira Nerys. In the September 10 bible, she's described this way.

**MAJOR KIRA NERYS**

**She is properly addressed as Major Kira since Bajorans put their family name first. Early 30's. A former member of the underground who, upon liberation of Bajor, was granted the rank of 'Major' in the newly formed provisional forces. She has been assigned as the Bajoran attaché to DS9 and is Sisko's first officer. Kira is an outspoken critic of the provisional government. Having fought for freedom all her life, it angers her to see the world she fought for splintered into dissenting factions. It's very possible that she was sent to DS9 simply to get her outspoken voice out of earshot. She's aggressive, hard-edged and passionate about her people. At first Kira is not a supporter of Bajor joining the Federation, preferring her world to remain independent of all outside interests. As the representative of the Bajorans on board the space station, she has no confidence in Sisko when he arrives.**

**Kira loathes the Cardassians. She committed atrocities against them in the name of freedom, some of which bother her. When others in the Bajoran underground eventually begin a new wave of terrorism, she will be forced into a moral quandary about tracking them down and bringing them to justice. Former terrorists consider her a turncoat.**

**She will come to respect and bond with Sisko although they will continue to have different agendas as new issues arise.**

Another slight character change concerned Jadzia Dax, the Trill science officer. In the April 8 bible, mention is made of the sexual tension between Sisko and Jadzia Dax, arising from a failed romance between them when they both served on Mars. However, viewers will remember that in the series as produced, Sisko and Jadzia Dax shared only a close, same-sex friendship in the past, not a potential male-female romance, primarily because when they first met, Dax—the slug half of the symbiotic life-form—was inside his previous host, the old man, Curzon.

In the September 10 bible, the change is addressed as follows.

**Dax and Ben Sisko have worked together before. The only trouble is that, back then, Dax was still in the body of an elderly man . . . and was something of a mentor to Sisko. Her sexually appealing new form will create a certain tension between her and Sisko, which they will both resist. After all, he's still having a hard time getting used to the fact that she's a three-hundred-year-old worm. But he does not hide the respect and affection he has for her.**

This change served a useful purpose by making Sisko one of the few males on the station who wasn't blatantly lusting after Jadzia Dax, as well as adding an amusing science-fiction element to their relationship by having Sisko refer to Jadzia as "old man."

A story point that had to be altered to match this change in the bible was Jadzia's age when she became "joined." In the treatment, the memory she relives under the Orb's influence shows her as a child of six when she received the sluglike symbiont. However, with the new back story between Sisko and Curzon Dax suggesting that Jadzia must have received the symbiont within the past three years (that is, in the time following the death of Sisko's wife and his posting to Mars, where he met Curzon), Jadzia's age was increased so that she was already an adult when the process occurred.

Other character changes were minor. Two occur in Odo's description: the first reflecting a characteristic brought to him by Rene Auberjonois, the acclaimed actor who brought Odo to life; the second to add a restriction to Odo's shapeshifting ability, in order to keep the character from becoming too all-powerful.

In the revised bible, the changes were described this way.

**His voice is gruff . . . his in-your-face manner is designed to keep everyone at a distance and disguise his inner vulnerability which he cannot bear to reveal.**

**He can only maintain his shape for about six hours before he must rejuvenate[4]—this occasionally puts him and others in jeopardy.**

Note Odo's "inner vulnerability which he cannot bear to reveal"—if conflict is good, then a *character* in conflict with himself is storytelling gold. *The Original Series'* Mr. Spock, whose human half was constantly at war with his Vulcan half,[5] is surely a prime example of the kind of tortured character that fascinates the audience.

An interesting addition was placed in the description of Dr. Julian Amoros, now renamed Bashir. In the second paragraph, where it explains that he was second in his class, the revised bible adds the following reason why:

**He mistook a preganglionic fiber for a post ganglionic nerve during the orals or he would have been first.**

[4]This was changed again and later established to be sixteen hours.

[5]STAR TREK purists will note that this inner conflict ended in STAR TREK: THE MOTION PICTURE.

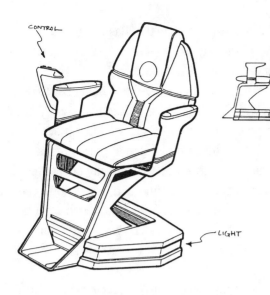

CONTROL

JIM MARTIN

LIGHT

## HOVER CHAIR

Preliminary design for Melora's hoverchair
when it was hoped she could use a
twenty-fourth-century model.

Preliminary design for Melora's
exoskeleton.

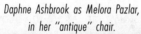

# MELORA

EXO.

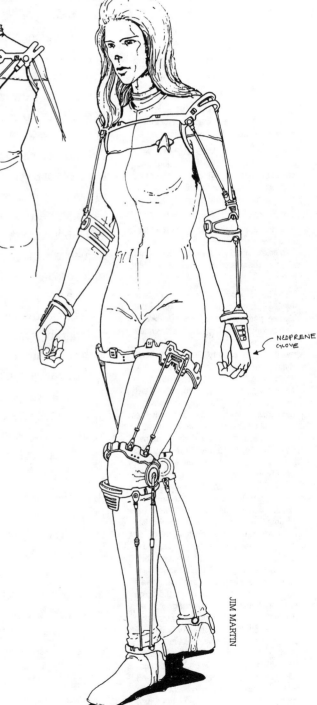

NEOPRENE
GLOVE

JIM MARTIN

Daphne Ashbrook as Melora Pazlar,
in her "antique" chair.

[6]Actually, the line as written by Michael Piller was:

**AMOROS**

I mistook the **MEDTECH** with the **MEDTECH** during the orals or I would have been first.

The use of TECH or MEDTECH in a *Deep Space Nine* script is a call for input from one of the series' consultants. In this case, technical consultants Rick Stembach and Mike Okuda suggested preganglionic fiber and postganglionic nerve be used.

[7]The scene involving Jake and Nog and their prank with the Garanian Bolites was also deleted from the pilot, but showed up intact in the first-season episode "A Man Alone."

[8]"Melora" is also an illustration of how ideas can occasionally go awry under the intense time pressure of episodic-television production. As originally envisioned for this episode, Melora was to appear in a twenty-fourth century floating "wheelchair," utilizing the antigrav technology that has been part of STAR TREK since *The Original Series*. Since an earlier *Next Generation* story, "Too Short a Season," had shown a character in such a chair, the production team decided they could pull it out of storage, remodel it slightly, and use it in this episode. However, the chair had been designed with the relatively larger sets of the *Enterprise* in mind, and would not work properly in the cramped Cardassian corridors of DS9. By the time this incompatibility was discovered, there was no time left to design and build a smaller twenty-fourth-century chair, and a restrained sense of panic set in. Then the writing staff came to the rescue. They revised the script to establish that some aspect of the Cardassian artificial-gravity system on the station prevented the operation of a standard antigrav chair, and that the replicators could only produce an antique twenty-first-century wheelchair. A twenty-first century wheelchair could then be quickly mocked up by taking a present-day, 1990s motorized wheelchair, adding a sleek cover to its batteries and motor, and creating a sound effect to make it sound different from wheelchairs today. Problem solved.

This explanation arrived in the bible by way of a line that Bashir was to say in one of the pilot's early drafts.[6] The line eventually was deleted from the pilot, but it showed up a year later in the second-season episode "Melora."[7]

"Melora" also provides another example of a character idea being set aside but not abandoned. As noted earlier, in their initial discussions Berman and Piller had considered having a regular character who had been raised on a low-gravity world and who would therefore be confined to a wheelchair in normal-gravity areas on the space station, but who would then be able to fly in the microgravity environment of her quarters. Unfortunately, the added scene setup time and associated costs of realistically depicting microgravity flying in each episode led to the character being set aside, along with the Denorios asteroids. However, the character, who came to be called Melora, was intriguing enough to be brought to life for a single story in which she visits DS9, requiring flying effects for only one episode.[8]

Another early character type who was considered—the alien who existed as two joined individuals who had to remain close together—was also missing from the bible. However, the concept of the alien's dual nature resurfaces in Jadzia Dax.

The final character change in the revised bible has to do with the Kai Opaka and elements of Bajoran mysticism. The Kai was changed from a man to a woman in order to place another strong female character in the series. Disrobing for the Kai and having her explore the *pagh* by foot massage might look silly, and would eat up story and production time by requiring all such scenes to take into account the disrobing sequence. For simplicity's sake, the location of the *pagh* was switched to the earlobes, and the disrobing idea was shelved.

The original bible also mentions several story points from the pilot treatment that were dropped from the final script. Among them that DS9 is towed to the wormhole, and that ships need to stop at DS9 to be outfitted with special impulse-energy buffers so they can travel through the wormhole without harming the entities who live within it. These altered story points bring us now to the changes that were made between the first pilot treatment and the final shooting script.

Treatment to script changes occur in two distinct categories—story and character. The story changes for the pilot are relatively minor, reflecting the overall strength of the initial treatment's dramatic structure.

First, Rulod, the odd-looking alien grifter, is gone. The reason, quite simply, is that he served no important story purpose other than being in the right place at the right time to see the wormhole open, and thus inform the Cardassians of the wormhole's existence. Consider: How big is the Denorios Belt? How many asteroids are in it? And Rulod just *happened* to hide his supplies on the one asteroid that would be passing by the wormhole *just* as it opened? It's one thing to get a story started by using such a strong coincidence, but it is generally unsatisfying to use such a huge one to add a twist so late in a story.

For the script, Michael Piller came up with a simpler solution. On page 76, just as Dax is ejected from the wormhole as an Orb . . .

O'Brien at his station . . . Kira at master . . . Bajoran
supernumeraries at various stations . . .

> O'BRIEN
> (reacting to sensors)
> Another neutrino disruption . . .

> KIRA
> Scanners are picking up an object
> near their last known
> coordinates . . . it isn't a ship . . .

> O'BRIEN
> (checking)
> Major, there's something inside
> it . . . some kind of lifeform . . .

More information in from the sensors.

> KIRA
> Are the Cardassian sensors picking
> it up?

> O'BRIEN
> They should be back on line by
> now . . . We have to assume they know
> everything we know . . .

Kira takes a moment to consider the consequences . . .

---

That one line of O'Brien's—"We have to assume they know everything we know . . ."—eliminates the need for Rulod's coincidence, and the need for the unresolved subplot about him smuggling medical supplies.

A key story point in the bible and the treatment that has disappeared completely is the notion that impulse engines somehow are dangerous to the entities who built the wormhole. This idea is given great weight in the treatment by having Sisko emerge from the wormhole to announce that he has the secret for safe passage through it. In the bible, it adds to the importance of DS9 by setting the condition that all ships that wish to pass through the wormhole have to be outfitted with special equipment at the station.

Yet this key idea has been completely eliminated from the *Deep Space Nine* back story. Why?

The main reason is logic. If, to pass through the wormhole into the Gamma Quadrant, a ship needs special upgrading available only at DS9, then how could ships *from* the Gamma Quadrant ever come through from the other side? Part of *Deep Space Nine*'s appeal is that unknown Gamma Quadrant aliens can emerge from the wormhole at any moment. With this condition still in place, they'd never make it.

The elimination of this idea also removes the nagging inconsistency of entities with godlike powers being subject to destruction by mere human technology. Besides, if they exist in all times at once, why didn't they see this coming? Better they should just be disturbed by the human concept of linear time, rather than be threatened by human machines. Then their decision to stay out of sight becomes an emotional one that is not subject to human intervention. After all, *Deep Space Nine* stories might get awfully repetitive if every time the station faced a terrible crisis, someone could slip inside the wormhole, fire up a disruptive impulse engine, and blackmail the entities into helping out.

Less obviously, but more importantly, the decision to eliminate the idea of there being a secret to safe passage through the wormhole changed the nature of Sisko's encounter with the entities. And the way that encounter was changed for the script changed the emotional context of the episode and of the series. Which brings us to changes in character.

The key character changes between the initial treatment and final script, other than those necessitated by replacing Ro with Kira, are apparently minor, but actually produce quite profound effects in the emotional content of the story. A look at two of them offers considerable insight into the process of writing quality material for television.

The first scene to examine is Sisko's initial meeting with Quark. In the treatment, Sisko enters Quark's bar and joins Odo and Quark in a conversation. A fight breaks out at a gaming table. Odo intervenes and, when he is attacked, displays his shapechanging ability to evade the weapon. Sisko stops the fight by firing his phaser overhead. Odo states his policy of not allowing weapons on the Promenade, then exits. Sisko and Quark have a conversation that exists primarily to establish Odo's back story. Then O'Brien calls and the scene ends.

There's nothing really wrong with the scene as written, but there is something missing from it. Remember conflict? It certainly exists between Odo and Sisko. Both demonstrate their differing agendas by taking action. Clearly there is friction between them and that part of the scene works well. But what of Quark and Sisko? Quark's involved with illegal activities. Sisko represents law and order. Yet they just have a bland conversation in which information is exposed. Where is *their* conflict? Where is the emotion between them? For that matter, throughout the entire treatment, how is Quark defined? He's just a guy behind the bar serving as a conduit for information. Not very interesting.

But the scene didn't stay uninteresting for long. Here's how it appears in the final script, moved out of Quark's bar and into the ruined Promenade.

---

33 INT. ASSAYING OFFICE

    A nervous teenage Ferengi (NOG), watching guard at the
    door, glances back . . .

NOG

Hurry up.

Following his look to see the interior of the office
is burned out . . . finding a huge, hideous looking adult
alien looting a safe of some valuable mineral
samples . . . putting them into a pouch. And as he moves
toward the door . . .

34  INT. PROMENADE

. . . they EXIT . . . react as they see Odo arriving . . .

                    ODO
          All right, just stand where you are.


The thieves turn the opposite direction and take a few
steps before they see Kira and Sisko arriving, cutting
off that route of escape too . . . Nog knows he's caught,
gives up (NOTE: He doesn't put up his hands) but the
other alien takes out a knife-like weapon . . . and
throws it at . . .

35
thru OMITTED[9]
37

38  ODO (OPTICAL)[10]

who twists his entire mid-section out of shape . . . and
the weapon flies by harmlessly and embeds itself in a
wall . . . meanwhile, the alien tries to sprint by him
but Odo reforms . . .

39  WIDER (OPTICAL)

. . . and grabs him roughly . . . the alien's bulk makes him
difficult to contain . . . and it looks like it could be
a long fight but before it even gets started, they are
interrupted by a phaser blast above their heads . . .
they both react[11] and turn to see

40  SISKO

holding a phaser . . .

                    SISKO
          That's enough.

                    ODO
          Who the hell are you?

[9]These deleted scene numbers are left over
from an earlier version of the script, which
had a different number of scenes up to this
point. But no action was deleted from this
sequence.

[10](OPTICAL) is an indication that this shot
requires visual effects. In this case, it calls
out Odo's "morphing" sequence.

[11]Note the spareness of the description
Piller uses. He does not presume to tell the
actors exactly *how* to react to the phaser
fire, e.g., fearfully, indignantly, angrily,
etc. It is the actor's job to create the proper
reaction that is true to the character. Good
scriptwriters keep their directions to actors at a minimum, relying on dialogue to
suggest to the actor an interpretation of
the character. Only when an emotional
reaction is a necessary story point should
the writer call it out.

                              KIRA
                    This is our new Starfleet
                    Commander, Odo.

                              ODO
                         (unimpressed)
                    I don't allow weapons on the
                    Promenade. That includes phasers.

                              QUARK
                    (O.C.)[12]
                    Nog? What's going on?

They turn to see Quark arriving (we saw him earlier in
the bar).

                              ODO
                         (to Quark)
                    The boy's in a lot of trouble.

The boy looks away from Quark's inquiring look . . .
Quark turns to Sisko . . .

                              QUARK
                    Commander, my name is Quark. I
                    used to run the local gambling
                    establishment . . . this is my
                    brother's boy . . . surely you can
                    see that he only has a peripheral
                    involvement in all this . . . we're
                    scheduled to depart tomorrow . . .
                    if we could be permitted to take
                    him, I promise you he will be
                    severely . . .

Sisko's mind is working . . . Interrupting—

                              SISKO
                    That won't be possible.
                         (to Odo)
                    Take him to the brig.

Odo acknowledges, leads Nog and the alien away as
as Quark stares bitterly at Sisko . . . then follows the
others . . .

                              KIRA
                         (shakes her head)[13]
                    Quark probably sent the two of
                    them here to steal the ore samples
                    in the first place . . .

[12]Off camera. It means the character is present, but is not visible from the camera's current angle. Some writers use O.S. for offstage, an older term. O.C. is different from V.O. for voice-over, which indicates that speaker is not in the scene at all. For example, it is used for Station Log entries, when we might hear Sisko's voice while seeing the station.

[13]This direction is just a way to suggest to the actor how she might deliver the line, without prescribing a specific emotional response. In the actual scene, Nana Visitor does not literally shake her head, but she does deliver the line with the same sense of mild exasperation the direction implies.

SISKO
(thoughtful)
Major, there's a Ferengi legal
tradition . . . it's called Plea
Bargaining. I might let the boy
go . . . but I want something in
exchange from Mister Quark . . .
something very important . . .

She looks at him curiously, before she can ask what
he's talking about . . .

O'BRIEN'S COM VOICE
O'Brien to Commander Sisko.

SISKO
(presses his combadge)
Go ahead.

O'BRIEN'S COM VOICE
Sir, the Enterprise hailed us
again. Captain Picard is waiting
to see you.

SISKO
(frowns)
Acknowledged.
(tight, to Kira)
This won't take long.

Leaves toward the airlock . . . as she watches him

FADE OUT.

END OF ACT ONE

---

Sisko's introduction to Odo, which worked well in the treatment, still plays the same way. But the whole dynamic of Sisko's introduction to Quark has completely changed. They're no longer just two people chatting in a bar. Sisko has had Quark's nephew arrested, so they're in conflict right away. Quark has made plans to leave the station, but now his long-term goals are thwarted.[14] Sisko has an unspoken reason for wanting to "plea bargain" with Quark—what is it? The audience wants to know. There's added excitement in this scene now, plus character development and story advancement—the hallmarks of good scriptwriting. This change has brought a previously flat part of the story to life.

But this scene is not all that's changed because of the conflict between Sisko and Quark. The rest of the first half of the story is changed as well when Sisko tells Quark his price for having Nog released: Sisko wants Quark to stay on DS9.

[14]As Quark tells Sisko in a later scene:

QUARK

Commander, I've made a career out of knowing when to leave. This Bajoran provisional government is far too provisional for my taste. And when governments fall, people like me are lined up and shot . . .

The end result of this story line in the script is the same as was achieved in the treatment—Quark's bar is open for business. But by making the fact that Quark is open for business a victory for Sisko and his somewhat devious negotiating skills, Piller has told us a great deal about DS9's new commander and firmly established the ongoing battle of wills to be waged between him and Quark.

The most intriguing and powerful change in character development, which affects the entire script, has to do with Sisko and his experience within the wormhole. Piller did not have to add any new elements to the treatment to create this change—everything was already in place and only needed to be tweaked. Like a tiny snowball causing a giant avalanche, the little bit of tweaking Piller did had a major result.

In the treatment, Sisko has the unenviable role of bringing enlightenment to an alien race. That's an arrogant position to take in these politically correct days, it doesn't make for a truly compelling story, nor is it a STAR TREK sentiment. The bottom line is, Who really cares if the entities in the wormhole understand humans or not?

One can almost hear Michael Piller asking, What makes it *personal?*

Interestingly, what makes it personal is already hiding in the treatment, half-formed. It begins with the wrenching opening in which Sisko must abandon his dead wife. Then, when Sisko first enters the wormhole, the treatment reads: ". . . he will eventually experience an emotional passage that will allow him to move beyond the grief of his wife's death." It ends when the entities take on their last personification in the form of Sisko's son, Jake: "As Sisko reaches a sense of peace within himself, he inadvertently provides a key to an understanding between the two species."

But what is the emotional passage? What brings on the sense of peace? And why is this passage important for achieving the secret for moving through the wormhole?

That was the starting point for the first tweak: Sisko's emotional passage *wasn't* necessary to learn the secret of wormhole passage because there now was no secret to learn—the story element about the disruptive impulse engines had been deleted. So the emotional passage became necessary solely for providing a key to the establishment of understanding between the two species. But in episodic television the main concern must rest with the main characters. Since we really don't have any vested interest in what the entities think of humans, it becomes apparent that the whole focus of Sisko's experience in the wormhole should be . . . Sisko.

A useful technique used by writers to bring a fresh approach to a story problem is to turn a situation upside down. Instead of an old and experienced doctor, create a young and naïve one. If Quark is going to be a regular on the series, show him wanting to leave. Change the Kai from a man to a woman. And change the story so that only *part* of the pilot episode would deal with the commander's discovery of the wormhole, while the rest of it would deal with the commander's discovery of *himself.*

It's about this point that we can understand why the title for the pilot changed from "The Ninth Orb" to "Emissary." It was no longer a story about a thing, it was a story about a person—*our* person, a person whose life we would want to follow for years to come, a person whose life experiences would resonate with our own.

Here's how Sisko's encounter in the wormhole came out in the final script, as Sisko bounces from memory to memory, talking to the entities who take on the appearance of people from his past, only to keep returning to his Starship minutes before its destruction by the Picard-led Borg.

---

240 INT. SARATOGA—SISKO'S QUARTERS

As before . . . Sisko and the Tactical Officer alien . . .
the fire and the smoke billowing up around them . . .

> SISKO
> What's the point of bringing me
> back again to this?

241 ANGLE[15]—JENNIFER ALIEN AND JAKE ALIEN

are there (Jennifer is dressed in her park costume,
Jake is wearing his fishing pond costume) . . . standing
by Jennifer's dead body and Jake's unconscious body
still on the floor . . .

> JAKE ALIEN
> We do not bring you here.

> JENNIFER ALIEN
> You bring us here.

> TACTICAL OFFICER ALIEN
> You exist here.

Sisko blinks, not entirely understanding . . . but is impatient to be done
with it . . .

> SISKO
> Then give me the power to lead
> you somewhere else.

242 ANGLE—KAI OPAKA ALIEN

is there . . .

> KAI OPAKA ALIEN
> We cannot give you what you deny
> yourself . . .

Sisko reacts, looks at her . . . as she says the familiar words . . .[16]

> KAI OPAKA ALIEN
> Look for solutions from within,
> Commander . . .

[15]"ANGLE" is a generic camera instruction. Just as a writer does not presume to tell actors exactly how a character should be interpreted, a writer should not force specific camera instructions on the director unless there is a specific story point to be made. In this case, ANGLE tells the director that at this point we should look at the scene from a camera perspective in which the Kai alien is not visible, until we change viewpoints on the next ANGLE and suddenly discover that she is present. Whether the scene is shot in close-up, from a low angle, from overhead, or even with a camera movement is a decision left to the director.

[16]The real Kai Opaka said these same words to Sisko earlier in the script.

SISKO #2 (O.C.)
Just help me get her free . . .

Sisko turns to see . . .

243 THE SAME SETTING

and a replay of the actual events (as we did with the
picnic in the park) . . . Sisko and the alien versions of
Jake, Jennifer, Opaka and the Tactical Officer watch
Sisko #2 and the duplicate Tactical Officer . . .

TACTICAL OFFICER
She's gone . . . there's nothing we
can do . . .

COMPUTER VOICE
Warning. Damage to warp core.
Containment failure in two
minutes . . .

Sisko #2 takes his dead wife's hand . . .

SISKO #2
You go ahead, Lieutenant. Take
the boy.

The security man ENTERS and the Tactical Officer gives
Jake #2 to him . . . The real Sisko watches, his eyes
glued to the horror, his mouth dry as cotton . . .

SISKO
I was ready to die with her . . .

TACTICAL OFFICER ALIEN
'Die'—what is this?

And it is Jennifer Alien who answers . . . as
understanding begins to grow . . .

JENNIFER ALIEN
The termination of their linear
existence.

244 JENNIFER ALIEN AND SISKO (OPTICAL)

As she studies him and sees his pain . . . and then
reaches out and places it on his shoulder with
comfort . . . he reacts to the touch of her hand and
looks into her eyes . . . and they aren't so alien

anymore . . . it is the first overt physical contact they
have made with him . . . a link . . . an understanding . . .
she looks back at the scene—

> TACTICAL OFFICER
> *Now*, sir . . .

As the Tactical Officer lifts him by the shoulder . . .
He continues to pull him out of the room . . .

> SISKO #2
> Dammit . . . we can't leave her
> here . . .

During the above, Sisko is beginning to make a
realization. . . .

> SISKO
> I've never left this ship . . .

> JENNIFER ALIEN
> You exist here.

> SISKO
> I . . . exist here.

The Tactical Officer leads Sisko #2 out . . . Sisko steps
slowly forward and moves to his dead wife taking the
place of his double . . . picks up her hand . . .

> SISKO
> (to the aliens)
> I don't know if you can
> understand. I see her like this
> every time I close my eyes . . . in
> the darkness in the blink of an
> eye, she's there . . . like this . . .

> JENNIFER ALIEN
> None of your past experiences
> helped prepare you for this
> consequence . . .

Sisko shakes his head, slowly . . .

> SISKO
> (softly)
> And I've never figured out how
> to live without her.

> JENNIFER ALIEN
> So you choose to exist here.

He nods, unable to speak . . . she moves closer . . .

                          JENNIFER ALIEN
                        It is not linear.

And of course it is so simple in its truth . . .

                              SISKO
                      No. It's not . . . linear.

Sisko gently places down the hand of his dead wife . . .
and as he accepts that this really is the end of their
life together, tears roll down his cheeks, and he
begins to truly grieve his loss. After a beat, he
stands, turns . . . and Jennifer alien is no longer
there. He understands, exchanges a meaningful look
with the remaining three aliens (Tactical Officer,
Opaka, and Jake). In this moment, two species have
finally come to understand one another . . . to learn
from one another . . . it is the end to the conflict . . .
and the beginning of a shared future. There is
something of a compassionate smile from Jake alien
that seals it . . . and as Sisko returns his smile with
an appreciation of what they've done . . .

245 THE WHITE SCREEN—SISKO'S EYES (OPTICAL)

thoughtful, showing the impact of what has occurred . . .
heartbeat . . . breathing . . .

---

See how the story has been turned upside down? Sisko enters the wormhole and finds entities who are baffled by the concept that humans live in linear time. They ask Sisko to explain it to them. He tries, *but as he explains to the entities the concept of linear time as a condition of being human, he realizes that* he himself *is not living that way*. Whether Sisko has enlightened the entities is ultimately unimportant. What *is* important, though, is that he has enlightened himself.

Best of all, by taking that new approach, not only had "Emissary" become a better story, it had become a STAR TREK story—examining the human condition.

But there were still many revisions and changes to come. Especially because now the production of *Deep Space Nine* was passing from the hands of its creators and into the group of specialists who would help bring Berman's and Piller's vision to life.

The blueprint had been set down. It was time to build a series.

# NINE

# THE

# READERS

# WRITE

*Please give me any reactions to what you read
as long as they're good.*

—Michael Piller[1]

**A**t this point in its development, the creation of *Deep Space Nine* became substantially different from that of other television series. Other series almost always begin in a vacuum, and only through an arduous and time-consuming start-up period is a staff and crew assembled who can deal with the unique production demands each different series has.

But *Deep Space Nine*'s start-up period was eased by the fact that a full team of people who could deal with the production demands of phasers and aliens and wormholes already existed, with five years' worth of experience—the team who made *The Next Generation*. Quite logically, Berman and Piller turned to key members of this team to begin the process of bringing the new STAR TREK series to life.

Among them were: Jeri Taylor, at the time a supervising producer[2] on the writing staff for *The Next Generation;* Naren Shankar, the series' science consultant; and two of STAR TREK's best-known technical consultants—Rick Sternbach and Michael Okuda, *The Next Generation*'s senior illustrator and scenic artist supervisor, respectively.

Over the next three months of preproduction—the planning and preparation stages for a series—each of these people received various drafts of the script and were invited to comment on everything from character names to technical background. Early drafts of the script also went to David Livingston, one of *The Next Generation*'s producers, so he could begin to prepare a budget for the episode and the series. Livingston's analysis of the script's costs and practicality would also lead to minor revisions as important as those effected by any of the other consultants.

The following examples of the specialized contributions made by Berman's and

[1]In a memo to Jeri Taylor and the writing staff for *The Next Generation*, accompanying the first bible and treatment for *Deep Space Nine*.

[2]In the past, producers were almost always associated with the logistical side of creating a television series. However, it has become common for producer credits today to be given on both the logistical as well as the creative sides of a production. See Appendix I for a detailed description of credits and their meanings.

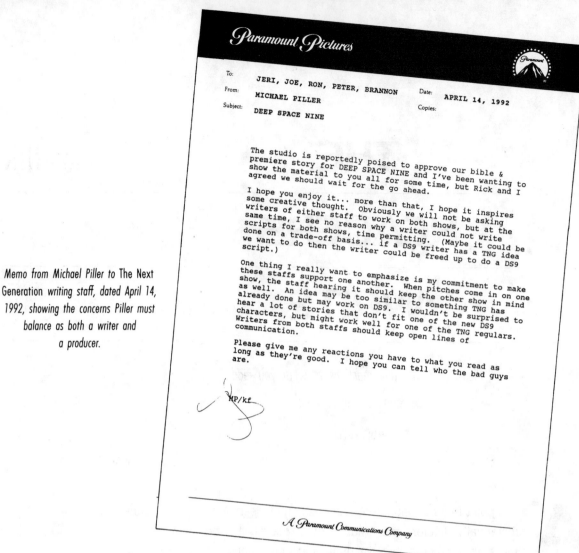

Paramount Pictures

To: JERI, JOE, RON, PETER, BRANNON          Date: APRIL 14, 1992
From: MICHAEL PILLER
Subject: DEEP SPACE NINE                      Copies:

The studio is reportedly poised to approve our bible & premiere story for DEEP SPACE NINE and I've been wanting to show the material to you all for some time, but Rick and I agreed we should wait for the go ahead.

I hope you enjoy it... more than that, I hope it inspires some creative thought. Obviously we will not be asking writers of either staff to work on both shows, but at the same time, I see no reason why a writer could not write scripts for both shows, time permitting. (Maybe it could be done on a trade-off basis... if a DS9 writer has a TNG idea we want to do then the writer could be freed up to do a DS9 script.)

One thing I really want to emphasize is my commitment to make these staffs support one another. When pitches come in on one show, the staff hearing it should keep the other show in mind as well. An idea may be too similar to something TNG has already done but may work on DS9. I wouldn't be surprised to hear a lot of stories that don't fit one of the new DS9 characters, but might work well for one of the TNG regulars. Writers from both staffs should keep open lines of communication.

Please give me any reactions you have to what you read as long as they're good. I hope you can tell who the bad guys are.

MP/kf

A Paramount Communications Company

*Memo from Michael Piller to The Next Generation writing staff, dated April 14, 1992, showing the concerns Piller must balance as both a writer and a producer.*

Piller's team highlight one of the most important and most frustrating elements of television production—the collaborative nature of it all.

## Jeri Taylor

Jeri Taylor joined the writing staff of *The Next Generation* as a supervising producer after she helped rewrite the fourth-season episode "Suddenly Human." Previously, she had served in various producer's roles on *Jake and the Fatman, In the Heat of the Night, Magnum P.I., Blue Thunder,* and *Quincy.*

Prior to her "Suddenly Human" script assignment, Taylor admits she knew nothing about STAR TREK—a situation she quickly changed by a marathon of watching *all* the original and *Next Generation* episodes, and the movies, though not all at once.

Today, Taylor is one of *The Next Generation*'s executive producers, and, with Berman and Piller, co-creator of STAR TREK: VOYAGER, involved in exactly the same type of conceptual development work Michael Piller was caught up in when she responded to his request for comments to the treatment for "The Ninth Orb."

Here are some excerpts from her memo to Piller, dated May 4, 1992.

. . . The story has many wonderful elements and will probably work exactly as written. It starts off terrifically, with the Borg flashback, the conflict between Sisko and Picard, and the troubled relationship between Sisko and his son. (One thought: We seem to do a lot of male-bonding/father-son stories. Would it be fresher if the child were a girl?)

The story then begins to feel a bit talky, drifting from talk scene to talk scene without real drive. Nothing happens, nothing pushes the story forward. One wants an event—maybe even the (early) discovery of the Wormhole, which now feels like it's late in coming.

The scene with the Kai, a pivotal one in which the events of the rest of the show are set up, seems to suffer from being just another in a string of talk scenes. It's hard to feel anything for the Bajorans or for the faceless "prophets," and yet we are expected to care that Sisko find them and warn them.

I'm sure when you've written the scene it will play better, but for my money the character of the Kai isn't very interesting—foot-massaging notwithstanding. He seems a straightforward, predictable combination of the Dalai Lama, the Maharishi, Ghandi, the guy who talked to Grasshopper . . . a cliché of the wizened, elderly guru. Would it be more interesting if he weren't so on-the-nose, maybe even possessed a sense of danger, of real mystery: Is he what he seems or what? Can the monks be trusted? Is Sisko getting into something that might really be perilous, but which he cannot resist anyway? I think there's more to be gotten from the character and the scene.

Sisko's spiritual "journey" and spiritual transformation is a unique and intriguing idea. I'm sure you have something in mind which will help clarify it for us; in story form it is somewhat confusing, and hard to tell just how the audience is going to be aware of what is happening to him. You've taken a big risk in isolating your major character and putting him in an essentially passive role; but big risks can pay off.

Ro's encounter with the Cardassians is good stuff, and provides a sense of urgency, drive, and action that energizes the story. If anything, I wouldn't give it such short shrift; it feels slightly truncated, and if there were a way to prolong it, I think it would sustain.

Minor observations: I'm sure I'm not the first to feel that Sisko's name will have people calling him "Kid." . . . "Quark" is a term in physics. Re Dax's flashback to receiving her symbiont: Why is an incision made on the old man, but not on the little girl? We established that Riker needed an incision, but of course he is human. Whatever the Trill do, it seems we should be consistent.

The characters are rich and interesting and will provide wonderful fodder for stories. The setting is great, lots of fun to be had there. It shapes up as a series that will be exciting, provocative, and challenging. Congratulations.

As we saw in the earlier chapter about the first revisions, Piller was indeed already addressing many of the areas Taylor suggested might be reworked. But one of the perks of being executive producer of a television series is that the final decision on creative matters rests with executive producers alone. Taylor wasn't the only one who wondered about the appropriateness of Quark's name, but Berman and Piller liked it so Quark's bar it was, and Quark's bar it remains.

## Rick Sternbach & Michael Okuda

Rick Sternbach remembers the first time he heard the announcement that a second STAR TREK series was going to be produced. He immediately exited the freeway, found the nearest phone, and called Gene Roddenberry's office.

Sternbach, a two-time winner of science fiction's prestigious Hugo Award for Best Artist, and an Emmy Award–winner for his work as an assistant art director on the PBS series *Cosmos,* had already worked on the STAR TREK features, and wanted to be back on the team. Roddenberry wanted him back, too, and soon Sternbach was designing the spaceships and technology of the STAR TREK universe, which he has continued to do for the features, for *Deep Space Nine*, and for the still-in-development *Voyager*.

Michael Okuda came to *The Next Generation* from television design production in Hawaii. His first contact with STAR TREK had come about when he submitted designs for STAR TREK IV: THE VOYAGE HOME. Not only did the producers approve of his artistic talent, they greatly appreciated his cost-saving technique for creating control panels and display screens. Instead of wiring consoles with actual switches and lights, and either back-projecting or adding through visual effects the images on a display screen, Okuda made those images in white on black on transparent film, then filled in the clear areas with blocks of transparent colored-plastic film usually used as stage light filters, also known as "gels." When the transparencies were backlit by a simple set of lights, they looked like crisp, state-of-the-art computer images for a fraction of the cost of the other two techniques.

Not only was Okuda's work accepted for STAR TREK IV, but he was hired as a scenic artist for *The Next Generation* as well. His responsibilities include overseeing the design of the distinctive graphics used in computer consoles and displays, and all the other signs and graphic elements that are used by Starfleet and the rest of STAR TREK's myriad alien cultures. Again, like Sternbach, Okuda's contributions now span the features, *Deep Space Nine*, and the upcoming *Voyager*. In fact, Okuda's contribution to the instantly recognizable visual environments of STAR TREK has led to the production staff referring to the graphics that he and his staff produce as "Okudagrams."[3]

But in addition to their work in creating some of the visual aspects of STAR TREK, Sternbach and Okuda also have technical-consultant credits on the two series. Technical consultant, in their case, refers to the impressive knowledge they have assembled about the physics of the twenty-fourth century, and the history of the future.[4]

[3]Okuda and his wife, Denise, who also works on *Deep Space Nine* as a scenic artist, rarely use this term themselves. They have a far more dry and technical vocabulary for the designs they use on the show, such as referring to the omnipresent Cardassian identification stickers as "squashed bugs."

[4]Rick Sternbach and Michael Okuda added Technical Consultant to their credits with the third-season *Next Generation* episode "Captain's Holiday." They are well known to STAR TREK fans as the authors of the *Star Trek: The Next Generation Technical Manual*. Michael and his wife, Denise, are also authors of the *Star Trek Chronology,* and, with Debbie Mirek, the exhaustive *Star Trek Encyclopedia*.

# STAR TREK: DS9 -- Control Panel Art
## CARDASSIAN USER INTERFACE

This is representative of the style
of control panel layouts unique to
Deep Space Nine and other
Cardassian vessels

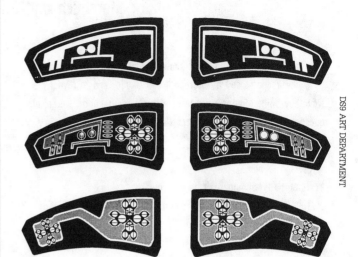

DS9 ART DEPARTMENT

A collection of Okudagrams. The circular
design surrounded by outstretched
"fingers" is known as the "squashed
bug" design. The fingers are part of a
Cardassian "bear claw."

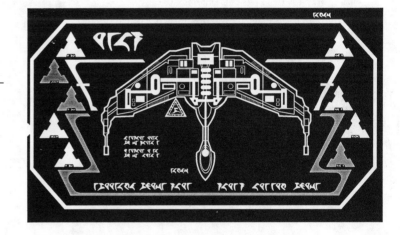

# Tech Wizards of The Twenty-Fourth Century:
## Rick Sternbach and Michael Okuda In Action

To investigate the detailed knowledge of twenty-fourth-century physics possessed by Sternbach and Okuda, and to reveal the way they work together, we tested them with a difficult technical question relating to the science of *Deep Space Nine*.

QUESTION: Why can't certain things be replicated? Specifically, gold-pressed latinum.

RICK STERNBACH: Latinum can't be replicated?

QUESTION: How could it be so valuable if it could be churned out by any replicator?

RS: Oh, well, Mike and I have had discussions about things like this. And then, when we can't come up with a decent answer, we—we sort of skip it. (laughter) I mean, certainly, if we had to think of a technical explanation, it might be that, you know, that the particular molecular structure just doesn't, you know, doesn't—Mike? Why *can't* you replicate latinum?

MICHAEL OKUDA: Uh, it's because—uh, when—uh, it's because the um, the uh, uh, the valence system and the molecular structure are, are arranged—the, uh, the, the, uh, replicator reads certain valence patterns—it recognizes that, that those are . . . *copyguarded!*

QUESTION: Copyguarded?

RS: Copyguarded! Oh, they're, they're "nudged," sort of "nudged quanta," and if they're—

MO: Hey, we talked about this before.

RS: That's right, that's right. Yes, and if they're, they're polarized in the, in the X plane, then they're, they're okay. If they're polarized in the, in the Y-Z plane, then they're bogus.

MO: Right.

RS: We have to do this stuff all the time.

Q: We knew there was a reason.

MO: You probably thought we just made it up.

RS: So how come when a ship goes by, it still makes a WHOOSH?

MO: We have to have very sensitive microphones.

RS: Oh, okay.

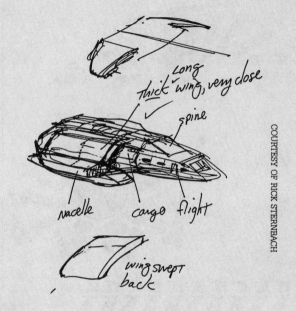

To: Rick Berman and Michael Piller
From: Mike Okuda and Rick Sternbach
Subject: Very preliminary tech notes on DS9: "Emissary"
Date: 2 June 1992

cc: Herman Zimmerman

Scene 5, page 2. Sisko: "Our phasers aren't penetrating their TECH at all." Suggest: "Our phasers aren't penetrating their shields at all." Or: "Absolutely no effect." Or: "Are we using the full frequency variation?"

Scene 10, page 3. Ops Officer: "Our shields are being drained... 94%, 85..." Suggest a smaller initial number and a bigger drop between the two numbers. Maybe: "Sixty five percent, fourty-two percent..."

Scene 26, page 12: O'Brien: "Those bloody Cardies! They didn't even leave us a TECH!" Suggest: Power outlet, instruction manual, usable data port, atmospheric regulator, gravity compensator, air filter.

Scene 26, page 14: O'Brien: "...I still haven't been able to find a TECH." Suggest: the master systems bypass, gravity systems controls, a way to adjust the gravity without pinning us all to the ceiling.

Scene 46, page 26: Sisko: "....Who served a year at Javos II?" Note: In "Ensign Ro," her term was served at Jaros II.

Scene 61, page 38. Kai Opaka: "This orb appeared in the skies over a thousand years ago..." Comment: In "Ensign Ro," we have established that Bajoran civilization flourished before humans were walking erect. Since Homo Erectus dates back about 450,000 years, this might mean that the Bajora go back at least that far. If this is so, then a 1,000 year old sphere seems like a rather recent event for such an ancient culture. Suggest the first orb might have been discovered "over 100,000 of your years ago." (Same comment for later lines relating to the age of the orbs.)

Scene 65, page 41. O'Brien: "Yessir... at least we have minimum shields now, but I had to steal a (TECH component) from the TECH system in order to make it work..." Suggest: "steal a field generator from the gravity system..."

Scene 67, page 44. Amoros: "I confused the MEDTECH with the MEDTECH during the orals or I would have been first." Suggest: "...I mistook a preganglionic fiber for a postganglionic nerve..."

*The memo from Sternbach and Okuda to Berman and Piller, dated June 2, 1992, in which Bashir's "preganglionic/postganglionic" line is suggested.*

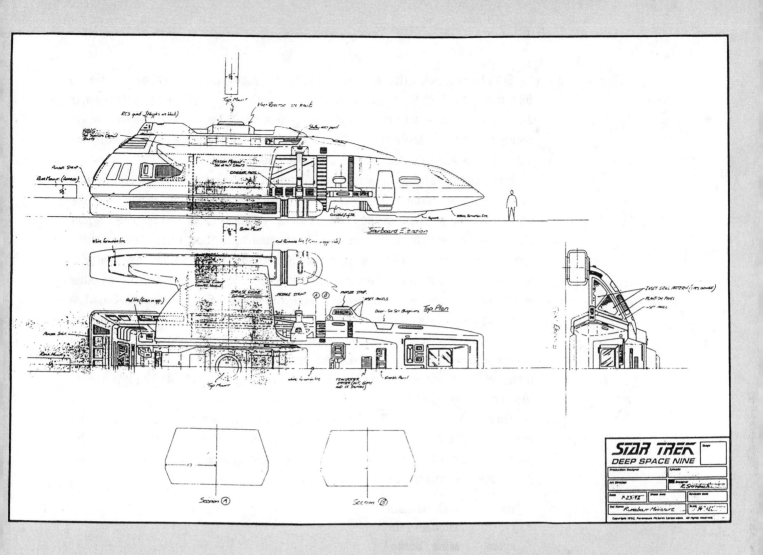

**Starboard Elevation**

**Top Plan**

Section Ⓐ

Section Ⓑ

## STAR TREK
### DEEP SPACE NINE

Designer R. Sternbach

Date 7·23·92

Runabout Miniature

Copyright 1992, Paramount Pictures Corporation. All Rights Reserved.

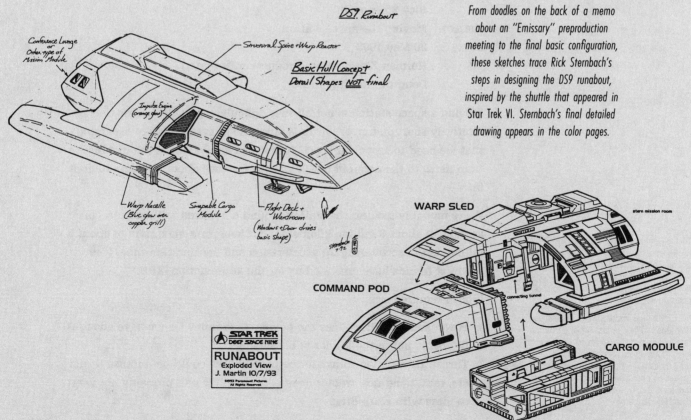

*DS9 Runabout*

From doodles on the back of a memo about an "Emissary" preproduction meeting to the final basic configuration, these sketches trace Rick Sternbach's steps in designing the DS9 runabout, inspired by the shuttle that appeared in Star Trek VI. Sternbach's final detailed drawing appears in the color pages.

Conference Lounge or Other type of Mission Module

Structural Spine + Warp Reactor

*Basic Hull Concept*
Detail Shapes **NOT** final

Impulse Engine (orange glow)

Warp Nacelle (Blue glow over copper grill)

Swapable Cargo Module

Flight Deck + Wardroom (Windows + Door drives basic shape)

**WARP SLED**

stern mission room

**COMMAND POD**

connecting tunnel

**CARGO MODULE**

## STAR TREK
### DEEP SPACE NINE
**RUNABOUT**
Exploded View
J. Martin 10/7/93
©93 Paramount Pictures.
All Rights Reserved.

Sternbach recalled that he and Okuda started providing technical and continuity information "to help the writers and producers fairly early on in the second season of *Next Generation*. A lot of the technical memos, the little bits and pieces that we handed off to them, seemed to make sense to them, I guess. They began trusting our views on not just the basic science, but the science fiction."

Sternbach notes that he was never a conventiongoing fan of STAR TREK, "but, ever since the original *Trek* series, I've been a fan of the design and the science-fiction concepts in the show. A lot of writers who worked on *The Original Series* were science-fiction writers, and they understood a lot of that. I think during the first season of *Next Generation*, we still had some of that. Dave Gerrold[5] was with us. Dorothy Fontana[6] was with us. They understood science fiction. A lot of the other writers did not have as comfortable a time with science-fiction concepts. So, Mike and I stepped in every so often with a suggestion: Try this name, try this term. And all the while, we were helping to shape exactly how a warp engine works, how a phaser works. If they needed the information, we would have it. We didn't want to dump an enormous volume on top of them and say: Here, read this. But if you want the help, we're here."

Thus, for the newest STAR TREK series, it was simply a continuation of Piller's practice on *The Next Generation* to give Sternbach and Okuda an early draft of the pilot script and ask for technical notes, on both dialogue and story points. Here are some excerpts from the resulting memos.

| | |
|---|---|
| **TO:** | **Rick Berman** |
| | **Michael Piller** |
| **FROM:** | **Mike Okuda** |
| | **Rick Sternbach** |
| **SUBJECT:** | **Moving the space station** |
| **DATE:** | **26 May 1992** |
| **CC:** | **Herman Zimmerman [Production Designer]** |
| | **Doug Drexler [Illustrator]** |

**Moving a space station is not all that difficult, especially across the relatively short distances within a single solar system. We're assuming that we need to move our space station the equivalent of the distance from Earth to the asteroid belt, and that we have about 48 hours to do it in.**

**We're probably moving the station around a hundred million miles, an average of about 3 million kilometers per hour, or a maximum of about 5 million km/h, accounting for acceleration and deceleration time. (Our scientist friends have criticized us for the abbreviation, KPH.)**

**What's required are:**

1. **Power source. Where does the power come from? Do we have enough? (Probably not without a lot of hassle.)**
2. **Thrust. How do we translate the power? This could be impulse thrusters, rocket engines, tractor beams, or sails. We will probably not want to mess with warp drive.**

[5]David Gerrold burst into STAR TREK fans' awareness by writing one of the most popular original episodes, "The Trouble with Tribbles," and went on to become both a noted television writer and science-fiction novelist.

[6]D. C. Fontana wrote several first-season episodes of *The Original Series*, including the highly praised "Journey to Babel," which introduced Spock's parents. She then became script consultant for the series' second season, and later cowrote the pilot for *The Next Generation* with Gene Roddenberry.

3. **Structural integrity.** Unlike a starship, a space station is generally intended to be a fairly static structure, meaning it is not designed to withstand the enormous accelerations involved in Star Trek-style spaceflight. This is not necessarily a problem. One can compensate for this by simply pushing very gently.

4. **Time.** Here's the kicker. We can move the station very slowly, but this means it will take a very long time. This is a benefit in terms of power requirements (you can get away with less power), but we have that time limit in which to get to the wormhole.

What follows is a page-long discussion of where the power to move the station might come from. Then the problem of how to translate that power into thrust is addressed.

**O'Brien might wish to strap some auxiliary thruster packs to the station (like we did to the waste freighter in "Final Mission"). The problem is that we do not have access to the resources of the Enterprise. Here again, time is the problem. What we might do is take the runabout, dock it to the station in some clever manner, and use the impulse drive to get us even more thrust. Even here, we might assume that it would take several hours to accelerate the station, then several hours to slow it down. Another thought. If we can get enough power out of the main reactors, we might be able to jerry-rig a low-level warp field around the station. This would not be to accelerate the ship to warp speed (which would literally take millions of times more power), but we might be able to re-create the trick we did in "Deja Q." By reducing the "apparent mass" of the station, we might be able to make the station light enough to move with the available power.**

Though the treatment for "The Ninth Orb" had DS9 towed to the wormhole by runabouts, the warp-field method suggested by Sternbach and Okuda is pretty much how DS9 was moved in the produced episode. Here's how the strategy was arrived at in the final script.

---

173 CONTINUED:

O'Brien is monitoring sensors on his panel . . . reacts as he sees something . . .

> O'BRIEN
> The Cardassians are leaving their
> position . . . on a course toward
> the Denorios Belt.

Kira frowns . . . stands . . .

KIRA

(beat[7], to O'Brien)

What would it take to move this
station to the mouth of the
wormhole?

O'BRIEN

This isn't a starship, Major.
We've got six working thrusters
to power us and that's it. A
hundred-sixty million kilometer
trip would take two months.

KIRA

It's got to be there tomorrow.

O'BRIEN

(reacts)
That's not possible, sir . . .

KIRA

That wormhole might just reshape
the future of this entire
quadrant. The Bajorans have to
stake a claim to it . . .
(beat, character
movement[8])
And I have to admit that claim
will be a lot stronger if there's
a Federation presence to back it
up.

DAX

(calm, to O'Brien)
Couldn't you modify the subspace
field output of the deflector
generators . . . just enough to
create a *low*-level field around
the station . . .

A beat. O'Brien begins to get her logic . . .

O'BRIEN

So we could lower the inertial
mass . . .

[7]A beat is simply a slight pause to indicate
that a character is thinking something
over, or otherwise considering his or her
next action.

[8]This is just a reminder that Kira has a long
speech and she shouldn't stand around
like a bump on a log. She's on the brink of
history. She should be doing something.
Exactly what, though, is left to the actor
and director.

```
                    DAX
                   (nods)
         If you can make the station
         lighter, those six thrusters would
         be all the power we'd need.
```

Interestingly enough, at the time the script was written and Sternbach and Okuda provided their technical notes, the idea of changing the value of inertia was a science-fiction concept as wild as faster-than-light travel and teleportation—the three main staples of STAR TREK science. However, a recent issue of the journal of the American Association for the Advancement of Science, *Science*, reports on a new theory of inertia that for the first time suggests that "inertia, once understood, might be controlled."[9] This is somewhat of a hat trick for science-fiction concepts achieving scientific respectability because 1993 brought the first theoretical basis for describing a technique of matter teleportation,[10] and an intriguing experiment involving the effect of filters on the transmission of light turned up repeatable evidence of photons travelling at 1.7 times the speed of light, which, of course, is impossible.[11] The science of the twenty-fourth century might be building its foundations even now.

Moving away from grand scientific concepts, Sternbach and Okuda sometimes provide technical notes that simply bring a STAR TREK flavor to a script, instead of suggesting a way to manage a plot point. Here are some other notes they provided to Berman and Piller in later memos.

**June 2, 1992**
**Scene 10, page 3. Ops Officer: "Our shields are being drained . . . 94%, 85 . . ." Suggest a smaller initial number and a bigger drop between the two numbers. Maybe: "Sixty-five percent, forty-two percent . . ."**

(In the final script, Piller used the percentages "sixty-four percent. . . forty-two . . .")

**June 10, 1992**
**Scene 176. O'Brien: Suggest: "I may still be able to pick up the runabout's transponder signal . . . and now that we know it's a wormhole, we can use a TECH compensator." The TECH device can be: field density compensator, waveform regulator, baryon field unifier, spatial compression compensator, spatial field regulator (you see where we're going? The old adjective-adjective-noun game), spatial density programmer, meson wave collimator. Whatever is picked can be used in Sc. 277, et cetera.**

Though the note above refers to a line cut from the final script, it's interesting to see one of the techniques Sternbach and Okuda use to come up with TECH replacements.

**Scene 219. O'Brien: Suggest: Are you sure it collapsed . . . it could have retreated deeper into subspace." Or: "Are you sure it collapsed . . . it could have submerged deeper into subspace."**

[9]*Science*, Vol. 263, February 4, 1994, page 612. "Inertia: Does Empty Space Put Up the Resistance?"

[10]*Discover*, Vol. 15 No. 1, January 1994, page 100. "Getting There Is Half the Fun." The article by Carl Zimmer reports that researchers at the University of Innsbruck in Austria are building an apparatus with which they hope to transport a single photon.

[11]*Nature*, Vol. 365 No. 6448, October 21, 1993, page 692. "Light faster than light?"

> **Dax: Suggest: "We haven't found any indication that it retreated . . . but we're still checking." Synonyms for *retreat* would be *withdraw*, or *recede*. Something to suggest it was pulled back.**

The synonym Piller used in the final script was "withdrawn."

> **Scene 237. Cory:[12] Suggest: "Mister O'Brien, can you re-establish a high energy subspace\* field before they get to within sensor range . . . I don't want them to be able to scan our defence systems . . ." Comment: The Cardassians used that against us in "The Wounded" to prevent us from seeing their cargo. We suggest the word *re-establish* because O'Brien did it once to move the station, so he ought to cobble it back together.**

> **\*If, by this time, you're sick of the word *subspace* in this context, you can substitute any fake particle or wave name (antilepton field, thoron field, dianon field, etc.).**

Piller chose to use "Thoron field."

In the next set of notes, we see that sometimes Sternbach's and Okuda's notes actually relate to their artistic duties as well as their technical consulting roles.

> **June 9, 1992**
> **Scene 101. Seeing the turbo car in a glass tube on the station exterior is probably not easily accomplished. We're imagining that almost all turboshafts are well-protected within the station structure; the scene could be rewritten to play in the airlock chamber attached to the runabout set.**

The scene was set in a new location, and all of DS9's turboshafts are inside the station, not exposed on the exterior.

> **Scene 128. Finding out where they are: We have a variety of ways of triangulating, even if we're on the other side of the galaxy. Some of these methods work today in the 20th century, with standard stellar observation techniques. Anyhow (scene okay up to first computer line):**

> **Computer Voice: Suggest: "Idran . . . trinary system consisting of a central red supergiant and twin O-type companions."**

> **(Later) Computer Voice: Suggest: "Identification of Idran is based on analysis of stellar magnetopause and hydrogen-alpha spectral analysis. Location correlates with region first studied in the late twenty-second century by the Quadros One probe of the Gamma Quadrant."**

> **Dax: Suggest: ". . . There were none of the usual IR resonance waves."**

And that scene, in the final script, went like this . . .

---

[12]An early name for Kira.

SISKO

Can you get a fix on our
coordinates . . . ?

DAX

(checking)

There's a star just under five
light years away . . . no M class
planets . . . Computer, identify
closest star system . . .

COMPUTER VOICE

Idran . . . a ternary system
consisting of a central supergiant
and twin O-type companions . . .

SISKO

(reacts)

Idran . . . that can't be right . . .

DAX

Computer, basis of identification . . .

COMPUTER VOICE

Identification of Idran is based
on the hydrogen-alpha spectral
analysis conducted in the
twenty-second century by the
Quadros-One probe of the Gamma
Quadrant.

SISKO

(stunned)

The Gamma Quadrant. Seventy
*thousand* light years from Bajor?
I'd say we just found our way into
a wormhole . . .

DAX

It's not like any wormhole I've
ever seen. There were none of
the usual resonance waves . . .

By now we see the pattern that emerges from Sternbach's and Okuda's contributions to STAR TREK scripts. The characters and their interactions are completely in the hands of the writers, while the science-fiction/STAR TREK context of those interactions are strengthened by Sternbach's and Okuda's detailed knowledge and command of background information, in the same way that the actors' eventual performances are strengthened by convincing sets and visual effects. The story is what's important, but a good setting can make the story even stronger. And Sternbach and Okuda do manage to show all the different ways the setting can be kept consistent and strong.

In reviewing the changes Sternbach and Okuda suggested and comparing them with the decisions Piller made in incorporating those suggestions into the script, sharp-eyed readers might have noticed that where Sternbach and Okuda suggested that Idran be a "trinary" star system, the term Piller used was "ternary." This wasn't a typo or a new science-fiction term. It was a contribution from another of STAR TREK's technical consultants, whose specialty is the real science of the twentieth century.

## Naren Shankar

Naren Shankar first participated in STAR TREK as cowriter (with Ronald D. Moore) of the fifth-season *Next Generation* episode "The First Duty." His initial position as a Writers Guild Intern on the series' writing staff eventually became that of science consultant for both series, based in part on his engineering doctorate from Cornell. Fortunately for STAR TREK, after receiving his doctorate Shankar decided he didn't really want to be an engineer after all, and, like so many others, came to Los Angeles to try and make a career as a writer.[13] For Shankar, that dream is coming true. For the seventh season of *The Next Generation,* he moved from being a consultant to a story editor.

But back in 1992, it was as *Next Generation*'s science consultant that Shankar was sent by Piller an early draft of "Emissary," asking for notes. Here are some extracts from Shankar's initial comments, which clearly illustrate his scientific knowledge as well as an engineer's fine eye for detail.

> **TECHNICAL NOTES**
> **July 20, 1992**
>
> **A few points . . .**
> • **Act 1, sc. 32, p. 19 (bottom)**
>   Odo: **"My security *array* has been down . . ."**
> **Suggest "grid" instead.**
>
> • **Act 1, sc. 40, p. 22 (middle)**
>   Sisko: **". . . Take *him* to the brig."**
> **Since Odo is taking both Nog and the alien away, Sisko should say, "Take *them* to the brig."**

[13]An old Hollywood joke says that if you ask any LA waiter, "How's the script going?" nine times out of ten, the reply will be: "Well, I've got this problem in the second act, but . . ."

```
                    DEEP SPACE NINE

                    TECHNICAL NOTES

                      "Emissary"
                   by Michael Piller
                    Draft Teleplay
           (including bf. revisions, 6/11/92)
                    June 11, 1992


 • Teaser, sc. 10, p. 4 (top)
    Conn Officer: "Attempting to come about... impulse engines
                    aren't doing it, sir..."

 I don't think this maneuver makes sense in the context of the
 battle, and furthermore, why bother with the impulse engines
 at all?  Maybe he should be "attempting to engage warp
 engines" or something like that.


 • Act 1, sc. 26, p. 12 (middle)
    O'Brien.

 A quick note: Has O'Brien been promoted?  Usually a transfer
 like this would be accompanied by advancement in rank.  Since
 it looks like he's going to be functioning as something like
 the Second Officer on DS9, he should probably be at least a
 Lieutenant.


 • Act 1, sc. 26, p. 12 (bottom)
    O'Brien: "...all the auto-TECH controls..."

 Suggest: "interlock servos", "auto-seal controls", or "auto-
 closure controls".


 • Act 1, sc. 26, p. 13 (top)
    O'Brien: "...We've got some TECH emissions..."

 Suggest: "stray nucleonic emissions".
```

*Part of a memo from science consultant Naren Shankar, commenting on an early draft of "Emissary."*

• **Act 2, sc. 64, p. 40 (top)**
**Kai: ". . . They [the orbs] have been studied and documented for a *millennium.*"**

**I would strongly suggest making the orbs much older than just one thousand years.**

**In sc. 16 of the TNG episode "Ensign Ro," Picard describes the "ancient" Bajoran civilization: ". . . they were architects and artists and builders and philosophers . . . *when humans were not yet standing erect.*" If you are going to maintain consistency with this statement, then the orbs should be something along the lines of *50 to 100 thousand years* old.**

**Furthermore, since the oldest faiths on Earth (e.g., Confucianism, Judaism) are well over two thousand years old, I think it would substantially heighten the mystery of the orb—as well as the Bajoran culture itself—if they were much older.**

Shankar then goes on to list the other places in the script where the age of the Orbs is mentioned. Sternbach and Okuda also recommended that the age of the Orbs be increased in order to be consistent with what had been previously established about Bajoran culture, and Piller subsequently did revise the script to suggest that the first Orb appeared in the skies over Bajor more than ten thousand years ago.

Shankar then continued with other suggestions.

- **Act 2, sc. 64, p. 40 (middle)**
  (in desc.): "She lifts the *arc* . . ."
  Typo: Should be spelled *"ark"* (meaning "container").

- **Act 4, sc 106, p. 62 (middle)**
  Sisko: ". . . Initializing pre-launch systems check (*TECH*)"
  Suggest simply *"Initializing pre-launch systems."*

- **Act 5, sc. 118, p. 65 (middle)**
  Sisko: "Adjusting course to fifty-three *by* one-fourteen . . ."
  If this is a course change, then the line should be: "Adjusting course to fifty-three *mark* one-fourteen"; if they're heading for a specific grid point, then the line should be: *"Setting course for grid point* fifty-three by one-fourteen."

- **Act 5, sc. 121, p. 66 (top)**
  O'Brien: "Lieutenant, *in that asteroid belt, you could be looking at chrondite echoes . . .*"
  This line seems a bit confusing. I'd suggest replacing it with something like: *"Lieutenant, considering the composition of those asteroids, you might be sensing chrondite decay emissions . . ."*

- **Act 5, sc. 136, p. 71 (middle & bottom)**
  Dax: *"Velocity* is still falling . . ."
  & Dax: *"Velocity* is five kph . . ."
  The word "velocity" should always be used with a directional modifier: e.g., "forward velocity," "lateral velocity." In the absence of a specified direction the word *"speed"* should be used instead.

Piller chose to add "forward" to one use of the word velocity in the scene, but that pesky "kph" which Sternbach and Okuda had mentioned remained, mainly because even if it were correctly written as k/h, it would still be read as "kay-per-aytch."

Shankar goes on to comment on the wormhole entities, who do not understand linear time, yet use the past tense in their conversation with Sisko. In the final script, the entities do end up speaking entirely in the present tense.

Another note had to do with a new bit of STAR TREK jargon that was evolving.

- **Act 9, sc. 247, p. 114 (middle)**
  Kira: ". . . Fire six *photons* across Jasad's bow . . ."
  O'Brien: "We only have six *photons*, Major . . ."
  While I know that we have occasionally used the term "photons" to refer to photon torpedoes, I would strongly discourage this use in the future. "Photons" are elementary physical particles of light; to use the term to describe a matter-anti-matter bomb (which is what a photon torpedo is) is confusing and technically incorrect. I'd suggest replacing both instances above with *"photon torpedoes."*

Piller went halfway on this and had Kira ask O'Brien to fire six photon torpedoes, to which O'Brien replied that he only had six photons.

In an earlier memo dated June 11, 1992, Shankar gave his reaction to the Ferengi barkeeper's name.

- **Act 1, sc. 29, p. 14 (bottom)**
  **Quark.**
  **In physics, "quarks" are elementary, sub-nuclear particles; it may be unwise to use this as a name for a Ferengi.**

We know how Piller decided to act on this one.

Then Shankar commented on the identification of the star in the Gamma Quadrant for which Sternbach and Okuda had offered changes.

- **Act 5, sc. 135, p. 73 (middle)**
  **Computer: "Idran . . . *trinary system* consisting . . . "**
  **The computer normally speaks in more complete sentences than this. Also, "trinary" is not typical astronomical usage; *"ternary"* would be better, although *"triple"* is preferred. Suggest the following: *"Star system identified as Idran . . . a ternary system . . ."***

Combining the astronomical data provided by Sternbach and Okuda, and the terminology provided by Shankar, Idran then became a ternary system. Only astronomers might catch the distinction, but the effort spent on this one small point shows the enthusiastic attention to accuracy that is shared by all members of Berman's and Piller's team—which is a good explanation for why they are on the team to begin with.

Taking a quick side step from issues of quality and technical correctness, there is one other vital aspect of any script that must be checked before it can ever hope to be made—is it *legally* proper?

America is a land of lawsuits and Hollywood often appears to be its capital. Each name Berman and Piller created, each alien word and rank, each science-fiction device and extraterrestrial location had to be checked to see if it might in any inadvertent way be linked to someone, something, or someplace. You've seen the disclaimers in thousands of movies and television shows: THE PERSONS AND EVENTS IN THIS PROGRAM ARE FICTITIOUS. ANY SIMILARITY TO ACTUAL PERSONS OR EVENTS IS UNINTENTIONAL. For *Deep Space Nine,* Joan Pearce Research Associates is the company that is entrusted to make that statement true. (Their researchers also have developed in-depth knowledge of the STAR TREK universe, resulting in some notes that have more to do with continuity than with legal matters. But this is a collaborative venture after all.)

Here are some excerpts from their initial report on the pilot script, dated July 30, 1992.

**COMMENT**
**This teleplay contains many allusions to the established series, STAR TREK: THE NEXT GENERATION. There are also characters in the script which were established in that series. Since this script is a pilot for a new series which we hope will see many years of production, we have rechecked those names and references which are not part of the *running* character names or established Star Trek lore. This is merely a precaution to be sure that items which appeared briefly in a previous episode and were clear at the time have no current conflicts.**

## CHARACTER NAMES

*Picard/Locutus p. 1*
**Established character.**

*Lieutenant Commander Benjamin Sisko p. 1*
**We find no current pertinent listing for this exact name.**

*Jake Sisko p. 6*
**We find no current pertinent listing for this exact name.**

*Miles O'Brien p. 11*
**Established character.**

*Quark p. 13*
**Single name only. We note the word was coined by living physicist, Murray Gell-Mann, to denote a theoretical particle.[14]**

The report continues, finding "no current pertinent listing for this exact name" for a variety of characters, until . . .

*Ty Cobb Alien p. 85*
**We assume the character will be costumed in an early Detroit Tigers uniform and will be made up to resemble the legendary player, Tyrus Raymond Cobb, 1886–1961. Possible permission from the Tigers Organization. Research can provide the telephone number if needed.[15]**

After dealing with the names of all the characters in the script, the report moves on to all other matters, as represented by these excerpts.

| PAGE | ITEM |
|------|------|
| 1/1 | *On Stardate 43997, Captain Jean-Luc Picard of the Federation starship Enterprise was kidnapped by the Borg*—reference to the previous Star Trek episode, "The Best of Both Worlds." Our records show the beginning stardate for that show as 43989.1. |
| 1/3 | *The Gage*—We find no pertinent listing for a warship with this exact name. There are other merchant and pleasure ships with the name. |
| 12/24 | (*the details of the set for the shopping area*)—Research will be happy to check names for the various shops if needed by the art department. Please advise.[16] |
| 14/29 | *Kumomoto*—Establishes the site of Keiko's mother's home. |
| 19/32 | *a map of the station*—We assume this will be designed by your art department and that no copyrighted materials will be included. |
| 32/51 | *chants*—Music clearance?[17] |
| 42/67 | *24th-century teenage paraphernalia*—Research can check any "tradenames," "artist names," etc. which might be needed for this set. |
| 43/68 | *alien music*—Music clearance. |

[14]Actually, Gell-Mann took the word from James Joyce's *Ulysses*, where it had no readily apparent meaning.

[15]Ty Cobb and the Detroit Tigers did not end up in the pilot episode. By the time the script went into production, the character called TY COBB ALIEN had been replaced by the generic, and less expensive in terms of rights payments, ALIEN BATTER, and the costumes he and his teammates wore during one of Sisko's sequences in the wormhole were from the Chicago Cubs, circa 1923. The next baseball player to appear on *Deep Space Nine* (in the episode "If Wishes Were Horses") was the legendary Buck Bokai of the London Kings—circa 2042. Any rights payments due for the use of that character won't have to be paid for at least another forty-eight years.

[16]Hmmm. Could there be a financial reason why all the shop names on the Promenade are in languages other than human?

[17]Music clearance means arrangements have been made to locate and pay the composer of the music used. This is seldom necessary for *Deep Space Nine* as the music chanted by Bajoran monks, or the music heard in Quark's bar, is written exclusively for the show. However, if the writers ever come up with a reason why someone on the series should be listening to a twentieth-century song, clearance has to be obtained and royalties paid.

Keone Young as the soon-to-be-legendary Buck Bokai of the London Kings, with Lieutenant Dax and Michael John Anderson as Rumpelstiltskin, in "If Wishes Were Horses."

43/69   *some games we recognize, some we don't*—If any proprietary games are used, permission will be needed. Research can provide any needed telephone numbers when the final selection is made. We assume the other games will be created by your art and prop departments and that no proprietary items will be duplicated.

43/70   *synthale*—We find no prominent proprietary listing for this exact term.

58/96   *the Denorios Belt*—No listing.

66/92   *some alien-looking glop-on-a-stick*—This term is a registered trademark of the Mars Exploration Symposium . . . just kidding, guys. Are you paying attention to these immortal words?[18]

65/118   *fifty-three by one-fourteen*—Better Startrekspeak: fifty-three *mark* one-fourteen.[19]

68/132   *Idran*—No listing.

69/132   *Quadros-One*—No listing.

69/132   *Gamma Quadrant*—No listing.

106/236   *Thoron field*—No listing.

109/239   *the Setlik Three massacre*—No listing.

115/250   *Roladan Wild Draw*—No listing.

116/252   *duranium*—Established previously.

[18]It was not until the final episode of the first season, "In the Hands of the Prophets," that the ever-popular "glop-on-a-stick" was finally given a real name—*jumja* sticks.

[19]When both the science consultant *and* the legal research company remark upon the same term, it's quite clear that STAR TREK *has* created a style all its own.

And was that final term *ever* established previously. "Duranium" dates back to 1966 and *The Original Series* episode "The Menagerie," written by Gene Roddenberry. This is the type of detail that Naren Shankar and Michael Okuda and Rick Sternbach love to throw into their script notes for the benefit of those paying *extremely* close attention to a STAR TREK show.

Of course, despite everyone's best efforts to check every word and reference and be as accurate as possible, little things still do manage to sneak by.

A science-fiction writer who had worked on *The Next Generation* noted with a sigh that for all the people who had read the script for "Emissary," over all those months of preproduction, apparently no one had ever caught the oxymoron that appeared in the first treatment and remained in every draft of the script up to the final.

How, the science-fiction writer asked, can an *orb* be *hourglass-shaped?*

Ah well, in the immortal words of Rick Sternbach, "When we can't come up with a decent answer, we—we sort of skip it."

# "A STRANGE, INTRIGUING OBJECT"

TEN

*The prime directive from the show's producers was that the
station itself must be a principal character in the
drama, just as the Starship Enterprise has been.*

—Herman Zimmerman

I n the previous chapter, one of the comments Rick Sternbach and Michael Okuda made about an early draft of "Emissary" had to do with the location of the turbolifts. Their note about the technical difficulty in showing a turbolift moving through a transparent tunnel, and their suggestion that all the station's turbolifts be contained safely inside, were only the tip of the proverbial iceberg. So far, we have only been concerned with words on paper, the flow of the story, and the believability of the characters. But television is a visual medium and no matter how good Piller's script was to begin with, no matter how much it would improve as he continued to polish it, taking into account the comments of his trusted first readers, all his efforts would be for naught if *Deep Space Nine* didn't end up *looking* good.

As one of the artists associated with the show later said, "Those who fail to remember style and color will be doomed to become *Space Rangers*."[1]

So how does one go about inventing the look of the future? *The Next Generation* had been doing it for years, but for the most part, the bulk of the design work was variations on a theme.

Starfleet installations had a sleek, comfortable look all their own. Starfleet technology was easily recognizable. Romulans had their own look, Klingons had theirs, ranging from their costumes to the interiors of their ships.

Certainly, almost every new episode of *The Next Generation* required new aliens, new sets, and new props, but they would be needed just for a single story. Longevity was not a great concern.

[1] *Space Rangers* was a short-lived network science-fiction series that debuted in most markets in the same week *Deep Space Nine* did. While the show had a distinct storytelling style that tried to focus on fast action and snappy dialogue, it did not hold an audience for long, and was canceled before all of the initial six episodes were aired.

Storytelling style aside, perhaps the flaw that hurt the series most was the quality of its special effects and overall design. Though each *Space Rangers* episode cost less than half of a *Deep Space Nine* episode, the producers did not address the fact that *The Next Generation* has set a high standard for how science fiction on television should appear. Any series that wishes to succeed in the market today must, as a matter of course, present itself with *at least* the same quality of visual effects and design as the STAR TREK series, or risk being categorized by the audience as cheap or unprofessional. *Babylon 5,* with its stunning computer-generated space sequences, is clearly poised to give both STAR TREK series some healthy competition when it comes to visual effects. Around *Deep Space Nine,* the production staff agree that *Babylon 5*'s continuing success will be good for the STAR TREK shows as well, as it can only increase the audience for well-produced, episodic science fiction.

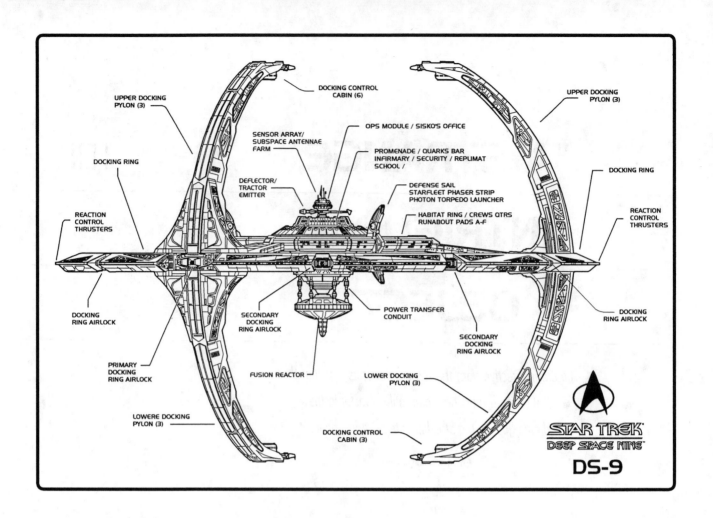

UPPER DOCKING
PYLON (3)

DOCKING CONTROL
CABIN (6)

UPPER DOCKING
PYLON (3)

DOCKING RING

SENSOR ARRAY/
SUBSPACE ANTENNAE
FARM

OPS MODULE / SISKO'S OFFICE

DOCKING RING

PROMENADE / QUARKS BAR
INFIRMARY / SECURITY / REPLIMAT
SCHOOL /

REACTION
CONTROL
THRUSTERS

DEFLECTOR/
TRACTOR
EMITTER

DEFENSE SAIL
STARFLEET PHASER STRIP
PHOTON TORPEDO LAUNCHER

REACTION
CONTROL
THRUSTERS

HABITAT RING / CREWS QTRS
RUNABOUT PADS A-F

DOCKING
RING AIRLOCK

POWER TRANSFER
CONDUIT

DOCKING
RING AIRLOCK

SECONDARY
DOCKING
RING AIRLOCK

SECONDARY
DOCKING
RING AIRLOCK

PRIMARY
DOCKING
RING AIRLOCK

FUSION REACTOR

LOWER DOCKING
PYLON (3)

LOWERE DOCKING
PYLON (3)

DOCKING CONTROL
CABIN (3)

STAR TREK
DEEP SPACE NINE

DS-9

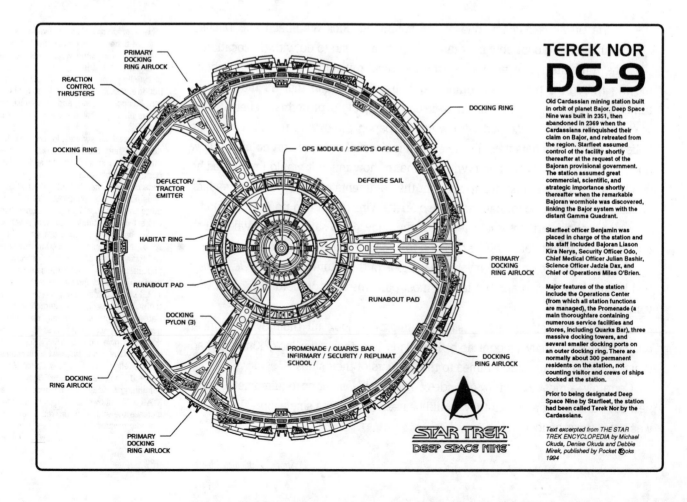

PRIMARY
DOCKING
RING AIRLOCK

REACTION
CONTROL
THRUSTERS

DOCKING RING

DOCKING RING

OPS MODULE / SISKO'S OFFICE

DEFLECTOR/
TRACTOR
EMITTER

DEFENSE SAIL

HABITAT RING

PRIMARY
DOCKING
RING AIRLOCK

RUNABOUT PAD

DOCKING
PYLON (3)

RUNABOUT PAD

PROMENADE / QUARKS BAR
INFIRMARY / SECURITY / REPLIMAT
SCHOOL /

DOCKING
RING AIRLOCK

DOCKING
RING AIRLOCK

PRIMARY
DOCKING
RING AIRLOCK

STAR TREK
DEEP SPACE NINE

# TEREK NOR
# DS-9

Old Cardassian mining station built
in orbit of planet Bajor. Deep Space
Nine was built in 2351, then
abandoned in 2369 when the
Cardassians relinquished their
claim on Bajor, and retreated from
the region. Starfleet assumed
control of the facility shortly
thereafter at the request of the
Bajoran provisional government.
The station assumed great
commercial, scientific, and
strategic importance shortly
thereafter when the remarkable
Bajoran wormhole was discovered,
linking the Bajor system with the
distant Gamma Quadrant.

Starfleet officer Benjamin was
placed in charge of the station and
his staff included Bajoran Liason
Kira Nerys, Security Officer Odo,
Chief Medical Officer Julian Bashir,
Science Officer Jadzia Dax, and
Chief of Operations Miles O'Brien.

Major features of the station
include the Operations Center
(from which all station functions
are managed), the Promenade (a
main thoroughfare containing
numerous service facilities and
stores, including Quarks Bar), three
massive docking towers, and
several smaller docking ports on
an outer docking ring. There are
normally about 300 permanent
residents on the station, not
counting visitor and crews of ships
docked at the station.

Prior to being designated Deep
Space Nine by Starfleet, the station
had been called Terek Nor by the
Cardassians.

Text excerpted from THE STAR
TREK ENCYCLOPEDIA by Michael
Okuda, Denise Okuda and Debbie
Mirek, published by Pocket Books
1994

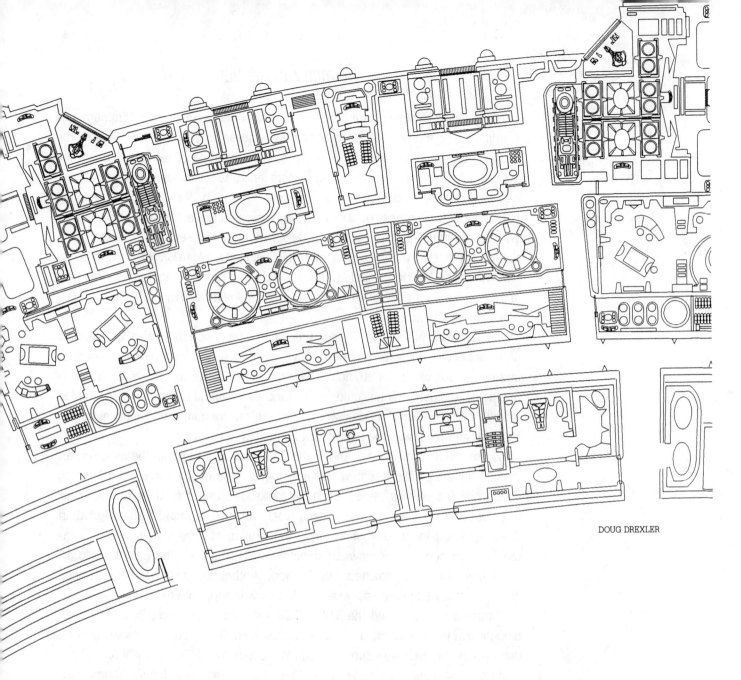

DOUG DREXLER

But in the case of *Deep Space Nine*, Berman and Piller needed a completely new setting which would anchor a series that could possibly run for six or seven years. We might recognize the uniforms that the crew of DS9 wore. We would certainly recognize their phasers and their tricorders. But the station itself, which had never been seen before, would have to have the same dramatic impact, the same visual interest, and the same long-term appeal as one of the most durable settings on television—the *Starship Enterprise*. In fact, Roddenberry had always exhorted STAR TREK writers to think of the *Enterprise* as a character, and Berman and Piller gave the same direction for the perception of DS9.

To accomplish that, there was only one person to whom Berman and Piller could go, the same person who had so successfully overseen the look of *The Next Generation*'s first season as production designer, the two most recent STAR TREK features, and a number of other notable films, including Ridley Scott's visually striking *Black Rain*—so they did.

*A generic detailed plan of the DS9 station. It doesn't show any ring or level in particular, but is used whenever a screen has to show a floor plan.*

# Herman Zimmerman

The production designer on a film or television series is, in Herman Zimmerman's words, "the person responsible for everything you see on the screen—except for the acting." This responsibility requires an intricate meshing of technical knowledge about everything from film stock and camera lenses to visual effects, wardrobe, set, and prop design, all combined with the eye of an artist. Fortunately, Zimmerman possesses all the requisite qualities, as can be seen each week on *Deep Space Nine*, without question *the* most beautifully designed show on television. (Zimmerman is the first to point out that no matter how well designed a television show might be, no one will notice the design unless it's photographed properly, and no one will care about the design if the stories aren't good. Once again, television is proven to be a collaborative enterprise.)

Like so many others who work in the film and television industries, Zimmerman didn't set out to do the job he's doing now. His original goal was to become an actor and singer, for which he studied at Northwestern University. However, when he graduated, the only way he could qualify for the assistantship position he needed in order to earn his master's degree was to switch his major from acting and directing to scene design. That was the inadvertent beginning of his career.

Zimmerman came to Los Angeles in 1965 and was hired as the assistant art director for the pilot of the new NBC soap opera *Days of Our Lives*. As a learning experience, the job was intense. Each day's episode required from five to seven sets, and there were five episodes shot each week. After three months, the original art director moved to another show and Zimmerman, still fresh from college, was promoted to become the new art director. He recalls sneaking into the NBC art department after hours to check out the work of other designers—not to steal their ideas, but to try and figure out exactly what he was supposed to be doing.

Zimmerman first joined the STAR TREK team when producer Robert Justman brought him in as production designer for *The Next Generation*'s first season. After that season, Zimmerman returned to film work, including STAR TREK V and VI.

Like many other key people in the STAR TREK production family, Zimmerman recognizes a crucial reason for the long-term appeal of the franchise—Gene Roddenberry's positive view of the future. After more than a quarter-century of STAR TREK's success in exemplifying this appeal, Zimmerman is still amazed that no other television or movie series has tried a similar approach.

## Thinking Like Cardassians

In March 1992, Berman and Piller anticipated the horrendous time pressure they would be under if Paramount gave a green light to the series in April 1992 for a January 1993 debut. Thus, with *The Next Generation*'s supervising producer, David Livingston, they organized a design group consisting of themselves, Herman Zimmerman, Rick Sternbach, and Michael Okuda to consider the design of the Cardassian space station. So far, the only description they had to go by was what

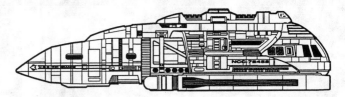

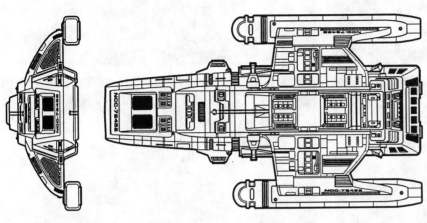

*Various views and control panels of a DS9 runabout—an example of what Ira Steven Behr calls "Starfleet-clean" design. The Cardassian approach to space vessel design would have to be extremely alien in comparison.*

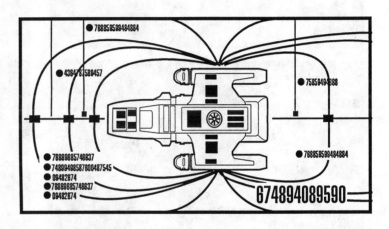

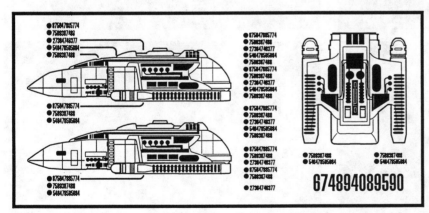

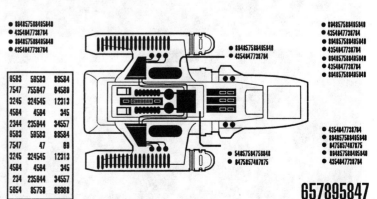

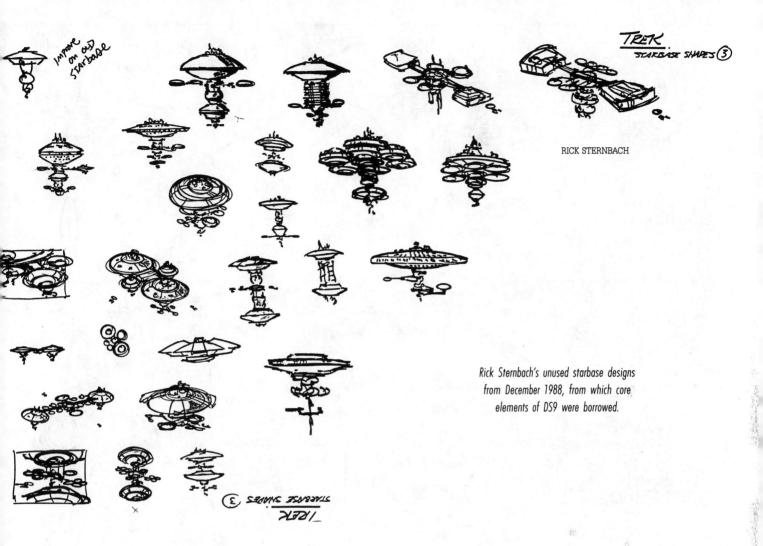

RICK STERNBACH

*Rick Sternbach's unused starbase designs
from December 1988, from which core
elements of DS9 were borrowed.*

appeared in the "Ninth Orb" treatment: ". . . a strange, intriguing object in orbit of Bajor. . . ." And the only visual precedent the group had to work from was the look of the Cardassians themselves, as created by makeup artist Michael Westmore and costume designer Robert Blackman, and of the Cardassian warship designed by Rick Sternbach. Other than those tantalizing hints of Cardassian psychology and history, the design group faced a blank slate.

There were, of course, many starting points to a project this broad, and the design group began with all of them simultaneously, under Herman Zimmerman's direction. At the same time, Zimmerman began working with set designers to begin to define the interior of the station even before the exterior was finalized. The major permanent sets—Ops, the Promenade, living quarters, and science labs—all had to be defined and created, even if no one was sure where these sets would eventually be in relation to each other.

Sternbach went back to his *Next Generation* files and pulled out sheet after sheet of discarded starbase designs that had been developed for the STAR TREK features, and everyone began poring through books and magazines, seeking visual inspiration.

Also during this initial stage, Berman and Piller created ongoing variations of the station's history. In one, it was 150 years old, built by a succession of different alien

*Facing page:
The Promenade takes shape on
Paramount's Stage 17. Meticulous
coordination between all members of
Herman Zimmerman's design team
insured that the live set design would
match the final space station miniature.*

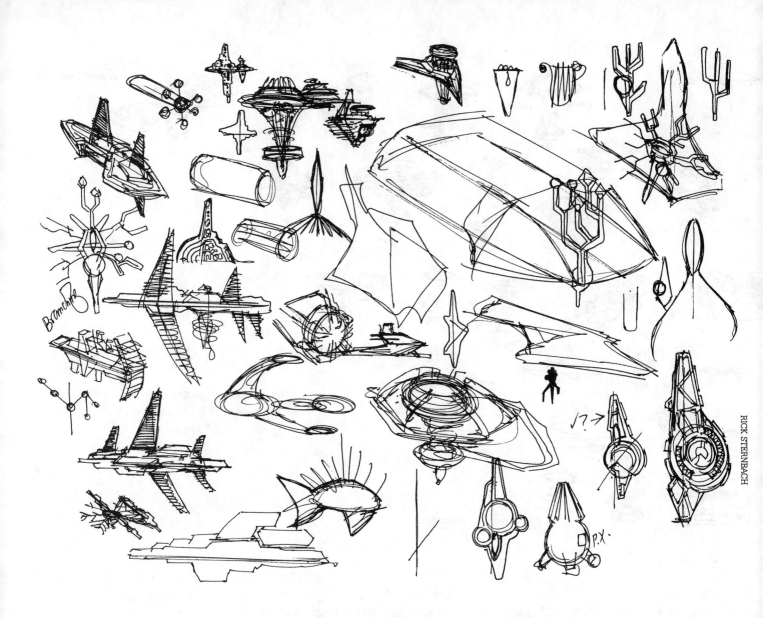

*Doodling is to the artist's creative process as asking questions is to the writer's. Rick Sternbach calls these quick sketches "Odd Directions."*

races, falling apart, badly repaired. In another, it was like a North Sea oil rig, more than 1,000 years old and built by aliens unknown, *or* like a combination of San Francisco's Fisherman's Wharf and Washington's Dulles International Airport. Yet another had it a haphazard collection of modules that had "grown" over the years, as if it were in the center of a Sargasso Sea of space junk. At the beginning, it was smaller than the *Enterprise*. Eventually, it would grow to have a diameter just over twice the *Enterprise's* length.[2]

They all worked at it. Zimmerman on his sketchpad, Okuda and Sternbach on their computers. "Otherwise," Sternbach said, "we would not have been able to turn out all the different designs we did in forms that could be rapidly changed. I think if we'd had to employ traditional drafting techniques, it would have taken us many, many weeks longer to come up with designs that would meet with the producers' approval."

And the producers' approval was not easy to come by. Okuda remembers one design meeting with Berman and Piller in which "in one horrifying fifteen-minute period, we went from 'these are really cool' to 'back to the drawing board.'"

[2]DS9's diameter is approximately 1,350 meters, which is 2.1 times the *Enterprise's* length of 642 meters. In old-fashioned measurements, that makes it a little over four-fifths of a mile. The station's mass is 10.12 million metric tonnes. These figures were calculated by Sternbach and Okuda, who, as we have learned, don't want anyone to think that they just make this stuff up.

But, in this case, the drawing board was a computer screen and the possibilities were endless. "Using some of the 3-D software that we were familiar with on *The Next Generation,*" Sternbach explains, "we started launching into designs based on what Berman and Piller described to us. In the early stages, no one really had that great an idea of what this thing would finally look like, but they had some general ideas about what the flavor of the station might be like. We hit a couple of dead ends, but we got back on track, and eventually refined the design into what you see in the final wheel shape."

Surprisingly, no one looks back at the dead ends and the lost work they represent with regret. "Those dead ends helped refine some of the design elements," Sternbach says. "We never threw everything away. Some things we did keep. From beginning to end, the design element that stayed with us was the core."

The core seen in the illustrations depicting the evolution of DS9 was always seen as the heart of the Promenade, which was considered to be one of the most important permanent sets. Even the designs that seemed to resemble bugs (based, initially, on the Cardassian graphics derived from their warship design, which Sternbach had

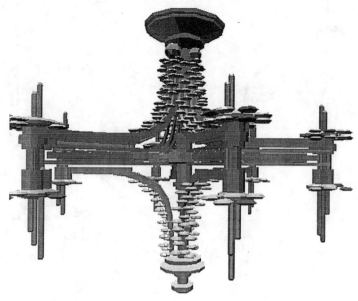

These preliminary designs were created by Mike Okuda, showing the terracing element, which would survive to the final stage.

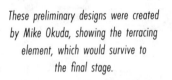

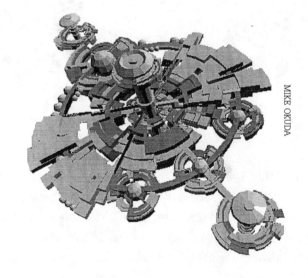

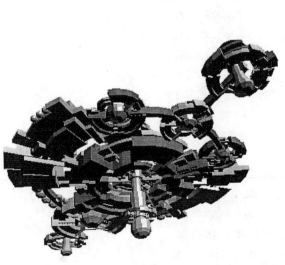

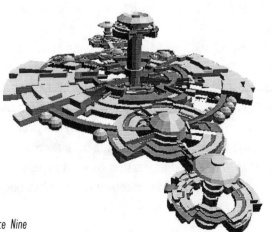

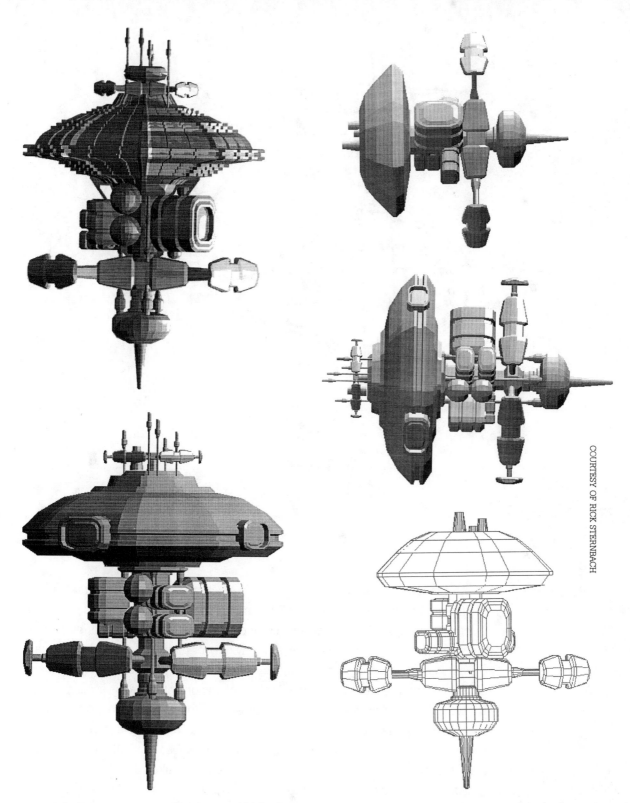

originally patterned on an Egyptian ankh) had a main core.

Though the nature of the design group's work and the constant back-and-forth commenting on computer-generated artwork made the effort to design DS9 truly collaborative, it is still possible to determine where certain specific design details came from.

Okuda came up with the terraced look in a preliminary design that was based on one of the old starbase designs, where the upper section was heavily terraced. That terracing can be seen today in the lower core.

*Several early, computer-rendered designs building from Sternbach's central core.*

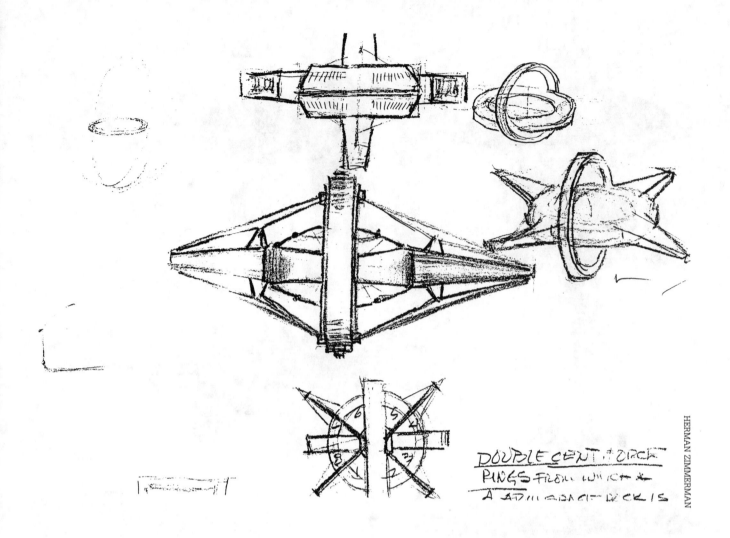

Handwritten: DOUBLE CENT. FORCE RINGS FROM WHICH A ADMIN SPACE DECK IS

*Herman Zimmerman's first sketches of DS9, showing spinning wheels within wheels.*

Also in the lower core is the fusion reactor, another design element introduced by Sternbach that survived to the end. "I was very much in love with this big fusion reactor," he says as he describes his approach to the design tasks at hand—practicality. "Space hardware, at least to my way of thinking, should be built in a certain logical, practical manner. So, a space station has to have a power plant and some habitation spaces. If this indeed was a mining operation as the scenario called for, we would need places for ships to come and go, to load up cargo, to off-load ore, and to process the ore. All of these various elements would have to be taken into account in arriving at the final design. But, as you can see from all the variants we had, there was more than one solution to this design problem."

After considering several of the initial design presentations, Sternbach credits Rick Berman with giving the design group a new consideration to add to the mix. "Berman told us, 'The design has to be as simple and elegant as the *Enterprise*. It has to be something you can draw in a couple of strokes.'"

Berman explained to the group that any child in the country can draw the *Enterprise*—a saucer, an engineering hull, two warp engines, and that was it. For DS9, he wanted the same simplicity to the basic shape. The engineering details could be as intricate and alien as the designers felt necessary, but the basic shape had to be something that could be drawn with just a few quick pen strokes.

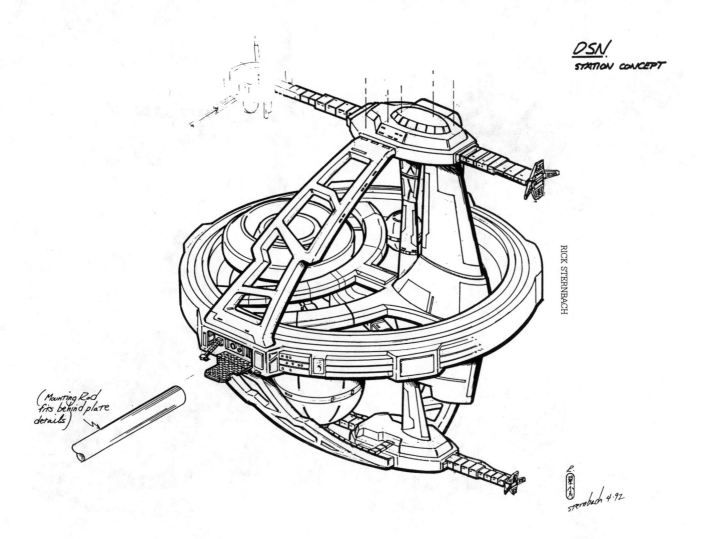

RICK STERNBACH

(Mounting Rod
fits behind plate
details)

sternbach 4.92

Again the design group went back to work, now striving for that simplicity along with everything else. Literally hundreds of drawings were generated, and at last they were closing in on key elements of what would be the final look of the station. Ironically, they went back to one of the first concepts Herman Zimmerman had sketched—a gyroscope-like assemblage of multiple rings. In a wonderful example of the unexpected twists and turns found in television production, the only reason these concepts existed was because Zimmerman had approached his initial designs of the station from the logical engineering hypothesis that to give the interior "gravity," it would have to spin. When Zimmerman was reminded that artificial gravity had always been a part of the STAR TREK universe, new designs began to incorporate features that would not be practical on a spinning model, and the hoops were left behind, though not for long.

Just as Rick Sternbach thought of space-station design from a practical view-point, the design group realized that there was another perspective they would have to adopt if the station was to be convincing—they had to start thinking like Cardassians.

For Zimmerman, the image that the Cardassians called to mind was of "a sophisticated, Spartan race: arrogant, intelligent, and cruel, for whom beauty only exists in strength." When they had first appeared in *The Next Generation* episode

*This design from April 1992 got far enough along that Sternbach determined how it could be mounted for motion-control photography.*

*More designs from Mike Okuda, showing a variety of modular approaches.*

"The Wounded," makeup designer Michael Westmore had given the Cardassians exoskeletons—twin spinal-type cords that ran up the outside edges of their necks. Costume designer Robert Blackman had given them peaked chest plates suggestive of crustaceans. Sternbach's *Galor*-class Cardassian warship, as constructed by STAR TREK modelmakers Ed Miarecki and Tom Hudson, had a scorpionlike quality to it. Slowly, a Cardassian aesthetic began to form.

Then came a key moment of serendipitous inspiration. In an architectural magazine, Zimmerman came across a cutaway drawing of an air terminal in Moscow. The drawing showed a control tower and the terminal below with shops and parking and other support features—it was a perfect arrangement for Ops and the Promenade. The design group saw the drawing and collectively said, "That's it!"

Two months had passed since the first meeting, and now everyone felt confident they were closing in on a final design.

Finally, building from Zimmerman's initial hoop designs, the group came up with a series of computer drawings depicting various combinations of interlocked rings surrounding a central core. Mounted presentation boards were prepared for Berman and Piller, displaying the various versions from different angles, and almost always with the *Enterprise* docked to give a sense of scale.

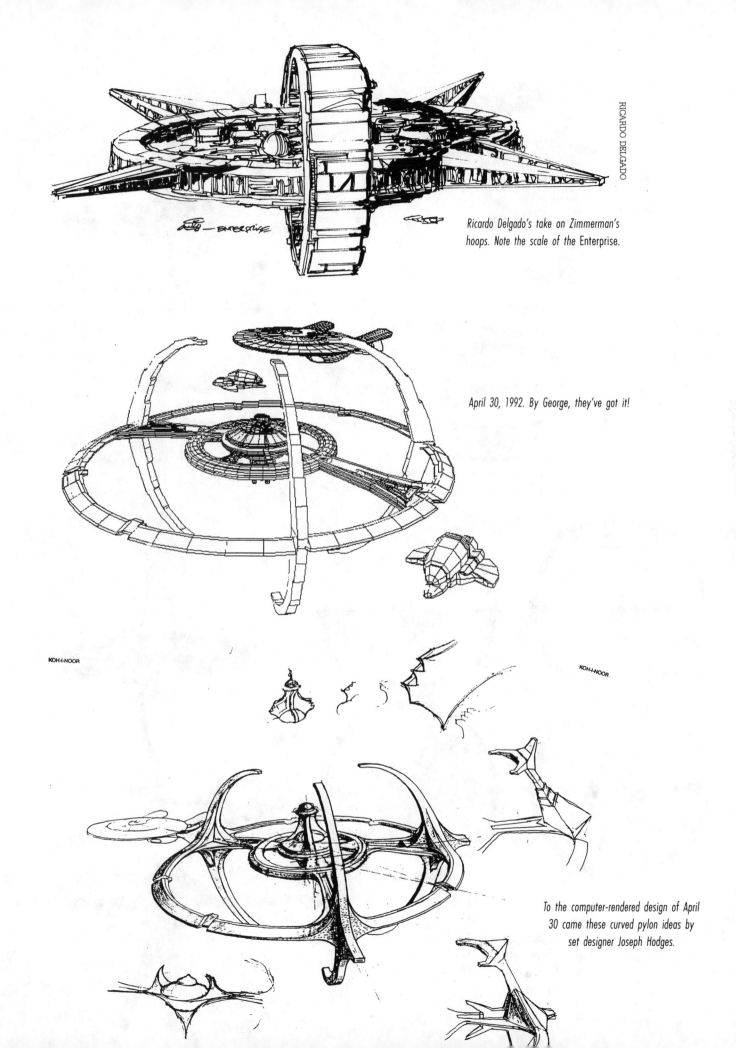

Ricardo Delgado's take on Zimmerman's hoops. Note the scale of the Enterprise.

April 30, 1992. By George, they've got it!

KOH-I-NOOR

KOH-I-NOOR

To the computer-rendered design of April 30 came these curved pylon ideas by set designer Joseph Hodges.

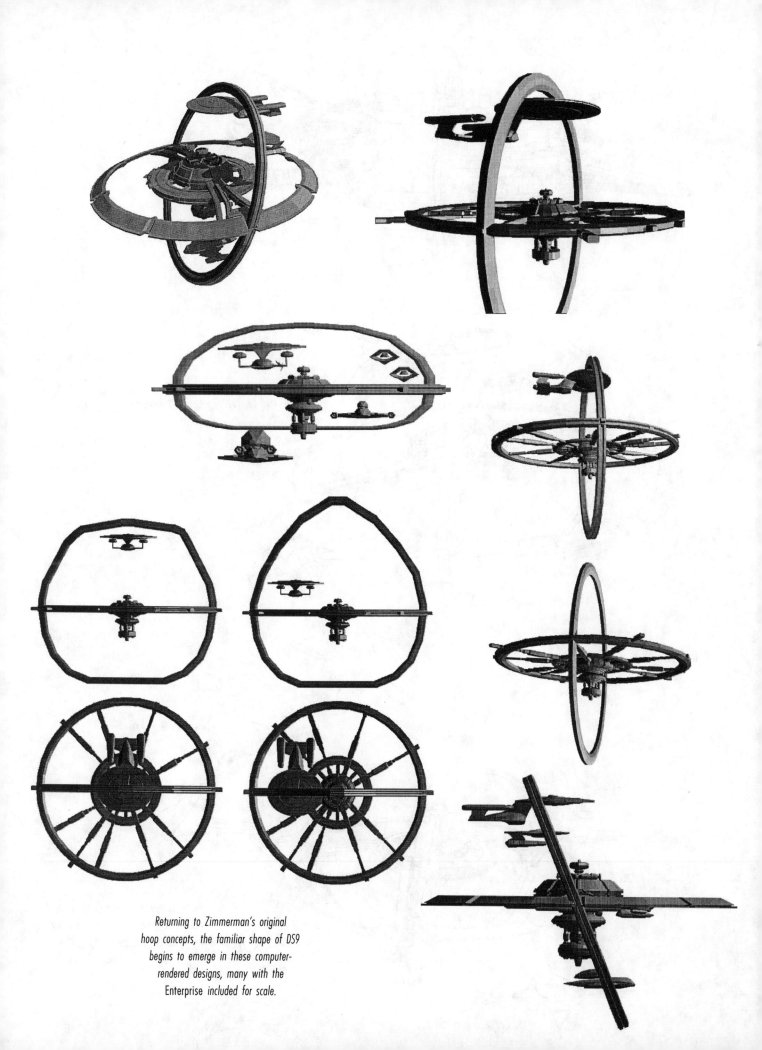

*Returning to Zimmerman's original
hoop concepts, the familiar shape of DS9
begins to emerge in these computer-
rendered designs, many with the
Enterprise included for scale.*

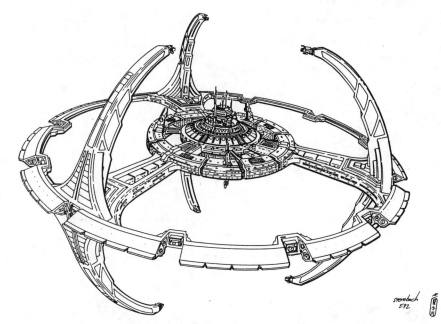

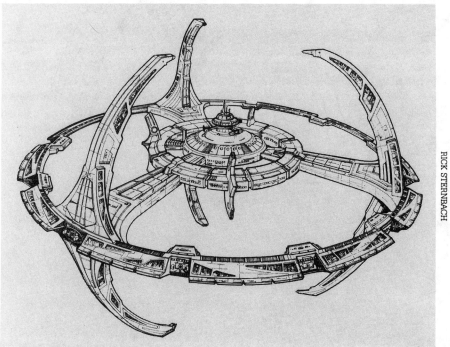

RICK STERNBACH

The final version. Now all they had to do was build it.

They were close. Very close. But there was still something . . . *un*alien about the design. Then Rick Berman wondered about not having the hoops complete. Break them, he suggested.

It was the final piece of inspiration for the station's basic shape—Zimmerman's hoops with Berman's breaks around Sternbach's core with Okuda's terracing topped by a Moscow air terminal, brought together through almost two and a half months of constant debate and refinement by everyone associated with the project, including *Deep Space Nine*'s scenic artists, Doug Drexler and Denise Okuda, set designers Joe Hodges and Nathan Crowley, series artists Ricardo Delgado, Jim Martin, and visual-effects supervisor Gary Hutzel.

DS9 was a true child of the collaborative television process, on its way to becoming a thing of beauty and an international icon for science-fiction adventure.

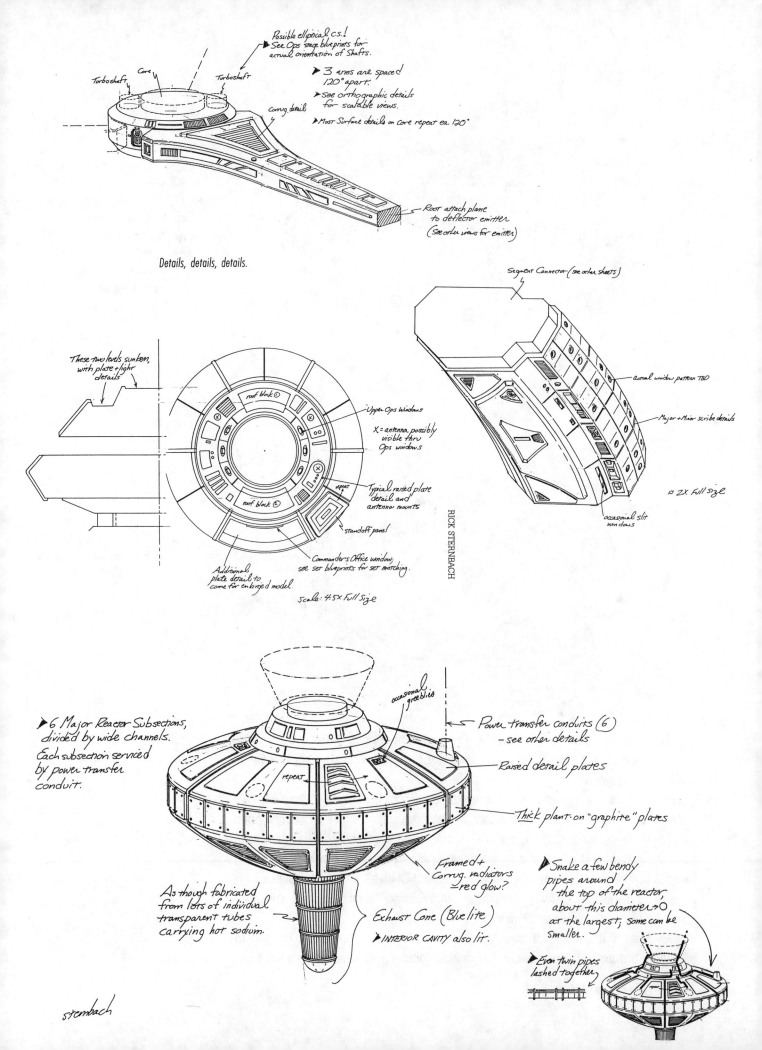

Possible elliptical c.s.!
See Ops stage blueprints for
actual orientation of shafts.

➤ 3 arms are spaced
  120° apart.
➤ see orthographic details
  for scalable views.
➤ Most surface details on core repeat ea. 120°

Turboshaft    Core    Turboshaft

Corrug. detail

Root attach plane
to deflector emitter
(see other views for emitter)

Details, details, details.

These two levels sunken,
with plate + light
details

roof block ①

roof block ②

Upper Ops Windows

X = antenna possibly
visible thru
Ops windows

Typical raised plate
detail and
antenna mounts

standoff panel

Commander's Office window;
see set blueprints for set matching.

Additional
plate detail to
come for enlarged model.

Scale: 4.5x Full Size

Segment Connector (see other sheets)

actual window pattern TBD

Major + Minor scribe details

☑ 2X Full Size

occasional slit
windows

RICK STERNBACH

occasional greeblies

Power transfer conduits (6)
— see other details

➤ 6 Major Reactor Subsections,
  divided by wide channels.
  Each subsection serviced
  by power transfer
  conduit.

repeat

Raised detail plates

Thick plant·on "graphite" plates

Framed +
Corrug. radiators
→ red glow?

As though fabricated
from lots of individual
transparent tubes
carrying hot sodium.

Exhaust Cone (Blue lite)
➤ INTERIOR CAVITY also lit.

➤ Snake a few bendy
  pipes around
  the top of the reactor,
  about this diameter →O
  at the largest; some can be
  smaller.

➤ Even twin pipes
  lashed together

sternbach

# THE

# ELEVEN

# CARDASSIAN

# WAY

*It's important to have continuity in Trek art because
that establishes credibility. I don't think of it as
background—it's part of the Trek world.*

—Michael Okuda

For the moment, all the design group had was a shape. Now they needed to add the details that would make it come alive.

Fortunately, the details had been building up in hundreds of other sketches. A Cardassian aesthetic *had* been found.

"The Cardassians like orderliness in all things," Zimmerman says. "And they prefer things in sets of three." We can see this reflected in the three top docking pylons, the three bottom docking pylons, the three crossover bridges, and the three concentric circles of the docking ring, the habitat ring, and the core. "The Cardassian mind prefers balance to symmetry," Zimmerman continues, "ellipses to circles, angles to straight lines, and hard metallic surfaces and dark colors. They believe in honesty in design and want to see the columns and beams which make up a structure, rather than disguise them."

Those distinctive Cardassian beams came from the work of set designer Joe Hodges, who was the first to sketch out some arms that were only partial, as Berman had suggested. Those arms instantly became the station's docking pylons, and were then refined on computer to forevermore become a part of Cardassian architecture, especially noticeable in the Promenade, where the walkway supports echo the docking pylons' design almost identically.

Illustrator Ricardo Delgado was another member of Zimmerman's team who helped refine the Cardassian approach to design. His early sketches of key *Deep Space Nine* sets created an almost *Blade Runner*-type depth of unexpected detail,

**This is representative sampling of signage as used on Deep Space Nine and other Cardassian facilities**

*Cardassian signage and engineering plaques.*

[1]On the ATM machine are a variety of symbols indicating the various monetary units that it can dispense. If you're ever fortunate enough to see it in person, you will notice the symbols for Klingon, Vulcan, Ferengi, and Bajoran currency, along with, for some inexplicable reason that couldn't have anything at all to do with the fact that two members of the *Deep Space Nine* graphics department are fervent *Man from U.N.C.L.E.* fans, the very distinctive logo of the United Network Command for Law and Enforcement. Surprisingly enough, it fits right in.

[2]With an unfinished alien space station intended to be the key image of those credits, time was becoming a factor. Though Sternbach and the others were hard at work creating the plan drawings that depicted the intricate details of DS9, the main model was still to be built. In order to keep on schedule, under the direction of visual-effects supervisor Dan Curry, a rough plywood-and-foamcore model of the station was quickly assembled and used in a black-and-white videotaped production to choreograph all the sweeping camera movements we see in the title sequence at the beginning of each episode. The camera moves that had been selected were stored in a computer program so that when the actual model of DS9 was available, it could take the place of the rough model on the computer-managed motion-control rig, and the same moves could be replayed exactly.

including twisted vines growing around metal posts, and the Promenade's Ferengi ATM machine,[1] which Delgado created without it being called for in any script.

Delgado had not previously worked on *The Next Generation,* and his unfamiliarity with all that had been established let him design alien artifacts and settings with a fresh eye, unfettered by the long-established style of Starfleet technology. Of course, Herman Zimmerman had his own techniques for maintaining a fresh approach. Delgado recalls giving Zimmerman a sketch of a shop in the Promenade. Zimmerman said he liked it, then turned it upside down, and announced he liked it even better that way. Obviously, the Cardassian aesthetic was getting to him.

Delgado also went to work on prop design and drew the storyboards for the show's opening title sequence under Dan Curry's direction, creating a visual collage of earlier STAR TREK images, from the establishing shot of a beckoning starfield to moving vistas of DS9 reminiscent of the dry-dock scene in the first STAR TREK feature.[2]

But set design, like the station's design, was not simply a matter for designers. Producers Piller and Berman were completely involved at all stages. In fact, Michael Okuda recalls that Piller "has an awesome grasp of the dynamics between sets and characters, and he was always suggesting ways to alter sets to match the way the characters would interact."

One of the most important sets in which the characters would interact was Ops, short for Operations.

Though it had not been a conscious decision at the time, during the long process of creating the DS9 station, the design group had replicated the heart of the two previous STAR TREK series—the bridge of the *Enterprise.* For twenty-seven years it had been the focus of STAR TREK stories, securely atop the highest part of both ships. Now Ops shared that same centralized location on DS9.

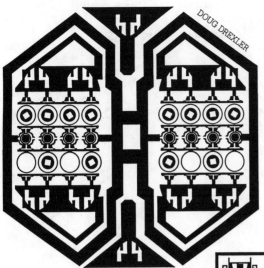

DOUG DREXLER

In case anyone asks, now you know
what Cardassian isolinear rods look like.

The Cardassian design aesthetic stretches
even to their circuit patterns, which don't
look anything at all like . . .

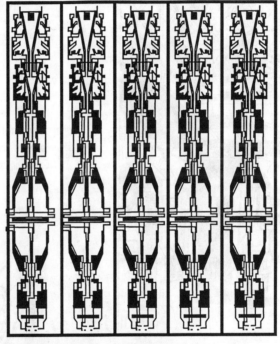

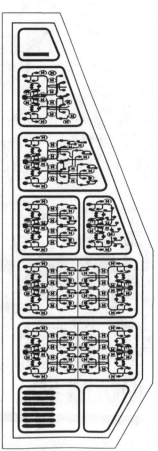

DOUG DREXLER

. . . Bajoran circuit patterns.

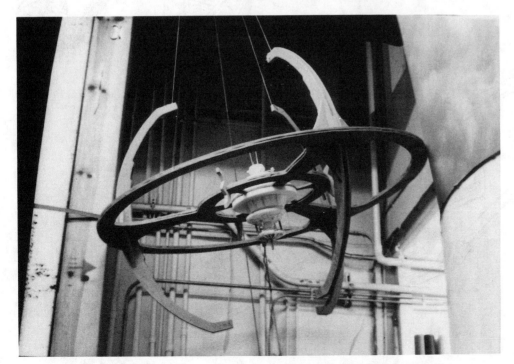

The first DS9, made of plywood and
Styrofoam, to stand in for the
not-yet-finished model during the
preliminary shooting of the opening
credits sequence.

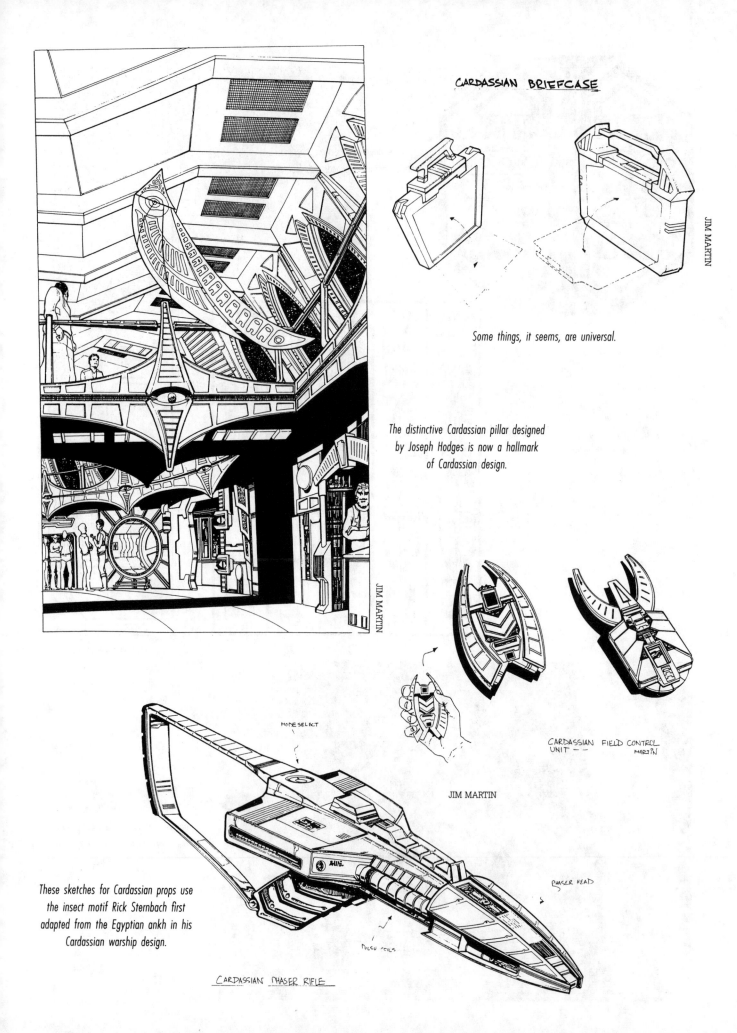

CARDASSIAN BRIEFCASE

JIM MARTIN

Some things, it seems, are universal.

The distinctive Cardassian pillar designed
by Joseph Hodges is now a hallmark
of Cardassian design.

JIM MARTIN

MODE SELECT

CARDASSIAN FIELD CONTROL
UNIT — — MARTIN

JIM MARTIN

These sketches for Cardassian props use
the insect motif Rick Sternbach first
adapted from the Egyptian ankh in his
Cardassian warship design.

PHASER HEAD

PULSE COILS

CARDASSIAN PHASER RIFLE

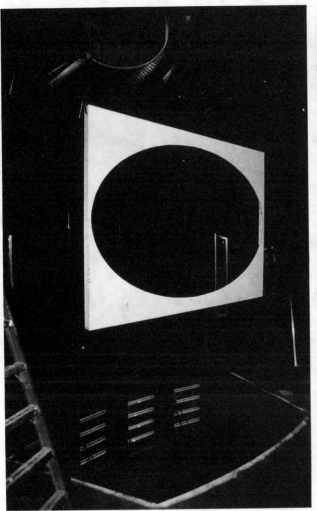

CHERYL GLUCKSTERN

Given that Ops would serve the same story functions as the bridge, it was logical to approach both designs from the same perspective, though with changes to reflect the station's alien builders, *and* improvements in television production technology. If this sounds familiar, it is—Herman Zimmerman was facing the same directives that Berman and Piller had faced in creating the series: Make it the same, but different.

Perhaps the most important storytelling feature on the *Enterprise*'s bridge is the main viewscreen. On it, we can talk to anyone, see anywhere, and track our progress through space and story. A large viewscreen also adds visual drama to many scenes. Zimmerman points out that the shots of Picard talking to the giant image of Q in *The Next Generation* pilot showed how valuable a large screen could be. Thus, a main viewscreen would be an important element of Ops, just the same as in the *Enterprise*. But what would make it different was that the screen could be turned off when not in use, and, as originally imagined by Zimmerman, it could be seen from both sides.

Storytelling required a method of getting people to and from Ops quickly, so the tried-and-true STAR TREK technology of turbolifts was also incorporated into the design of Ops. But here, the difference in their appearance is something that Zimmerman had always wanted to see—the turbolifts are not hidden by doors, they

*Above left:*
*A large sheet of Styrofoam is used to check the positioning of the Ops viewscreen while the sets are under construction.*

*Above right:*
*Part of the disorder in this construction scene is intentional—as related in the pilot episode, the Cardassians trashed DS9 before withdrawing.*

Not just any hole in the wall.

CHERYL GLUCKSTERN

During construction, cardboard fills in for
backlit Cardassian control panels still to come.

can be seen to actually move up and down with actors on them. While this necessitated a design that raised the floor of part of the set to give travel room for the lift, the circular, well-like structure that resulted, in which elevated tiers of decking surround a central computer "pit," served the show perfectly.

Since Cardassians had been defined as a military race, the station commander's office was placed at the highest level of the set so he could look down on everyone on duty in Ops, and everyone on duty had to look up at him. This part of the design logic even made it into Piller's pilot script, when Sisko sees Ops for the first time, along with the audience.

---

30  INT. OPS

> Sisko and O'Brien ENTER from a Turbolift . . . the
> multi-tiered facility lined with computer and life-
> support systems, tactical controls, a master
> communications panel and transporter pad. It is in
> disarray . . . panels are open . . . noticeable gaps appear
> where machinery has been removed . . . conduits hang out
> of panels . . . several Bajorans and a couple of
> Starfleet supernumeraries are busily working on
> various repairs . . . A beat as they move deeper inside,
> Sisko looking around . . .

*The layout of the Ops center table, in the center of the operations "pit."*

O'BRIEN

I'd like to ask the designer what he was thinking about when they built this place . . . I still haven't been able to find an O-D-N access . . . that's the Prefect's office up there . . .

Sisko looks up . . .

31 ANGLE

The office is on the mezzanine with a balcony like Mussolini might have designed for himself . . . Sisko shakes his head . . .

SISKO

So all others have to look up with respect. Cardassian architecture.

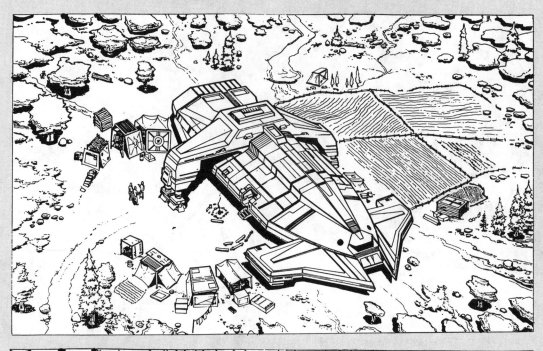

Perhaps the largest single expenditure for both the pilot and the ongoing production of *Deep Space Nine* is set construction, which, like all production costs, is something that comes under the watchful eye of supervising producer David Livingston.

"As a production manager on *The Next Generation*, I did the budgeting for both the pilot and the series. Then, as the supervising producer, which is really a line producer position, on *Deep Space Nine*, I had to do the same thing over again. Bobby Della Santino, who's the production manager, did all the work, and I supervised the budgeting process. But it was a lot easier than doing *The Next Generation*, because we had done it once and we knew the pitfalls. On *The Next Generation*, the wardrobe costs were a lot more than we had thought. Set costs, through—there were certain pitfalls that we knew to keep our eyes open for."

The largest pitfall was the incredible scope of the sets required for *Deep Space Nine*—more complex than any ever built for any television series. Livingston agrees that the sets for the series were "a huge undertaking. And at that level of complexity, when you want to change one little thing, it ends up costing a fortune. Whereas if you want to cut something big, it doesn't save you any money at all. That

Careful planning is the key to getting the most money on the screen for an episode of Deep Space Nine. These sketches by Jim Martin show two variations for an establishing shot for the community in "Paradise," which could be accomplished by means of a matte painting. The third sketch shows how the actual set would look, and the fourth sketch reveals just how little of the establishing shot and landed spacecraft would actually have to be built.

JIM MARTIN

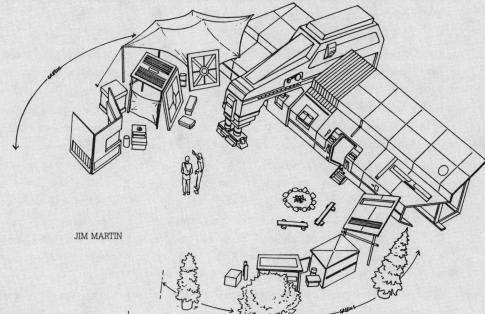

seems to be the traditional route in construction."

Given the record-setting cost of *The Next Generation,* and the Paramount executives' concern with the bottom line, it seems reasonable to think that perhaps the STAR TREK production team had been requested to make *Deep Space Nine* a less expensive series. But Livingston says that was never the case.

"They didn't give us any of those kinds of dictates. The studio had always said they wanted something equal to *The Next Generation.* My job was mainly to prepare the budget realistically. In fact," Livingston continues, "I wanted to make sure that we maintained or exceeded the level of production on *The Next Generation.* And, because from a production side I knew how to do that kind of show, my position always was that they were going to have to spend more money."

Livingston also points out that even simply *matching* the quality and complexity of *The Next Generation* required a greater expenditure, "because it was a first-season show and first-season shows always cost more." Why? "First of all, on a space show, it's been my experience with a couple of them now that you're surprised that things always cost more than you might have thought they'd cost initially—and the first season is when you find out these things. Also, you want to stretch a little bit and try and find out where the show's at. That means you might end up spending a little more money because you experiment." Referring back to his "other" space show, Livingston says, "I know that we experimented a lot with wardrobe on the first season of *The Next Generation,* and then when we made the changes in the wardrobe in the third season, we had to spend a lot of R-and-D money." Returning to the first season of *Deep Space Nine,* Livingston continues by pointing out that "the crew and the directors on a first-season show take a little bit longer with their work because they're getting to know the characters and the actors. They're not as familiar with the operation of the show and the crew is not as meshed as it is when you go into a second season."

During Livingston's discussion of the relationship between *Deep Space Nine*'s design and the resultant higher cost of production, director of photography Marvin Rush joined the conversation by phone, and added his own unique explanations for the increased costs of the show—giving a glimpse if not of the series' inner workings, then of the playful banter that goes on at every level of production.

Livingston took the call and repeated Rush's comments for us. Rush's first observation was to be expected, because it's what everyone says.

"*Deep Space Nine is* more complex," Livingston passes on to us. "There're more people involved, and whenever you have more people you have to cover them and stage them and light them, and move things around. And that takes longer to light and to photograph on *Deep Space Nine,* by the nature of the sets and the mood and the quality of it. On *The Next Generation,* the *Enterprise* has a higher key look [brighter background light resulting in an overall brighter screen], and a flatter lighting style—not in a negative sense, but in a more inviting, homey kind of look. Very bright."

Then Livingston asks Rush, "What else would you say?" And he relays Rush's answer. "'The cameraman is a slow . . .'" Did you say he is a 'slow pig'? Is that what you said? 'P-i-g. A slug, even.'" Livingston tries not to look embarrassed and tries to restart the conversation with a more serious tone. "But *why* does it take longer? Do the directors . . ." Livingston breaks off and listens carefully as Rush passes on more invaluable wisdom. "'All the directors suck, s-u-c-k,'" Livingston repeats, then tries again. "But, in general, though, don't we hire directors that take a little bit longer on *Deep Space Nine*?" Livingston smiles ruefully at Rush's reply. "Yeah, that's, that's a fact. I punish you." Another attempt. "I'm being serious now. What else is a difference between the two shows? In terms of why it takes longer to do *Deep Space Nine*?" Livingston listens carefully as his eyes widen. "Marvin, I can't tell them that," he says, and the conversation and the call end.

On his own, Livingston then goes on to explain the nature of the sets in detail. "It's the hard-wall construction, and the quality of the sets," he begins. "The Promenade, Ops, they're all multilayer sets. Quark's, for example, is infinitely harder to shoot than Ten-Forward, even though Ten-Forward has a stair up. But Quark's is much harder because it's a six-wall set—you're surrounded by walls and they have to be moved in and out, along with the bar unit.

"Ops is also very complicated because it's on three different levels. In fact, you can shoot three hundred and sixty degrees in Ops, where on the *Enterprise,* you very rarely turn around." The directors know how flexible the sets can be, Livingston concludes, and so they take more time to set up shots that show them off to their best advantage.

The second season usually brings respite from the birthing pains of the first. "Now we know where the pitfalls are," Livingston says. "We made adjustments in the pattern budget, and put in money into areas where we expressed significant overages last year, in effect protecting those areas. So now we can spend money in those areas without being concerned that we're going to go over budget. Also, we have a lot firmer control over the show after a whole season. Bobby and I know where the money needs to be spent, and where it gets spent, and, therefore, we have a lot better control over the show, financially. Even toward the end of the first season we did. And the show came out very well."

Despite the smoother operation of a second season, *Deep Space Nine* is still a more expensive show to produce than *The Next Generation* was. (Overall, in its last season, *The Next Generation* cost more per episode than *Deep Space Nine,* mostly the result of higher payments being paid to the cast and other key personnel after seven record-breaking years. If those personnel costs are set aside, *Deep Space Nine* is the more expensive show.)

"That's because we wanted more extras," Livingston explains, "and we wanted the look to be a little bit darker and moodier, and a little more gritty. And all that costs more money. For example, it takes longer to shoot that kind of show because the lighting takes a little bit longer to set up. More extras means more extras' cost, more costuming costs. Because you're on an alien space station, there's a lot more aliens—the Bajorans, plus all of the people who come to visit. So the makeup costs are tremendously more on *Deep Space Nine,* and the show takes longer to shoot in terms of hours.

"So, basically," Livingston states in summary, "when Rick and Michael gave me the script, I said this show is going to cost more to produce than *The Next Generation,* assuming you want to keep them both at the same level of production that we have been operating at. And that's indeed what has happened."

Of course, Paramount wasn't interested in giving the new show a blank check to begin production, and Livingston was asked to revise his budget downward. How he did that was the responsibility of Berman and his team. "That's usually what they do," Livingston says. "I mean, they've entrusted Rick and subsequently all of us for seven years on *The Next Generation* to make those kinds of judgments. So, they left it up to us. They don't come in and say, 'Well, you can't have that many extras or you can't have that set, or you can't have that piece of wardrobe.' That's why they pay us. The studio says you have to cut it, and our job is to then find out where to make the adjustments."

On the series in general, Livingston says those cuts are "an easy call. What you do," he says, "is to cut the two big items, which, unfortunately, are the two main visual items to any series, or particularly to a space series—the opticals and the construction budgets. Usually, all the other items in the budget are sacrosanct. If you cut them, you're just fooling yourself, because they're the day-to-day operations costs. So, what you have to do when you need to cut a series budget is usually to cut creative elements out of it."

The question then comes to mind, What about those episodes that are literally stuffed with new construction and optical elements? How can the budgets for those shows possibly be approved? We specifically asked Livingston about the third episode of the second season, "The Siege," which had new Bajoran sets, a new Bajoran spaceship seen in miniature and as a full-size mock-up with interior set, and perhaps the best miniature sequence yet in a STAR TREK television show—a dogfight between two spaceships in space, *and* within the Bajoran atmosphere. As Livingston says, "It was huge, and it went over pattern on just about everything."

However, such expensive episodes are possible because, Livingston explains, "over the course of a season, you just do some less expensive shows to make up for it. And the writing staff knows that they have to do that. Michael Piller knew that the second season's opening three-parter was going to be humongous, and knew that he had to get us 'well' during the course of the first half of the season. And he did, and we're in excellent shape right now—on budget and doing really well. So, that's where the writers' magic comes in. They know when they have to pull one out of a hat, and do something that's as compelling as any show, just less expensive. On *The Next Generation,* we call them 'ship shows,' which means you basically stay onboard the ship and you don't go to exotic locations or have to build some sets on Stage 16. On *Deep Space Nine,* we do a 'station show.' Most of the action takes place in isolated areas without a lot of people and extras." On other television series, this type of episode is also known as a "bottle" show.

A striking example of a "station show" is the first-season episode "Duet," in which Kira must deal with a Cardassian who claims to have been a death-camp commander during the Bajoran occupation. "It was a very inexpensive show," Livingston says, "but an incredibly compelling one."

In fact, Livingston goes on to say, "Duet" is a perfect illustration of what has made STAR TREK a hit since 1966. The sets and the special effects are just "trappings." The secret is that "STAR TREK is character driven. That's the magic of both *The Next Generation* and *Deep Space Nine.* It doesn't matter what screwy makeup you put on people, what kind of special effects you have. If you don't have the character, and people having conflict among themselves and resolving that conflict, you've got nothing. That's what Gene's magic was. All the rest, as far as I'm concerned, including everything I do, is gravy."

Overall, the set designs for *Deep Space Nine* eclipsed anything ever built for television before, primarily because of the multilevel approach to their construction, most evident on the Promenade and in Quark's bar. But there is another aspect to the sets' design that is not obviously apparent onscreen, though it adds immeasurably to the series' distinctive look.

On most television series, it is sometimes a disappointment to actually visit the sets in person. Things look smaller, the finish is rough, and everywhere there are missing pieces—a ceiling, a fourth wall, and the part of a hallway not immediately visible through a door.

But this is not the case with *Deep Space Nine.* Almost every room is complete with ceiling, walls, and windows looking out into a starfield. To get to Dr. Bashir's infirmary, it is necessary to exit the cargo bay to the left, walk down the corridor, and turn left again, just like following a map for a real warren of corridors. Want to take a look at the upstairs at Quark's? Head along the Promenade, go past the sign for Cardassian sushi, and watch for Quark's main entrance on the left. If you come to the Replimat by the staircase leading to the second level, you've gone too far. One warning, though: If you do make it to Quark's, try not to lean on the bar—it's on wheels.

Those wheels are the secret to *Deep Space Nine*'s permanent sets—they're constructed with what are called "wild" walls, to an extent seldom seen on television. Wild walls are portions of the set that can be disconnected and rolled away to give access for lights and cameras. For example, in a scene that takes place in Sisko's living quarters, we might see Sisko sitting on the couch, with a wall behind him on which we see a large painting hung above a table with a three-dimensional chess set, just like the kind on which Mr. Spock and Captain Kirk played.

Sisko might be talking with Jake, and when Sisko looks over at his son, we cut to see Jake standing with his back to a large window through which the stars of the Bajoran sector gleam. As far as we can tell, the scene has been shot in Sisko's complete quarters. Well, yes and no.

For the portions of the scene involving camera angles on Sisko, the wall with the windows has been rolled away to reveal the plain wood and concrete walls of Stage 4. In its vacated space, the camera has been set up, key lights have been put in place, and the first-unit production crew stands ready. When Sisko's lines have been filmed to the director's satisfaction, a break for the actors is called, which might last anywhere between thirty minutes to an hour. During that time, the window wall is bolted back into place and the large fabric backdrop on which squares of reflective Mylar plastic have been glued is stretched into place to create the starfield. At the same time, the wall with the picture is moved out of position and the camera and lights are repositioned in its place to shoot Jake's part of the scene. If more than two characters were to be in the scene, or if the action called for the characters to move from the sitting area into the bedroom or out into the corridor of the habitat ring, other sections of walls could be removed to accommodate the action.

The goal for the production value of the *Deep Space Nine* sets has been admirably met—anywhere the director can point the camera is a direction in which he or she can film. Watch closely the next time you view a television program other than *Deep Space Nine* and see if you ever catch a glimpse of a ceiling, or how many times a scene will be shot so that every wall can be seen. That's a luxury that previously belonged only to movie directors shooting on location.

Another unusual—for television—capability built into the *Deep Space Nine* sets is the exceptionally high quality of their finishing details. Typical television sets are designed to the limit of resolution on a typical television screen, which isn't high. Their rough surfaces, bad seams, streaked paint, and wobbly graphics are not indicative of shoddy work, but a result of the knowledge that no one will ever see those flaws on their television at home. But Rick Berman, in particular, refuses to accept that ''just good enough'' level of quality. The finishing detail of all STAR TREK sets, for *Deep Space Nine* and *The Next Generation*, are of the same quality we would see in sets built for motion pictures, in which any minor flaw would be blown up to gigantic, noticeable proportions on a movie-theater screen.

Once again, this attention to detail allows directors almost unlimited freedom in choosing shots for their production. They can shoot close on anything—a wall-panel control, a desktop monitor, an airlock seal—and be certain that the resulting image will be as finely detailed as if the shot had been made on location on a real space station.

But as should be obvious by now, it is not just the *way* in which the sets were designed and built that accounts for the distinctive look of *Deep Space Nine*. It is also a function of *how* they are *filmed*—a process with almost as many possible choices as the design of the station to begin with.

Visual-effects supervisor Dan Curry, who helped establish the differences between the Federation look and the Cardassian look, explains some of the technical considerations he and visual-effects supervisor Gary Hutzel and illustrator Robert Legato have addressed. "There were conscious decisions made early on about how to create a distinct look for the show. And it came right down to simple things, even the choice of camera lens we use for miniature photography.

"On *The Next Generation,* we normally shoot with a 24mm lens.[3] *Deep Space Nine* is shot with a 20, which gives a little bit more stretch to the space station."

Lenses were just one part of the technical equation, though. There was also the matter of choosing film stock and exposure. Curry explains, *"Deep Space Nine* has a darker look. The stars are printed in a little bit darker and the contrast ratio is a little bit greater. If you'll notice, the shadow side of the DS9 station is much darker than the shadow sides of the *Enterprise,* under most circumstances. Part of it is that we took our look from NASA orbital shots—real photographs of the space shuttle and other space vehicles. Gary and Rob decided they wanted to go with that real harsh look, so that's why the shadow sides are almost black.

"Even looking at the title sequence, you'll see that where the wheel of the station swings by in the foreground, there is no visual information. It's just windows and a silhouette against the light areas. What you get going for you there might be termed a grittier look."

If ever there was a misunderstanding about Berman's and Piller's intentions for *Deep Space Nine,* it was the way in which these visual terms were reported by the press. Much to the producer's chagrin, before *Deep Space Nine* ever aired, television columnists and reviewers focused on the series being "darker, grimmer, and grittier" than *The Next Generation.* The impression those early mentions left was of a series in which cannibalism, mass murder, and existential angst were certain to play a part. But, in fact, in their quest for an angle on the story, the media misconstrued comments about the *visual* look of the show and applied them to the *content. Deep Space Nine* does have the potential for more intercharacter conflict, which was one of Berman's and Piller's original goals, but it is not and never has been intended to be anything other than a forum for telling stories in the traditional STAR TREK manner. To do otherwise would be to risk damaging a billion-dollar franchise. John Pike, who was president of network television for Paramount at the time *Deep Space Nine* was green-lighted, said it best. "STAR TREK is one of the most important jewels in Paramount's crown. We would do nothing to fracture that asset. We would not attempt any changes in Roddenberry's vision for short-term gain if it might result in long-term damage." Truly dark, grim stories on STAR TREK will be a long time coming, if ever.

In contrast to this visual emphasis on darkness and shadow, *Deep Space Nine* also boasts intense, saturated colors that arise from the constant use of a slight diffusion filter by director of photography Marvin Rush. As a result, in the midst of high-contrast shadow, the colors on the DS9 station almost appear to glow—another departure from what Ira Steven Behr calls the "Starfleet-clean" look of *The Next Generation.*

This dark look broken by small patches of rich color was further developed by the new uniforms designed by costume designer Robert Blackman, who had joined *The Next Generation* in its third season. One of Blackman's first responsibilities on that

[3]This is what's called a "wide-angle" lens, because of the wide field of vision it has. The measurement refers to the distance from the outside edge of the lens's center to the film. The shorter the measurement, the wider the field of vision. The longer the distance, such as in telephoto lenses, the narrower. Because the average human eye has a field of vision roughly comparable to that of a 50 to 55mm lens, wide-angle lenses are popular in television because, by showing more of the background, they create the illusion that sets are larger than they actually are. Care must be taken not to choose a lens with too wide a field of vision, though, because those lenses lead to what's called "fish-eye" distortion.

show had been to direct the modification of the original *Next Generation* Starfleet uniform designed by William Ware Theiss.[4] The cast had complained about the lack of comfort in the spandex jumpsuits and Blackman came up with a two-piece version for men (which led to Picard's characteristic tug on his tunic) and a less-constricting one-piece design for women, all made from a lighter-weight wool gabardine.

Though some members of the production staff had argued against the expense of new uniforms for the cast of *Deep Space Nine*, especially given the logic that a Starfleet uniform is a Starfleet uniform, Rick Berman was insistent that a change of costume design was necessary to establish the series' new visual image. Working with a by-now traditional "same but different" approach, Blackman came up with a variation of the Starfleet Academy uniforms he had designed for *The Next Generation* episode "The First Duty." At first glance, they appeared to be a reversal of the typical Starfleet uniform. Instead of a color panel across the chest, with black at the shoulders, Blackman gave the smaller shoulder areas the color and left the rest of the uniform black. To give the outfit a more casual appearance, adding to the impression that these were real working clothes, he gave the tunics an "open collar" look and added a lilac undershirt.

For Bajoran military personnel, Blackman created an equivalent uniform in either Bajoran rust or Bajoran gray—two shades from the distinctive Bajoran color palette which can be seen on Bajoran props and in Bajoran sets. This constant use of specific colors for specific STAR TREK races is another of the many small details not immediately apparent in the design of the series, but which contribute to its cohesiveness and reality.

One of the final design decisions to be faced by the producers had to do with the nature of the graphics to be used on the series. From a technical point of view, would DS9 utilize computer screens that worked like the *Enterprise*'s—that is, with a combination of backlit transparencies and special-effects images added in post-production? Or had real video displays advanced enough since the first season of *The Next Generation* to warrant their inclusion in the sets, so that computer displays could be filmed live, along with the actors? More pressing for the art department, from a design point of view, would those computer displays be part of an original Cardassian system, or Starfleet-style retrofits? The answers to these questions would have ramifications in both the ongoing budget for the series, and the stories to be told.

Here's how Michael Okuda summed up the arguments for and against Cardassian computers and controls.

| TO: | **Rick Berman and Michael Piller** |
|---|---|
| FROM: | **Mike Okuda** |
| SUBJECT: | **Cardassian language** |
| DATE: | **21 May 1992** |
| CC: | **Herman Zimmerman** |
| | **Rick Sternbach** |
| | **Doug Drexler** |

**We're rapidly approaching the point where we will need to address the question of whether or not our heroes can read the Cardassian language. This is important for me because it affects the design of consoles and readouts. My thoughts on the matter are:**

[4]William Theiss had also designed the uniforms for *The Original Series* crew, as well as most of the fanciful sixties costumes worn by guest stars and extras over its two and a half seasons. Theiss died of complications from AIDS in 1993, but a Butterfield & Butterfield auction of his private collection of STAR TREK costumes in December of that year, supported by Paramount Pictures, raised more than $150,000 for Project Angel Food, a nonprofit organization that cares for AIDS patients. Among the items auctioned to devotees of Theiss's work and fans of the show was an original gold shirt worn by William Shatner as Captain Kirk, which sold for $16,000.

- **REASONS WHY OUR HEROES SHOULD BE ABLE TO READ CARDASSIAN:**

1. It is logical for them to be able to do so. Riker learned Klingon before being assigned to a Klingon ship. Our people could certainly learn Cardassian, especially when being assigned to a Cardassian facility.
2. It would be visually fun. Having a more alien style to the hardware and readouts would be more interesting visually, and would help to distinguish the two STAR TREKs from each other. Alien computer screens are almost always more fun than readouts in English.
3. It might be a source of humor. Maybe Ro knows more Cardassian than O'Brien, but he is loath to ask her for help, so he muddles along without asking.

- **REASONS WHY OUR HEROES SHOULD *NOT* BE ABLE TO READ CARDASSIAN:**

1. It might be confusing to our audience. Even if we do not normally care if our audience can read the panel labels, this may be important on story-point insert graphics.
2. It would be technologically unnecessary. Our people should be able to come up with a computer program to instantly translate all the Cardassian into English (or Bajoran, for that matter).
3. It could be a valuable source of problems at critical moments. "Don't push that button . . . I think it will blow up the station."

- **POSSIBLE COMPROMISES**

1. We might establish a translation program which only works on command. For example, we might scan an approaching ship, then Sisko asks the computer, "Translation, please." At this point, a new window appears on the readout with English subtitles. We could thus retain the fun of the Cardassian styling, but let the audiences read what we want them to.
2. We might gradually introduce standard Starfleet-style monitors to replace Cardassian screens. This would presumably be because our people are continually "upgrading" the station over the course of the series.
3. Note that graphics rarely convey story points unaided. Even if the graphic is critical to understanding something, we usually have a character voice-over explaining what we're seeing.

In a move that substantially helped in creating the distinctive visual quality of *Deep Space Nine*, Berman and Piller decided that all equipment on the station should be Cardassian in appearance. From that design mandate came the additional decision to use actual video monitors in the sets, suitably redesigned so they didn't look too obviously like ordinary, twentieth-century television sets.

In the past, the use of live video monitors had been problematic in science-fiction productions. To begin with, the film cameras used on set operate at a standard speed of twenty-four frames per second while a television monitor displays its images at thirty frames. The result of this difference in timing is the annoying black band that can sometimes be seen crawling up a television screen filmed for newscasts or in home videos. Fortunately, there are several pieces of equipment on the market that allow the display rate of a monitor to be adjusted until it is synchronized with the film camera, though the process does add an extra degree of difficulty to the filming.

From a simple artistic standpoint, since television sets are so recognizable, the question that must be asked in many science-fiction productions is What are present-day television sets doing in the future? To be sure, televisions can be "redressed" to look futuristic. James Cameron added plastic frames to the monitors used in *Aliens* to make them appear to be wide-screen. Several science-fiction productions have also turned television screens sideways to give their images a different look caused by vertical scan lines instead of horizontal. But overall, the use of recognizable technology in productions about the future is one of the surest ways to date it. As Michael Okuda commented, "If the designers of the original STAR TREK series had had the money to use real monitors and the latest in batwing toggle switches, the show would have been obsolete in two years!"

That was one of the main reasons why real monitors were not used in *The Next Generation*—they didn't look like twenty-fourth-century technology. Watch the classic science-fiction movie *2001: A Space Odyssey*. Many of the ubiquitous computer graphics were filmed using traditional animation techniques, then back-projected on control consoles, and they still hold up remarkably well today. But the old-fashion tubes used to display numbers are a jarring bit of 1960s technology that does not maintain the illusion of the future.

So with all those reasons against using monitors in STAR TREK, why was the decision made to use them in *Deep Space Nine?* Because there *was* one big advantage.

With live video there can be constant visual activity in the background of scenes, helping establish Ops, for instance, as a nerve center inundated with information. *The Next Generation* background screens are, for the most part, static, except for Okuda's clever trick of rotating polarizing material behind them to create an inexpensive "Weather in Motion"-type illusion. That style of screen is in keeping with the more sedate Starfleet look, but *Deep Space Nine* was to be different, alien, Cardassian. And who said the Cardassians had to build display screens that were as crisp and movement-free as Starfleet's? Certainly not Berman and Piller, so live video monitors were installed.

By July 1991, the preproduction phase of *Deep Space Nine* resembled the familiar spinning-plate routine from the old *Ed Sullivan Show,* with Berman and Piller rushing back and forth, seeing how many plates they could keep in the air at the same time—not just involving themselves in script rewrites and space-station and set design, but in alien makeup, budgeting and scheduling, transferring and replacing some personnel from *The Next Generation* while hiring new personnel for the new show, lining up composers and directors and editors, continuing discussions on what a wormhole should look like, and all the while gearing up for the sixth season of *The Next Generation*.

But despite all these pressures, it was time to address the final set of preproduction decisions to be made, decisions that were also the toughest and, arguably, the most important.

It was time to think about the unthinkable—actors!

# FOLLOWING

# IN THE

# FOOTSTEPS

# TWELVE

*At the beginning, I was very conscious that I was following
in the footsteps of great actors.*

—Armin Shimerman

There was a time when the fate of what was to become *Deep Space Nine* rested in one person's hands. Then Rick Berman called Michael Piller, and the shaping of the series-to-be became the responsibility of two people. Berman and Piller, in turn, gathered together the nucleus of the *Deep Space Nine* production team, and once again responsibility spread. This is why the key word we have stressed is "collaboration," because that's what the creation of any television series is.

Up to a point.

That point is casting.

As soon as actors enter the television equation, the clock rolls back, collaboration and shared responsibility fly out the window, and all that hundreds of people have worked and struggled to achieve once again rests solely with only a few individuals. There's nothing to be done about it, either. It's the nature of the beast and the reason that actors in Hollywood are both respected and resented, usually at the same time by the same people. To understand why, try answering the following questions.

When was the last time you tuned in to an episode of a specific series because it was written by a particular writer whose work you enjoy? Name a director of photography whose work will always induce you to watch a television show he has worked on. How many times have you talked to your friends the next day about the impressive editing in a television episode? And, finally, name all the television actors whose work you enjoy.

*That's* a long list, isn't it?

Our point, exactly.

Unless involved in the television industry, or an extremely avid fan, no one really pays much attention to the myriad other names that come after those of the actors in the credits of a television show. The millions of people who watch *Deep Space Nine* each week *aren't* tuning in because they're hoping Berman and Piller have written tonight's episode; they aren't tuning in to enjoy Dick Rabjohn's dynamic editing or David Livingston's fluid tracking shots or Dennis McCarthy's haunting musical score. They're tuning in to see Quark and Odo spar with each other. They're tuning in to share a quiet moment between Sisko and his son, and to see Miles and Keiko and Molly talk around the dinner table. In short, people are tuning in to catch up with their friends because the inescapable truth of weekly television drama is exactly what the old cliché says it is—the audience is inviting the cast into their living rooms.

If the audience likes the cast, if they become friends, then they'll be invited back week after week, and the advertisers will like them, too. But if the audience doesn't like the cast, more than a hundred of the cast's coworkers are out of a job through no fault of their own.

This is not to say that the incredible expenditure of hard work and money that goes into every other part of *Deep Space Nine* is for naught. A key part of the series' appeal is its unearthly look, its special effects, its imaginative aliens and science-fiction technology. But all those elements, ultimately, are window dressing.

If people didn't like the dynamic interaction between Quark and Odo, if Sisko's relationship with his son were unappealing and unrealistic, if O'Brien family life were monotonous and boring, people might tune in to the series for a week or two to check out the visual effects and aliens, but interest would soon wane.

The bottom line is that no matter how good every other aspect of a production is, it will ultimately live or die solely on the audience's reaction to the performance of the actors. The good news is that once those actors have established their characters and connected with the audience, they can help a series survive those occasional instances when a script is less than clear and the visual effects less than ideal. The bad news is that unless the people responsible for casting a new show do their job exceptionally well, everyone else's work for that show is effectively wasted. The pressure, therefore, is enormous, and helps explain why the same actors keep returning to television again and again—everyone likes a known quantity.

Berman and Piller are no exception.

Of the seven actors portraying regular characters on *Deep Space Nine,* three had previously worked in other STAR TREK productions—Rene Auberjonois, Colm Meaney, and Armin Shimerman—and four had already proven themselves with television audiences by starring in other series—Auberjonois again, Avery Brooks, Terry Farrell, and Nana Visitor. Only Siddig El Fadil[1] had no American television experience, though he had starred in several British television productions.

So who are these people who have so successfully lived up to the expectations of the producers by bringing to life memorable characters whom audiences *are* inviting into their homes each week? Is there some common attribute that binds them all? Is there a shared outlook? A united drive to fulfill group goals?

[1]Cirroc Lofton, who plays Benjamin Sisko's son, Jake, is the youngest regular cast member, though Hannah Hatae, the toddler who plays Molly O'Brien, is the youngest recurring actor.

Above left:
Cirroc Lofton as Jake Sisko.

Above right:
Rosalind Chao as Keiko O'Brien, with
Hana Hatae as Molly.

Forget it.

For all the talent these actors have, for all their magical ability to transform themselves into their characters, they are all, at the end of the day, ordinary people doing their jobs. Each has a different approach, and each has different expectations and goals for his or her work. About the only thing they do share is an intense commitment to the professionalism of their craft, and a slightly bemused but respectful reaction to their sudden ascendancy into the pantheon of STAR TREK heroes.

The importance they now play in the world of STAR TREK—with the constant invitations for personal appearances, the thousands of fan letters, and their transformation into action figures[2]—is, of course, no surprise to them. To the actors who starred in *The Original Series,* STAR TREK was just another job. What happened to them afterward as the popularity of the series grew was completely unexpected.

To the actors who starred in *The Next Generation,* there was at first some uncertainty as to how they would be received. But as the show's ratings grew and the episodes rolled on, they could look to the experiences of the first series' stars to see what would soon happen to them.

Thus, by the time *Deep Space Nine* was getting ready to begin production, it was generally assumed that a similar sort of success also awaited the actors who took part in that series—provided the series caught on. Indeed, the responsibilities and demands of this type of success were what accounted, in part, for Michelle Forbes's decision not to continue her role as Ensign Ro on the new series. Most television shows don't last. But a multiyear contract for a STAR TREK series is as close to a sure thing as there is in television.

[2]Brent Spiner, who portrayed the android Data on *The Next Generation,* was originally uncertain about how he felt in having his likeness used for an action figure. But then, he says in a reference to the *Star Wars* action figure of Obi-Wan Kenobi, "I figured if it was good enough for Alec Guinness, it was good enough for me."

# Star Trek Fans: The Not-So-Silent Minority

The cast and crew of *Deep Space Nine* have great respect for the way they have become revered by devoted STAR TREK fans. Intriguingly, this respect is not absolutely necessary for the show's continued success, because the most dedicated STAR TREK fans—those who regularly buy collectibles and attend STAR TREK conventions—make up only a small percentage of the series' viewing audience.

How small?

Well, in an average week, between thirteen and fifteen million people in the United States watch an episode of *Deep Space Nine* (about seventeen to twenty million watched *The Next Generation* in its final seasons), yet the core of dedicated STAR TREK fans, as measured by merchandise sales and convention attendance in the United States, is, at most, about 300,000 strong—just over two percent of the total viewing audience.

Of course, STAR TREK's *total* appreciative audience is considerably larger than any of the above figures suggest. According to a survey conducted just prior to STAR TREK's twenty-fifth anniversary, in 1991, more than fifty-three percent of the American population at that time considered themselves to be STAR TREK fans—which is about the same percentage who tuned in to watch Nancy Kerrigan win her Silver Medal in the 1994 Winter Olympics, making it the sixth-highest-rated television show in American broadcast history.

Paramount executives lie awake at night—or at least have several meetings a year—trying to come up with ways to encourage *all* those self-confessed STAR TREK fans to watch episodes and to buy tickets to STAR TREK features on a regular basis.

---

*Avery Brooks as Commander Benjamin Sisko.*

These then are the actors who took the gamble to commit a sizable percentage of their working career to a role in STAR TREK's latest installment. Some did so on the advice of their agents, some did so *despite* the advice of their agents, but all knew exactly what they were getting into and have succeeded grandly in their roles. As Armin Shimerman said, "At the beginning, I was very conscious that I was following in the footsteps of great actors." These new cast members are leaving impressive footsteps of their own.

Let's meet them.

## Avery Brooks

Avery Brooks is every bit as commanding in person as his character, Benjamin Sisko, appears onscreen. But where Sisko must often be solemn and intense in his position as DS9's commander, Brooks leavens his own impressive presence with a ready smile and a sparkling quickness of thought. A simple conversation about acting in a television series can easily become a multifaceted discussion ranging from the history of popular culture to philosophy to his work as the artistic director of the National Black Arts Festival. Such digressions are fitting, because Brooks does not consider himself just an actor, but an artist involved in many fields. And he has the credits to prove it.

As a stage actor, Brooks has won critical acclaim in the title role of the Phillip Hayes Dean play *Paul Robeson,* which he performed on Broadway, as well as in Los Angeles and Washington, D.C. In fact, Brooks seems to be one of the few people working in television who is actually doing one of the first jobs he wanted to do—he was the first black Master of Fine Arts graduate in acting and directing at Rutgers University.

**Teaser**

1) Promenade - As written (jealous Keiko?)

2) Promenade - As written

3) Keiko's Schoolroom - Keiko in mid lecture on wormhole - as Bajoran Abbess enters and observes - Keiko retrieves her lesson - the Abbess begins to challenge her teachings - Keiko defends herself - Abbess accuses Keiko of blasphemy

**Act I**   Anara adjusting waggets

1) Security Office - as written - didn't know where his wrench was - establishing relationship

2) Sisko's Office - Keiko comes to Sisko - she tells him about her confrontation with Abbess - Sisko understands the issues - He's sympathetic with the need to respect religious beliefs - Sisko calls in Kira to discuss what to do next - Kira is aligned with the philosophy that the religious leaders must take a part in the secular life of Bajor - Conflict between Keiko & Kira

3) Bajoran Shrine - As written

**Act II** (lose last line)

1) Ops - (IB) as written - Conduct internal scan by computer that locates trace materials - After that, Keiko and Jake remain - Jake listens in as a

2) Schoolroom - Bajoran parent comes to ask Keiko not to teach wormhole - "We like you but" - Keiko says I'm not teaching the wormhole any more, this semester -

---

3) Power Conduit - O'Brien & Anara find melted tools and more - tricorder - not good enough - Decide to get Dax to do a complete analysis

4) Promenade - Near airlock Odo sees several monks

4b) O'Brien & Keiko talking - O'Brien supporting her - Bajoran won't serve them glop-on-a-stick

5) Science Lab - Dax calls Kira - somebody got killed
Ext Space

6) Promenade - New Monks & Winn & children & parents outside school - Winn asks Keiko "Will you recant?" - Keiko gives speech - Bajorans take kids, leaving Jake and another kid - Keiko will teach class - go off on Jake's worried expression

**Act III**

1) Ops - Bashir reports on DNA residue - unable to positively identify body
      - "It looks like an industrial accident" Bashir will continue to investigate - Jake arrives - Sisko asks what's wrong they go into...

2) Sisko's Office - Jake tells Sisko what happened - Sisko explains Bajoran/Federation differences - "What're you going to do?" says Jake

3) Ext Bajor - Matte shot

4) Int. Temple - Religious leaders won't meet with Sisko - Eniyo speaks with Sisko - explains situation, gives Sisko some advice - He's reluctant but he'll do what he can - He shares his view of wormhole

5) Ops - Sisko returns - Tensions are rising - more outside agitators, more monks - Bajorans not reporting to work but Anara is there explains what's been going on

---

6) Replimat - Sisko meets with Bajoran leaders, urges thoughtful resolution - Winn arrives challenges Sisko, disrupts meeting she's annoying persistent - Sisko loses his temper a little bit - He regrets it - The meeting breaks up - Sisko & Kira have a moment together. Bashir approaches -

7) Infirmary - It's murder & it's crewman John

**Act IV** (All senior officers)

1) Commander's Office - Odo reports to Sisko - John's last day - (est. murder occurred prior to Bajoran protests) - He went up to the Runabouts to chase down loose ends: "loose ends...something up there"

2) Ops - O'Brien asks Anara to come with him - Odo called to Quark's

3) Quark's - Odo breaks up fight between two Bajorans - Quark tells Odo that alot of outside agitators from the surface are on station

4) Runabout Pad - O'Brien & Anara have panels open - find nothing - O'Brien contacts Odo, Nothing here to suggest foul play

5) Quark's - Odo wonders "Are you sure?" - There's an explosion

6) Promenade - Schoolroom on fire

**Act V**

1) Promenade - Fire out - Crowd of people & Keiko, Jake, Sisko & crew survey damage - Sisko speaks with Abbess - Kira interrupts with news that Eniyo's enroute - Abbess gives Anara a look

2) Ops - Sisko returns, calls Eniyo on new screen - they discuss what he's going to do & how he's going to do it (back to schoolroom) - Odo enters during conversation - We need security precautions - Eniyo signs off -

---

2) Cont - Sisko gives security instructions - Odo reveals he found override of security at another exit - "I've fixed the problem" - my theory was that someone wanted to steal a Runabout and John found them and was killed so they moved to another Runabout - Anara reacts

3) Bajoran Shrine - Anara comes in - Abbess why are you here - Anara says my escape route's been shut down - Abbess says the prophets will care for you

4) Ext. Space - Eniyo's ship arrives

5) Ops - Sisko goes to greet Eniyo - O'Brien still immersed in mystery of who would want to steal a Runabout - he investigates step-by-step, all security programs and commands looking for clues

6) Airlock - Sisko greets Eniyo - They begin to move forward - & senior officers

7) Ops - O'Brien finds something very odd Security office anomaly

8) Promenade - Sisko & Eniyo & entourage emerge from airlock, greeted by a large crowd - they move thru with security officers guarding them - O'Brien arrives on Turbolift, pushes his way thru crowd to Security Office - Find Anara moving thru crowd to

9) Int. Security - O'Brien alone uses tricorder to track down anomaly - realizes waggets were used to disable weapon scan on Promenade - Anara!

10) Promenade - O'Brien fights his way thru crowd - Anara's moving thru on a collision course - O'Brien hits Com "Sisko, Anara" - Sisko tackles Anara, weapon discharges - Sisko is hero

11) Ops - Act 6 Scene 8 - as written from Abbess Winn enters...

JCF

---

The story breakdown board for "In the
Hands of the Prophets."

## Good Ferengi Are Made, Not Born

Two-time Emmy winner Karen Westerfield at her makeup station, showing off Quark's "six-pack"—the set of distinctive colors that are used to bring a healthy flush to his Ferengi skin.

Armin Shimerman starts his day two hours before he's needed on set.

Even though it's six A.M., Shimerman knows which way is up. The headpiece can be reused several times.

Westerfield "feathers" the edges of the appliance to make it blend into Shimerman's own skin without apparent seams.

The adhesive used to hold the latex appliances in place was originally designed as a medical adhesive for colostomy bags.

Some seams can be hidden in the natural angles of the face.

A short break while Westerfield mixes Quark's custom colors.

The only reason a Ferengi needs a hair dryer is to dry the adhesive holding his face on.

Westerfield suggests using the surgical adhesive on the book writers who have been pestering her for an hour. Shimerman gives the suggestion thoughtful consideration.

Like painting a portrait, Westerfield begins creating Quark's coloring with underlayers of coarse shading, which will gradually be blended together.

At the next station, Dean Jones applies Rene Auberjonois's makeup. Auberjonois and Shimerman often use this time together to run over their scenes for the day—when they aren't being interviewed.

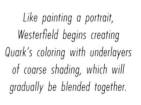

Time for the final details.

Westerfield applying her own blend of color around the eyes which Shimerman credits with bringing Quark's eyes to life within the shadows of the heavy Ferengi brow.

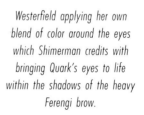

What's a Ferengi without nose wrinkles?

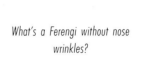

One last brush stroke . . . or not?

Another masterpiece . . . to be retouched throughout the day, then pulled off and discarded after sixteen hours.

Michael Westmore's makeup studio is always heads above the rest.

This is either a wall in a monstrous trophy room or Michael Westmore's studio.

*Dr. Bashir's infirmary takes shape.*

*The DS9 art department details again!*

Though Monty Python fans might suspect it's a blancmange on its way to Wimbledon, this is how the DS9 model spends its downtime at Image G, wrapped in foam rubber and a white sheet. So far, it's been used so often that it hasn't made sense to build a box for it and ship it off to storage with the rest of the STAR TREK models.

Forget the complicated Okudagrams—this is the computer display that controls the real DS9 on the motion-control rig at Image G. On second thought, this looks more complicated than an Okudagram, doesn't it?

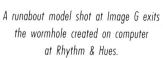

A runabout model shot at Image G exits the wormhole created on computer at Rhythm & Hues.

All the components of a STAR TREK production come together in this composite exposure from the pilot episode.

A new kind of viewscreen for a new kind of STAR TREK.

If you paid attention to Chapter 14, you should be able to name the almost thirty separate exposures that were combined to create this image.

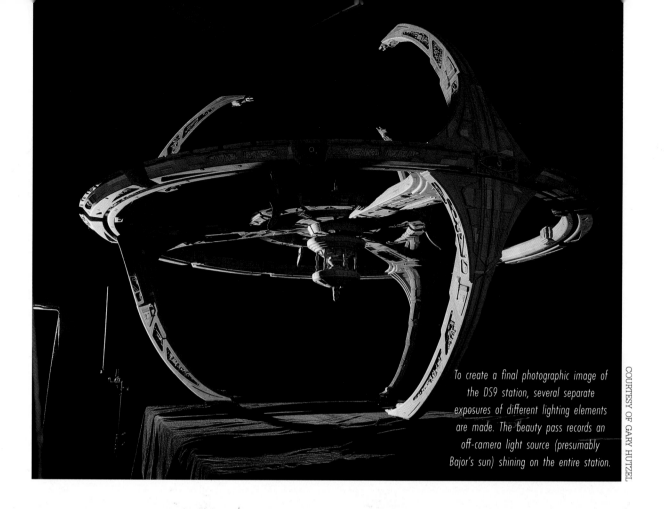

To create a final photographic image of the DS9 station, several separate exposures of different lighting elements are made. The beauty pass records an off-camera light source (presumably Bajor's sun) shining on the entire station.

With all other lighting squares switched off, another exposure records only the light coming through the station's windows. (Custom neon tubes have been built into the model for this purpose.)

Nicknamed the "Malibu" pass, this exposure records the floodlights that shine on the station's exterior. The name refers to the popular garden lights, also known as Malibu lights.

In actual filming, the strobe pass records the blinking lights on the station by exposing a few frames with the lights switched on, then a few more with the lights switched off, and so on.

The indelicately named "dingus" pass records the reactor's glow.

Finally, all the different exposures of all the individual lighting elements are combined—or composited—to produce a complete image of the station. For the actual show, individual exposures are made on film, and then composited on videotape. When a spaceship appears in a shot with the DS9 station, its final image is also the result of several composited exposures.

*Gary Hutzel prepares an upside-down runabout model for a matte pass.*

*Chris Schnitzer prepares the runabout for a shot in which smoke will create the impression of atmospheric haze.*

MARTIN
DEEP SPACE
NINE 6·92

*A preliminary design for the runabout interior, from June 1992.*

JIM MARTIN

Early concept drawings for Ops,
here called the bridge.

RICARDO DELGADO

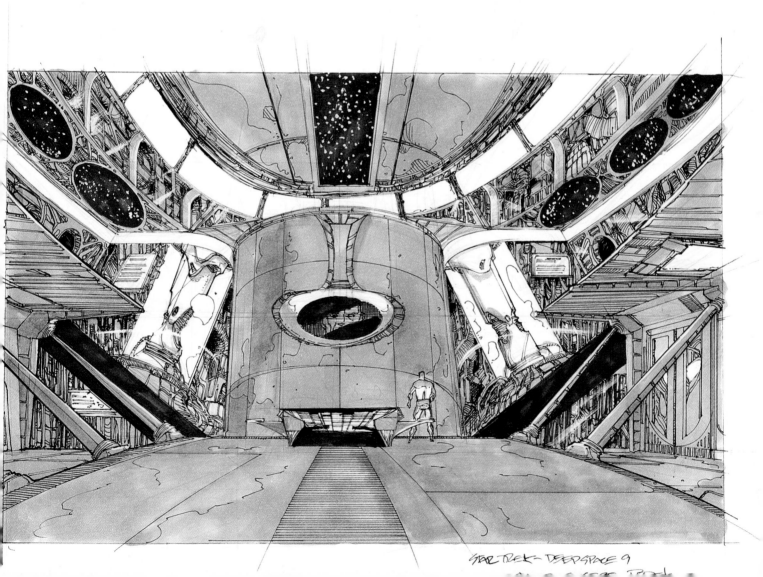

STAR TREK - DEEP SPACE 9

*The first-season cast photo. As someone once said, we're all just one big, happy fleet.*

ANALYSIS
MONITORS

LAB                                    R.DELGADO. 7·92

A lab concept from July 1992.                    RICARDO DELGADO

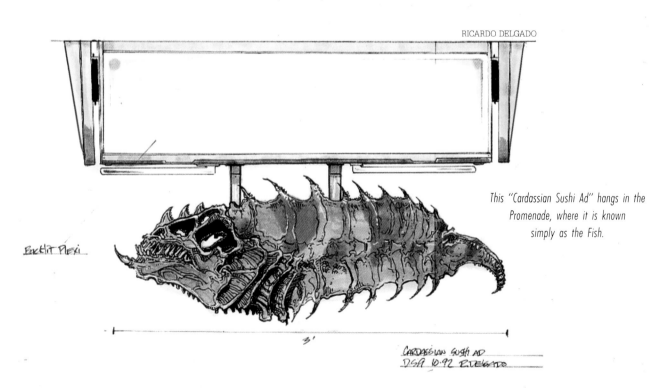

RICARDO DELGADO

BACKLIT PLEXI

This "Cardassian Sushi Ad" hangs in the
Promenade, where it is known
simply as the Fish.

3'

CARDASSIAN SUSHI AD
DS9 10·92 R·DELGADO

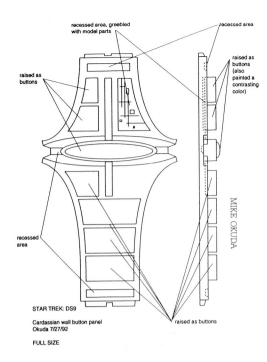

recessed area, greebled with model parts

recessed area

raised as buttons

raised as buttons (also painted a contrasting color)

recessed area

MIKE OKUDA

STAR TREK: DS9

Cardassian wall button panel
Okuda 7/27/92

FULL SIZE

raised as buttons

*Contributing to the cohesive nature of the STAR TREK design philosophy, certain basic shapes recur in everything Cardassian.*

Cardassian Design

ROBBIE ROBINSON

*The Cardassian wall unit designed by Michael Okuda, modified by Herman Zimmerman's unique, "let's turn it upside down" approach.*

CARIN BAER

*Mark Alaimo as Gul Dukat. Makeup design by Michael Westmore. Costume design by Robert Blackman.*

Getting close to the final, "pit" design of
Ops. Note the round windows and
compressed viewscreen frame.

An early wormhole concept,
from June 1992.

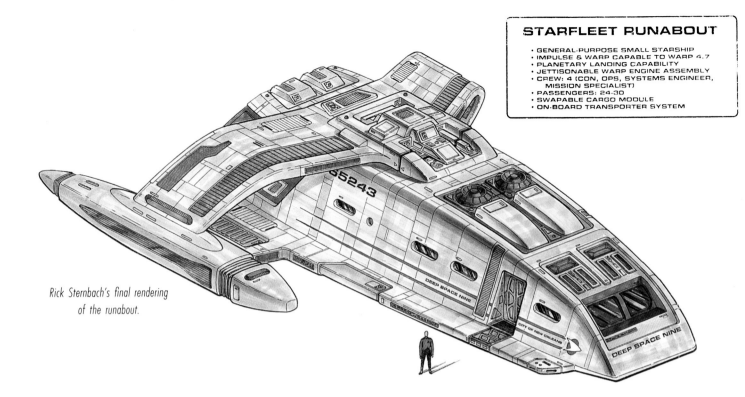

*Rick Sternbach's final rendering of the runabout.*

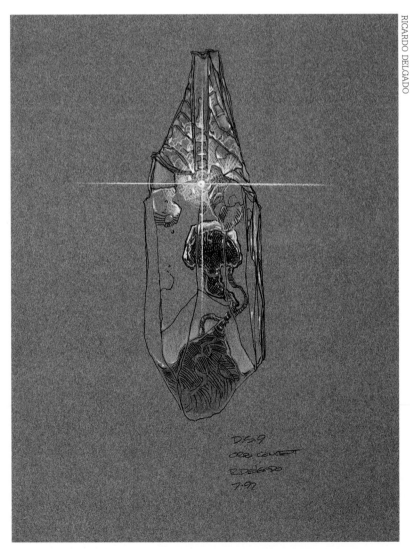

RICARDO DELGADO

*An early concept for a Tear of the Prophets—neither orb- nor hourglass-shaped.*

As a singer, he has performed the role of Malcolm X in the American Music Theater Festival production of the Anthony Davis opera *X: The Life and Times of Malcolm X.*

As a pianist, he has performed with jazz greats Jon Hendricks, Butch Morris, Henry Threadgill, Lester Bowie, and Joseph Jarman.

As a teacher, he has been affiliated with the prestigious Rutgers University for more than two decades, and has been a tenured professor of theater at the Mason Gross School of the Arts for fifteen years.

In addition, as a television actor, Brooks played the title role in the American Playhouse presentation of *Solomon Northup's Odyssey,* earned a CableACE Award nomination for his portrayal of Uncle Tom in the Showtime presentation of *Uncle Tom's Cabin,* and to millions of viewers is remembered as Hawk, Spenser's mysterious partner on *Spenser: For Hire,* who then became the lead character in his own series, *A Man Called Hawk.*

When asked how he manages to keep all his interests and careers going at once, Brooks replies simply, ''I don't know.''

But Brooks does know what attracted him to the role of Benjamin Sisko, and it was exactly what Rick Berman and Michael Piller had invested in the character to begin with—Sisko's *personal* story.

As a student of popular culture, Brooks understands the strength and depth of STAR TREK's quarter-century-plus history, but as an actor, he tries not to let that foundation influence his work. ''There's no reason to complicate it,'' Brooks explains, quickly adding that he's not discounting STAR TREK, simply recognizing it as an extensive and complex backdrop for storytelling. He leaves it to other people to describe and maintain that backdrop. For Brooks, the main concern is character.

''What really attracted me was the *story* of 'Emissary.' I still feel very connected to the story of having a man who is trying to begin the journey to find peace, to come to terms with the past, and at the same time have to defend humankind from some other intelligence in the universe. It's a fascinating idea. We may yet have to do that for real.

''It's also a story of a man who is trying to raise his son, alone, and I think it's extraordinarily well written. All that attracted me—in addition to the fact that, of course, knowing what STAR TREK is, to have a chance to show a brown man be in charge. That's very important. It's called contemporary mythologism.''

Perfect color-blindness has always been part of Gene Roddenberry's positive vision for the future, an aspect of *The Original Series* that made it groundbreaking in the 1960s for depicting a racially mixed crew. Berman and Piller have since kept Roddenberry's dream alive in their stewardship of the STAR TREK universe, and though, at first, the commander of DS9 might have been male or female of any race, as Berman and Piller refined their conception of their show, they decided it was time for a black Starfleet officer to have center stage. Along with Avery Brooks, actors such as James Earl Jones and Carl Weathers were also considered for the role of Sisko.

Still, the real world has not caught up to Roddenberry's dream, and Brooks is pleased to be part of the ongoing educational process.

''I'm thinking about children looking at the show—I'm thinking about people

*''If I were to really step back and look at the size and the scope of STAR TREK, I'd be scared to come to work.''*

dealing with it. It's about time it should be easy for us to accept that kind of reality, that we are able to get past this notion of the black and white of it and look at the 'human' of it."

Because *Deep Space Nine* scripts make nothing of the fact that Sisko is black, Brooks says that part of the character doesn't enter into his performance. Instead, he simply plays a person, the color of whom is no longer important in the twenty-fourth century. "I am who I am. It's who I am. So I mean, this is the way I speak. The *only* way I can speak. To the world, it happens to be I am an African-American male person. That's true. But I'm not playing that."

Brooks also sees his role as Sisko as part of a continuum linked with his other major television role—Hawk.

"Let's go back even further," Brooks says in discussing his television roles, "to *A Man Called Hawk*. That was the first time, as far as I understand it, that we had a brown, contemporary, mythological *hero* in the history of television. You can go back and look. Tell me another one who did not answer to anybody, who didn't have a badge, who did not need to be sanctioned by white males. Maybe I've missed something somewhere in the history of television. But I think that's the first one. A hero."

There can be no better description of Sisko—a single father, a man seeking peace with himself, and a commander on the edge of the final frontier. He is clearly just as Avery Brooks portrays him, and just as Berman and Piller envisioned him—a hero who is very human.

## Rene Auberjonois

Rene Auberjonois as Security Chief Odo.

*"We'll just see who looks better on the lunch box."*

Unlike Sisko, the character played by Rene Auberjonois is not human. In fact, no one on DS9 is exactly certain what Odo is, other than that he's a shapeshifter. But in keeping with the tradition of STAR TREK, and following in the successful footsteps of two other nonhuman characters—Mr. Spock and Data—Auberjonois has found the secret to bringing an alien to life by finding what is human about him. As in the case of STAR TREK's earlier, most intriguing characters, it is the search for identity, the quest to belong. And, as Auberjonois has observed, what better metaphor for an individual seeking identity than the ability to take on any shape?

Following in another STAR TREK tradition, that of drawing on actors with solid classical experience, Auberjonois, like Brooks, has impressive credits, both on stage and in television. And also like Brooks, Auberjonois is doing exactly the kind of job he first set out to do. Knowing he wanted to be an actor since age six, he first took to the stage at age sixteen, with the encouragement and instruction of family friend, John Houseman.

His first appearance on Broadway was in the musical *Coco*, starring Katherine Hepburn, for which he won a Tony Award. He was also honored with Tony Award nominations for his performances in the Broadway productions of *Big River*[3] and *The Good Doctor*, and for his role as movie mogul Buddie Fidler in the musical *City of Angels*.

His film debut was in Robert Altman's classic *M\*A\*S\*H*, which he followed with appearances in films such as *Brewster McCloud*, *The Hindenberg*, the Dino DeLaurentis version of *King Kong*, and—in his first STAR TREK appearance—STAR TREK VI: THE UNDISCOVERED COUNTRY. (Auberjonois accepted his small part in that film at the urging of his friend, director Nicholas Meyer. The role was the nefarious "Colonel West," Meyer's dark version of Oliver North. Unfortunately, the role was cut from the theatrical release, though added back in the home-video version.) Auberjonois also delighted millions of people in his celebrated "nonappearance" in the hit animated Disney film *The Little Mermaid*, in which he provided the unforgettable speaking and singing voice for the manic French Chef who attempts to cook Sebastian the Crab.

As a television actor, Auberjonois has earned two Emmy nominations, one for his performance in the ABC special *The Legend of Sleepy Hollow*, and the second for what is, perhaps, his best-remembered role, as Chief of Staff Clayton Endicott III, on the hit series *Benson*.

In person, Auberjonois can sometimes appear as intense and curmudgeonly as his character, though in the actor's case a dry sense of humor is often in evidence, as is a realistic outlook on life. Commenting on one, rather mundane aspect of being involved with STAR TREK, Auberjonois likes to remember the first day of the first season. "We were all standing, getting pictures taken, and I was posing, and Colm was teasing me about my posing, and I said, 'Well, we'll just see who looks best on the lunch box.'"

But Auberjonois's humor does not hide the seriousness with which he treats his role. In fact, so concerned was he about his characterization that in the first season he began to watch finished episodes of the series in order to see how Odo played against the others in the cast.

Watching one's own performance is something many actors prefer not to do. As Auberjonois says, "It can be uncomfortable, like listening to your voice on a tape recorder—you just don't sound the way you think you should."

Contrary to expectations, it is not the fact that Auberjonois must perform in a full-face appliance that has him concerned about his performance.[4] Not only has Auberjonois often performed in masks, he has taught mask work at Julliard. Craig Reardon, the makeup artist who sculpted Odo's features under Michael Westmore's direction, agrees with Auberjonois's outlook by saying, "You cannot submerge an actor who has character. A wonderful actor will always come through the appliance."

Certainly Rene Auberjonois is proof of that.

[3]Proving it's a small universe, when Auberjonois left *Big River*, his role was taken over by Brent Spiner.

[4]In the series' first season, Odo's makeup was a source of some concern. Though Michael Westmore's initial design was intended to match the bible's description of Odo as "an unfinished man," the practicalities of applying three latex appliances to Auberjonois—for his forehead, nose and cheeks, and chin—in addition to his almost-solid ears, created problems with visible seams, especially around the mouth, traditionally the most troublesome area of the face for gluing appliances. On other designs, such problems can be disguised by designing appliances so that seams fall within folds and wrinkles where they are not noticeable. But because of Odo's smooth, unlined features, such techniques were unavailable. For the first few episodes, Auberjonois was appreciative of the care and skill with which director of photography Marvin Rush set the lighting of Odo's scenes, in order to lessen the shadows that might call attention to the makeup's seams.

After trying several different design variations over the course of the first season, Michael Westmore tried to lessen Auberjonois's concerns by pointing out that on *The Next Generation*, attentive viewers could tell the season of a given show simply by looking at Worf's makeup, which changed regularly. However, by the end of *Deep Space Nine*'s first season, Odo's makeup had become a single, full-face appliance, obviating the need to hide connecting seams. According to Michael Westmore, Odo's design is now set, and will not be changing as did Worf's.

# Between the Lines: Actors at Work

The creative complexity of developing characters on episodic television is a surprisingly informal process, despite its incredible importance. Nana Visitor, who portrays Major Kira Nerys, reports that after about the third episode of the first season, she rarely heard from the writing staff or producers about her character and the directions she might take Kira. "As a matter of fact, I've never felt any pressure from them in that sense that 'They' want it this way—which is wonderful and lovely. They give us the space and the respect to do what we do."

Avery Brooks describes his "dialogue" with the writers and producers as a roundabout process in which he replies to the content of the script by putting his interpretation on film. The writers continue the dialogue by adapting their work to his performance, and he, in turn, adapts his performance to their work, so that in time, a consensus is reached. All the other actors on *Deep Space Nine* work in a similar fashion, asking direct questions about the script only on rare occasions.

As to what, exactly, an actor brings to his or her role—other than an ability to endlessly repeat the same line of dialogue so it sounds fresh each time—the following scene from the first-season episode "A Man Alone" serves as a striking example. In this episode, Odo is the prime suspect in a murder committed on DS9, and some of the station's inhabitants are convinced he is guilty and no longer deserves to be their constable. Some of them, therefore, take matters into their own hands, and trash Odo's office.

---

61 INT. SECURITY OFFICE

Odo reacts as he sees it has been vandalized . . . his chair knocked over . . . things that used to be on top of his desk have been thrown to the floor . . . a file cabinet turned over . . . on the wall in red letters, there is simply scribbled the word: "SHIFTER." And in that moment, alone, we can see the vulnerability within the man sneak through, the hurt is revealed, as it would never be revealed to another living soul. From behind him—

QUARK (O.C.)
I can find out who did it for you . . .

Odo pulls it all back inside, turns and looks evenly at Quark . . .

ODO
Not for me. Tell it to Starfleet.
I'm not in charge here any longer.

QUARK
Well now, there's a piece of good news to brighten my day . . .

ODO
Better take advantage of my absence while you can, Quark . . .

QUARK
Oh, I will, I will. Count on it.
I'll have every confidence man in the sector on board by tomorrow . . .

ODO
You do and I'll . . .

Beat. Quark grins. Realizing Quark was just trying to get a rise out of him, Odo shuts up . . .

ODO
You're going to get sloppy without me to keep an eye on you . . .

QUARK
I don't think so. You've kept me on my toes for too long now.

ODO
Sure. I've turned you into a better crook.

QUARK
Like it or not.

ODO
(beat, straight)
Think you could use a shape-shifter in your organization?

Quark reacts, taking him seriously a beat,

then breaks into a smile . . . Odo almost
grins . . . .

> QUARK
> You had me going . . .

> ODO
> I did, didn't I . . .

> QUARK
> Yes, you did . . .

A moment of awkward silence, two adver-
saries closer in their way than most friends
. . . Quark turns to leave, pauses at the
door . . .

> QUARK
> I've been asking some friends at
> Kran-Tobol prison about Ibudan . . .
> if he made any enemies while he
> was there.
> (he shakes his head)
> Couldn't find any. Mostly he
> stayed around the Bajoran
> dissidents the Cardassians locked
> up . . .

Odo nods thanks for trying . . . and Quark
hits the touch pad and EXITS. Odo begins to
straighten his office . . .

As mere words on a page, it's clear that the writer, Michael Piller (from a story by Gerald Sanford and Michael Piller), has captured the essence of the relationship between Quark and Odo. As Armin Shimerman says, "We knew early on that this relationship was something special, reminiscent of Spock and Bones from the first series." But, as viewers of the new series know, that relationship transcends the words on a page, as this scene in its final form shows so well.

When the time came for Shimerman and Auberjonois to film this scene, as actors they searched for and found what is called "subtext"—the meaning hidden between the lines, which can make dialogue and character relationships more complex and thus more interesting. In this instance, Odo's office is in a shambles. Among the scattered debris are several computer padds, which are used for entering and checking data. Though the script doesn't call for it until the end, Auberjonois chose to begin the scene with Odo straightening the office. Shimerman followed Auberjonois's lead, and Quark began to help. However, the first two times Quark picked up a computer padd, everything about his body language conveyed the impression that he intended to keep it. Without breaking the rhythm of their dialogue, Odo snatched the padds from Quark's grasp.

But the third time Quark picks up a padd, just as he's giving his last speech about checking the prisons, he's across the office from Odo, and when he finishes speaking he takes a step out through the door. But then he pauses, glances down at the padd in his hand, smiles, and turns and holds the padd out to Odo without saying a word. Odo takes it, not with a snatching motion, but as someone receiving a gift. And with a final, knowing grin from Quark just before he does exit, the whole tenor of the scene has changed. Though the words they exchanged were little more than insulting banter, their actions underscored the more complex relationship that exists between them. It was an insightful character moment, and it enriched what was already a good scene, and made it wonderful.

That enrichment of the written scene, created and developed by Auberjonois and Shimerman, and encouraged by the episode's director, Paul Lynch, is part of the magic that occurs when the sum of the parts is greater than the whole. And enriching the whole is what the best actors do—bringing the written word to unexpected life.

# Siddig El Fadil

Siddig El Fadil as Dr. Julian Bashir.

"Deanna Troi's long-lost brother?"

About a year before he was cast as the youthfully arrogant yet naive Dr. Julian Bashir, Siddig El Fadil had the youthful arrogance and naïveté to tell his agent that he wouldn't accept any roles on American television—except for *The Next Generation*.

El Fadil—a Sudan-born, English actor—claims his statement wasn't made for political reasons, "It was actually the truth. I'm very familiar with series television in England, and STAR TREK was different because it was actually genuinely different from everything else."

Of course, El Fadil was not suggesting to his agent that she get him a starring role in a STAR TREK series, only a guest role. "I was thinking how on Earth I could get into *The Next Generation*," El Fadil explains. "Maybe I could be Deanna Troi's long-lost brother. That was the only thing I could think of that I could possibly do and get away with."

Fortunately for El Fadil, instead of getting a one-shot guest part on *The Next Generation*, he was cast as King Faisil in a British television production of *A Dangerous Man: Lawrence After Arabia*. El Fadil's performance was so striking that when Rick Berman saw the show on PBS, he had Paramount's London office track down the actor with the idea that he would be perfect for the role of Commander Sisko. However, Berman reconsidered when he learned that El Fadil was only in his mid-twenties, and asked, instead, that he audition for the role of Bashir.

Unfortunately, El Fadil had to appear in his first audition with a black eye he had received the night before.

"I was sitting on the subway in London," El Fadil explains, "and there was a very drunk Brazilian guy who had seen me on a show in England, and must have been one of the only people who had seen it, so it was very odd and very weird.

"He wasn't drunk enough *not* to recognize me, but he came out with the most extraordinary stuff. He went, 'Okay, so what's it all about?' I mean, he came at me like that, with one of those art and philosophy general questions. Now, I was reading the paper and I was really toast, it was about eleven-thirty at night, and I'm saying to myself, I don't want to talk right now, to anybody. And he says, 'Well, come on then, tell me what it's about, you're an artist, you're an actor.' And I'm saying, 'You're very kind but I've just got to read this,' and he went, 'Come on! You people are all dead! You have no life! That's the trouble with the world, there's no life in the world, there's no joy,' and all this sort of stuff. And I continued to cower and got on to my tube and he followed me and then just finally got so angry after fifteen minutes of spouting that he just hit me. I mean, complete Ernest Hemingway—you know, I've got to go and fish marlin now.

"But that was the day before my audition, and so I ended up with a slightly green eye. It went perfectly, though for my second test they were probably disappointed that I didn't have one green eye like David Bowie and one black eye like I had for the screen test in London."

Though El Fadil taped his first audition in London, Paramount flew him to Los Angeles for a second test in front of studio executives. Apparently, they were not too disappointed that his eye colors didn't match his London tape, because he was offered the role on the spot—and given three days to close up his London apartment and move to Los Angeles.

Perhaps because he had no American television experience and was largely unknown to the audience he would soon appear before, El Fadil chose to attack his characterization of Bashir with a gamble—he was going to fly in the face of conventional wisdom and make the doctor unlikable.

"There was a definite proviso from the production office to make Bashir naïve and arrogant," El Fadil explains. "So, for me, it was just the most ideal opportunity in the world, because I had time to think about the role before I did it. And I thought, Well, what I'll do is something that won't necessarily go down very well, but will be real life—or as *near* to real life as something on some planet in the middle of nowhere can be—that is, start a guy off who is completely imperfect in almost every aspect, knowing that I've got a chance to get myself out of trouble, hopefully, in the second season. Or the third season.

"That's a real privilege. No other actor, I'm sure, on Earth, gets that kind of privilege with episodic television—to know that your show could at least go for three years, probably for six, and you might as well start off 'underground,' and work your way up. That runs a risk, but it's a modicum of risk. So I have the freedom to do that.

"I didn't have to do a *90210* thing where I start off sexy because if you don't start off sexy you get fired. I could start off completely 'un' everything—antihero, in fact. And so that's what I did."

But, proving the reason why conventional wisdom got its name, many viewers of the series did not respond favorably to El Fadil's experiment. In fact, he says, the experiment "hit the fan," and hundreds of letters came in complaining about Bashir's personality. Fortunately, though, El Fadil had friends in the highest place—the producers' office. In fact, acknowledging the power structure of television production, El Fadil says that in the end, it is Berman and Piller who are responsible for his continued characterization arc for Bashir, "because they have the guts to let it go on."

Now into his second season, El Fadil is following through on his plan to have Bashir evolve into a more likable hero, with the help of the writers, he points out. "Now they're beefing me up a bit. Bashir started off lost and now he's finding a way back."

# Terry Farrell

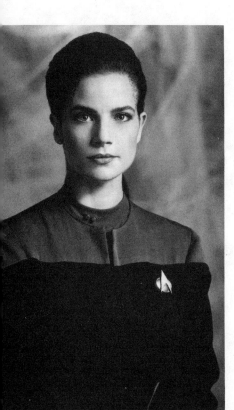

Terry Farrell as Lieutenant Jadzia Dax.

"When they're taking your picture forever, it's nice to be awake."

Terry Farrell's role of Jadzia Dax, the science officer who is half beautiful young woman, half three-hundred-year-old slug, was the last to be filled for *Deep Space Nine*. As Rick Berman says, "A beautiful young woman is always the most difficult role to cast on television, especially one who can act." In most cases, young female actors want to move directly to films, and an ongoing commitment to a successful series can severely interfere with the actor's availability for feature work. But in Terry Farrell's case, though she is young, she has already achieved the success that most actors her age are still struggling for, and a television role was not an interruption of her career, but an extension of it.

Farrell began her career early by signing with the prestigious Elite modeling agency at age sixteen. Over the next several years she appeared on the sought-after covers of magazines such as *Vogue* and *Mademoiselle*. Seeking to expand her career opportunities, Farrell began studying acting in Los Angeles and New York, and quickly landed the costarring role of Laurie Caswell in the ABC series *Paper Dolls*, playing a young woman caught up in the machinations of the modeling and cosmetics industries.

Farrell then went on to numerous guest roles in such hit series as *The Cosby Show*, *Family Ties*, and *Quantum Leap*, as well as costarring with Faye Dunaway in the NBC telefilm *L.A. Madame*. Farrell's credits don't end with television, either. Her feature-film credits include the Rodney Dangerfield hit *Back to School*, and the lead in Miramax's *Hellraiser III*.

In keeping with the chaos theory of television, though she couldn't know it at the time, all these roles relate directly to her performance as Jadzia Dax.

"Everything you do prepares you," Farrell says, "whether you do a series or a feature." However, she does feel that of all her previous roles, making the feature film *Hellraiser III* was the experience most like making *Deep Space Nine*. And not just because of that film's special effects and odd creatures.

"You shoot a low-budget feature the way we shoot *Deep Space Nine*," she explains. "On *Hellraiser III*, we shot fast. There were a lot of setups every day. It wasn't like some slow pace. It was, Hurry up! Oh, my God! You go into overtime and the producers have a heart attack. The producers come down, and go, ARGHHH! What are you *doing?*" Farrell laughs as she remembers her work on the *Hellraiser* film.

"But *Paper Dolls* was a drama," Farrell continues, "like a soap opera. As an actor, you're not saying anything particularly bizarre that couldn't happen to you in real life—at least, in a dramatized version of it. You're not wearing anything odd, you don't have anything odd happening to you, really—I mean, certainly nothing that you have to imagine." *Deep Space Nine*, of course, despite the personal core that lies beneath all the stories, is science fiction, and as the station's science officer, Farrell has to contend with more than her fair share of STAR TREK's trademark "technobabble."

"The pilot for me was all technobabble," Farrell says. "I tried to have it sound like

I knew what I was talking about—but I had no idea what I was saying." Finally, she came up with a method for coping with this part of her character—"Memorize it. Straight memorize it. Instead of trying to find an intention, just memorize it, then find stuff later."

Fortunately, she soon found out she was not alone. "Later, when I got to work with Colm more often, I felt great because he forgets all the time, too. That made me feel a lot better."

Like her fellow cast members, Farrell has found that creating her role has become easier over time. In the first season, Farrell recalls that she would start her preparation for an episode by reading and memorizing the "white pages"—which is the first draft of a script released by the writing staff.[5] That was a difficult approach to take, for the simple reason that multiple script revisions would follow, and in each her lines might have been changed and/or increased or reduced. But, as Farrell says, though reading the white pages is harder, she did it "because you don't know the character yourself, and you want to work on it to know your character better. But now, a year later, it's a little easier because you can read it to get the idea and know what the script's about, and wait until you get changes to actually start breaking it down, or break it down without memorizing it. In the beginning, you're so excited, you *want* to memorize it."

Farrell's practical approach to her role mirrors that of her costar, Rene Auberjonois. Auberjonois has often said that as a father with two children in college, from a strictly financial point of view he welcomed the chance to have a steady role for the next few years. Similarly, when Farrell was cast as Jadzia Dax, Rick Berman gave her a hug and told her her life was now going to change; but when Farrell is asked what the impact of being on the series has been, her simple answer is to smile and say, "I still have my house."

Like several other members of the cast who play nonhumans, Farrell's day begins several hours before she's actually due on set, with a hair and makeup call. Farrell calls it the only routine part of her work on *Deep Space Nine.* "Every day, the second AD[6] greets me out here and I get my coffee and that's my warm up for the day. Then, the mission to find Michael Westmore in the morning is probably the biggest deal."

Westmore, who designs and supervises the makeup for *Deep Space Nine,* was sometimes hard to track down in the first two seasons because he had the same responsibility for *The Next Generation.* "Michael does my makeup, and he does Brent and Gates on *The Next Generation,* so it can get kind of crazy when they need both Brent and myself at the same time. Last time, I won out and I got done first, and this time Brent won, and I had to sit and wait forty-five minutes."

All told, though, Farrell is pleased with her morning routine. After refining her makeup during the first episodes, it now takes about forty-five minutes for her hair, and forty-five minutes for her distinctive Trill markings to be hand-painted by Westmore. She finds that the approximately two hours of preparation gives her time to wake up before going on camera, "which is pleasant," Farrell says. "When they're taking your picture forever, it's nice to be awake."

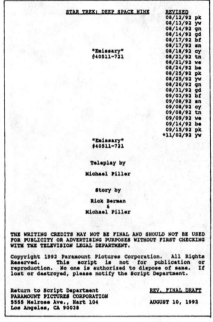

The title page for "Emissary," which was revised twenty-two times after the Revised Final Draft of August 10, 1992.

[5]Because scripts invariably go through multiple revisions, sometimes involving only a few scenes or even a few lines, television production studios use a system of color-coding revision pages. On *Deep Space Nine,* the following order is used.

| | |
|---|---|
| FIRST DRAFT | WHITE |
| FIRST REVISION | BLUE |
| SECOND | PINK |
| THIRD | YELLOW |
| FOURTH | GREEN |
| FIFTH | GOLDENROD |
| SIXTH | BUFF |
| SEVENTH | SALMON |
| EIGHTH | CANARY |
| NINTH | TAN |

After the ninth revision, the sequence begins again with white. The pilot script, "Emissary," ended up with three sets of white pages after going through the full color sequence more than twice. However, now that the series is in ongoing production, five to six revisions is more often the norm.

[6]Second assistant director, whose duties often include keeping track of the cast when they're off the set, so that they will be able to go to the set when the director is ready for them.

# Colm Meaney

Colm Meaney as Chief Operations Officer Miles O'Brien.

*"Colm, just try saying it—try saying, 'Yes, yes, yes.'"*

[7]Actors in a similar position on *Deep Space Nine* include twenty-four-year-old Aron Eisenberg, who portrays Quark's nephew, Nog; Max Grodenchik as Quark's brother, Rom; Rosalind Chao as Keiko O'Brien; Marc Alaimo as the Cardassian Gul Dukat; Philip Anglim as Bareil, the Bajoran Vedek and Kira's potential love interest; and Wallace Shawn as the delightfully obnoxious Ferengi Nagus, Zak. Though not having a regular contract for a certain number of episodes each season can be hard on an actor, the rich variety of recurring characters that is part of *Deep Space Nine* contributes to the ongoing sense of continuity that has served all the STAR TREK series so well. And who among them can know if his or her character might someday be selected to become a regular, on this or some new STAR TREK series?

[8]A frustrating example of Meaney's comment is the experience of Pierce Brosnan, a fellow Irish actor who had long ago set his professional sights on someday playing James Bond in films. In American television, Brosnan achieved considerable fame as the title character in *Remington Steele*, and when that series' cancellation was announced, he was indeed offered the role of Bond following Roger Moore's decision

Like Michelle Forbes, Colm Meaney wasn't certain if he was ready to make the commitment to being a regular on a series. Though he had actually appeared in the pilot episode of *The Next Generation* as a nonspeaking, nondescript crew member on the battle bridge, he had spent several years gradually establishing an ongoing presence on the series as Transporter Chief O'Brien, acquiring his first names—Miles Edward—and being married to Keiko Ishikawa in the fourth-season episodes "Family" and "Data's Day," respectively.

As a recurring character on *The Next Generation*, Meaney had no contract and was hired on an episode-by-episode basis,[7] which left him considerable time to advance his stellar career as an actor—a career that he began at the age of fourteen, when he began studying acting in Dublin, Ireland, where he was born.

After high school, Meaney entered the Abbey Theatre School of Acting, which was part of the Irish National Theatre. Eventually, he joined the company as a professional.

After eight years of stage work in England, Meaney won his first roles in British television—including appearances on the BBC police drama *Z Cars*—and moved to New York. Further stage work in the United States led to his first American television roles, including appearances on *Remington Steele*, *Moonlighting*, the syndicated horror anthology *Tales from the Darkside*, and *The Next Generation*. At the same time, Meaney created a wide range of characters in hit movies as diverse as *Dick Tracy*, *Die Hard II*, *Last of the Mohicans*, and *Under Siege*. One of his most noteworthy roles was as the father in the box-office success *The Commitments*—a role he reprised to unanimous critical acclaim in *The Snapper*.

Now that he has a contract, and knows how much of his year will be committed to *Deep Space Nine*, Meaney does admit that balancing his two careers can be awkward. "I mean, there's always something you'd love to go and do but you can't. The producers here are very good about it—they're very cooperative in terms of working a way around the schedule to let you do other work, especially feature films. It reflects well on the show if a film does well."

Meaney also appreciates the way in which today's audience relates to actors who work in film and television at the same time. "There's a much bigger crossover, today, between television and film acting. There's far less of a stigma, almost a *class* thing, than there was some time ago. You know, 'Film actors don't do television, it's beneath them,' and 'Television actors can't get films because producers won't hire them because they're television actors.'[8] I think that's largely disappeared, that those lines have been blurred to a great extent, so there's a much bigger crossover. And I think that's obviously to our benefit, being around today as opposed to being around twenty years ago. Back then, I think there was much more of a kind of a pigeonholing, a classification of actors, too. You know, 'Certain types didn't play other types because that's not how the audience knows them.'"

Not only has this new, more enlightened way of perceiving actors made Meaney's work more varied, he also appreciates its effect on the quality of other actors he's able to work with on *Deep Space Nine*. "That's one of the great things about this show, it

Max Grodènchik as Rom whispers things
Quark would rather Pel (Helene Udy)
didn't hear.

Aron Eisenberg as Nog doing the
twenty-fourth century equivalent of
hanging around the mall with Jake Sisko.

Wallace Shawn as Grand Nagus Zak puts
the moves on Jadzia.

**Recurring Guest Stars of
Deep Space Nine**

attracts actors of an extraordinary caliber—guest stars like Frank Langella, Louise Fletcher, Richard Beymer, and Richard Kiley. There're not many TV shows attract that caliber.''

Meaney is very pleased with the way his role as O'Brien has worked out on *Deep Space Nine*, especially since he wasn't initially drawn to the idea. ''I was kind of like the 'irregular' regular over on *The Next Generation*,'' he says ''It was basically a freelance relationship.'' His dilemma in deciding whether or not to take on the role of O'Brien on a more-or-less full-time basis ''was more to do with committing to being a series regular and not being able to do what I was doing outside STAR TREK.'' Meaney reports that it took about six months for him to say yes to Berman and Piller. ''Finally it came down to my agent on the phone to me, saying, 'Colm, just try saying it—try saying, Yes, yes, yes.' ''

He did say yes and has not regretted anything that has followed. ''Obviously, there're things come up that you'd like to do, that you can't do. So, that's the

to retire from the movie series. Brosnan accepted the role, only to learn that the producers of *Remington Steele* retained an option for his services for a number of months past the cancellation of the series. When the producers realized that Brosnan was going to be the new Bond, they immediately made plans to make new episodes of *Remington Steele* to capitalize on Brosnan's impending rise in stature. Unfortunately, when the producers of the Bond films learned that their new Bond would be appearing in more television episodes, which they felt would devalue his image, they withdrew their offer. Brosnan, bound by his contract, could do nothing but continue the role of Remington Steele as Timothy Dalton became the new Bond. However, happy endings being the Hollywood tradition, Brosnan finally became the new James Bond in June of 1994, with his first film in that role scheduled for the summer of 1995.

Louise Fletcher as Vedek Wynn, who ended the second season as Bajor's newly elected Kai.

Philip Anglim as Vedek Bareil, Kira's love interest.

Frank Langella as Wynn's fellow conspirator, Jaro.

trade-off. When you've made a decision, you've got to realize what the trade-off was, that there were reasons for being here, for doing this."

Meaney explains that one of his best reasons for accepting the role of O'Brien was his nine-year-old daughter. "It's important to be around a bit. The year before this show began, I was away on location for about eight months. But here, even though we work long hours, at least you do get home every evening."

With the relative luxury of having a well-defined character so early on in the life of a new series, and the experience to know both sides of the actor's dilemma of whether or not to commit to an ongoing series, Colm Meaney has the air of someone who is settled and confident in his work.

Other roles, though, will continue to be part of his work, as well, especially movies made on hiatus.[9] As Meaney says, "It's nice to get out of your spacesuit for a while."

[9] A break in the production of a television series . . . at least, for the cast and production crew. The writers and producers of *Deep Space Nine* work almost continuously throughout the year, as do the production design and art departments, though at a slightly less frenetic pace when actual production has ceased.

Brian Keith as Mullibok, a stubborn Bajoran farmer who refuses to leave his home in "Progress."

The grand old man of classic science-fiction films such as The Thing, Kenneth Tobey, as Rurigan in "Shadowplay."

**Special Guest Stars of Deep Space Nine**

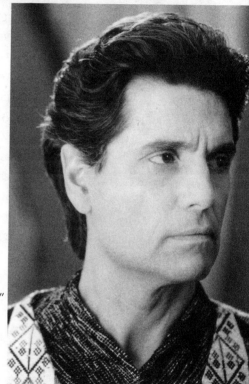

Chris Sarandon as Martus, intent on putting Quark out of business in "Rivals."

John Glover as Verad, intent on stealing Jadzia's worm in "Invasive Procedures."

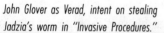

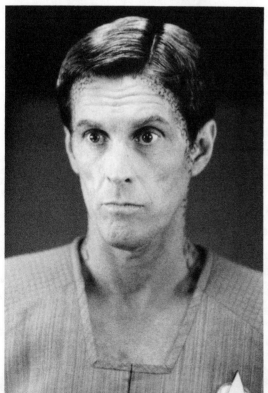

Barbara Basson on DS9 by way of Hill Street, as Roana, in "Rivals."

# Armin Shimerman

Armin Shimerman as Quark.

"The actor must be as sneaky as the character."

Armin Shimerman is everything his character, Quark, is not—*almost*.

Where Quark is always looking for an angle in order to increase his chances for profit, Shimerman is unselfishly gracious with his fellow actors and the production crew of *Deep Space Nine,* as well as with the constant stream of visitors who arrive to watch him work. Where Quark can be dynamically greedy, eagerly seeking to gain everything for himself, Shimerman gratefully acknowledges all those who have contributed to his portrayal of DS9's favorite barkeep—including, but not limited to, Michael Westmore, who designed his makeup; Craig Reardon, who sculpted his Ferengi features with an "extra something" just for Shimerman; Karen Westerfield, who spends each working day with Shimerman, applying, maintaining, and finally removing his makeup; and the producers and writing staff of *Deep Space Nine,* who have allowed Shimerman to lift the Ferengi race beyond the realm of stereotype and caricature, to make them every bit as complex and multilayered as those other great STAR TREK inventions the Vulcans and the Klingons.

Of course, we did say that Shimerman is *almost* unlike Quark in every way. The actor and the character do, in fact, have two qualities in common. Both are passionate about their work. And both are more devious than anyone imagines. But that should come as no surprise because, as Shimerman himself says, in his position, "The actor must be as sneaky as the character!" Why he says that, we'll get to in a moment. First, some biographical notes.

By now it should be a familiar pattern that though many people in the nonperforming areas of television production sought first to begin their careers as actors, almost everyone who has a career as an actor set out from the beginning to do exactly that. Armin Shimerman is no exception.

He was born and raised in New Jersey, and, when he was seventeen, moved to Los Angeles with his family. It was in LA that his mother enrolled him in a drama group, hoping it would help him meet new friends. What it did was convince him he wanted to become an actor.

After graduating from UCLA, Shimerman went to New York for stage experience, and received it in regional theater productions for the Tyrone Guthrie Theatre, the American Shakespeare Festival, and the New York Shakespeare Festival. Continuing his upward path, he won roles in the Broadway productions of *I Remember Mama, Broadway, St. Joan,* and *Three Penny Opera.*

Returning to Los Angeles, Shimerman obtained the obligatory guest appearances on such series as *L.A. Law, Married . . . With Children,* and *Who's the Boss?* One notable guest-starring role, which found him playing a large-headed alien seeking profit several years before the advent of *Deep Space Nine,* was in the "Gimme, Gimme" episode of the Fox Television series *Alien Nation.*

But Shimerman's talents were not limited to guest-starring roles alone, and he became known to millions of viewers in the recurring roles of Pascal on *Beauty and the Beast,* and of Cousin Bernie on *Brooklyn Bridge.* Shimerman also endeared himself to science-fiction fans by playing the part of Weasel in the low-budget and, consequently, little-known science-fiction film *Arena,* which is one of those movies known as "buried treasures" in local video-rental stores. The film's story of combat matches between aliens on an interstellar space station would be at home in the *Deep Space Nine* universe, as would many of its grotesque aliens. However, before those roles, Shimerman took on one part that was to prove pivotal not only to the world of STAR TREK, but to his own career—that of the first Ferengi seen on *The Next Generation:* Letek.[10]

In that series' first-season episode, "The Last Outpost," Shimerman played the leader of the Ferengi landing party that was the first group of the aliens encountered directly by the Federation. As originally conceived, the Ferengi were to be *The Next Generation*'s Klingons—a dangerous race that would become the Federation's greatest foe. Appearing with Shimerman as his fellow Ferengi were Jake Dengel as Mordoc, and Tracey Walter as Kayron. The Ferengi, as a race, were developed by Gene Roddenberry and Herb Wright, and first were mentioned in the *Next Generation* pilot episode. As Shimerman remembers, "We all had hopes that there would be some threat, some 'bite,' to the Ferengi." But, at first, that was not to be.

Shimerman believes the Ferengi's downfall began with the decision to shoot them in "The Last Outpost" as if they were part of a comedy film. "Except for the viewscreen sequences, we were usually shot together," Shimerman says, and that lessened the chance for the Ferengi to have a powerful impact. "To make a character threatening on TV," he continues, "you have to be able to see his eyes."

Shimerman remembers that one of his first inputs into the definition of the Ferengi was to suggest to the director that they not "jump up and down like crazed gerbils in the final scene of the episode, which is what he wanted. I knew if we did that, the Ferengi would never be a threat," Shimerman says. In the episode as filmed, the three Ferengi do scuttle back and forth in great agitation, though there is no jumping. But as Rick Berman later put it, "their silliness quotient" effectively ruled them out as a major adversary.

Shimerman, no stranger to collaboration in television, understands that the Ferengi grew to become a valuable part of the STAR TREK universe by providing comic relief, and he sees nothing wrong with that. "But now I want to change that," he says, and he lays out his plan for what he hopes Quark might become.

"At the beginning, I realized that the writers saw Quark as an extension of all the Ferengi they had seen before—comical, sort of two-dimensional characters. My agenda was to change that, to make Quark three-dimensional, a little less obvious, so that in the years to come, he'll be less transparent, and the audience will not be quite sure what Quark will do in certain situations." Knowing that he's straying into character-development areas that are usually the province of the writers and the producers, this is where Shimerman adds with a smile that to pull this off, "The actor must be as sneaky as the character."

However, looking back at how the character of Quark did develop over the first and second seasons, it's obvious that Shimerman has succeeded in his goals. Quark is certainly out for profit, but in a curious way he has his own sense of honor and duty to his family and his customers. Now when Quark is faced with a difficult decision that might put profit over the well-being of others on DS9, the audience really can't

[10]With tongue firmly in his Ferengi cheek, Shimerman has been known to proclaim his very *first* role in *The Next Generation* as his "most influential guest appearance." The role he refers to is that of a metallic face that briefly comes to life on the side of a Betazoid gift box, in the first-season episode "Haven." The role, such as it was, was uncredited.

be sure what choice he'll make—which is a testament to Shimerman's talent and insight.

As an actor, Shimerman begins his day earlier than any other regular cast member, arriving at the makeup trailer outside Stage 5 at least three hours before he's needed on the set, so he can meet his personal makeup artist, Karen Westerfield.[11]

Westerfield, a two-time Emmy winner as part of Michael Westmore's makeup team, starts Shimerman's transformation by slipping on him his Ferengi cranium and ears—a multiuse appliance on which sharp-eyed followers of the Ferengi might notice a few creases and ripples behind the ears that other Ferengi makeup never had.

Those extra folds behind Quark's ears were added by Michael Westmore and Craig Reardon at Shimerman's request, owing to his experience as Letek several years earlier. "It was painful—*very* painful," Shimerman remembers, "because the original Ferengi appliances had no ear pockets." Thus, the actors wearing the Ferengi headpieces had their ears flattened against their heads, as if wearing a very tight bathing cap.

"After nine hours, flattened ears are extremely uncomfortable," Shimerman says, "to the point where on a sixteen-hour day, they become psychologically enervating."

Shimerman's solution was to request that his headpieces for Quark incorporate spaces for his ears, and Westmore arranged to have them sculpted into the final model, literally taking a great deal of pressure off the actor.

As noted, Shimerman is a great believer in the power of an actor's eyes, and he is especially appreciative of a detail that Karen Westerfield brought to Westmore's design for Quark's features—a subtle use of magenta around Quark's eyes that serves to make Shimerman's pale eyes jump out from the deep shadows of the thick Ferengi brow. Once again, collaboration has combined three separate components— makeup design, application, and an actor's talent—to create a character as remarkable in a visual sense as he is in his ongoing performance and in the writing. Commenting on his new role in STAR TREK's latest installment, Shimerman says, "STAR TREK is a legend, there's no doubt about that, and I'm a very lucky boy to be part of it."

The viewers of *Deep Space Nine* are lucky that he is, as well.

[11]When the Northridge earthquake hit Los Angeles on January 17 at 4:31 A.M., Shimerman was just finishing up in the makeup trailer after having arrived on the lot at 2:00! Karen Westerfield, who was working on Shimerman at the time, recalls, that "Everyone standing felt before everyone sitting down. When it started, I said, 'Earthquake.' And Armin said, 'Are you sure?' And then he said, 'YUUUP!' as everything started shaking."

Fortunately, there were no injuries in the trailer or anywhere else on the *Deep Space Nine* sets, though those in the makeup trailer did have a bizarre close call. "Because there were eight of us in there," Westerfield says, "the weight was holding the trailer down so we didn't lose anything and no one got hurt." Like most everyone else in Los Angeles that morning, Westerfield and those with her in the trailer decided to wait it out until dawn, and, because power was out, they lit emergency candles throughout the trailer. Then, when it got light, "Armin decided he had to go back to his house to check on his family." Westerfield thought it was a good idea and got out the alcohol she uses to take off Shimerman's makeup. But as Shimerman put on his jacket, Westerfield recalls that just as she was warning him to be careful, "he whipped it around and he knocked the candle over into the alcohol and, just like that, it went WHOOSH!"

Westerfield continues the story with nervous laughter. "It was *wild*—it lit up the whole trailer. We were all laughing, even though it would have been bad if it had spilled on us. But we were lucky." After extinguishing the fire, Westerfield remembers asking, "Where's pestilence? It's got to be around here somewhere."

## Nana Visitor

While Colm Meaney's agent was trying to talk him into accepting a regular role on *Deep Space Nine*, Nana Visitor's manager was trying to talk her *out* of doing the same. That was the only reason why she didn't accept the role of Major Kira Nerys when it was first offered to her after what was only her second audition. As Rick Berman said, Visitor "nailed the role of Major Kira on her first reading."

Visitor also recalls the speed with which the role was offered. "I had two auditions. One for the producers, and one for Paramount. It was really short. It was very quick. The only thing that made it a little longer is that my manager at the time didn't really want me to do this show, because it was syndicated. He felt I should hold out for network.[12] But my love for my character—and it's hard not to recognize the quality of the writing—made me go, Well, all right, you think I'm throwing my career away at this time of my life—which is a critical time for an actress:[13] So be it. This is the way I'm going. This is what I became an actor to do. This kind of role. Not playing a woman in relation to other people: a mother, or a wife, or a prostitute, or a killer. She's fully realized. My agent's reluctance made the decision-making process a little longer, but once that conflict was resolved, getting the role was very quick."

One thing that didn't come quickly to Visitor, though, was the realization that the role she was going to be auditioning for was in a STAR TREK series. Berman played with her a bit because of this, and once she did accept the role, he solemnly discussed with her the nose she'd have to wear. Having no idea of the delicate ridges that are Bajoran noses, Visitor asked about the appliance, and Berman showed her a novelty elephant nose. It took a few moments for Visitor to realize Berman was joking.

Today, of course, that Bajoran nose is so much a part of her life that her infant son doesn't even notice it. "The first time saw it he made a quizzical face. He touched it, bounced it, gave a great belly laugh—and he never looked at it again."[14]

Her son's reaction might have something to do with the acting genes he has inherited from his parents. Visitor's husband is also an actor, and Visitor herself was born and raised in and around New York's theater district. Her father was a Broadway choreographer, and her mother a ballet instructor. Visitor began studying dance in her mother's studio at age seven, and by the end of high school was heading for a career onstage.

Early on, Visitor had the distinction of touring with Angela Lansbury in *Gypsy*, and later appeared in the acclaimed Broadway musical *42nd Street*, the last choreographed by the legendary Gower Champion. Her other stage credits include *My One and Only*, *The Ladies Room*, and *A Musical Jubilee*. But stage is not the only outlet for actors in New York, and Visitor also appeared in the ABC daytime soap operas *Ryan's Hope* and *One Life to Live*.

In 1985 Visitor came to Los Angeles and began her run of television guest appearances. (Perhaps it's becoming obvious by now why Los Angeles is a mecca for actors.) Among the shows she appeared in were *Empty Nest*, *Murder, She Wrote*, *Baby Talk*, *thirtysomething*, *Jake and the Fatman*, *L.A. Law*, *In the Heat of the Night*, and *Matlock*. Her first regular starring role was as the "company witch," Bryn Newhouse, on the NBC sitcom *Working Girl*, based on the hit film.

*Nana Visitor as Major Kira Nerys, in her pilot-episode hairstyle.*

### "You can't have a big butt and be a freedom fighter."

[12]This prejudice against non-network shows is akin to the class distinctions Colm Meaney noted that once existed between film actors and television actors. But, in the 1990s, at the dawn of the five-hundred-channel universe, the truth is that just as there is more acceptance of actors crossing over between movie and television roles, shows like *The Next Generation* and *Deep Space Nine* have proven that a syndicated series can have the same quality and size of audience that any network show might aspire to.

[13]Nana Visitor was thirty-six at the time we spoke with her. The critical phase she refers to is that time when female actors move from being typecast as "pretty young things" to being typecast as "old." Good female actors who are fortunate enough to combine hard work with luck sometimes slip between these two extremes to establish themselves as actors who, like Visitor, can play fully-realized characters, adding years and many good parts to their careers. Male actors do not face this crossroads as early in their careers, because far more emphasis is placed on a woman's age than on a man's. For having survived in such a cutthroat, arbitrary, and unfathomable industry as television acting, we were constantly surprised at how good-natured the cast of *Deep Space Nine* remained. But then again, they *are* all actors, aren't they?

[14]Two of Visitor's coworkers didn't fare as well, however. On his frequent visits to the

Above left:
The revised hairstyle, more befitting a
career military officer.

Above right:
A different look for Kira from five years
earlier, during the Cardassian occupation,
in "Necessary Evil."

set to spend time with his mother, the
baby became good friends with Rene
Auberjonois and Armin Shimerman, displaying no fear of or curiosity about their
alien makeup. However, Visitor recalls, "It
finally happened. He turned a year and a
half, and it was WAUUHHH! whenever he
saw them. Which, of course, just killed
Armin and Rene."

[15]The standard Screen Actors Guild contract stipulates that actors shall not be
required on the set any earlier than twelve
hours after their last appearance there. If a
slipping production schedule requires an
actor to come in before the twelve-hour
limit, then the actor is said to be "forced"
and the studio pays a preset penalty fee.

Working as a regular on a sitcom, Visitor says, was unlike appearing on *Deep
Space Nine*. "It was a totally different experience. On a half-hour show, you're a
nine-to-five worker. You have one long day a week, And most of the time you don't do
even nine-to-five. Once you get into a rhythm, once you've done about three shows,
you come in for an hour, and then go home.

"But *Deep Space Nine* is a challenge because of the hours. It's interesting
because guest stars will come in and say, 'Oh my God, I'm going to fall down dead,
I've been forced[15] three times and I'm exhausted and I've got all this dialogue.'
Inevitably, they turn to us and say, 'How do you do it?'" Visitor answers her own
question by saying, "I think part of it is you get into shape, you get into the rhythm of
it. And you know when to expend the energy and when not to. So you pace yourself
and become like an athlete.

"The other part—and for me this is the biggest part—is interest. I'm interested
not only in what Kira does and being true to that, I'm also interested in the bigger
picture. I'm interested in the show, and the quality of the show. And I think that at
two o'clock in the morning, you really do have to have a bigger picture to be able to
concentrate and do what's necessary. Otherwise, if it gets down to a basic
level—you're just sleepy, you want to say, Get this shot over, I don't care if it's
good—and you can *never* have that attitude. Not on a show like this."

The athlete image is one that Visitor keeps close to heart. Not just because she's
an actor coping with the grueling schedule of episodic television, but also because
she's also a mother coping with the equally—perhaps even more—grueling
schedule of raising a young child. How does she manage both full-time jobs at once?

"Again, it's discipline and having an incredible partner. We sat down when I got
this job, and he knew how much I loved the part. That wasn't hard to see. He's an
actor, as well, and he was excited by it, too. And he was amazing. He said, 'You've

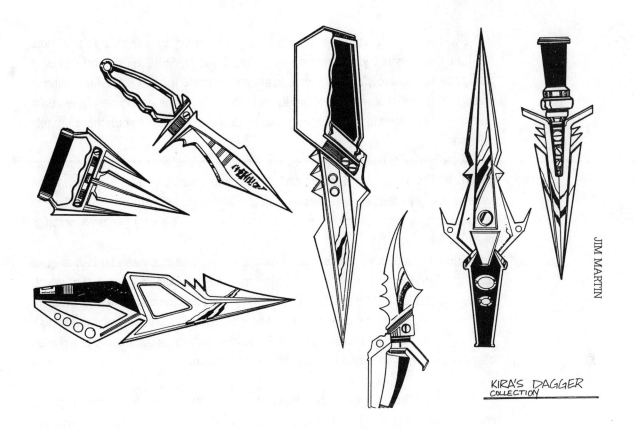

JIM MARTIN

KIRA'S DAGGER COLLECTION

Kira's dagger collection—an indication of hidden character traits yet to come?

got to do this. There's no question. I will stay home with Buster,' because Buster was three and a half months old. 'You do this,' he said. So I did.

"There are difficult moments where I'm not where I want to be. But, for the most part, all it's taken—besides having a mate that will enable me to do this, and who brings Buster to the set, which really helps in these eighteen-hour days—is discipline. Just discipline. Being a soldier. When I lost the weight during the pilot from having the baby, I used to be on the Stairmaster and I'd say to myself, 'You're a soldier. You're a freedom fighter. You can't have a big butt and be a freedom fighter. Doesn't make sense.' So, that's it. At lunch, I go and work out, and I just try to have time for everything, and when I get home, if my son's up, or he needs something, I'm up. It's just less sleep."

Visitor has such dedication to her work and enthusiasm for her role that she even sees the positive aspects of going without sleep. "The great thing is that Kira has a face that can age—that has more than just glamor—so if I don't sleep all night, and I look tired—hey! It's part of what Kira is. She lives life.

"It's almost more of a European take," Visitor explains. "It's like being a woman in Paris, smoking a cigarette and wearing a black turtleneck and looking like she had a wild night and whatever, and there's nothing wrong with that! You're living life! You're having fun. Something's going on in your emotional life. So," she says with a grin, "since I don't have a choice, I've taken the European view! The more lines on my face the more interesting."

With an attitude like that, it's no wonder that Kira has become one of *Deep Space Nine*'s most interesting characters, *and* a role model to thousands of viewers.

"I've had women write to me," Visitor says, "and say they're trying to be more like Kira, that they're trying to get down to their feelings. And I'm realizing that even though there's a perception that women are very close to their feelings, I'm seeing in these letters that that's not necessarily true. Women have a hard time. They might know what the feeling is, but to express it, to act on it, that's something entirely different.

"As a matter of fact, Kira's helped me, personally, in that way. It's like a muscle, you know. I'm in this world of Kira and dealing with what she deals with, and those traits in me and that way of thinking are being exercised within me, so Nana is becoming more like Kira in certain ways of thinking. She's a very healthy woman in many ways.

"The only bad thing is that sometimes it's very hard because she had a lot of tragedy. Everything that we can imagine in today's world, she went through it. Starvation and killing the enemy, all of it. But when I see the response from women, and from men, and from fourteen-year-old boys who aren't having a problem seeing a woman be first officer, and seeing a woman in charge, I think this character's maybe changing one person's views, and that's terribly important."

And with that thought of the ability of one fictional character in an imaginary setting to change some people's views and to provide inspiration to others, we have moved 180 degrees from the simple, nonemotional business decisions that first led to *Deep Space Nine*'s creation, and found the true core of what can be so good and so worthwhile in television.

Make no mistake: Episodic television is a business, first and foremost, pure and simple. But the inspiring part of what television can be, and what *Deep Space Nine* illustrates so well, is that once the financial machinations have been set in motion, once the studio sales staff has contracted with independent stations, once the advertising has been sold . . . talented people put business aside and pour their hearts and souls into their work.

In coming up with the stories for *Deep Space Nine*, Michael Piller asks, "What makes this personal?"

The actors of *Deep Space Nine*, guided by the writing staff's scripts, clothed in artful makeup and costumes and inhabiting otherworldly sets, are perhaps the most important answer to that question, by creating characters the audience can care about, identify with, and want to know more about. And in that equation, writ with the talent and skill and experience of the seven regular cast members and their supporting cast of recurring and guest actors, money matters and business decisions and corporate balance sheets have no part. Nor should they.

To be corny, it's called the magic of television, and in this case the actors are the magicians.

As for the stage on which they perform, that's what we'll look at next.

# THE MOST

# THIRTEEN

# CLOSED SET ON

# THE LOT

*I ain't no Ansel Adams—I'm*
*not waiting for the light.*

—David Livingston

T hey had the script, the sets, the crew, the makeup, the costumes, the props, and—more or less—a schedule. The only thing to be done now was to mix them all together, and the place where that mixing takes place is, of course, the set.[1]

For the pilot episode of *Deep Space Nine*, the first day of principal photography[2] took place on Stage 4, on August 18, 1992. Fittingly, the first scene filmed was Scene 30, in which Sisko arrives in Ops for the very first time. (The opening of that scene is reproduced in Chapter 11, page *162*.) However, by the afternoon of the first day, the scenes being shot took place four days after the first scene, and it would not be until two and a half weeks into production that the actual first scene of the script—on the bridge of the *Saratoga* during the battle of Wolf 359—would come before the camera. As an example of the out-of-sequence nature of filming episodic television, note that Scene 30 appears on page 16 of the shooting script, two-thirds of the way through the first act, and that the last scene shot that day was Scene 90, which begins Act Four on page 54.

Scene 90 is interesting for another reason, too. Let's take a look at it.

[1]Occasionally, some scenes will be shot on location, though because *Deep Space Nine* is set in the twenty-fourth century on alien worlds, most location shots are limited to naturalistic settings, such as gardens, forests, and scrubland. Location shooting adds variety to the look of the series, but any money saved by not having to construct a naturalistic set is usually eaten up by the cost of transporting the entire company off the lot, and dealing with the uncontrollable lighting and sound conditions of Southern California's great outdoors. Plus, permit fees, security arrangements, and other assorted local charges can cost the production almost $6,000 a day in additional expenses.

[2]"Principal photography" refers to filming involving the director and the first-unit crew, and the day it begins is generally considered to be the official first day of production. The term is used to distinguish first-unit work from second-unit photography and special-effects shots, which, when a series is in full production, usually begin one or two weeks after principal photography. In the case of "Emissary," second-unit filming did not begin until about a month after the first unit had begun.

# Fractured Time: Filming out of Sequence

It's apparent why television episodes are filmed out of sequence—cost-effectiveness. Once the Ops set has been lit and prepped for shooting one scene, it makes sense to then film *all* the Ops scenes one after the other, so the set will only have to be prepared once.

While out-of-sequence filming is beneficial to the production overall, it can make crafting a performance by an actor very difficult. For example, one of the pivotal sequences in "Emissary" was Sisko's conversation with the Entities in the wormhole, a key scene leading up to his transfiguring realization that he has not let go of his past (as reproduced on page *115*).

222 THE WHITE SCREEN - SISKO'S EYES (OPTICAL)

Heartbeat. Breathing.

        SISKO
Talk to me. Are you still there?
What just happened?

223 EXT. BEACH - DAY - JENNIFER ALIEN (OPTICAL)

walking along the shore as seen in Act Two . . .

        JENNIFER ALIEN
More of your kind.

               INTERCUTTING:

224 THE WHITE SCREEN - SISKO'S EYES (OPTICAL)

        SISKO
Another ship . . . in the wormhole?

        JENNIFER ALIEN
'Wormhole' - what is this?

        SISKO
It is how we describe the kind
of passage that brought me here . . .

225  INT. OBSERVATION LOUNGE [on the Enterprise]

        PICARD ALIEN
It is terminated.

225A  REVERSE ANGLE - SISKO IN THE OBSERVATION LOUNGE

        SISKO
Terminated . . .

        PICARD ALIEN
Our existence is disrupted
whenever one of you enters the
passage . . .

226 INT. SARATOGA BRIDGE

        CONN OFFICER ALIEN
Your linear nature is inherently
destructive.

        OPS OFFICER ALIEN
You have no regard for the
consequences of your acts.

        SISKO
That's not true. We're aware that
every choice we make has a
consequence . . .

        CAPTAIN OFFICER ALIEN
But you claim you do not know what
it will be . . .

        SISKO
We don't . . .

227 EXT. FISHING POND - DAY - JAKE ALIEN

        JAKE ALIEN
        (interrupting)
Then how can you take
responsibility for your actions . . .

        SISKO
We use past experience to help
guide us.
        (beat)

For Jennifer and me, all the
experiences in our lives prepared
us for the day we met on the
beach . . . helped us recognize that
we had a future together. When
we married, we accepted all the
consequences of that act, whatever
they might be . . . including the
consequence of *you.*

                    JAKE ALIEN
          Me?

                    SISKO
          My son, Jake . . .

228 INT. STARSHIP SICKBAY - CLOSEUP ON A
NEWBORN BABY BOY

and Sisko finds himself holding his child in
his hands for the first time . . . as a
Starfleet doctor and nurses, all aliens, tend
to Jennifer in bed . . . who looks up in her
post labor flush . . .

                    JENNIFER ALIEN
          The child with Jennifer.

                    SISKO
          Yes.

                    JENNIFER ALIEN
                    (beginning to
                    understand)
          Linear . . . procreation . . . ?

                    SISKO
                    (acknowledges)
          Yes. Jake is the continuation
          of our family . . .

                    JENNIFER ALIEN
                    (remembering)
          'The sound of children playing'.

229 A CATCHER'S MITT

as a bat swings and misses a ball as it pops
into the glove. Pan up to find Jake Alien is

the catcher . . . and a batter stands in front
of him, both dressed in Chicago Cubs uniforms of the early 1920s . . .

                    BATTER ALIEN
                    (accusing)
          Aggressive. Adversarial.

230 REVERSE ANGLE - EXT. BASEBALL FIELD - DAY

Sisko is standing on a pitcher's mound,
wearing a Cubs cap circa 1923 . . . and his
Starfleet uniform . . . in the background,
the rest of the Cubs' team works out . . .
playing catch, hitting fungos, fielding . . .
few spectators and reporters in straw hats
mill about . . .

                    SISKO
                    (correction)
          *Competition.* For fun. It's a
          game . . . that Jake and I play . . .
          on the Holodeck . . . it's called
          baseball.

And Jake alien stands out of his crouch and
as he takes off the mask and looks at it
curiously . . . and then looks around at the
environment . . . joining Sisko on the
mound . . .

                    JAKE ALIEN
          'Baseball' - what is this?

                    SISKO
          I was afraid you'd ask that . . .

A beat . . . How the hell do you explain
baseball to an alien . . . he takes a deep
breath, well, here goes . . .

                    SISKO
          I throw the ball to you . . . and
          this other player stands between
          us with a bat, a stick . . . and
          he . . . he tries to hit the ball
          in between these two white
          lines . . .

Jake alien blinks with confusion, Sisko pauses . . . regroups . . . getting another idea . . . his delivery growing with confidence as he continues . . .

> SISKO
>
> The rules aren't important . . . what's important is—it's *linear.* Every time you throw this ball a hundred different things can happen in the game . . . he might swing and miss, he might hit it . . . the point is you never know . . . you try to anticipate, set a strategy for all the possibilities as best you can . . . but in the end it all comes down to throwing one pitch after another . . . and seeing what happens. With each new consequence, the game begins to take shape . . .

> BATTER ALIEN
> (grasping the meaning)
> And you have no idea what that shape is until it is completed . . .

> SISKO
> (beat)
> That's right. In fact, the game wouldn't be worth playing if we knew what was going to happen.

> JAKE ALIEN
> (flabbergasted)
> You *value* your ignorance of what is to come?

> SISKO
> (acknowledges, driving home his point)
> That might be the most important thing to understand about humans. It is the unknown that defines our existence. We are constantly searching . . . not just for answers to our questions . . . but for new *questions.* We are explorers . . .

> we explore our lives day by day . . . and we explore the galaxy, trying to expand the boundaries of our knowledge. And that is why I'm here. Not to conquer you either with weapons or with ideas. But to co-exist and learn.

231 JAKE ALIEN

    studies him curiously for a beat . . .

232 SISKO

    waits hopefully for a response . . . reacts as he looks down at

233 HIS HANDS

    bloody and burned as they were at the Saratoga.

234 INT. SISKO'S QUARTERS

    and he's back on the Saratoga . . . his quarters in flames . . . his wife dead . . . his son unconscious . . . standing with the Tactical Officer . . .

> TACTICAL OFFICER ALIEN
> If all you say is true . . . why do you exist *here?*

Sisko reacts, confused and . . .

234A THE WHITE SCREEN - SISKO'S EYES (OPTICAL)

    Heartbeat. Breathing.

In the episode as filmed, this sequence, which is vital to the story's emotional core, runs three minutes and fifty-five seconds, and Avery Brooks delivers a compelling performance that begins with Sisko's feelings of concern, touches on his frustration at being unable to explain himself to the Entities, grows with confidence as he expounds on his baseball metaphor, then collapses into fear as he returns to the *Saratoga.* For an actor of Brooks's ability to give such a performance on a single set in a single scene would be just as moving, but perhaps not as remarkable as under the circumstances in which Brooks actually had to create this particular performance—a few lines at a time, out of sequence, on *eight* diffent sets and locations, over a period of almost three weeks!

The order in which the scenes composing this sequence were filmed was: 223 and 224, jumping up to 227, jumping again to 229 through 232 (233 deleted), then back to 225 and 225A, up to 228, back to 226, and ahead again to 234.

Adding to the potential confusion for Brooks was that when he was on a particular set—for example, the *Saratoga* bridge—he would have to play the scenes relating to actual story events, e.g. the battle of Wolf 359, then slip into a frame of mind suitable for Sisko's first sequence with the Entities, then for his second, and so on.

The skill with which Brooks managed to keep distinct all these different aspects of Sisko at different times is truly impressive. As Brooks himself says, "The out-of-sequence notion in episodic is very difficult, *always* a challenge. Especially in the small amount of time in which you're doing it, because the moments become more dense in some ways. If you work twelve hours to fourteen hours a day, then in the third day of that you have to really struggle to thumb back through the performance to find it again. But if my performance can become seamless, then somehow, I'm doing what I'm supposed to be doing."

---

ACT FOUR

FADE IN:[3]


90  INT. COMMANDER'S OFFICE (DAY #4)[4]


Sisko presses a control panel on a monitor and watches a recorded transmission from a university chancellor on Earth . . .

> CHANCELLOR (MONITOR)[5]
> Just a follow-up, Ben . . . that old
> house you asked about on Moravian
> Lane is available . . . it's yours
> if you want it . . . we look forward
> to hearing your decision.

A panel appears noting the end of transmission. Sisko stares at the screen.

> KIRA'S COM VOICE
> Kira to Commander Sisko. A
> Cardassian warship has just
> entered Bajoran space . . .

He rises . . .

> SISKO
> On screen.

Walks out to his balcony . . .

---

[3]The traditional way in which a new act begins, referring to the way the picture slowly appears on the screen, rather than just beginning with an abrupt jump from the black screen following a commercial break to the first frame of a scene. Often you'll notice that the very first shot of a new act (or scene) opens on a ceiling or a window or some other detail, and then begins to move to find the characters, giving the audience a chance to ease into the show again without missing any important visual information.

[4]This refers to the episode's time line. In this case, four days have passed since Sisko first arrived on DS9. On any other show, this notation would be a cue for the costuming department that characters should not be wearing the same clothes they wore on Day #3, or will wear on Day #5. However, in a show where almost everyone wears the same clothes all the time, the day notation is more a convenience for the cast and crew who film the script out of sequence. (Though for the pilot episode, Sisko first appeared on DS9 in a starship uniform, switching over to the standard DS9 uniform only after his meeting with Picard on the *Enterprise*.) The Day #4 notation here would indicate to Avery Brooks that Sisko would probably be familiar with the operation of his Cardassian viewscreen by now, where he might have displayed some confusion about its operation on Day #1.

[5]If this scene had been shot for *The Next Generation*, the word "MONITOR" would not be used here, and up on the slug line—INT. COMMANDER'S OFFICE—we would have seen the word "(OPTICAL)" to indicate that a special-effects shot would be required to matte an image of the Chancellor into the blank monitor screen on Sisko's desk. However, the decision to equip the *Deep Space Nine* sets with video monitors eliminated the need for a special-effects shot in this scene. Instead, the actor playing the Chancellor sat in front of a backdrop for a video camera, which transmitted him directly to the real video monitor on Sisko's desk.

For those with a good memory of "Emissary," Scene 90 should be about as familiar as the foot massages Kai Opaka was supposed to give. The fact is, Scene 90 was cut from the final version of the show, along with every other instance of Sisko actively trying to get another job in preparation for leaving Starfleet. From a story point of view, Berman and Piller decided that Sisko might appear to be unsympathetic if he spent time looking for another job when he should be doing the one he had been given. Also, from a technical point of view, the story as filmed was running long, so some scenes had to be cut anyway. Eventually, about half the footage shot on the first day of principal photography was consigned to the vaults, never to be seen.[6] As someone once said, that's showbiz.

But worrying whether or not a particular scene will make it to the final cut of an episode is not what anyone is concerned with when filming is underway. On set, with the clock ticking at close to $5,000 per hour, with the specter of overtime charges cresting above the budget like a tidal wave about to break, the only concern is making the schedule. As supervising director David Livingston says when he's on the set as a director, "I ain't no Ansel Adams—I'm not waiting for the light." The goal is to set up, shoot, and move on as quickly as possible while maintaining the high quality the series is known for. Of all the different stages in the production of *Deep Space Nine,* the working set is the one where a sense of nonstop urgency is most pronounced.

This urgency helps explain why the STAR TREK sets are the most difficult sets to visit on the Paramount lot.[7] No one wants to risk a delay caused by a visitor talking or tripping over a cable while the film is rolling, or becoming a dreaded "bogey"—the term used for "civilians" who wander into a shot, or who are reflected in viewscreens or any other reflective surface.[8] The strictness with which access to the sets is enforced applies equally to people who work on the Paramount lot and to people who work on the show itself. Surprisingly, even production designer Herman Zimmerman says he rarely ventures onto a working set unless he's been invited.[9]

So, for all those who aren't related to a Paramount producer, what's it like on the set of *Deep Space Nine?* The best analogy we can come up with is that it's like visiting a Las Vegas casino. Here's why.

Entering a working stage building is like entering a cocoon. There are no windows, sound is muffled, and the high ceilings disappear into dark shadows. Once you've moved into the stage's labyrinthine interior, away from the outside doors, there is nothing that provides any cue as to what time it might be. Like a casino, the environment is the same whether you're there at ten in the morning, five in the afternoon, or three the next morning.

The smell is a combination of a new home and a photo-finishing lab. Most of all, there's the scent of cut wood, fresh paint, new carpet, and a subtle chemical smell that comes from the lights and the heated gels that add color to them. The only time that that intermingling of scents is overpowered is just before the end of lunch break, when the enticing aroma of fresh-baked cookies helps inspire tired workers who must go back to their jobs—a not-so-subtle trick of the trade practiced by the caterers.

The caterers, known as "craft services," are also responsible for the ten-foot-long wooden tables stocked with doughnuts and Danishes, fruit, bagels, deli sandwich

[6] In addition to straightforward insurance liability concerns, the two other chief reasons for keeping visitors on the set to a minimum are to insure the security of props and the security of ideas. Unfortunately, there is a thriving market in stolen STAR TREK memorabilia, which Paramount combats by vigorous prosecution and extreme security measures that include putting serial numbers on certain props so they can be traced (and also so that collectors will realize that props that are legitimately on the market must carry a verifiable Paramount identification plate as proof that they are real, and not forgeries).

As for security of ideas, there is extreme—yet understandable—determination on the part of everyone connected with the show that story developments and special prop designs not be leaked ahead of the scheduled broadcast of an episode, in order to insure that what viewers see will be fresh and new. The concern over well-meaning fans who post inside information on computer bulletin boards has even reached Michael Piller's office. In the past, the STAR TREK office distributed lists of story premises under development as a courtesy to writers, to save them from inadvertently working on similar and, therefore, unusable ideas. But that practice has been stopped. Premise sheets from *The Next Generation* invariably ended up circulating among fans, spoiling what the writers hoped would be story surprises.

[7] Sharp-eyed viewers with frame-by-frame capability on their VCRs will notice that it's hard enough to prevent reflections of legitimate production crew in windows and viewscreens.

[8] Note that we're talking about *working* sets, also known as hot sets—that is, sets prepared for filming. Dark sets—sets not currently in use—are open to the crew of the series at any time, especially to directors of upcoming episodes who study them in person in order to plan the shots for their episodes. However, for the general public, hot or dark, STAR TREK sets are strictly off limits.

[9] Strangers constantly come up to question crew members foolish enough to wear these on the street, either asking to buy the clothing then and there, or wanting to know what it's like to work for Commander Sisko.

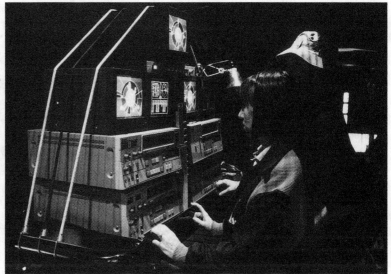

In the hurry-up-and-wait atmosphere, camera grips can take a break while the gaffers change the lights. When the lights are set and the camera crew has to go to work, the lighting crew can take its break.

makings, cooler chests of pop and bottled waters, and never-empty metal coffee dispensers. Time is so important on the set that it is far less expensive to keep free and bountiful food and drink only a few steps away than to risk having one vital member of the team go missing on a trip to the commissary exactly when she or he is needed.

These craft tables also serve as a social gathering spot at the beginning of the day and during breaks. Depending on the scenes being shot, it's here you're likely to spot Bajoran supernumeraries wearing decidedly un-STAR-TREK-like eyeglasses and drinking colas while discussing the traffic on Melrose with Dabo girls and Ferengi. Usually, one or two hideous aliens can also be spotted gingerly slipping a straw through a mouth hole, or taking delicate bites from a sandwich, hoping not to strain the makeup around their mouths.

In addition to the costumed extras, there are a seemingly inordinate number of civilians around, dressed in jeans and work clothes, sometimes wearing a *Deep Space Nine* crew jacket or sweater.[10] The first thing you notice about these workers is that at any given time, half of them don't seem to be doing anything except talking, reading the newspaper, or leaning back in a chair, eyes closed. But the apparent lack of activity isn't a sign of featherbedding—like soldiers waiting for the command to move out and establish a beachhead, these workers are waiting for their time to spring into action. They're the gaffers and electricians and set technicians whose jobs are done the moment a set is properly assembled, dressed, and lit for shooting. While the director works with the actors, these people wait for the call to move to the next setup—and when they get that call, stand back or you're likely to get run over

Lurking in the dimly lit Cardassian corridor, you're apt to find the video playback cart sending Okudagrams and other images to monitors on a "hot" set. Here, scenic artist Denise Okuda and video playback operator Joe Unsinn check tapes of images being sent to monitors in the cargo bay.

[10]Fittingly, not even the security guards are immune from the team spirit that fills the *Deep Space Nine* production. One of the guards, Russ English, has drawn some ingenious alien makeup designs, which he has submitted to Michael Westmore.

# BRINGING IT ALL HOME: STAR TREK PRODUCTS

Official STAR TREK licensed merchandise, including this very book, enables fans to extend their appreciation of the series, as well as serving the important purpose of cross-promoting the series in a variety of venues. After all, it costs money to buy *Deep Space Nine* ads in *TV Guide*. How much nicer to have thousands of tiny *Deep Space Nine* ads in the form of action-figure packages in toy stores, or in the form of book covers in bookstores. Plus, in return for approving the manufacture of particular items and trying its best to insure that the items accurately reflect the series, Paramount receives a royalty on the sale of each piece of *Deep Space Nine* merchandise. Overall, it's been estimated that total sales of all licensed STAR TREK merchandise has reached one billion dollars at the retail level.

Paramount's licensing division began to develop its plans for *Deep Space Nine* about the same time the public announcement for the series was made. The first product on the shelves was the novelization of the pilot episode, by J. M. Dillard, a noted science-fiction and horror writer who has written other original STAR TREK novels, as well as novelizations for the most recent STAR TREK features. Compared with the rush to have Dillard's novelization reach the stands at the same time the first *Deep Space Nine* episode was broadcast, other products for the series followed a more leisurely schedule. A series of comics from Malibu Graphics began publication in August 1993, and a line of wonderfully detailed action figures from Playmates was released in February 1994.

With the STAR TREK line of licensed merchandise, Paramount rarely has to initiate any ideas with potential licensees. Instead, manufacturers come to Paramount with their own proposals for products that they feel would be of interest to fans.

One suggestion came from production designer Herman Zimmerman, who responded with delight to a handmade present a fan had sent him. The creation was a small ball of fur to which had been added an ominous neural interface plate and a frightening weapon muzzle—that's right, it was a fully assimilated Borg Tribble!

Unfortunately, licensing had to reject Zimmerman's request that it look into manufacturing Borg Tribbles. The unwritten rule of licensing STAR TREK goods is that if it hasn't appeared on an episode or in a movie, then it can't be licensed. Of course, Zimmerman was told, if he would like to convince Rick Berman to produce an episode in which Borg Tribbles played a part, licensing would be happy to reconsider his request. Today, the lonely Borg Tribble occupies a place of pride atop Doug Drexler's computer monitor in the *Deep Space Nine* art department. (Among the other requests licensing has received and declined over the years, our favorite is the suggestion for children's contact lenses to make their eyes look just like Data's.)

These meticulously detailed action figures are part of a successful line of STAR TREK toys from Playmates, including both The Original Series and The Next Generation. Though the majority of these toys are purchased for children, the company estimates that a sizable percentage is also purchased by adults who simply want their favorite character to sit on their desk.

STAR TREK DEEP SPACE NINE EMISSARY #1

The extraordinary novel, based on the blockbuster pilot episode for the exciting new television series!

The Novel by J. M. DILLARD
Based on the Teleplay by MICHAEL PILLER
Story by RICK BERMAN & MICHAEL PILLER

The first in the new series of Deep Space Nine novels from Pocket Books.

MALIBU
AT THE EDGE OF THE FINAL FRONTIER
STAR TREK DEEP SPACE NINE
1
MIKE W. BARR · GORDON PURCELL · TERRY PALLOT

The first edition of the Deep Space Nine comic book from Malibu Graphics.

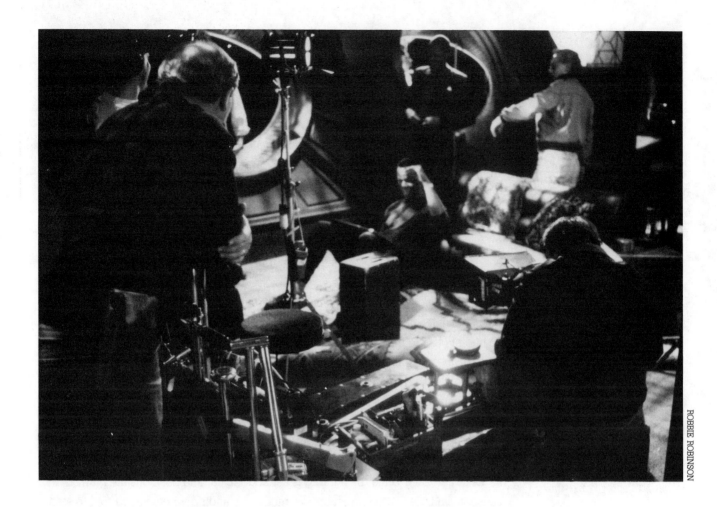

by a ladder, a rolling space-station bulkhead, or a lumbering equipment cart festooned with coiled cables and electrical switching boxes. When the stage crew moves, they *move*.

A uniformed fire marshal continually moves through the set, insuring that among the controlled confusion of hot lights and special-effects equipment, no inadvertent fire hazard springs up. Uniformed security guards are also a fixture around the stage doors, making sure that the only people on the set are those who are *supposed* to be on the set, but always with a friendly smile.[11]

During the setup period, the stars of the show—regular cast members and those making guest appearances—usually leave the set and go to their trailers. The trailers *are* actually trailers: small rooms on wheels parked outside the stages. For a regular cast member, a trailer contains a small sitting area up front, with a fold-down table, a phone, a television set, and, in Siddig El Fadil's case, a well-used Nintendo game, as well as a small bathroom and, at the far end, a minuscule bedroom where it's sometimes possible to stretch out during a long wait between scenes. Scattered about the trailer are an assortment of personal effects—books, scripts, carryall bags, as well as occasional bits of STAR TREK merchandise sent over by licensing, such as the latest *Deep Space Nine* novel with the cast member's face on the cover.

These trailers exist to preserve the cast members' sanity and peace of mind. After sixteen hours of work, when the actor steps on set to deliver her or his lines in the last

*The same design that makes the DS9 sets so realistic also makes for cramped working conditions. Here a shot in Sisko's quarters is set up with Avery Brooks's stand-in.*

[11]Of course, the trailers are also prime targets for practical jokes played by the cast on each other. When life-sized *Deep Space Nine* character stand-ups were first released, many of the cast members were startled to find their coworkers apparently hiding in their bathrooms and bedrooms.

*Director of photography Marvin Rush checks a camera angle with the stand-in for Avery Brooks.*

[12]On one memorable visit to the Paramount lot, we rounded the corner of a stage and found ourselves face-to-face with about forty Coneheads (from the Dan Aykroyd/Jane Curtin movie of the same name) on their break, drinking coffee, giving each other shoulder massages, and generally horsing around, all watched over by one lonely Borg who stood with his hands behind his back by another stage door, observing the Coneheads with a sad expression, as if his parents had forbidden him to play with the other aliens. It was a quintessential Hollywood moment.

[13]During the filming of the first-season episode "Dramatis Personae," Nana Visitor slipped on a rain-slicked stairway and wrenched her back. Even though she was prepared to do her scenes for the day, Rick Berman insisted she go to the hospital to be checked while a frantic search began for a Kira stand-in to take her place. When Visitor arrived at the hospital in full Bajoran makeup, she tried to tell the doctor about her back, but the doctor was far more concerned with doing something about her terribly broken nose.

[14]Supervising producer David Livingston, who has directed several superb *Deep Space Nine* episodes, including "Crossover," and the memorable "The Nagus" with Wallace Shawn, stands just under six feet and has a hairline moving into Jean-Luc Picard territory. However, he likes to

shot of the day, it's absolutely crucial that the actor look and sound the same as she or he did in the first shot of the day, and as she or he *will* sound in the middle of the next day. Having a quiet retreat where the urgency of the stage can be forgotten, even if for only a few minutes, is not a luxury, it's a necessity.[12]

The extras, of course, don't have the luxury of trailers, and when they're not congregated around the craft table, they can be found sitting on the chairs in the Replimat, or on the Promenade benches—anywhere they're out of camera range, so they can read paperbacks, knit, or wander outside to catch some fresh air.[13]

Also on the set are people who are clearly actors, yet who aren't in costume, wearing only twentieth-century street clothes. These are the stand-ins for the principal players. Note that stand-ins are not stunt doubles. Stunt doubles are a special class of actors who have a wide range of physical skills, and who win their roles by being able to resemble a specific character closely enough to take his or her place in potentially dangerous scenes. How dangerous? Well, anything from crashing over a railing and into the bar at Quark's to any instance where one of the main characters has to make sudden physical contact with another actor. All of the *Deep Space Nine* main cast are fit and capable of doing the bulk of their own physical stunts, but with the responsibility of the series resting on their shoulders, the studio quite rightly doesn't want to risk even the slightest chance of a sprained ankle or twisted back.[14]

But stand-ins never double for an actor in final film. For the most part, they are actors who are the same size and complexion as a main character, who literally stand in his or her place while the lighting is set and the camera positions are marked. In a sense, it's a little like being an artist's model—standing where you're told to stand, looking where you're told to look, and moving where you're told to move. Adjusting the lighting for the set and determining the focus settings for the camera are critical steps, but they can also be tedious. Thus, rather than add another hour or so of standing around to a principal actor's day, stand-ins are used to relieve some of the pressure of the principal's day.

The lighting of stand-ins and the setting of the camera positions are directed, naturally, by the director, who works closely with the directors of photography and lighting. The director is usually the most harried-looking person on the set, because he or she is the one responsible for keeping the principal photography on schedule.[15] Directors can usually be found in a tall folding chair, off to the side of the camera, watching the scene come together on a beat-up, twelve-inch black-and-white television set balanced on a plywood box.[16] During rehearsal—what little there is of it—they move among the actors, interacting with them. During shooting, they either sit or stand near the camera, sometimes walking along beside it if the shot involves a camera movement. And while the camera is being relocated and the lighting is being changed, the directors do what they do best—they worry.

Directors are not paid simply to worry on the set for seven or eight days, either. The Directors Guild sets fifteen days as the time a director has to complete an assignment for a one-hour, network, prime-time episode. Since a production incurs overtime charges for working on weekends, that works out to three weeks of worry because directors don't stop thinking about their assignment on weekends. Roughly

206    *The Making of Star Trek: Deep Space Nine*

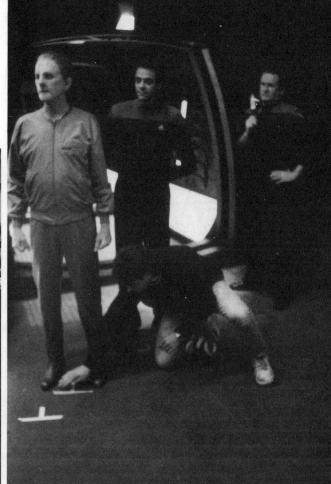

ROBBIE ROBINSON

speaking, the assignment breaks down into a week of preproduction, in which the director plans the shoot and attends preproduction meetings; then a week of shooting; followed by a week of postproduction in which the director talks over the episode with the editor and has input into the first rough cut. Past that first cut, though, the show passes directly into the hands of the producers.

Though we have not researched the contracts Paramount enters into with directors for *Deep Space Nine*, the Directors Guild minimum for directing a one-hour, prime-time, network episode is $21,542, plus 5.5% payable to the Guild as a pension contribution, and 7% payable to the Guild for health and welfare funds. In the case of "Emissary," the director, David Carson, would also have been entitled to additional compensation in recognition of the importance of a pilot episode in setting the look, feel, and characterization of a series.

Like actors and writers, directors also earn residual payments, starting roughly at 40% of the original minimum for a replay of an episode shot for syndication, and eventually reaching 5% for the thirteenth and each subsequent run.

Interestingly enough, as Rick Berman earlier noted, the role of a director on a television show is quite different from that of a director on a film. The film director is responsible for virtually everything that ends up on the screen, from costumes and makeup to sound effects and scoring. But on a television production, the producer is responsible for those things. The director's role is essentially limited to overseeing the photography of the acting. Where a film's director can make wholesale changes in a script on the fly, once the production is on the set the director of a *Deep Space*

*As rehearsal ends, the "marks" the actors must hit to stay in focus are taped to the ground.*

say that when he started as a director, he was six-four and had hair. . . .

[15]Previous to the production reaching the set, however, the director does have the opportunity to have input into the script during discussions with the producers, and during production meetings. Also, actors may generally have their own way with minor changes in the rhythm of the words they are to say, provided the content of their speeches doesn't change. For example, here's a comparison between written lines and filmed lines from the first-season episode "Past Prologue."

### AS WRITTEN

#### GUL DANAR

He is Khon-Ma! Even the Bajorans would not grant his kind asylum . . .

Sisko raises an eyebrow, glances at Kira . . .

#### GUL DANAR

He has committed heinous crimes against the Cardassian people . . . and I demand you release him to our custody . . . if you do not . . .

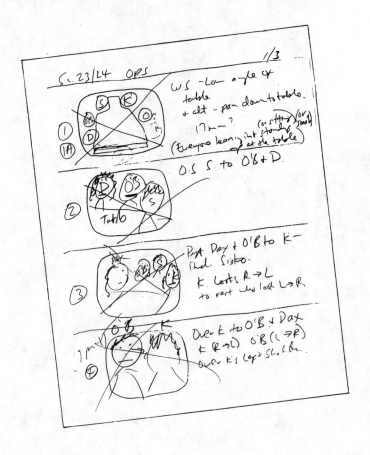

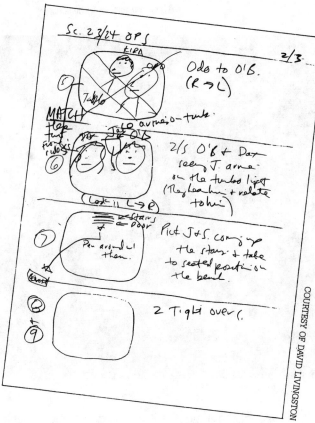

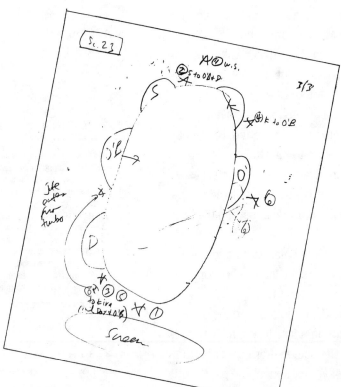

### A Director's Notes

Despite his misgivings about exposing an unsuspecting world to his, shall we say, "rough" artwork, David Livingston has generously provided these pages from his working script of "In the Hands of the Prophets," the last episode of the first season, which he directed. These sketches, which, to be fair, were intended for Livingston's eyes only, show his approach to covering scenes 23 and 24—a complex task because six actors must be accounted for. With the cost of production so high, it is imperative that directors do this type of visual planning before arriving on the set so the cast and crew aren't left waiting while the director searches for inspiration while the clock is running.

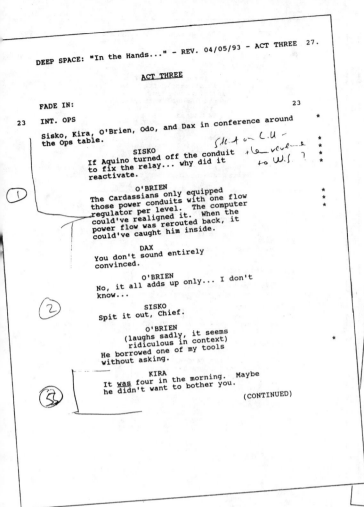
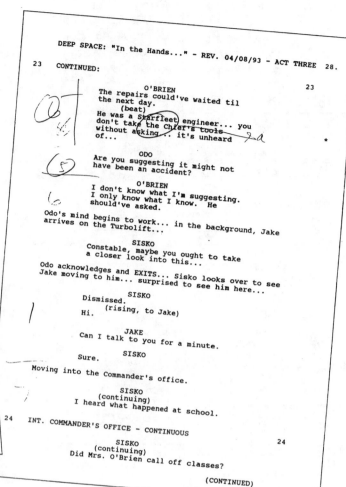

*Nine* episode must not allow a single word to change without specific permission from the producers.[17] In fact, just in case the director lets an inadvertent ad lib or changed line slip by, there is a vital member of the production team sitting right beside him—the person responsible for continuity, also known as the script supervisor.[18]

The script supervisor for *Deep Space Nine* is most often Judi Brown—a woman with an enormous talent for detail and the ability to keep accurate notes in fast-paced situations. She keeps track of every word spoken by the actors in a scene to make certain they match the script. She makes certain each scene goes before the camera, as well as tracking how many times it's shot—called "takes," as when the assistant camera operator calls, "Scene Thirty, take five"—and which of those takes are printed—as when the director calls, "Print it!"[19]

In an off-the-record discussion with one of *Deep Space Nine*'s directors, we commented on Rick Berman's reputation for allowing first-time directors to direct episodes of *The Next Generation*.[20] We speculated that Berman's generosity in this matter reflected either an extraordinary willingness to gamble on his part, or the fact that, in episodic television, directors are narrowly restricted in what they can bring to a show. The director conceded it was the latter. In fact, he continued, considering that by now (the end of the first season) the lead actors know their roles better than any director, all a director needs to be on these shows is an expert in scene blocking and lighting.

SISKO

(interrupting)
I'll immediately investigate the
matter. In the interim, if you'd
care to dock your vessel, I'll
be glad to hear your explanation
for having violated Bajoran space
and threatened a Federation
facility.

**AS FILMED**

GUL DANAR

*He is Khon-Ma! Not even the Bajorans*
*would grant his kind asylum . . .*

[Not as filmed, he doesn't.]

GUL DANAR

*He has committed heinous crimes*
*against the Cardassian people . . .*
*and I demand that you release him to*
*our custody . . .*

SISKO

[does not interrupt]
*I'll investigate the matter*
*immediately. In the interim, if*
*you'd*
*care to dock your vessel, I'll*
*be glad to hear an explanation*
*for having violated Bajoran space*
*and threatened a Federation*
*facility.*

[16]In film and television productions dating
back to the bad old days, the position of

## Top-left continuity log

| 59 | SR 23 | 4/16 | PROMENADE |
|---|---|---|---|
| 1 | :20 | COMPL | START ON THEIR BACKS 2/S WINN + BAREIL TURN TO FACE BACK GROUP AS SISKO ENTERS R. 1 FROM SCHOOL ROOM. |
| 2 | :51 | COMPL | |
| 3 | :51 | COMPL | |
| 4 | :54 | COMPL | |
| (5) | :50 | COMPL | |

| 59A | SR 23 | 4/16 | P/U W.S. WINN + BAREIL AS SISKO ENTERS |
|---|---|---|---|
| (1) | :24 | INCL | |
| | :25 | COMPL | |

| 59B | SR 23 | 4/16 | OU SISKO TO CROWD |
|---|---|---|---|
| 1 | :11 | COMPL. | |
| (2) | :12 | COMPL | |
| (3) | :08 | COMPL | |

| 59C | EFX | 4/16 | 24-72 FPS NEELA IN CROWD - THEY APPROACH SHE X FWD |
|---|---|---|---|
| (1) | :12 | COMPL | |
| 2 | :08 | INCL | |
| 3 | :08 | COMPL | |
| 4 | :07 | INCL | |
| 5 | :10 | INCL | |
| (6) | :10 | COMPL | |
| (7) | :11 | COMPL | |
| (8) | :10 | COMPL | |

| 59J | SR 24 | 4/16 | A - OU BAREIL + WINN TO CROWD B - X ON CROWD. REACT TO SPEECH THEN TO SISKO: "NO". CHAOS. |
|---|---|---|---|
| 1 | :09 | INCL | |
| (2) | :35 | COMPL | |

| 59R | MOS | 4/19 | 72 FPS, 200 mm SISKO'S POV OF BACK OF BAREIL'S HEAD |
|---|---|---|---|
| (1) | :07 | COMPL. | |
| (2) | :11 | COMPL | |

| 59S | MOS | 4/19 | 24 FPS, 200 mm SISKO'S POV OF BAREIL |
|---|---|---|---|
| (1) | :19 | COMPL | Dick This shot is OK |

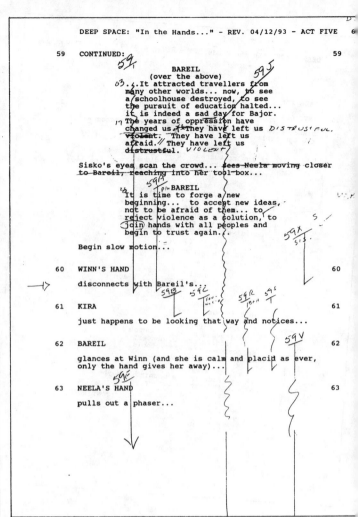

59 CONTINUED:           59

BAREIL
(over the above)
63.4 ...It attracted travellers from many other worlds... now, to see a schoolhouse destroyed, to see the pursuit of education halted... it is indeed a sad day for Bajor. The years of oppression have changed us ~ They have left us DISTRUSTFUL. violent. They have left us afraid. // They have left us distrustful. VIOLENT

Sisko's eyes scan the crowd... sees Neela moving closer to Bareil, reaching into her tool box...

BAREIL
It is time to forge a new beginning... to accept new ideas, not to be afraid of them... to reject violence as a solution, to join hands with all peoples and begin to trust again...

Begin slow motion...

60    WINN'S HAND           60

disconnects with Bareil's...

61    KIRA           61

just happens to be looking that way and notices...

62    BAREIL           62

glances at Winn (and she is calm and placid as ever, only the hand gives her away)...

63    NEELA'S HAND           63

pulls out a phaser...

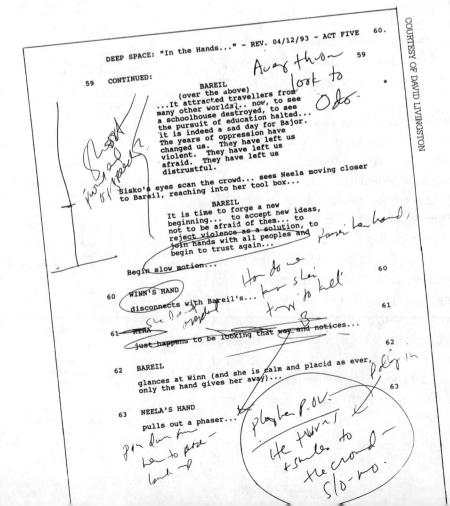

These pages are an example of the careful notes taken by Judi Brown, responsible for continuity during shooting. On the lefthand side, the numbers under each scene number keep track of each take and show how long each lasted in seconds. Circled takes are those to be printed. On the righthand side, the markings show what was recorded in each take, note script alterations, and record extra shots not specifically called for in the script—59A, 59B, 59C, etc.—which the director has added for extra coverage.

This is the director's copy of the same page shown from the continuity script. The difference in legibility is because only the director has to work from his script, while the continuity script becomes an important document for tracking the postproduction of an episode and must be read and used by many people.

Director Cliff Bole watching a scene play
out on a tiny, black-and-white television
set that shows what the
camera is filming.

Director Cliff Bole shows Colm Meaney
what the producers will rip from their
chests if the episode doesn't
wrap on schedule.

Rene Auberjonois checks Judi Brown's
detailed notes on her continuity script.

"Continuity" was often credited as "Script Girl."

[19]All live-action scenes for *Deep Space Nine* are shot on 35mm film negative. Any given reel of exposed film might contain several versions of a particular scene. For example, the first two takes in which actors missed their lines, a third take in which the actors said their lines in a way the director felt could be improved, and a fourth take, which the director and the actors feel is perfect. Of these four takes, the director might call for take three and take four to be "printed." That is, after the film negative of *all* the takes has been developed, takes three and four will be printed to a new negative to make a positive version of them. Those positive "printed takes" are then transferred to videotape and viewed by the producers, who will approve one or the other—or parts of both—for use by the editor in assembling the final version of the episode.

[20]Because the first season can be so critical in defining a series, Berman specified that only veteran directors of *The Next Generation* would direct first-season episodes of *Deep Space Nine*.

[21]Directing the actor to get up from his seat at the table. However, in the scene as shot, Garak did not get up until he began the last half of his final speech, with "Now, good day to you."

There is some truth in what this particular director says, but we think he's being too modest. Certainly directors must be expert in blocking a scene—that is, the mechanics of arranging and moving the actors to keep specific shots well composed, pleasing, and logical in terms of maintaining a natural flow of action. But directors also set the pacing of a show and, just as actors add shadings and subtext to their lines to make the sum of the parts equal more than the whole, directors can define the emotional content of a scene by the camera angles and movements they choose. The same line spoken in the same tone by the same actor can have entirely different emotional meanings depending on whether the actor has been shot in extreme close-up with an ominous slash of light across his face, or in a two-shot, or even from an unusual angle.

Take, for example, the humorous scene with which the first-season episode "Past Prologue" begins. Set in the Replimat, it shows Dr. Bashir's first contact with Garak, DS9's lone Cardassian, who claims to be a tailor though he's rumored to be a spy. As written—by Kathryn Powers—the scene ends like this.

---

Bashir tries tentatively to take the offensive . . .

> BASHIR
> You know . . . there are some who
> say you've remained on DS Nine
> as the . . . eyes and ears of your
> fellow departed Cardassians.

> GARAK
> You don't say. Doctor, you're
> not intimating that I'm considered
> some sort of . . . 'spy', are you?

> BASHIR
> (too quickly)
> No. Not at all. I don't even know
> you, Sir.

> GARAK
> Ah! An open mind. The essence
> of intellect.
> (rising)[21]
> As you may know, I have a
> clothing shop nearby, so . . . If
> you should require any apparel,
> or merely wish, as I do, for a
> bit of enjoyable company now and
> then, I'm at your disposal,
> Doctor.

Andrew Robinson and Siddig El Fadil as plain, simple Garak and his new friend at the Replimat.

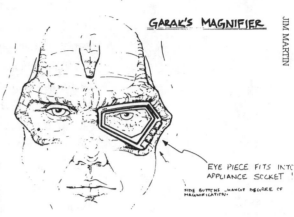

JIM MARTIN

GARAK'S MAGNIFIER

EYE PIECE FITS INTO APPLIANCE SOCKET !

SIDE BUTTONS CHANGE DEGREE OF MAGNIFICATION.

A plain, simple prop for Garak.

> BASHIR
> You're very kind, Mr. Garak.
>
> GARAK
> Oh, it's just Garak. Plain,
> simple Garak. And now, good day
> to you, Doctor . . . I'm so glad to
> have made such an interesting new
> friend today.

As he watches Garak depart, HOLD on Bashir—his face reflecting an enthusiasm which will carry over into:

---

This scene is a wonderful example of how an actor can enrich a script without changing a word. As Garak, Andrew Robinson[22] delivered his lines with a ingratiating smile while constantly shifting his eyes to keep track of everything going on around him. There should be no doubt in anyone's mind after this that he *is* a spy, or at least hopes to be thought of as one.

But Robinson's performance was enriched even more by the way in which the episode's director, Winrich Kolbe, chose to shoot the scene, and especially Garak.

The scene begins with an establishing shot of Bashir sitting alone at a table in the Replimat, drinking tea and reading a padd as Garak approaches.[23] After Garak speaks his first words of self-introduction, the scene then becomes a succession of alternating over-the-shoulder shots—we look over Garak's shoulder at Bashir, then cut to look over Bashir's shoulder at Garak, visually going back and forth, just as the

[22]A favorite to genre fans for his role as Larry, and later the resurrected Frank, in the first *Hellraiser* movie.

[23]At the beginning of almost every scene in a television episode, there will be a shot that should firmly establish where the actors are in relation to the set and to each other. This is called a master shot, and sometimes an entire scene will be filmed from this angle. Then the camera will move in and concentrate on just one or two characters at a time (a one-shot and a two-shot, respectively), while the entire scene is played out again with some actors off camera altogether. A scene involving four characters in Ops might result in five or six printed takes—one master, one close-up for each of the four characters, and one two-shot for part of the scene when two characters exchange a few lines of dialogue between themselves. This practice is called "coverage," as in, "The editor wanted to insert a close-up of Kira's reaction to Sisko's order, but the director didn't shoot enough coverage of her." Or, "The production is half a day behind schedule because the director shot too much coverage in Ops, yesterday."

dialogue goes back and forth. With this simple one-two treatment, Kolbe has created a rhythm for the scene.

But then, at the end of the scene, Kolbe breaks the rhythm and thereby adds more visual punch to Robinson as he delivers his last line.[24] The break comes when Garak stands and we cut back to the same view of Bashir we've had over Garak's shoulder. But this time, instead of cutting back to Garak as he speaks, the camera *moves in* on Bashir as Garak places his hands on the doctor's shoulders. Thus, just as Garak gets more personal with Bashir by touching him, we get more personal with Bashir by seeing him from a closer distance. This new vantage point also heightens the discomfort we see on Bashir's face. After all, how could we tell if Bashir *were* feeling more uncomfortable if we still saw him from fifteen feet back, as we did at the beginning of the scene? By getting close to him, his feelings are apparent, *and* magnified.

A final fillip is added to the scene when we finally do cut back to Garak. This time, we don't see him at eye level; we're looking up at him as he says, ". . . interesting new friend today." Looking up at actors generally makes them appear larger and, therefore, more imposing. This angle takes Garak's innocuous statement and weights it with vaguely threatening intent. Thus the director has added emotional resonance to the scene, just as skillfully as Robinson did with his shifting eyes and Siddig El Fadil did with his awkward hands and wide eyes.

These descriptions of the additional elements that actors and directors bring to *Deep Space Nine* might create the erroneous impression that the actors and directors have ample time for rehearsal and discussion of each scene, as they often do while making movies. But in episodic television, rehearsal is most often a quick run-through of starting and ending positions for the actors and the camera. The set is just too expensive a place for action and motivation to be worked out. One of the most important skills any television actor or director must have is the ability to instantly see a way to do something, and then instantly do it that way. The more time spent thinking about something inevitably means the longer the day, and the more onerous the overtime penalties will be.

Rehearsal for the principal actors can sometimes resemble a pajama party gone bad—almost no one is in his or her complete outfit. Armin Shimerman might be in full Ferengi makeup and wearing a terry-cloth bathrobe. Nana Visitor could run through a scene wearing a black leotard top with her jumpsuit open and flopping around her waist. Rene Auberjonois might be out of uniform in a black T-shirt worn under an incongruous gray windbreaker. Comfort is all important when it comes to enduring sixteen-hour days, and no one wants to wear bulky, constricting costumes until it's time for the camera to roll.[25]

The director takes the lead in the rehearsal, explaining to the actors how he sees them moving through the scene about to be shot. But one thing a director will rarely do is tell the actors how he thinks their character should deliver a line. In episodic television, it's understood that the character belongs to the actor, and no one will understand that character more fully than the actor. Thus, a director might suggest that the regulars try a particular scene with a bit more or less of whatever they're doing, but he will never dictate their performance the way a movie director might.[26]

[24]Breaking rhythm is a standard technique for setting an audience on edge by creating a sense of anticipation. Stand-up comics will deliver several setup lines in a fluid manner, pause to build expectation, then . . . give the punch line. In many horror films, the eerie background music (often augmented by a heartbeat pulse) will stop for a beat just before something jumps out at the heroes. An audience does not have to be aware of an existing rhythm in cutting or dialogue for them to become subliminally aware that the rhythm has suddenly been broken, making it an effective method to heighten suspense and interest.

[25]Colm Meaney, who is familiar with the uniforms worn on *The Next Generation*, feels that the *Deep Space Nine* uniforms are less binding and more comfortable.

[26]In STAR TREK, of course, it often happens that the regular characters are possessed by alien intelligences, offering the actors a chance to act outside the normal boundaries of their characters. In these instances, the director might become more involved with creating a performance, the way he might give more direction to a guest star creating a new character.

Rehearsals generally end with stagehands putting tape on the floor to indicate the actor's ''marks''—that is, the precise spots he or she should move to in order to remain in focus and in frame. Focus is set by extending a tape measure from the camera lens to the actor's position, and then setting the appropriate distance on the lens. If a scene requires movement on the part of the camera and a change in focus, it is the responsibility of the operator's assistant to manually change the lens settings at the correct moment in the scene.

While it seems a given that precise focus is critical in the filming of *Deep Space Nine*—or any series—new technology is giving the producers unparalleled techniques to correct errors after the fact.

For example, on one of the last days of filming for ''In the Hands of the Prophets,'' the final episode of the first season, a vital reaction shot of Sisko turned out to be out of focus. The shot—a close-up of Sisko realizing that an assassin was approaching through a crowd—was necessary for the episode's climactic sequence, but because it was such a simple shot, there was only one take, and it was unusable. Other producers might have torn out their hair and spent the money to relight the entire Promenade for just that one, split-second shot, or else cringed and allowed the shot to air as it was. But Rick Berman looked at the out-of-focus footage and simply asked, ''Can that be enhanced?'' Producer Peter Lauritson said, ''Yes,'' and that was the

*Cliff Bole gestures hypnotically as Judi Brown and Avery Brooks seem to reenact a favorite scene from E.T. Hey, when we talk about the chaos of producing a television series, we mean it.*

extent of the crisis. The out-of-focus footage was sent to Unitel, the supplier that transfers all filmed STAR TREK footage to digital videotape, and it came back in sharp focus! The contrast was a bit higher on the enhanced footage than it was on the other footage that came before and after, but on an ordinary television in the context of the whole scene, that increased contrast is barely perceptible.

Another element in the same episode also bothered Berman's sharp eye for detail. During an over-the-shoulder shot of another character talking, the actor with his back to the camera swayed ever-so-slightly back and forth throughout the scene. In person, or in a long shot, the movement would be almost unnoticeable. But since the actor's head and shoulder framed the shot in the foreground, Berman found the movement distracting. Again, rather than having the footage reshot, Berman asked that when the actor had swayed all the way to the left, the image from that specific frame be captured and printed on all the frames that followed. The result is that in the final shot, the actor sways gently to the left, then holds his position while everything else in the frame continues in action. The correction took less than ten minutes to make and, given the short time the shot remains on the screen, cannot be noticed.

After rehearsal, the principal actors leave the set while stand-ins take their positions and the lighting for the set is adjusted to be proper for the scene to be filmed. The actors use this time to memorize their lines for the upcoming scene, or to read a new script, make phone calls in their trailers, or be interviewed by inquisitive book writers. But it is also during this time, and other free moments during their long days, that they might arrange their own rehearsals with each other.

As an example of impromptu rehearsal, Armin Shimerman and Rene Auberjonois make use of the time they share having their makeup applied in the same trailer, side by side. On those days when their call times in makeup coincide, the two actors use the hour or so they're seated next to each other to run over any lines they might have together. For the second-season episode "The Siege," when Terry Farrell read the script and saw that she and Nana Visitor had many pages of dialogue on their own, to be filmed in the cramped quarters of a Bajoran spaceship, Farrell called Visitor and said, "My God, did you see what we have to do next episode?"

Farrell explains that "because we were shooting ten pages in two days and it was a ship called a 'rider'—smaller than a runabout—we knew we'd have a lot of added actions to perform, and to try to learn our lines over external sound and all the other confusion in a small set would be hard." So the two actors arranged to meet for breakfast and run over their lines, which helped them prepare for their two difficult days.

Given that every day sounds difficult for the cast of *Deep Space Nine,* what really makes the difference between an easy day and a truly hard day? Overall, the first two days of an episode's shoot are generally easier because, in most episodes, there hasn't been enough time to fall behind schedule. Actors don't tend to be forced at the beginning, and overtime is kept to a minimum. However, by the time the company has reached the last two days of an eight-day shoot,[27] the schedule is likely to be strained, the cast suffering from sleep deprivation, and the director fending off the producers who are worried about cost overruns.

For individual actors, whether a show is easy or hard is usually a function of how

[27]Ideally, it takes an average of six and a half days to shoot the live-action, first-unit portion of a *Deep Space Nine* episode. Seven days is the average.

large a part the actor has in that episode's script. Because *Deep Space Nine* is an ensemble show, the burden of carrying the show each week does not depend solely on one particular actor, as, for example, the series *Murder, She Wrote* depends on lead actor Angela Lansbury. Instead, it's possible to have an episode that focuses on Odo one week, giving Rene Auberjonois seven days of early calls and long hours, while Terry Farrell and Colm Meaney might only have to appear in two or three scenes filmed on one or two days. However, the next episode might have Odo in the background—giving Auberjonois time to catch up on his sleep—while Meaney and Farrell have to stay on set until two in the morning, reciting technobabble to each other. As a character who once played poker on *The Next Generation* said, "It's all relative."

However, even though we might expect that, given the ensemble nature of the series, the principal actors would make full use of their light schedules by staying away from the lot, we observed an unexpected situation on the set of *Deep Space Nine* that we'd never seen on any other set we've visited—that is, the extent of the camaraderie that already exists among the principal cast members. On our first visit to the set, the morning schedule was to film a long scene between Sisko and Odo in Sisko's quarters. Yet, long before they were needed in makeup or wardrobe, the other actors wandered on to the set in their street clothes to see how things were progressing. They traded tabloids to check up on the latest gossip about themselves, passed around a magazine with an article about the show, drank coffee, and basically caught up with one another before it was time to go to work. Most people tend to avoid their workplace until the last possible second, but to the cast of this series, their workplace is something to be enjoyed.

Of course, being the star of a television series gives an actor more freedom than is granted those who are hired as extras, which might account for the relaxed attitude the principal actors have toward their working conditions. For extras and minor performers, instead of being made up in a trailer, they are likely to be part of a gang makeup session in an unused stage, where rows of lighted mirrors have been set up.[28] They are herded onto the set as a group, instead of being politely called by an AD, hurriedly given their assignments by the AD to listen attentively to Sisko when he gives a speech, or murmur discontentedly among themselves,[29] or wander back and forth along the Promenade, then are warned to remove all jewelry, watches, and glasses, and are expected to be able to repeat each of their moves exactly for each new take.

Extras on *Deep Space Nine*, indeed on any show, are then faced with the dilemma of their trade. Ostensibly, they have been hired to be background characters who will not stand out, yet most of them have their sights set on an acting career and are eager to prove themselves. Hollywood tradition has it that sometimes all that needs to be done to accomplish that is to bring yourself to the attention of the director by some distinctive action or expression. Unfortunately, extras who try that kind of tactic on *Deep Space Nine* are sure to run afoul of Rick Berman's infamous eye for detail. While viewing dailies, he can pick out an errant extra from a crowd of forty. Anyone who attracts attention to himself or herself at the expense of the principal actors in the scene is not doing the job right, and Berman makes note of it.[30]

[28]A rule of thumb when it comes to budgeting and scheduling is that one makeup artist can handle four Bajoran noses (two, if they're going to be put on children), or one Cardassian. A team of forty extras, which includes only ten humans, with everyone else some kind of alien, can easily result in the need for ten to fifteen extra makeup artists.

[29]Any extra who utters a distinct line of dialogue that is written in the script must be paid a higher rate plus residuals each time the episode is rebroadcast. (See page 34 for a note about residuals.) However, for crowd scenes, extras are permitted to "ad-lib" certain lines at no extra charge, provided that the lines are not written in the script, but, instead, are merely "suggested" by the assistant director. Thus it's possible to have a crowd of extras murmur among themselves for the same cost as a silent crowd. In practice, though, the sound effect of a murmuring crowd is added by the sound editors in postproduction.

[30]Experienced extras passed on the following tip for those who want to succeed: At the beginning of the day, do all that you can to remain in the far background of scenes, never drawing attention to yourself. The logic behind this advice is that most of the extras are used in the establishing or master shots, and subsequently are hired only for half a day. Once those shots have been taken, fewer extras are needed as background in the close-up shots that follow and, if you have stood out in the first round of shots, directors will dismiss you so that you don't appear too often. Meanwhile, those extras who haven't been seen clearly will usually be asked to stay for the rest of the day, doubling their money *plus* getting a free meal—always an important consideration for beginning actors.

*A gang makeup session for DS9.*

[31]Adding sound effects is almost a universal pastime on *Deep Space Nine*. Actors add the sounds of doors opening and closing during rehearsal, Rick Berman adds phaser whistles and equipment beeps while watching dailies, and special-effects artists and editors add sound effects to every scene they work on. Presumably, they're gaining an impression of how the final scene will play when the actual sound effects have been added to the final cut. But one half of the team writing this book used to make similar sounds while playing with toy spacemen as a child, and suspects something much more primal is going on—these people are just plain having fun!

When it finally comes time for the principal actors to return to the properly lit set and perform their lines, every other activity on the set comes to a halt. The assistant director calls out, "Rehearsing," which is an instruction to all present that a "first-team rehearsal" is in progress and that they must speak softly and not move anything that could distract the actors. The actors then run through their lines and go for their marks. A camera assistant might double-check a measurement with a tape measure. The actors' personal makeup artists hover around with makeup-laden belts to perform quick touch-ups. Stagehands open and close airlock doors with ropes and pulleys while the rehearsing actors add their own sound effects.[31] Then, in a matter of minutes, the assistant director announces, "The next one will be picture," and it's time for the first take.

In the parlance of the set, when the camera is set to roll the company is "on a bell." The bell refers to the loud buzzer that sounds just before the camera rolls. Outside the stage on the busy streets of the lot, flashing red lights by every door wink on, warning those outside not to enter. On some stages, the flashing red lights extend to portable units mounted on platforms that keep trucks from rumbling past while a shot is in progress.

On the set, some actors sit patiently, others shake their hands and rotate their shoulders, others stretch their mouths and faces. No one talks, no one moves—

except for the old hands among the production crew who know exactly how loudly they can whisper without incurring the wrath of the director.

The assistant director announces, "Rolling," to let everyone know the camera is in operation. A camera assistant calls out "Speed!" to let the director know that the camera has reached and is maintaining its operational speed—twenty-four frames per second for normal motion, faster for slow motion. With that, a camera assistant holds the marker board in front of the camera and slaps down the clapper arm on it to make a sharp noise. The writing on the marker board will serve to identify the shot if it is chosen to be printed. The sharp noise combined with the movement of the clapper arm will serve to synchronize the film with the sound recording, which is being made on a separate piece of equipment.

If there are extras in the scene, such as shoppers on the Promenade or technicians in Ops, the assistant director gets them started by calling out, "Background." If something special is to happen at the top of the scene, such as an airlock door opening, then the director will call out an instruction for the door to open or close or whatever. And *finally* the director does what all directors live to do—call, "Action!"

This is when the real fun begins.

Consider a simple scene set in Quark's bar, involving Quark behind the bar and Odo in front of it, with some extras playing Dabo in the background. Perhaps five lines are going to be filmed in the exchange between Quark and Odo, during which Quark will pour a drink and Odo will check a tricorder. Even with those simple elements in the scene, the number of things that can go wrong approaches infinity.

First of all, actors miss their lines. *Every* actor. Those with stage experience, those without. Those with a ten-line speech, those with just one line. There is no shame and no stigma attached to missing a line, provided it doesn't happen *all* the time, and that it doesn't happen too often at two in the morning when the missed line is the only thing keeping everyone from going home.

Second of all, even when actors say their lines perfectly, they must at the same time remember to hit their marks. And if they remember to hit their marks, then they must hit them perfectly. Those are two more things that can go wrong.

Then there's continuity. Perhaps the first time the scene was filmed in a master angle, Quark began to pour a drink halfway through Odo's second line. Therefore, the close-up on Quark won't match unless he remembers to pour the drink again on exactly the same word. This is where the continuity checker is so important, because she marks up her script to indicate exactly where and when specific actions took place in previous takes.

Then there're props, sets, and mechanical effects. Will the tricorder light up properly? Will the bar stay motionless when Odo leans against it? Will Quark be able to pour the drink without making the pitcher and the glass clink together, ruining a word or two of dialogue?

And then, when everything has worked perfectly, will the extra shout "Dabo!" at the right moment? Or will the sound engineer announce that he could hear someone burp over his headphones? And last but not least, when the scene has gone perfectly right to the moment the director calls "Cut and print!" will the camera have operated cleanly? After every good take, the "gate" on the camera is checked to make sure it's

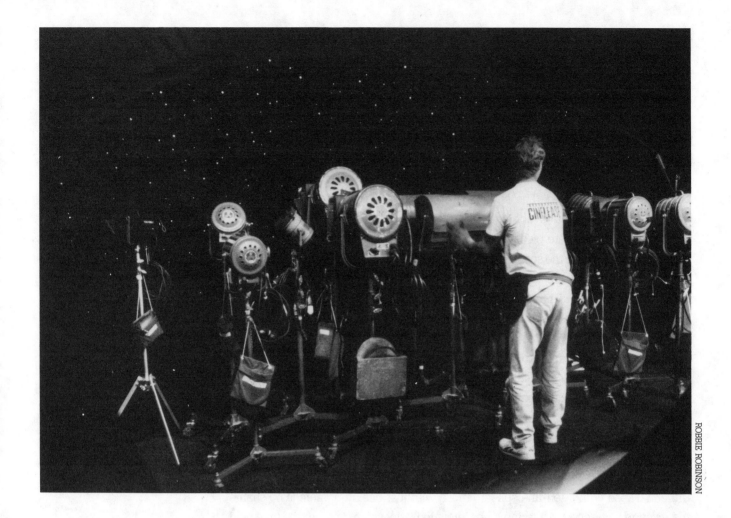

*When one looks out the windows of DS9, sometimes not all the lights in the sky are stars.*

free from dirt that might have left specks on the film. Only when the gate is pronounced clear can the director be relatively certain that he's got the shot he needs. And even then, more often than not, if there's the slightest reason for concern, the director is liable to tell everyone to resume their places and do it again for a "safety"—one additional shot just in case something unpredictable went wrong with the first one.

Eventually, though, the scene is completed to the director's satisfaction,[32] and the company starts to move to the next shot or, at the end of the shooting day, the AD announces, "That's a wrap," and it's time to head home.

But just because the *Deep Space Nine* stages shut down at night, or on a weekend, doesn't mean that work on a particular episode has stopped. Because the filming of live action on full-size sets is only part of what goes into a STAR TREK series.

Since the moment the first starship *Enterprise* blurred across the screen in the opening credits of *The Original Series*, there has always been one important element of STAR TREK that sets it apart from any other show on television—

—Visual effects.

Which are what we'll look at next.

[32]The critical factor here is the visual component of the scene. If there has been inadvertent background noise, or if an actor wearing prosthetic teeth has had trouble articulating certain words (for example, according to Armin Shimerman, the word "hellhole" is an absolute impossibility to say around Quark's teeth), dialogue can always be rerecorded in "looping" sessions after the episode has been edited.

# SEEING THINGS

FOURTEEN

# THAT AREN'T

# THERE

*The best visual effect is the one that*
*no one knows is there.*

—Adam Howard

T he human eye is endlessly adaptable. Put it in a dark room and its light-gathering ability increases, by the eye first opening its iris to admit more light, then changing the chemical receptivity of its retina. Move it to a brightly lit room and the iris closes and the chemistry changes again. Likewise, it can adjust its color-perception capabilities. Look into a house at night, and all the light inside coming from ordinary electrical tungsten lightbulbs looks orange. But go inside for a few minutes, and all colors appear normal as the eye adjusts. Reverse the process in the daytime and the sunlit outside will look harshly blue. But after a few minutes more under the sun, daylight looks natural again while tungsten lights resume their orange glow.

By comparison, film is a one-trick pony. Its emulsion can be formulated to achieve the correct color balance for tungsten light *or* for daylight, but not for both at the same time. And fluorescent lights will look sickly green under either extreme.

In the past ten years, research has yielded film and even computer-driven sensing devices that respond to a wide variety of lighting conditions, but still nothing has come close to the human eye's ability to discern color balance, shadow detail, and highlights at the same time.

Couple the human eye's light-sensing abilities with its further capability to determine distance and size based on three-dimensional binocular focusing, and almost any camera-film system might as well be built out of stone knives and bearskins, to coin a phrase. Even the digital-recording formats that are poised to

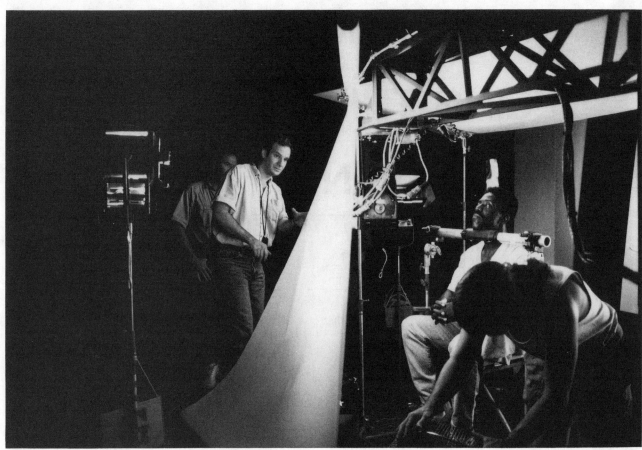

*Visual-effects supervisor Robert Legato, Director of photography Marvin Rush, and a stand-in for Avery Brooks conducting a test of Piller's "optical effect to be determined" at Image G.*

```
                                                           77.
        DEEP SPACE: "Emissary" REV. FINAL 8/10/92 - ACT FIVE

                                                           156

 156    CONTINUED:
                          KIRA
                 Yellow alert... secure Ops. Beam
                 it aboard Mister O'Brien, but put
                 it in a level one security
                 field...

                          O'BRIEN
                 Aye, sir... locking on...

        He presses some panels...
                                                           157

 157    ANGLE ON THE TRANSPORTER PAD (OPTICAL)

        As the orb MATERIALIZES... and the orb disintegrates
        into spinning light and disappears revealing Dax.  Off
        reactions.
                                                           158

 158    WHITE SCREEN (OPTICAL)

        Discovering a state-of-the-art optical effect to be
        determined... that suggests Sisko in an altered
        state... no reality we've ever experienced... it may
        be just his eyes in some disengaged fashion... for this
        draft, it will be described as 'WHITE SCREEN   SISKO'S
        EYES'.  A heartbeat and breathing the only sounds...
        suddenly --
                                                           159

 159    A RUSH OF IMAGES (OPTICAL)

        Five separate shots, each less than a second:

                 --Jennifer looking up at the beach...
                 --Sisko's bloody burned hands...
                 --A baseball landing in a catcher's
                 mitt...
                 --Locutus on a viewscreen...
                 --Jennifer's lifeless hand on the
                 Saratoga...
                                                           160

 160    THE WHITE SCREEN - SISKO'S EYES (OPTICAL)

        As before.  Heartbeat... breathing...

                          SISKO
                 Who are you?

        No response... only --
```

*This is where visual effects begin—the written word. Check out Michael Piller's challenge to STAR TREK'S optical-effects wizards: ". . . a state-of-the-art visual effect to be determined . . ."*

replace many of film's uses in the next decades suffer from limited capabilities when compared to the natural eye.

Yet the camera/film system—or, for futurists, the camera/recording-medium system—is the only technology currently available that allows us to record events in a manner and with details similar to the way we see them in person. Digital filming technology *is* fast approaching, though for now, matching the resolution of film is an expensive and time-intensive proposition. In any event, a lens system—or at least a holographic replica of a lens system—is still required to focus light on CCDs (charged coupling devices for sensing light, such as those found in video cameras), just as lenses focus light on film today.

The art of visual effects, then, is to manipulate all the individual components of the camera/recording-medium system to create images of impossible (or expensive or dangerous) things and events that can trick our eyes into perceiving those images are real. For the record, in television *"special* effects" refers to a class of effects that are created on the live stage, such as explosions, automatic doors, flying, etc. These are also known as practical or mechanical effects. On the other hand, *"visual* effects" are those effects created off the set, including starships in flight, phaser bursts, alien landscapes, and so on. And when it comes to creating visual effects for *Deep Space Nine,* when we say *all* the components of the system are used, we mean *all.*

*Above left:*
*Chris Schnitzer hauling the DS9 model into position on the Bulldog rig at Image G.*

*Above right:*
*Dennis Hoerter checking the DS9 model before a "window pass." The camera on the Bulldog rig can be maneuvered to within a fraction of an inch of the model.*

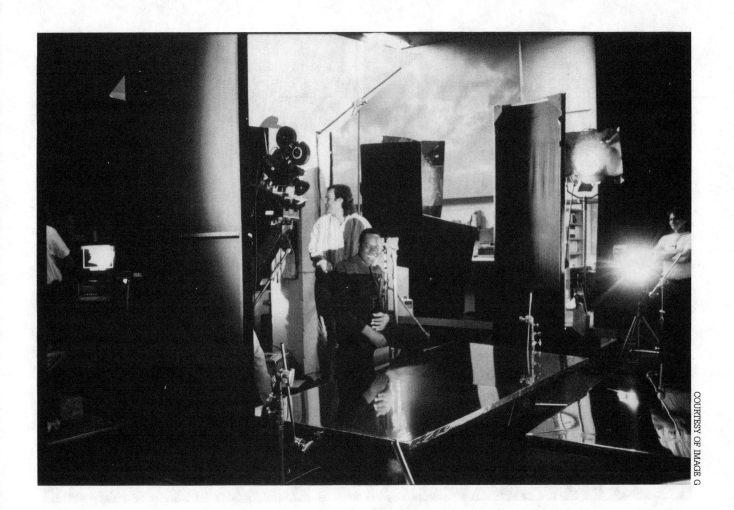

*For the episode "Move Along Home," Avery Brooks prepares to film his fall into a bottomless pit at Image G. The bottomless pit was shot separately.*

The techniques used on *Deep Space Nine* run the gamut from miniature photography, to matte paintings, to computer manipulation *and* creation of images. As visual-effects producer Dan Curry says, "We use a variety of techniques—whatever works for a particular shot. And sometimes we invent a technique for the problem at hand."

Though the techniques used to create visual-effects shots for *Deep Space Nine* are many and varied, the people responsible for them all share the same characteristic—in addition to being artists, they are also technicians of the first order, combining aesthetics and technology to deceive our eyes and effortlessly transport us to the twenty-fourth century, when Starships can emerge from wormholes and orbit alien worlds, without betraying the trickery that has brought these wonders to visual life.

That they're technical wizards is proven each week as their effects dazzle and entertain viewers. That they're artists is proven by the fact that even though they all use the same equipment, no one uses the exact same method as another. Invariably, when we asked one visual-effects specialist how a particular shot was achieved, the details we were given didn't match what a second specialist had told us. In trying to explain to Specialist One what Specialist Two had told us, we would usually get quizzical looks and be asked two questions in return—"He does it *that* way? I wonder why?" Fortunately, because the creation of visual effects *is* an art form,

differences in style and technique are not as important as the final result, which for *Deep Space Nine* is always of the highest quality.

Here's an inside look at how these artist-technicians work some of their magic.

*The Bulldog rig filming a "cloud bank" made of cotton fibers.*

## Miniatures

Don't tell the Cardassians, but Starfleet's vast armada of ships is safely stored in wooden packing crates on the Paramount lot. Come to think of it, the vast Cardassian armada is there, too, along with the Klingon armada, the Ferengi armada, the Romulan, and a horde of other alien ships. It makes no difference that some of these armadas number no more than a single ship—photograph it ten times and you'll have ten of them easily enough.

One important miniature space object that is not stored with the others is DS9 itself. It's so big—six feet in diameter—and is used so often that even now, toward the end of the series' second season, a packing crate for it has not yet been built. Instead, it spends its downtime wrapped in foam rubber and covered by a large white sheet, lodged behind some old theater seats in the studio where all of *Deep Space Nine*'s miniature work is done—Image G.

Like most of the suppliers of visual effects for Hollywood, Image G is an independent company located off the Paramount lot, and contracts with the studio

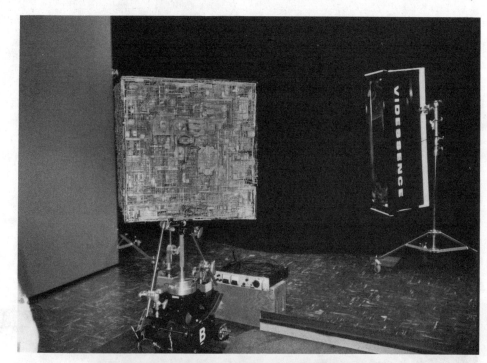

The Borg ship mounted for filming for the pilot episode re-creation of the Battle of Wolf 359. Note the movable platform to which the ship is attached.

The back side of the Borg ship, showing access to interior lighting and another mounting point.

on a season-by-season basis. In keeping with Rick Berman's pursuit of excellence—a continuation of Gene Roddenberry's edict that *Next Generation* visual effects look "real," and not like *The Original Series'* effects—Image G is a company renowned for its work in feature films, including the technically demanding *Flight of the Intruder.*

Image G's specialty is what's known as "motion control" photography.

Back in the days of the *Flash Gordon* serials, model rockets were hung on strings and pulled through a shot while being filmed at a normal camera speed of twenty-four frames per second. Sometimes a rocket might be double-exposed onto a

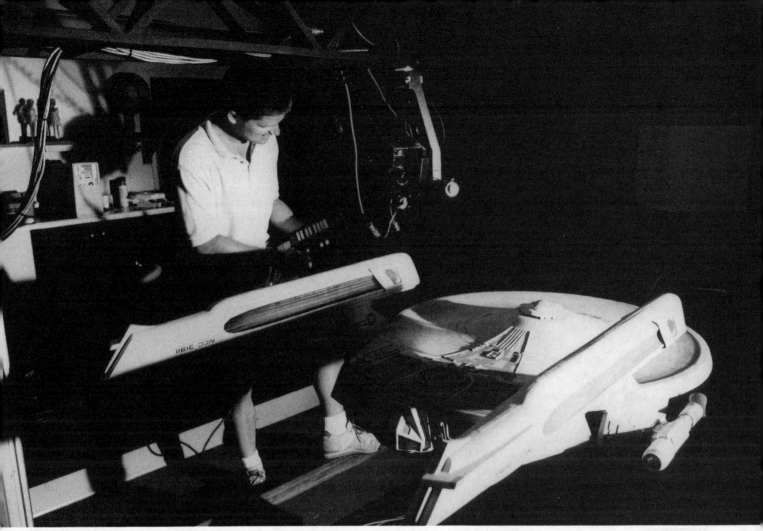

background plate showing stars or an alien planet, but that was the extent of the camera trickery involved. Any lighting effects, such as a rocket's burning exhaust, were filmed at the same time as the rocket, so the scale of the model was often given away by tendrils of smoke that viewers could recognize as coming from a sparkler and not a full-size, spacegoing vessel.

Needless to say, as audiences became more demanding, the technology of visual effects improved by necessity.

The hallmark of motion-control photography is the ability to photograph different visual elements of a model *on separate exposures*. For example, if you think of low-budget science-fiction films of the fifties, and even the sixties, you can probably remember scenes in which spaceships were obviously models because only parts of them were in focus at any one time. This was a result of the use of close-up lenses that had a limited depth of field—if the front of a twelve-inch-long spaceship was in focus, the back of it would be out of focus.

One way out of this technical dilemma was to add considerably more light to a scene. Then the camera lens could be "stopped down." That is, the opening—called an aperture—through which the light passed on its way from the lens to the film was made smaller. When this happens, the lens's depth of field increases. Pump lots of light onto a twelve-inch model and with a small enough aperture, the whole thing will be in focus, exactly as if it were a life-size rocket seen at a distance.

*Camera operator Erik Nagh programming a move for Sisko's ship, the Saratoga. Depending on the camera angles required, models can be mounted rightside up or, as in this picture, upside down.*

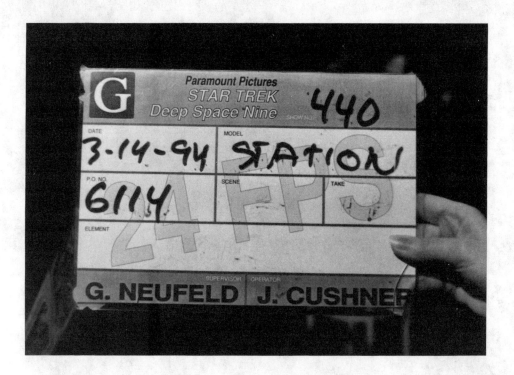

A title card for a motion-control shot, showing it's being shot at normal speed—24 frames per second.

If adding more light to a shot was not practical—because it might melt the plastic detailing, for example—another way to solve the problem was to increase the exposure time for a frame. Film exposure follows, for the most part, a clear-cut mathematical pattern. If a given amount of light will properly expose a shot for, let's say, an exposure of one sixty-fourth of a second, then half that amount of light will yield the same results for an exposure that is twice as long—one thirty-second of a second.

However, this solution raised several new problems. First of all, there were definite limits as to how long a given exposure could be, especially if the rocket model was swinging by on a length of black thread or fishing line. If an exposure was too long, the rocket would be blurred. If the exposure was too short, then the other lighting effects might not be bright enough to expose the film.

The ideal situation was to photograph the model and the lighting effects separately—a simple matter if the model was still, but how could this be accomplished if the model was moving?

The answer was to arrange a system by which the model could make the identical movement over and over again. Hence, motion control.

The first large-scale use of a motion-control system was for the groundbreaking science-fiction film *2001: A Space Odyssey*. The models—several of which were so large that they could not be easily moved—were fixed in place while the *camera* was put on special tracks on which it could advance increment by increment. (On film, it makes no difference to the final visual effect if the camera is moving toward the model or the model is moving toward the camera. Yet another example of relativity.)

A model, such as the lengthy spaceship *Discovery*, was lit to yield the proper exposure for its bright white surface. The camera was locked in position. A single frame was exposed. Then the camera was manually moved forward to the next

The DS9 model, dwarfed by the Bulldog rig.

position, where another frame would be exposed, and so on until the camera action had been completed.

Then, the camera was moved back to its original starting position and *the film was rewound in the camera.* The outside lights shining on the model were extinguished and the interior lights showing windows were turned on. Then, on the very same exposed frame of film on which there was already a latent image of the fully lit *Discovery,* a second, double exposure was made, calibrated for the intensity of the interior lights.

After the frame was exposed, the camera was once again moved forward by the identical increment it had been moved before, and the second frame of film was advanced into position for a second double-exposure.

On and on the process went, with each exposure and each camera position tediously marked down by hand. A mistake in the last set of exposures meant starting the whole process from the beginning.

But the hard work was worthwhile. *2001* set a new standard for excellence in science-fiction imagery, and the techniques pioneered in its creation reached their greatest heights in the third *Star Wars* film, *Return of the Jedi*.[1]

By the time *Jedi* was made, motion-control photography had evolved to the point where film was being exposed dozens of times on dozens of separate passes. A single X-Wing Fighter could be placed in position and photographed on three separate passes. Then, with the camera returned to its original starting point, the X-Wing would be placed in a new position and the same set of exposures would be made. When this was repeated often enough, by the time the film was developed that single Fighter had created an entire formation of spacecraft banking through space. The breakthrough that had made this level of complexity possible was, of course, computer control.

Today, operating out of a nondescript studio about ten minutes from the Paramount lot, Image G[2] continues to push the envelope of what is possible with motion-control photography. Owner Tom Barron, who has been in the business for almost twenty years, started Image G the year before *The Next Generation* began production. His original intention was to focus on the production of commercials, because in its constant search for new techniques and effects commerical production helps propel the visual-effects industry.

However, one year later, when *The Next Generation* was in full production, visual-effects supervisor Robert Legato came to Image G with the first Ferengi Starship. He wanted it photographed to match footage of the *Enterprise* that had already been shot at George Lucas's Industrial Light and Magic in Marin County.[3] The Ferengi ship footage turned out so well that Image G has ended up shooting all the motion-control photography for *The Next Generation* ever since, and has shot all motion-control footage for *Deep Space Nine* as well.

Motion-control work for *Deep Space Nine* is considerably different from that done in the early days of *2001*, or even the more advanced system used in the *Star Wars* films. In fact, Tom Barron says, the software that drives his motion-control rigs changes almost weekly as new advances are brought on-line.

A key capability of the motion-control rig—called "the Bulldog"—used for *Deep Space Nine* is that as the camera moves, so can the model. To be sure, it is the camera that provides the linear motion, but at the same time the camera approaches or recedes from a model with graceful arcs, the model itself can be moved in three axes on its own platform. Each movement of the platform is recorded along with the camera position, so each combined motion can be replayed endlessly. And "endlessly" is an important word. For the pilot episode, "Emissary," the shot through the window of Sisko's escape pod leaving the *Saratoga* required *sixty-seven* separate film elements.[4]

Why so many? Let's take a look at a simpler shot from the pilot—the Act Two opening shot of DS9, looking up at its pylons to see the *Enterprise* docked with Bajor in the background. On the printed page, the scene was simply described like this.

[1] For a convoluted piece of STAR TREK trivia, the story is that the working title for *Return of the Jedi* was *Revenge of the Jedi*. While it was in production, Paramount announced the second STAR TREK film as *The Vengeance of Khan*. Lucasfilm took exception to Paramount using a title it felt was too close to its own, so Paramount changed its title to *The Wrath of Khan*. Then Lucasfilm realized that Jedi knights should be above such petty concerns as revenge, and changed *its* title to *Return of the Jedi*. Some early promotional materials for both films that use their original titles are sought-after collector's items.

[2] Why Image *G*? Well, one version has it that in the industry, properly exposed footage is considered a "G" image, while improperly exposed footage is "NFG." We leave the rest up to you.

[3] In terms of receiving the most recognition for the least work done, one of the best credits in the history of television appears at the end of every episode of *The Next Generation*: "Special Visual Effects—Industrial Light and Magic (ILM) a division of Lucasfilm Ltd." Whoever negotiated that credit was a master of the trade, because ILM didn't shoot a frame of film for *The Next Generation* series other than for the pilot episode in 1987. However, because of that credit, it has been reaping the positive association with the show's visual effects ever since. To be fair, however, ILM is an industry leader and will provide many of the key visual-effects shots for *Star Trek: Generations*.

[4] Unlike earlier motion-control systems in which film was rewound and reexposed for subsequent passes, each pass shot at Image G is exposed on fresh film. In this system, if something goes wrong with one of the passes—power failure, someone bumping a light, scratched film, or a city-destroying earthquake, to name just a few possibilities—the other passes aren't lost as well. Because the Image G system stores every camera movement, it's possible for one sequence of passes to be filmed, then to reconfigure the rig for a different shot, and two days later come back and reshoot just one element of the previous sequence in order to correct a flaw.

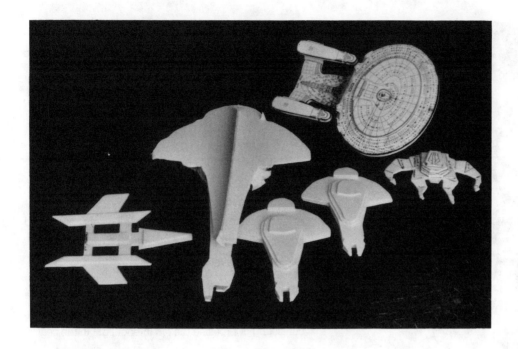

*Some of the quick-and-dirty foamcore models used for positioning guides on "reference passes."*

---

FADE IN:

41  EXT. SPACE - THE ENTERPRISE (OPTICAL)

docked at DS9.

---

But the photography required to create that three-word scene breaks down like this:

| MODEL | EXPOSURE |
|---|---|
| DEEP SPACE NINE & FOAMCORE *ENTERPRISE* | 1. Reference Pass<br>—The *Enterprise* and DS9 models are built to different scales,[5] so for the final sequence they are photographed separately at different distances from the camera to make them appear at the same scale.[6] However, as a positioning guide for the visual-effects supervisors, a flimsy, rough foamcore model of the *Enterprise* at the same scale as the station is filmed in position on the docking pylon, and then removed. |
| DEEP SPACE NINE | 2. Beauty Pass<br>—For this pass, the model is lit only by a strong directional light source, with a small amount of "fill" light, which enables some detail to be seen in the shadow areas. |

[5] Just as there are several different-sized models of the *Enterprise*, there are three different models of DS9. Unlike the *Enterprise*, though, the two additional DS9s are only partial models. One is a cut-in-half version of the station, rarely used, constructed so the camera can look out from the interior rings. The second is a large detail of a runabout launch platform on the exterior ring, which was used for a shot in the pilot, and, to date, has not been used since.

[6] In fact, even in scenes such as the one in "Sanctuary," in which seven ships are shown docked or docking with DS9, each model is shot separately.

The visual-effects supervisor and camera operators can quickly review each motion-control shot by means of a video pickup on the film camera. In the past, a motion-control rig would have to remain set up for hours while film was developed and printed in order to see if a shot had worked.

3. Window Pass

—Now, the exterior, directional light source is switched off and the model's interior lights (lit by neon tubes inside the model) are exposed, using a slight diffusion filter to give them a glow.[7]

4. Second Light Pass

—The window lights are turned off, and the exterior lights shining along the docking pylons (known as the "Malibu" lights) are exposed.

—At the same time, the exterior strobe lights are turned off and on for the appropriate frames to make them appear to blink in the final footage.

5. Power Station Pass

—This is also indelicately known as the "Dingus" Pass, consisting of exposing the red interior light in the central power core, again shot with a diffusion filter.

6. First Matte Pass

—The purpose of a matte is to create a stark silhouette of the model to be used to drop out visual information from the background, thus avoiding a double-exposure in which we might see stars shining through the station. The First Matte Pass involves using an orange card to block the left side of the frame holding the station in position.

7. Second Matte Pass

—The right half of the frame is covered.

8. Third Matte Pass

—Now the orange card is used to mask the platform the model sits on.

9. Star Pass

—The starfield behind DS9 is most often generated by a half-cylinder core of Plexiglas, painted black, through which thousands of tiny holes have been poked to allow backlighting to shine through.[8]

BAJOR

10. Planet Pass

—There are many different ways in which planets are created for *Deep Space Nine*, but one common method is to project a 4 × 5 transparency of a planetary surface onto a white half-sphere.

11. Planet Matte Pass

—Shot so the background stars will not shine through the planet.

[7]Strictly speaking, in the vacuum of space, lights don't glow as they do within an atmosphere clouded by water vapor and dust. This is the same artistic license that lets STAR TREK spaceships make noises in space.

[8]Experiments are under way to try and render stars through computer graphics, though a cost-effective technique for realistically combining computer-generated stars and filmed models hasn't yet been satisfactorily developed.

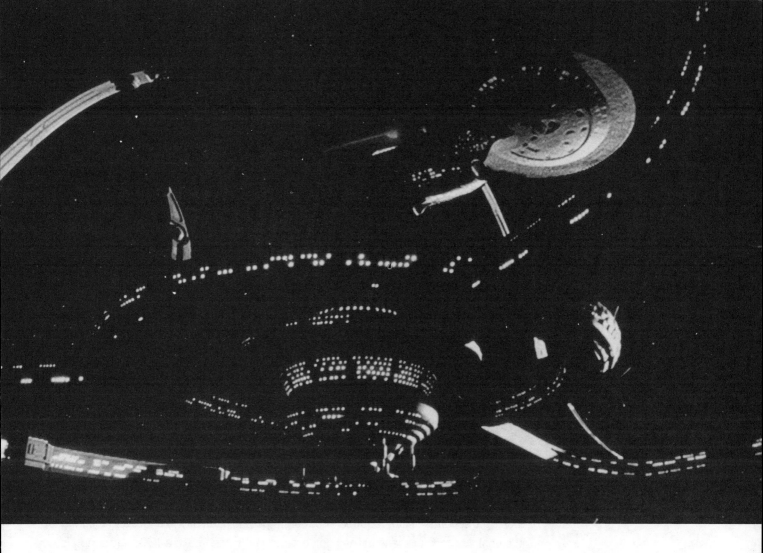

ENTERPRISE

12. Beauty Pass

—This pass is lit from the same source as that which lit
the station model so all the shadows will match in
intensity and direction. For *Next Generation* episodes,
the *Enterprise* was shot with more fill light so the
shadows were not as deep.

13. Window Pass

—The same as for the station.

14. Second Light Pass

—The same as for the station, this exposure is for the
exterior lights and strobes.

15. Nacelle Pass

—This pass adds the glow to the warp nacelles.

16. Matte Pass

—A single pass works for the *Enterprise* because it is
smaller than DS9.

*This shot of the Enterprise docked at
DS9 is a composite of more than ten
different exposures of the two
models shot separately.*

Now think of what was required for the sixty-seven-exposure scene in which the Borg destroy the *Saratoga*. In addition to the Borg ship and the *Saratoga* in the scene, there are an *Excelsior*-class Starship, three escape pods, and the debris from the *Saratoga*'s explosion. Adding to the shot's complexity is the number of light sources—an off-camera nearby star, along with energy beams and an explosion. Because the Borg ship had to appear to be illuminated by the *Saratoga*'s explosion, it required an additional pass for what is called "interactive lighting." In this exposure, the model is brightly lit so every detail is visible. Then, when all the various exposures are being put together—a process called compositing—for the frames of film in which the light from the explosion must play over the Borg ship, the artist responsible for the shot takes regions of the fully exposed model and overlays them on the darkly lit model. The effect is as if another light source has been added to the model. This interactive lighting element is then colored to match the color of the explosion, and the illusion is complete.

As far as sixty-seven exposures seeming complicated, visual-effects producer Dan Curry holds a personal record of a shot on *The Next Generation* with more than 140 exposure elements. And when computer-generated effects are added to the mix, the sequence from the pilot in which Dax disappears into the Orb inside the wormhole had *200* separate "layers" of images.

Going back to the relatively simpler shot of DS9 and the *Enterprise*, each of the sixteen passes took about ten seconds to shoot—five seconds for the actual shot, with standard, two-second-long "heads" and "tails" at the beginning and end. But those 160 seconds of film required about eight people a full day to shoot and resulted in a final five-second scene in the pilot, covering only one line in a 124-page script. Is there a faster and less expensive way?

Yes and no.

Certainly there are shortcuts that can be taken regarding the complexity of the models. Occasionally, alien ships will be constructed without built-in interior lights. To give the impression of interior lights, though, a bundle of small lights called "strap-ons" are artfully arranged over the model for the light passes. Viewed in person, this makes a spaceship model look as if it has been buried in a coil of discarded Christmas lights. But onscreen, when the light pass is combined with the beauty pass, the spaceship will appear to be studded with brightly lit windows.

For shots in which whole fleets of ships have to be shown, as in the first-season episode "Sanctuary," four or five small models can be shot at once, instead of one at a time. We must note, however, that these time-saving techniques are used only when the nature of the shot is such that there's no chance that visual quality will suffer. Certainly, if an episode required many close-ups of an alien ship, a model would be built with interior lights. Likewise, if a shot of an armada of ships was going to remain onscreen long enough for viewers to study it in detail, each ship would be shot individually. With Rick Berman's sharp eye watching over every detail, it could be no other way.

With the examples of the motion pictures *The Abyss, Terminator 2,* and *Jurassic Park* before us, an obvious question is: How much longer will *Deep Space Nine* and other STAR TREK series be shot with miniatures instead of being created by

These two ports are usually hidden on the DS9 model—they're the plugs that control the interior lighting.

CGI—computer-generated imagery? We asked this question of almost everyone connected with the series' visual effects, and their answers were identical: Someday, almost all visual-effects work will be done in the computer, but that day is still a few years distant for STAR TREK. The reason, most visual-effects workers said, is that for now it is faster and less expensive to build a miniature spaceship as a physical model than as a computer model, and that, again for now, filmed miniatures, with their real-world textures and imperfections, impart a more realistic look to the final shot than the too-perfect crispness of CGI spaceships.[9]

However, anyone who's watched first-season episodes of the syndicated science-fiction series *Babylon 5* knows that that final statement is open to debate—all of that show's space sequences are created by CGI on the Amiga Video Toaster system.[10] Certainly, the unnamed moon around which B5 orbits is obviously a computer graphic with smeared and unconvincing surface detail. However, some shots of the various spaceships that fly around the station are coming startlingly close to the look of filmed miniatures. Given the increase in quality between *Babylon 5's* pilot in January of 1993 and the beginning of its first season in February 1994, it is very reasonable to assume that within a year or two, the realism of the CGI effects will consistently come close to or be equal to that of filmed miniatures. Then the miniatures vs. CGI debate will be over artistic content, not technical ability.

[9]In fact, Image G goes to great lengths to avoid computer perfection even in the computer-driven motion-control of its model photography.

The computer system that runs the Bulldog rig is able to plot a camera move once the operator has specified a starting point and ending point. However, the result is a smooth and perfect arc. Therefore, in designing motion-control camera moves for *Deep Space Nine*, the operators don't let the computer do all the work. Instead, the camera is moved by the operator using a remote control, almost as if it were a handheld-camera shot. The result is a more realistic-seeming camera move with odd shakes and direction corrections at an almost subliminal level. The computer then remembers the camera's position at each point along the path and reproduces it exactly each time the move is rerun.

[10]By the end of its first season, the *Babylon 5* CGI unit consisted of a four-person

All STAR TREK models—except DS9 itself—are kept in sturdy plywood boxes for storage. Polaroids on the outside keep track of what's inside.

animation crew operating a computer system that includes Macintoshes, PCs, and, for image rendering, twenty-two 2000 Amiga/Toasters, coordinated by a 15-gigabyte DEL XE 4000 server.

[11] Model kits have saved considerable money for *Deep Space Nine*'s ongoing production as well. When a second-season script called for a runabout to be destroyed, rather than using a multi-thousand-dollar, hand-built miniature, the art department assembled an ordinary runabout model kit for Image G to explode.

[12] First-season visual-effects supervisor Robert Legato was responsible for the station's exterior color scheme, and for the addition of the outside "Malibu" spotlights shining up the docking pylons.

[13] Movies are another matter. As of this writing, Industrial Light and Magic will use a CGI model of the *Enterprise* 1701-D for some of the visual-effects shots in the *Next Generation* feature.

However, the intriguing point that it is sometimes quicker and less expensive to build a physical model than a computer model does have some merit—though it is not an absolute statement. For example, once plans had been approved, the six-foot DS9 model took several months to be built by Brazil Fabrication, the sophisticated modelmaking company owned by Tony Meininger. Meininger and his crew began with a welded steel frame weighing sixty-five pounds, over which molded epoxy fiberglass was applied. Then the basic surface design of each distinct section of the station was built from plywood, and sheets of styrene plastic were vacuformed over them.

Continuing with a tradition begun on *2001: A Space Odyssey,* these plastic forms were detailed with small plastic parts from model kits to add realistic texture to the surface.[11] Then these detailed sections were cast in silicon rubber, the rubber was used as a mold to cast epoxy, and the resulting castings were assembled on the steel frame, leaving room for the neon tubes, transformers, and wiring that are needed to produce the station's interior lights.[12]

No one wants to talk about how much money this lengthy process cost, but the result is one of the most realistically detailed models ever built for filming, which is also rugged enough to withstand the rigors of almost weekly use.

The *Babylon 5* station was also originally conceived as a physical model like DS9. The show's visual-effects supervisor, Rob Thornton, had estimated that it would take six to eight people a month and a half to build the model, using between ten to fifteen thousand dollars in materials. However, working on his Amiga Video Toaster, Thornton was able to "build" a computer model of the B5 station in two weeks, with no charge for materials.

Clearly, for major undertakings, CGI does have the ability to save time and money. However, in television production, major undertakings are few and far between.[13] Extensive attention was lavished on both the DS9 physical model and the B5 CGI model, because both space stations would serve as the visual focus for their respective series over, the producers of both shows hope, many years. But the reality of day-to-day television production is such that the "alien ship of the week" usually has to be slapped together in a day for no money.

That *can* be done with physical models. Appropriate shapes can be carved out of styrene foam in less than an hour. Plastic skin and model-kit parts can be glued on by skilled fingers on the only side of the ship to be photographed. Likewise, painting and lettering can also be confined to half or three-quarters of the vehicle. Given the machine shop at Image G, the modelmaking experience of top modelmakers like Greg Jein and Tony Meininger, the extensive collection of ships built for previous episodes, and the boxes of parts available, vast fleets of new space vehicles can be and are turned out at a moment's notice. True, they won't be as finely detailed or as sturdy as the DS9 model, but they will photograph perfectly.

On the other hand, creating an alien ship from scratch on a computer is a more time-consuming task, not as suited to the seat-of-the-pants approach of model photography. A less complex model than B5 will still take a designer several days to complete on a computer screen—a luxury of time not available on most shows.

Another advantage model photography has over CGI—and again we stress, *for*

now—is the ability to shoot interactive elements along with the model. For example, in the second-season *Deep Space Nine* episode "Invasive Procedures," DS9 encounters a plasma storm. Visual-effects supervisor Glenn Neufeld was in charge of translating the script's single line—"a violent plasma storm enshrouds the station"—into visual reality, on time and on budget. Neufeld says it was the most difficult shot he's attempted on the series. To give an idea of how complex visual-effects shots are created, here's how Neufeld describes that sequence.

"The first question is, of course, what is a 'plasma storm' and then you go on from there. So it's always a matter of deciding what you've done or what you've seen done that's interesting that fills the bill—and then finding a way to do it including the station.

"The plasma-storm shot was the most difficult for me because Rick Berman's dictate on the show is that model shots move. They always move. They never stop moving. At the same time, a lot of great elements—blowing smoke is a simple

*Above left:*
Note the warning sign on this miniature.
As a cost-saving measure, miniatures are
often finished only on the side
that will be filmed.

*Above right:*
As a further cost-cutting measure,
miniatures are often built with existing
materials, sometimes from model kits,
and other times from things as simple as
the coffee-cup lid that forms the
roof of this model.

example—look best when they're shot at high speed.[14] So you deliberately get the smoke moving really fast, faster than the eye can see, and then you shoot it at very high speed. The look of the smoke drifting when it's being blown very hard, going at high speed—which is extreme slow motion—makes even a tiny bit of smoke look very massive. But the more camera motion you have in the shot, the more the [motion-control camera] rig moves, and the lower the top speed that you can shoot it

Thus, Neufeld couldn't photograph smoke blowing around DS9 by actually having smoke blow around the *model,* because the moving smoke would have to be shot at a different frame speed than the station, and for motion-control photography to work, all the frames must match exactly.

"So, the first thing you have to do is you have to limit the scope of the camera move so that the film can be rolled at twenty-four frames or higher. For the plasma storm, I limited the move so the camera would run at twenty-four frames a second—real time. Then the trick was to find an organic element [the smoke] that I could shoot, and that I could control enough. What we did was, after we shot the station, we took the station out and we made a black satin table that was tilted at a very slight angle. It was about eight feet square. We used a combination of liquid nitrogen and dry ice and water to create smoke at one end of the table so the smoke would drift very slowly across the table. Then, once we had a very thin layer drifting, we ran the same camera move on it.

"Of course, smoke has to be lit completely differently from a model, yet the angle of the light has to match the angle of the light that had been on the station. So we very carefully lit the station where we knew that the smoke would also look good later. I got a very thin layer of smoke going, and I shot it at twenty-four frames. Then I also shot it at twelve, and at six, so I would have a slow pass, a fast pass, and a very fast pass. We loaded up the nitrogen part of the smoke and used a little bit of $CO_2$, because the nitrogen boils very violently. So we'd come out of the edge boiling and there'd be some variation in the smoke. We shot this effect at three speeds, too."

However, because the resulting footage showed only a single, thin layer of smoke, Neufeld then adjusted the camera's position and reshot the same sequence several times so he would end up with multiple exposures showing several layers of smoke, much the same way that a single spaceship model can be shot several times to create several spaceships in different positions.

"When we shot the station, we also used extra matte cards [to mask out the back portions of the station model in order] to hold the front arms out away from the station, and to hold the inner part of the front ring away from the station. The idea was that I couldn't bury the entire station in smoke the whole time. So what we agreed to in the production meeting—because these shots were very long and there wasn't a lot of money—was that when you were looking east you would see stars and you would see a little bit of smoke blowing across. And as the move turned, you would see a big background structure like V'Ger [the alien space probe from STAR TREK: THE MOTION PICTURE], which is actually a cloud-tank element. [In this case, the "cloud-tank element" was a separate exposure of billows of smoke shot in a special, glass-sided tank, and then added to the background of the final shot.] When

[14]Cameras run at high speed to film slow motion. The standard rate at which film goes through a camera is twenty-four frames per second. If a camera is run at high speed, say 240 frames a second, and then played back at the standard twenty-four frames per second, an action that took one second to complete will take ten seconds to play back. If a camera films at a slow speed, say twelve frames per second, when that film is played back at normal speed, actions will appear to move twice as quickly.

the cloud-tank element became visible and we started looking right into it, the smoke would start to blow into the camera.

"Then we arranged the move so that when we were looking down the table, the smoke was almost front-lit, and as the move comes around, it becomes fully backlit. So it went from being very thick to being very thin to being very thick again. Then, we composited the smoke layer by layer. I used the extra matte pieces, so that as we turn around the station, it looks as though the arm is disappearing into the smoke. And we did that with all the layers so as the station turns, and the smoke starts to blow toward us off the station, you get the appearance that Wow, the storm's over *there* and it's really blowing *this* way—and when you look the other way, you don't see it.

"Then, as a final touch, we carved a foam replica of the inner ring and Ops and all of the little bits and pieces, which we placed on the table. We scaled the move so that we could get very close to it, placed it on the table, and poured triple the amount of smoke over it so that as the smoke went down the table, it actually jumped up over Ops and swirled around it. Then we printed that in very lightly so that at the very end of the move, as you come around and the smoke is very thick, you get a little sense that the smoke is actually blowing around Ops. It's very subtle because the foam model was not precise enough. There was a little piece of it that was misaligned and you can see where the smoke is actually going *through* Ops. But," Neufeld concludes with a smile, "it was a plasma storm, and plasma storms can do that."

However, on a television budget and schedule, CGI can't yet create convincing smoke effects—though CGI-created water and fire, once notoriously hard, have become more realistic over the past few years.

To be fair, though, there are some things that CGI can do which model photography can't. One impressive shot in *Babylon 5*'s pilot episode began about thirty yards off the station, looking back at crew members standing at a window. Then, the "camera" zooms back to a distance of thirty miles! Not even Image G's biggest motion-control rig could stage a pullback like that.

Of course, *Deep Space Nine* does not film physical models for all its visual effects. Two of its most notable recurring images—the wormhole and Odo's morphing—are completely computer-generated.

## Computer-Generated Imagery

Odo's morphing ability is a direct descendant of the first crude morphing technique seen in Lucasfilm's feature *Willow*, and the more sophisticated renditions seen in James Cameron's *Terminator 2* and Michael Jackson's "Black or White" video.

To create one of Odo's morphing sequences, at least three pieces of real film footage are required. The first is a background "plate"—that is, a shot of the set or location against which Odo's morph will take place. Depending on the shot's requirements and the director's choice of camera angles, two or three background plates may be required. The second piece of film required is of the actor, Rene Auberjonois, against a blue screen, usually going through a movement that will be continued by the computer-generated version of his body. The third piece of film is a blue-screen shot of whatever it is Odo is to morph into or out of.

These live-action shots are digitized, then sent to Vision Arts, the CGI company that quite literally twists Odo out of shape—creating the computer-generated in-between stages derived from various combinations of the visual characteristics of the beginning and ending shapes. Once a horrendously complex process that required tens of thousands of dollars and months of computer effort, today each morph is a two-week process costing approximately $10,000, with the likelihood of further enhancements to come.

But where Odo's morphing ability can vary from week to week according to story needs, the Bajoran wormhole is a constant.

The wormhole's chief visual designer was Michael Gibson, a designer-director at Rhythm & Hues—the visual-effects company hired by Paramount to produce the seven key wormhole shots used throughout the series. Those shots included three exterior shots, three interior shots, and a separate "burst" effect that is used to show ships emerging from the wormhole.

However, though the number and length of these seven shots were established by producer Peter Lauritson and Robert Legato, the actual appearance of the wormhole itself was left to Rhythm & Hues, whose team consisted of Gibson, technical director Larry Weinberg, head animator Juck Somsaman, and software specialist Mark Henne.

Though no one knows what a wormhole might look like, Gibson tried doing research to at least make an attempt at some kind of scientific accuracy. His efforts led him in the direction of a shifting, organic shape for the wormhole, rather than the sharp, solid planes of a purely mathematical construct.

To achieve that organic effect, just as Glenn Neufeld shot many layers of smoke to create his plasma storm, Gibson decided on a similar layered look for the interior of the wormhole, allowing many levels of visual information to be seen at once, as if the wormhole's boundary walls were transparent.

As in all arenas of television production requiring constant feedback and collaboration, the wormhole was constructed with several distinct stages. First, sketches and storyboards were prepared for Paramount's approval. Then, low-resolution, "wire-frame" models were constructed in the computer to establish the timing and movement of each shot.

When timing and movement were set, Gibson and his team began the finishing details—adding swirling particles and rays of light. The overall wormhole color scheme emphasizing different shades of turquoise, blue, and purple was deliberately chosen to avoid any connotation of the wormhole exploding, which might have happened if reds and oranges were used.

Though the wormhole effect is completely computer-generated—on a Silicon Graphics system using, for the most part, Rhythm & Hues's own software—Gibson worked closely with Image G in order to make sure the effect would combine properly with the model photography for the series. In fact, large, high-contrast transparencies of various stages of the wormhole's opening were made so light could shine through them onto spaceship models on the motion-control rig. Also, detailed animation

*Interesting objects abound at Image G. On this one table off to the side are foamcore Cardassian warships used for positioning tests, and a verteron node, usually found only inside a wormhole.*

notes had to be prepared so that when film was shot of a model spaceship's exterior or full-size set's interior, Robert Legato could insure that the lighting on both would match the flickering light created for the wormhole's interior,[15] effectively tying together all the major visual elements that go into *Deep Space Nine*—live action, model photography, and computer generated and enhanced images.

Despite the seemingly clear-cut differences between model photography and CGI, as used on *Deep Space Nine* and *Babylon 5,* it is wrong to think of the two systems of visual effects as two competing systems. Instead, these two approaches to visual effects are in some ways actually moving toward synthesis. After all, once a model has been photographed for *Deep Space Nine,* the developed film is immediately digitized and all further work on it is carried out by CGI-style equipment and techniques.

Which brings us to the next phase of visual effects, where everything comes together.

[15]In order to check the effects of the interior lighting conditions on an object passing through the wormhole, Rhythm & Hues prepared a test sequence in which they created a computer-generated object to travel along the path that spaceship models would eventually use. Unfortunately, the company did not have any computer-generated spaceships in its database of objects, so the team combined the physical attributes of two objects they did have—a biplane and a cow. Thus, in case the question ever comes up in the STAR TREK edition of Trivial Pursuit, the first object to travel through the Bajoran wormhole was a flying bovine, nicknamed ''aero-cow.''

# Digital Magic

Every physical element of *Deep Space Nine* is shot on film, not videotape. However, that film is just a first step. As soon as it's printed, it's sent to Unitel Video, where it is transferred to D2 videotape. Then the film is put into storage and—provided no disasters occur while an episode is in postproduction—it never sees the light of day again.[16]

The film elements that are transferred include everything shot on sets and on location by the first and second units, all the passes of models shot at Image G, and all film of *physical* matte paintings executed by Illusion Arts.[17] Live-action footage is also duped onto standard VHS cassettes so the producers can review them as dailies. All "V-takes"—shots that require visual effects—are then sent on to the company called Digital Magic. Here, on banks of video equipment that would look at home on the *Enterprise,* the myriad passes of models are composited, and phaser, transporter, and all other types of visual effects are created.

One of the key artists to create these effects is Adam Howard, an Australian who trained as a graphic designer and who arrived at his first job the same week a computer graphics system was installed. As the new employee, Howard was asked to master the system and teach the rest of the company how to use it. Seven years and two Emmys later,[18] Howard is one of the top artists who works on a sophisticated digital image system called a HARRI.

The HARRI gives Howard the ability to retouch photographic images one computer pixel at a time. At the highest resolution—used when Digital Magic works on feature films, such as digitally removing the safety wires holding Sylvester Stallone securely to the mountain in *Cliffhanger*—Howard's work can be transferred back to film stock at a resolution greater than the film, so that there is virtually no image degradation and no evidence of electronic scan lines.

As a workplace, Digital Magic is a soothing environment—complete with a twenty-four-hour kitchen to help workers like Howard through their twenty-four-hour days.[19] And in the quiet, darkened confines of the HARRI Bay, a day can pass easily as all concentration is focused on the images on the multiple video monitors.

In a way, Howard's work is somewhat like a video game. He uses a graphics pad, a mouse, and a keyboard to move cursors over the screen, enclose boundary areas, and select colors and shading, all with the apparently effortless skill of a kid going for a high score on a Nintendo game. But Howard's quick movements and subtle artistry are the result of finely developed talent and skill that viewers of *Deep Space Nine* and *The Next Generation* have come to take for granted. (Howard himself is modest about his skills, describing them as "highly complicated techniques requiring years of finger-painting experience.") Howard wouldn't have it any other way. As he says, "The best visual effect is the one that no one knows is there."

What visual effects are in *Deep Space Nine* that viewers might not have noticed? Everything from replacing a live video-monitor display in Ops that didn't photograph properly, to blanking out an inadvertent appearance by the overhead microphone boom or by a "bogey" reflected in a window, and even, in the first season, smoothing the seams on Odo's early makeup.

[16] In the planning stages of *The Next Generation,* an important decision was made that still affects *Deep Space Nine* today. The choice Gene Roddenberry and the production team faced was whether to do the visual effects for the new series using film techniques, or on video. Video effects were faster and less costly, but only worked on the television screen. Because of video's low resolution at the time, there would be no final negative print from which film versions of *The Next Generation* could be edited together for theatrical release in other countries. Ultimately, the decision was made to go to video, and *Deep Space Nine* continues that process today. Thus, although the resolution of the visual effects is much higher today than was possible in 1987, there are no final film prints of any episode of either series, and the episodes cannot be rescanned at the higher resolution necessary for high-definition television broadcast in the future. Theoretically, it would be possible to return to the original raw film and redo all the visual effects at higher resolution, but such a step would be the equivalent of putting the show through the complete postproduction process again. It will be much less expensive to wait for enhancement technology to be developed so the final video versions of *Deep Space Nine* episodes can reprocessed, rather than being remade.

[17] Some matte paintings for *Deep Space Nine* are created directly on the computer. Others begin as paintings, then are digitized and retouched on computer. For example, "Emissary" includes a shot panning over the ruins of Bajor's major city. This image began as a painting, with three separate foreground and background elements. These elements were digitized into the computer, where glistening water effects and speeding traffic were added. Then, at the end of the first season, for "In the Hands of the Prophets," the same digitized art was used, but this time the foreground damaged buildings were removed, the background damaged buildings and the road were retouched to show they had been repaired, and the whole scene was brightened to illustrate the progress of Bajor's reconstruction after the Cardassian occupation.

[18] For his contributions to the visual effects in *The Next Generation* episodes "Conundrum" and "A Matter of Time."

[19] One of the benefits of working such long hours in television production is that when work gets extremely busy, between craft service tables on the set and employee kitchens at postproduction companies, the crew rarely has to spend any of their own money on food.

But it's the effects that viewers *do* see, and *do* recognize as visual effects even as they accept the reality of them, that are most associated with *Deep Space Nine* in most people's minds. And for good reason. Because the time and effort expended on creating them is the equal of any model photography at Image G.

Take that pinnacle of STAR TREK technology, the phaser—Gene Roddenberry's answer to the ray guns of Flash Gordon and Buck Rogers.

Back in the days of the old science-fiction serials, ray-gun beams were created by the simple process of actually *scratching* off the emulsion on the film footage. By the time of the original STAR TREK series, solid, animated bars of light were added to film footage of the actors pointing their weapons. Unfortunately, the constraints of the technology used in the sixties required the actors to freeze while they fired their phasers because the animated phaser beam couldn't move. This led to the regrettable instances where viewers can see a phaser move in the actor's hand, while the beam appears to float in place. Also, for all the energy the phaser beam appeared to be emitting, no one was ever lit up by it. But that was then and this is now.

Today, the creation of a STAR TREK phaser beam has been elevated to an art form. On Adam Howard's HARRI system is a menu of phaser types: Federation, Cardassian, Bajoran, Klingon,[20] you name it. Calling up this menu reveals a selection of black-and-white glowing bars that stretch from one side of the screen to another. Some bars appear to be straightforward representations of nothing more complicated than a fluorescent light tube. But others include convoluted swirls of light that twist around the main beam. In fact, sharp-eyed viewers will have noticed that every different weapon type on *The Next Generation* and *Deep Space Nine* has its own, distinct, beam. For example, a Federation phaser beam is composed of five light elements and is predominantly orangish-red in color, while a Bajoran phaser beam is composed of three elements and is distinctly more golden.

The black-and-white phaser beams that stretch across the menu screen on the HARRI are not just two-dimensional images, either. They are computer-generated, three-dimensional cylinders. Howard, or one of the other HARRI artists who work on *Deep Space Nine*, selects the beam pattern called for by the script with a quick mouse click, and that cylinder appears on the screen, which displays the actual live footage to which the phaser fire will be added.

We watched Howard create a burst of phaser fire for the first-season episode "In the Hands of the Prophets." The sequence—filmed in slow motion by director David Livingston—occurs in Act Five, when Neela fires her phaser almost directly into the camera, cutting to a shot of Vedek Bareil as the phaser beam hits part of the Promenade walkway behind him.

Onscreen, the two-shot sequence lasts twenty-three frames—not quite one second—and it took Howard just over an hour to create the phaser beam by adding eighteen different layers of visual information to the live photography. This is how he did it.

First of all, Howard had to identify the frame in which Neela "pulls the trigger." Early on in *The Next Generation,* some phasers were built with lights in their muzzles that were intended to guide the visual-effects artists as to when to lay in the beam. But Howard points out that the built-in lights were far more trouble than they were

[20]We know, we know—Klingons use disruptors, not phasers. But on the HARRI, the disruptor's distinctive energy beam is filed under "phaser."

worth, because actors seldom pulled the trigger and released it at the right time.

Today on *Deep Space Nine,* none of the phasers has built-in lights. Instead, Howard studies the footage carefully and chooses the moment when the actor playing Neela *appears* to have fired, based on her expression and movements. That frame becomes his starting point.

In *The Original Series,* a phaser beam was a solid core of light that sprang out of the phaser within a few frames. Today, the process is more complex and—it is hoped—more realistic.

First of all, Howard adds a preignition glow to the tip of the phaser. This glow comes from another menu of stock images called "Trek Starbursts." Howard selects the glow he wants—an image that looks like a tiny, bright light pointing directly at the camera—makes it appear on the still frame of Neela, and nudges it directly overtop the tip of her phaser, pixel by pixel.

At this point, the starburst glow is not actually a visual element. Instead, it is a digital mask that will be used to alter the visual information already in the still frame. In effect, what Howard does is to take a duplicate of the still frame, strip away all colors except the specific golden glow of the Bajoran phaser, brighten that glow, and then matte it into the original still frame just in the area marked by the starburst. The key to this process is that Howard has not added a solid object to the image—he has added a burst of transparent light. Think of what a searchlight beam looks like as it passes through dusty air and hits the side of a building. We can see right through the beam, and where its circle of light hits an object, it's as if everything within the circle has been overexposed. Howard follows the same visual rules of appearance in creating a phaser beam. To further add to the realism of the image, Howard also adds a faint blue lens flare to either side of the glow, to add what we would expect to see if someone shone a bright light into a camera lens.

For the second frame, Howard adds a "hot spot" to the phaser's muzzle by hand, just as anyone using a computer paint program might. This is an area that will appear to be so overexposed on the frame that no information exists within it—in other words, it's so blinding we can't see anything beyond it.

In the next frame, Howard adds the Bajoran phaser beam from the menu of STAR TREK phasers. It's clear that the image is three-dimensional, because as Howard moves its end point to the muzzle of the phaser, it changes shape so that it acquires perspective—very narrow where it touches the phaser, widening dramatically as it falls off the screen.

When Howard has the origin point of the beam at the proper point on the phaser's muzzle, he "locks" it into place, then moves the widening beam around until it appears to be perfectly aligned with the angle of the phaser's barrel. This is where an artist's eye is a necessity, because unlike *The Original Series,* Neela's phaser will continue to fire as she moves it up. Thus, the phaser beam will change shape as Howard realigns it to match the moving position of the phaser.

Again, this element is not a computer-generated object being *added* to the live-action image. The Bajoran phaser-beam elements are digital masks that are used to increase the light intensity already existing in specific areas of the frame. Howard also increases the light intensity in other areas by hand, as if the energy leaving the phaser is illuminating Neela's face and the people around her.

Moving to the shot of Vedek Bareil, Howard must match the end point of the moving phaser beam to a small explosion that takes place on the edge of the Promenade walkway behind him—just about where Jake and Nog can often be seen sitting together in other episodes.

The beam, which is now traveling away from the camera's point of view and so doesn't require lens flares, is much smaller, appearing as the traditional narrow beam of bright light as it burns its way up the walkway support. Though few people will ever notice the detail, Howard marks the trail of the phaser with a blackened burn mark along the support, adding red edges as if the phasered metal is glowing. Then, in the frames where the explosion takes place (presumably the phaser beam hit a power conduit), Howard ends the beam, but adds a glow to that side of the screen in order to visually increase the apparent power of the explosion.

Playing back the twenty-three frames over and over in order to judge the effectiveness of his work, Adam Howard does what everyone else involved with the show does at these times—he adds his own sound effects, explaining that they help time out the scene. (Yeah, right.) Finally, an hour and twenty minutes after he began—less fifteen minutes to discuss various approaches to a diaper commercial involving an invisible baby, and helping to solve a problem with a viewscreen shot elsewhere in the episode—Howard declares the shot complete by giving it Robert Legato's ultimate benediction for an effects sequence that is exceptionally good: "The kids are going to piss!"

While a typical *Deep Space Nine* episode is shot in about seven days, "Emissary," as the pilot, had an initial schedule of twenty-two days, and ran longer. This was usual for a complex new show where newly constructed sets were being filmed for the first time and the cast and crew were developing their unique style of working together. But even on the last day of principal photography, when the actors had spoken their last lines and the AD had called "That's a wrap!" for the last time, the pilot episode was nowhere near finished.

Over at Image G, the battle of Wolf 359 was being re-created on the Bulldog; Rhythm & Hues was flying aero-cows through an incomplete wormhole; Tony Meininger and crew were detailing DS9 so it could finally take the place of its plywood and foamcore stand-in; Illusion Arts was creating a destroyed Bajoran city; Vision Arts was melting images of Odo; and Adam Howard was laying in the first images to appear on the Ops viewscreen.

Eventually, however, all the separate creative elements of "Emissary" were completed.

But the show itself was still nowhere near finished.

It was time for all the different parts to be finally put together.

It was time for "the Machine" to take over.

# FIFTEEN

# "THE MACHINE"

*Don't mess with me on math.*

—Rick Berman

**T**hey all call it "the Machine."

The actors, the directors, the office staff, the postproduction crew, the producers—*everyone.*

And they're right.

The Machine is the awesomely complex, amazingly efficient, and virtually unstoppable production process that drives the making of *Deep Space Nine.*

Its birthplace is the inviolable airdate schedule, set by Paramount's domestic television sales division, arranged so that original episodes will be available for the crucial February, May, and November ratings sweeps.[1] *Deep Space Nine* has never missed an airdate. According to visual-effects coordinator Laura Lang-Matz, even when a visual-effects shot is being delivered only forty-eight hours before a show ships,[2] there's no excitement or sense of panic because it is an absolute given that *Deep Space Nine* will *never* miss an airdate. The Machine won't let it.

About the only segment of *Deep Space Nine*'s production cycle in which this overwhelming pressure to stay on schedule isn't felt is in the initial writing stages. The writing staff always keep many stories and scripts in development at the same time. On *The Next Generation*, scripts would sometimes be worked on over several seasons until they were considered ready for production. If a particular story is proving difficult to develop, there's not a lot of pressure on the staff to rush the process because there are—or there should be—other stories to choose from.

*But,* once a script is given a definite slot, its airdate is set in stone and the Machine begins chugging along in earnest.

[1] The national audiences for network broadcasts are measured on a daily basis by the two key audience measurement companies—Nielsen and Arbitron. But in February, May, July, and November of each year, both companies measure *local* broadcast markets—Nielsen, 211, and Arbitron, 209. The results of these ratings help set the prices local stations can set for commercial time. Therefore, it's essential that original episodes be scheduled during these months to insure that viewers don't switch to another channel because of reruns.

[2] "Shipping" a show refers to its delivery to the syndicated stations. About sixty percent of the local television stations showing *Deep Space Nine* receive their episodes by satellite transmission. (Many fans with satellite dishes also intercept these commercial-free downloads.) The rest of the stations receive their episodes on 3/4″ videotape cassettes.

The first half of the process, as we've seen, involves the creation of all the unique visual elements that will be assembled into the final episode—set, prop, costume, graphics, and model design and construction, live-action filming, motion-control photography, and computer visual effects. The second half of the process involves the assembly itself.

The artist who is the linchpin of this postproduction process—the person who works on the show longer than any other individual except for the producers—is . . . the editor?

We all know film editors. They're the people we see with Oscars at the Academy Award ceremonies each year, as we wonder, "Why do they give out an Oscar for *that?*"

The truth is, editing is one of the most important and—outside the industry at least—one of the least understood creative processes in the making of a television episode, or a movie. We once commented to a heavyweight movie producer that we understood enough about the film industry to know that the real power to shape a movie lay with the producer. But the producer shook her head and said the *real* power lies with the editor.

How can editing be so important and so unappreciated at the same time? Because it's like breathing. As long as someone is breathing normally, breathing isn't noticed. But the instant something goes wrong, it has our full attention. With editing, the same dynamics apply—we only notice it when something goes wrong. Thanks to

*At some point in its production cycle, even a STAR TREK series becomes like any other network-quality, shot-on-film television show—one part of a larger process.*

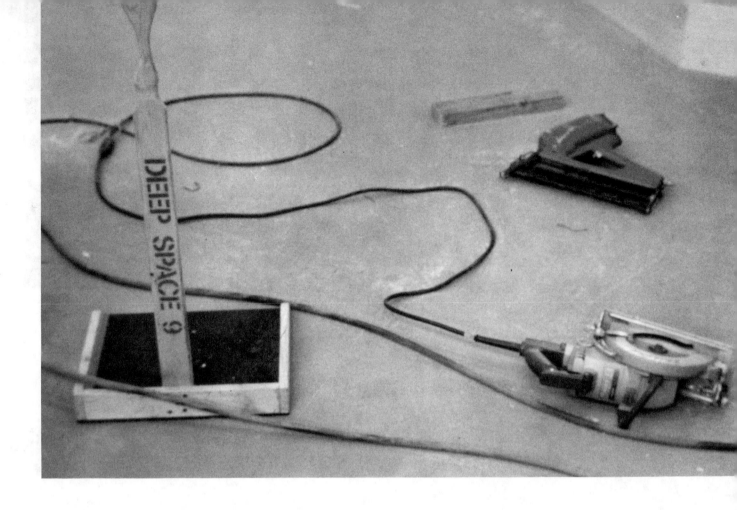

the quality of editors working on *Deep Space Nine*, viewers are rarely, if ever, given reason to notice the editors' hard work.

Editors start that work on an episode of *Deep Space Nine* at the same time the director does—when they're given a copy of the first-draft script, about two to three weeks prior to the first day of principal photography. This allows for some creative-thinking time before the actual hands-on work begins under a strict schedule.

That hands-on work starts as soon as the first dailies are approved by the producers and transferred to low-quality videotape for what is called the ''off-line'' cut. The term off-line is used because none of what the editor works with is final video or film—only copies. On *Deep Space Nine*, editors work in small rooms on the lot, sitting at a console with at least six screens—called a Montage system. (In the case of Richard Rabjohn, an editor we watched at work assembling ''In the Hands of the Prophets,'' his six screens are topped by a watchful tribble. Like many people who work on the series, Rabjohn remembers *The Original Series* with fondness.) One large screen allows the editor to view the work in progress, and five smaller ones are used to preview available clips. Several clips may come from one take. For example, the director might have filmed Dax for an entire conversation and printed it as one take. However, in editing the conversation to go back and forth between all the characters involved, the editor might select several separate clips from that take to show Dax taking part in the scene.

The clips are brought to the screens by a bank of seventeen video playback units in another room, dutifully loaded and maintained by the assistant editor. Each playback unit, called a work bin, contains the same collection of cuts on four hours' worth of tape. By having the same material available on so many machines at once, delays resulting from searching for a particular clip are greatly reduced. When the editor requests a specific clip by number, a computerized controller is able to select the playback unit on which that clip is most quickly available, saving the editor the time-consuming chore of searching back and forth through a single, four-hour long tape. (Digital-editing systems like those used at Digital Magic allow near-instantaneous access to clips, but because of their cost it will be several seasons before *Deep Space Nine* editors switch over to them.)

Working at his console, the editor brings up all the clips required for a particular scene and then assembles them into a whole, while at the same time noting when the soundtrack from one clip will play over another, such as when we cut away from a character who is speaking to see the silent reaction of another character.[3]

If you're thinking that sounds complicated, you're right. Here's a sample of what Richard Rabjohn had to keep track of during his work on "In the Hands of the Prophets."

You might recognize the sequence presented here as the attempted assassination that begins on the sample continuity pages in Chapter 13.[4] Sixteen cuts in less than thirty-three seconds, displaying action that was only briefly described in the script, incorporating visual effects, first-unit action, a stunt double for Avery Brooks, slow-motion footage blended with normal-speed footage, and an actual explosion on the Promenade—all put together so seamlessly that most of the viewers who saw it never once thought about how complex the sequence was.

In the editing storyboards, each top and bottom pair of images corresponds to the first and last frame of a clip. The numbers below give the start and end codes of the clip's visual and audio components, the cumulative total of the act's length, the total number of clips used so far, and the identifying code for the take each clip came from. That's a lot of numeric information, but that's exactly what is generated by an off-line edit—not a final cut of the episode, but a computer disk of start and stop codes for sound and picture.

In essence, all the editor is doing during the ten days or so he has to complete an episode is generating a list of frame numbers corresponding to the actual, first-generation quality video that will be electronically spliced together during the "on-line" editing session. The process can be likened to a designer completing a rough assembly of the text and illustrations for a book, checking to make sure the content is the right length and in the right order, then passing over that rough assembly to someone else—a computer—who will do the precise layout for reproduction. Adding to the complexity of the job a *Deep Space Nine* editor faces, however, is the fact that the final images come from so many different sources. Often, while waiting for a visual-effects sequence such as a viewscreen conversation or an Odo morph to be completed, the editor will have to leave a hole in his work, estimating the time to be taken up by the missing sequence by inserting a handwritten title card in the rough cut.

[3]In the event the editor discovers a "hole" in the filmed action, he refers to the continuity script to see if there is a take that was filmed but not printed. *Very* occasionally, an editor will request that a specific shot be filmed to complete a sequence.

[4]The close-up of Sisko labeled S59Z/2 was the shot discussed in Chapter 13 in which the focus was "enhanced." Try to spot it when you watch a rerun of this episode.

Timing, of course, is the immutable target of the editor. Somehow, all the different elements that have been created by the first unit, second unit, and visual-effects teams must be assembled so they come out to forty-two minutes and thirty seconds. In the final stages of editing, skillful editors shave seconds off the beginning and endings of scenes to reach that goal. Occasionally, when it's apparent that an episode is going to run extremely long or short while it's still filming, the writing staff will be dragooned into quickly adding scenes to give the editor an extra ninety seconds to work with, or into rewriting two-page scenes to fit into half a page.

But all that concern with timing is simply the technical end of the editor's job. There is subtle and impressive artistry involved as well.

First, there is the sense of pacing. Just as we saw Winrich Kolbe create a visual rhythm for the memorable scene between Garak and Bashir (in Chapter 13), an editor must also match the rhythm of his cuts to the filming style of the director and the pacing of the script. Watch almost any *Deep Space Nine* episode, and as the action builds to a climax in the fifth act, notice how many more back-and-forth cuts there are. Ideally, this quickening of the visual pace of a story will also be matched by shorter, snappier dialogue, quick camera moves, and driving music. But imagine what might happen if that same rapid-fire, back-and-forth technique were used during a romantic scene between Kira and Vedek Bareil—the jarring visual construction of the scene would war with the slower dialogue and gentler emotional context. Appropriate rhythm is important in all aspects of television storytelling, and editors must be masters of it.

On a subtler level, editors also must have innate knowledge of the movement of people and things. When we see Odo exit through the door of his office, though the average viewer might not notice that he's leading with his right foot, almost everyone *will* notice that something's wrong if the next clip shows him coming through the door from a vantage point in the Promenade, leading with his left foot. Similarly, if a clip ends with Sisko turning in place on his chair to answer a viewscreen call, all viewers instinctively know what position he should be in when the next clip picks him up from a different angle in front of the viewscreen, as he completes his turn. The sad reality of an editor's job is that if the two clips are cut together perfectly, no one will notice except other editors.

And Rick Berman, of course.

As executive producer, Rick Berman is the person to whom all aspects of postproduction are presented for approval. His discerning eye and personal style have such a profound influence on the final product that the people responsible for editing, sound effects, and musical scoring often present Berman with what they know is a few percentage points less than a complete job. It's those final finishing touches that almost every department confidently leaves to Berman's direction, knowing that the person responsible for developing *The Next Generation*'s technical excellence is bringing the same attention to the detail and quality of his latest series.

It is when a *Deep Space Nine* episode clocks in at forty-two minutes, thirty seconds, and Rick Berman gives his approval, that the off-line edit is said to be "locked." Now that episode is swallowed totally by the Machine and goes into the

*Following pages:*
*These storyboards were generated by the Montage editing system used at Paramount for Deep Space Nine, and show the final two and half minutes of the last first-season episode. They also give us an idea of the complexity the editor faces in assembling all the disparate parts of a Deep Space Nine episode, created by so many different people, into a coherent and entertaining whole.*

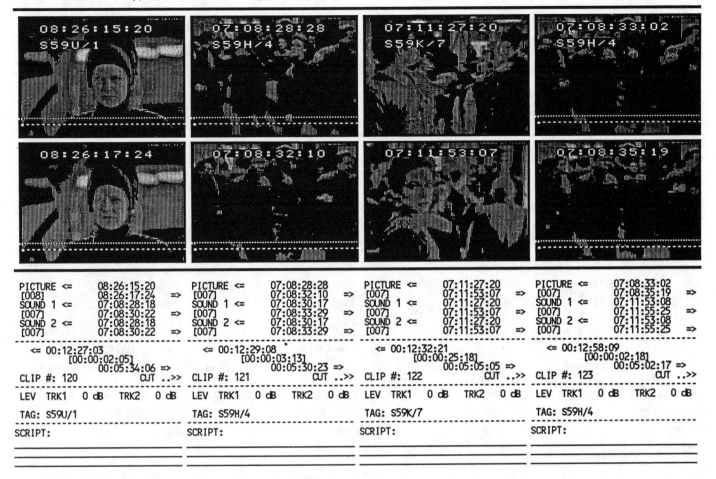

PICTURE <=      08:26:15:20        PICTURE <=      07:08:28:28        PICTURE <=      07:11:27:20        PICTURE <=      07:08:33:02
[008]           08:26:17:24  =>    [007]           07:08:32:10  =>    [007]           07:11:53:07  =>    [007]           07:08:35:19  =>
SOUND 1 <=      07:08:28:18        SOUND 1 <=      07:08:30:17        SOUND 1 <=      07:11:27:20        SOUND 1 <=      07:11:53:08
[007]           07:08:30:22  =>    [007]           07:08:33:29  =>    [007]           07:11:53:07  =>    [007]           07:11:55:25  =>
SOUND 2 <=      07:08:28:18        SOUND 2 <=      07:08:30:17        SOUND 2 <=      07:11:27:20        SOUND 2 <=      07:11:53:08
[007]           07:08:30:22  =>    [007]           07:08:33:29  =>    [007]           07:11:53:07  =>    [007]           07:11:55:25  =>
---------------------------        ---------------------------        ---------------------------        ---------------------------
  <= 00:12:27:03                     <= 00:12:29:08                     <= 00:12:32:21                     <= 00:12:58:09
      [00:00:02:05]                     [00:00:03:13]                     [00:00:25:18]                     [00:00:02:18]
            00:05:34:06 =>                   00:05:30:23 =>                   00:05:05:05 =>                   00:05:02:17 =>
CLIP #: 120          CUT ..>>      CLIP #: 121          CUT ..>>      CLIP #: 122          CUT ..>>      CLIP #: 123          CUT ..>>

LEV  TRK1   0 dB    TRK2   0 dB    LEV  TRK1   0 dB    TRK2   0 dB    LEV  TRK1   0 dB    TRK2   0 dB    LEV  TRK1   0 dB    TRK2   0 dB

TAG: S59U/1                        TAG: S59H/4                        TAG: S59K/7                        TAG: S59H/4
---------------------------        ---------------------------        ---------------------------        ---------------------------
SCRIPT:                            SCRIPT:                            SCRIPT:                            SCRIPT:

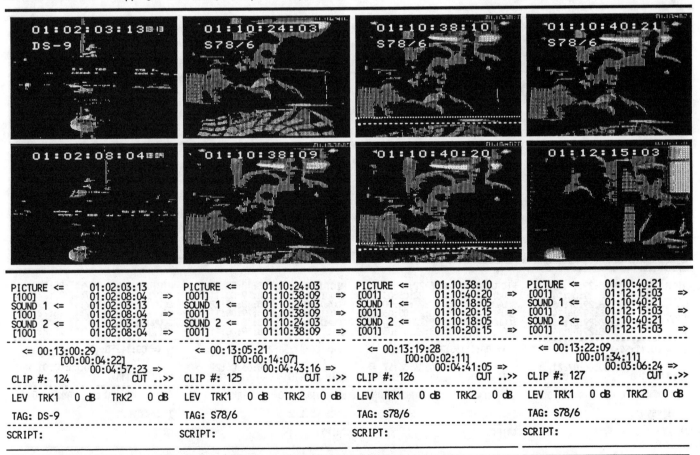

PICTURE <=      01:02:03:13        PICTURE <=      01:10:24:03        PICTURE <=      01:10:38:10        PICTURE <=      01:10:40:21
[100]           01:02:08:04  =>    [001]           01:10:38:09  =>    [001]           01:10:40:20  =>    [001]           01:12:15:03  =>
SOUND 1 <=      01:02:03:13        SOUND 1 <=      01:10:24:03        SOUND 1 <=      01:10:18:05        SOUND 1 <=      01:10:40:21
[100]           01:02:08:04  =>    [001]           01:10:38:09  =>    [001]           01:10:20:15  =>    [001]           01:12:15:03  =>
SOUND 2 <=      01:02:03:13        SOUND 2 <=      01:10:24:03        SOUND 2 <=      01:10:18:05        SOUND 2 <=      01:10:40:21
[100]           01:02:08:04  =>    [001]           01:10:38:09  =>    [001]           01:10:20:15  =>    [001]           01:12:15:03  =>
---------------------------        ---------------------------        ---------------------------        ---------------------------
  <= 00:13:00:29                     <= 00:13:05:21                     <= 00:13:19:28                     <= 00:13:22:09
      [00:00:04:22]                     [00:00:14:07]                     [00:00:02:11]                     [00:01:34:11]
            00:04:57:23 =>                   00:04:43:16 =>                   00:04:41:05 =>                   00:03:06:24 =>
CLIP #: 124          CUT ..>>      CLIP #: 125          CUT ..>>      CLIP #: 126          CUT ..>>      CLIP #: 127          CUT ..>>

LEV  TRK1   0 dB    TRK2   0 dB    LEV  TRK1   0 dB    TRK2   0 dB    LEV  TRK1   0 dB    TRK2   0 dB    LEV  TRK1   0 dB    TRK2   0 dB

TAG: DS-9                          TAG: S78/6                         TAG: S78/6                         TAG: S78/6
---------------------------        ---------------------------        ---------------------------        ---------------------------
SCRIPT:                            SCRIPT:                            SCRIPT:                            SCRIPT:

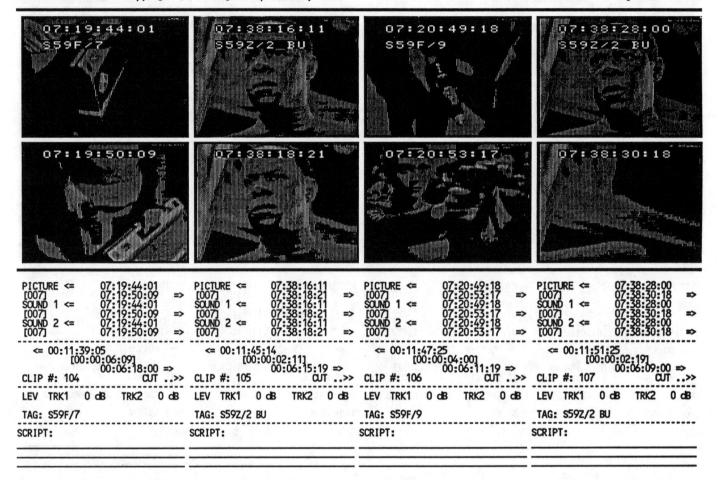

```
PICTURE <=     07:19:44:01       PICTURE <=     07:38:16:11       PICTURE <=     07:20:49:18       PICTURE <=     07:38:28:00
[007]          07:19:50:09  =>   [007]          07:38:18:21  =>   [007]          07:20:53:17  =>   [007]          07:38:30:18  =>
SOUND 1 <=     07:19:44:01       SOUND 1 <=     07:38:16:11       SOUND 1 <=     07:20:49:18       SOUND 1 <=     07:38:28:00
[007]          07:19:50:09  =>   [007]          07:38:18:21  =>   [007]          07:20:53:17  =>   [007]          07:38:30:18  =>
SOUND 2 <=     07:19:44:01       SOUND 2 <=     07:38:16:11       SOUND 2 <=     07:20:49:18       SOUND 2 <=     07:38:28:00
[007]          07:19:50:09  =>   [007]          07:38:18:21  =>   [007]          07:20:53:17  =>   [007]          07:38:30:18  =>
----------------------------     ----------------------------     ----------------------------     ----------------------------
  <= 00:11:39:05                   <= 00:11:45:14                   <= 00:11:47:25                   <= 00:11:51:25
     [00:00:06:09]                    [00:00:02:11]                    [00:00:04:00]                    [00:00:02:19]
          00:06:18:00 =>                   00:06:15:19 =>                   00:06:11:19 =>                   00:06:09:00 =>
CLIP #: 104        CUT ..>>      CLIP #: 105        CUT ..>>      CLIP #: 106        CUT ..>>      CLIP #: 107        CUT ..>>
LEV TRK1  0 dB   TRK2  0 dB      LEV TRK1  0 dB   TRK2  0 dB      LEV TRK1  0 dB   TRK2  0 dB      LEV TRK1  0 dB   TRK2  0 dB
TAG: S59F/7                      TAG: S59Z/2 BU                   TAG: S59F/9                      TAG: S59Z/2 BU
----------------------------     ----------------------------     ----------------------------     ----------------------------
SCRIPT:                          SCRIPT:                          SCRIPT:                          SCRIPT:
```

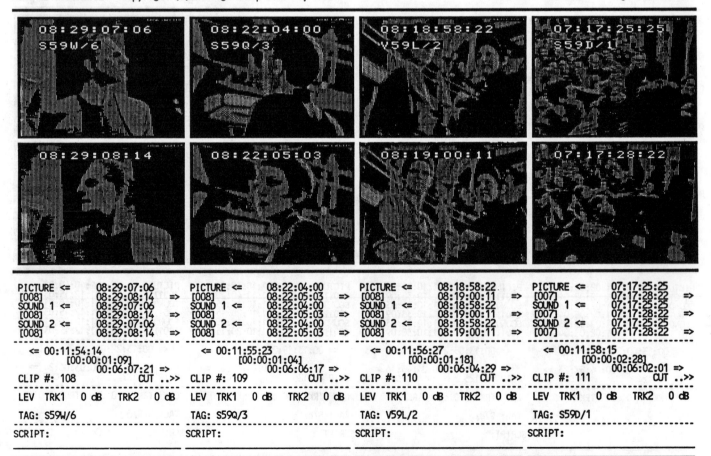

```
PICTURE <=     08:29:07:06       PICTURE <=     08:22:04:00       PICTURE <=     08:18:58:22       PICTURE <=     07:17:25:25
[008]          08:29:08:14  =>   [008]          08:22:05:03  =>   [008]          08:19:00:11  =>   [007]          07:17:28:22  =>
SOUND 1 <=     08:29:07:06       SOUND 1 <=     08:22:04:00       SOUND 1 <=     08:18:58:22       SOUND 1 <=     07:17:25:25
[008]          08:29:08:14  =>   [008]          08:22:05:03  =>   [008]          08:19:00:11  =>   [007]          07:17:28:22  =>
SOUND 2 <=     08:29:07:06       SOUND 2 <=     08:22:04:00       SOUND 2 <=     08:18:58:22       SOUND 2 <=     07:17:25:25
[008]          08:29:08:14  =>   [008]          08:22:05:03  =>   [008]          08:19:00:11  =>   [007]          07:17:28:22  =>
----------------------------     ----------------------------     ----------------------------     ----------------------------
  <= 00:11:54:14                   <= 00:11:55:23                   <= 00:11:56:27                   <= 00:11:58:15
     [00:00:01:09]                    [00:00:01:04]                    [00:00:01:18]                    [00:00:02:28]
          00:06:07:21 =>                   00:06:06:17 =>                   00:06:04:29 =>                   00:06:02:01 =>
CLIP #: 108        CUT ..>>      CLIP #: 109        CUT ..>>      CLIP #: 110        CUT ..>>      CLIP #: 111        CUT ..>>
LEV TRK1  0 dB   TRK2  0 dB      LEV TRK1  0 dB   TRK2  0 dB      LEV TRK1  0 dB   TRK2  0 dB      LEV TRK1  0 dB   TRK2  0 dB
TAG: S59W/6                      TAG: S59Q/3                      TAG: V59L/2                      TAG: S59D/1
----------------------------     ----------------------------     ----------------------------     ----------------------------
SCRIPT:                          SCRIPT:                          SCRIPT:                          SCRIPT:
```

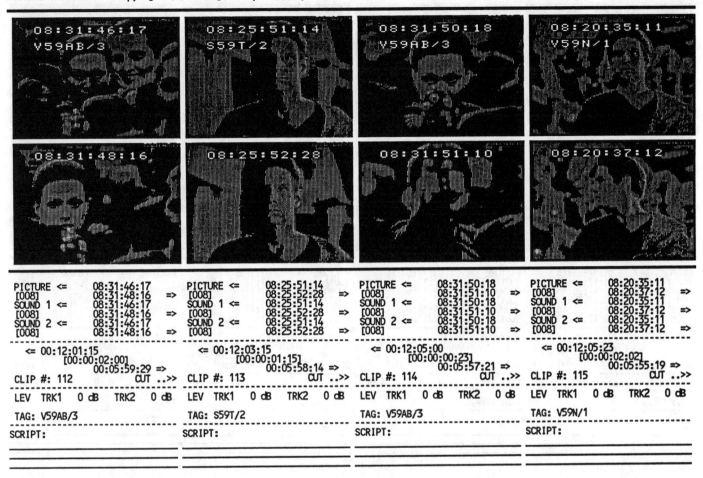

```
PICTURE <=      08:31:46:17        PICTURE <=      08:25:51:14        PICTURE <=      08:31:50:18        PICTURE <=      08:20:35:11
  [008]         08:31:48:16 =>       [008]         08:25:52:28 =>       [008]         08:31:51:10 =>       [008]         08:20:37:12 =>
SOUND 1 <=      08:31:46:17        SOUND 1 <=      08:25:51:14        SOUND 1 <=      08:31:50:18        SOUND 1 <=      08:20:35:11
  [008]         08:31:48:16 =>       [008]         08:25:52:28 =>       [008]         08:31:51:10 =>       [008]         08:20:37:12 =>
SOUND 2 <=      08:31:46:17        SOUND 2 <=      08:25:51:14        SOUND 2 <=      08:31:50:18        SOUND 2 <=      08:20:35:11
  [008]         08:31:48:16 =>       [008]         08:25:52:28 =>       [008]         08:31:51:10 =>       [008]         08:20:37:12 =>
```

```
  <= 00:12:01:15                    <= 00:12:03:15                    <= 00:12:05:00                    <= 00:12:05:23
    [00:00:02:00]                     [00:00:01:15]                     [00:00:00:23]                     [00:00:02:02]
              00:05:59:29 =>                    00:05:58:14 =>                   00:05:57:21 =>                    00:05:55:19 =>
CLIP #: 112          CUT ..>>    CLIP #: 113          CUT ..>>    CLIP #: 114          CUT ..>>    CLIP #: 115          CUT ..>>

LEV  TRK1   0 dB  TRK2   0 dB    LEV  TRK1   0 dB  TRK2   0 dB    LEV  TRK1   0 dB  TRK2   0 dB    LEV  TRK1   0 dB  TRK2   0 dB

TAG: V59AB/3                     TAG: S59T/2                     TAG: V59AB/3                     TAG: V59N/1

SCRIPT:                         SCRIPT:                         SCRIPT:                         SCRIPT:
```

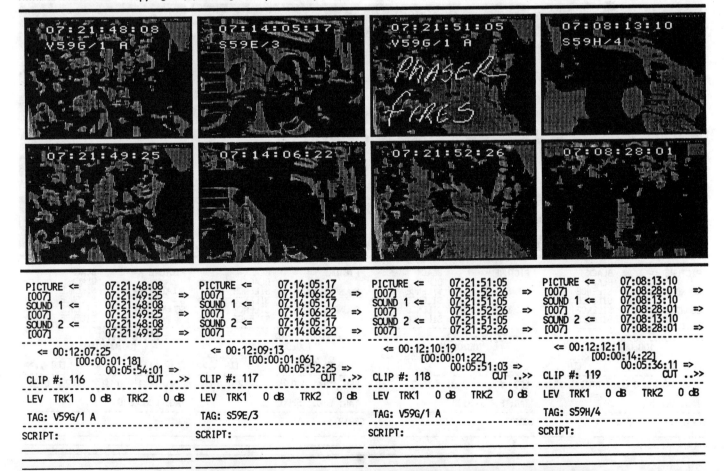

```
PICTURE <=      07:21:48:08        PICTURE <=      07:14:05:17        PICTURE <=      07:21:51:05        PICTURE <=      07:08:13:10
  [007]         07:21:49:25 =>       [007]         07:14:06:22 =>       [007]         07:21:52:26 =>       [007]         07:08:28:01 =>
SOUND 1 <=      07:21:48:08        SOUND 1 <=      07:14:05:17        SOUND 1 <=      07:21:51:05        SOUND 1 <=      07:08:13:10
  [007]         07:21:49:25 =>       [007]         07:14:06:22 =>       [007]         07:21:52:26 =>       [007]         07:08:28:01 =>
SOUND 2 <=      07:21:48:08        SOUND 2 <=      07:14:05:17        SOUND 2 <=      07:21:51:05        SOUND 2 <=      07:08:13:10
  [007]         07:21:49:25 =>       [007]         07:14:06:22 =>       [007]         07:21:52:26 =>       [007]         07:08:28:01 =>
```

```
  <= 00:12:07:25                    <= 00:12:09:13                    <= 00:12:10:19                    <= 00:12:12:11
    [00:00:01:18]                     [00:00:01:06]                     [00:00:01:22]                     [00:00:14:22]
              00:05:54:01 =>                    00:05:52:25 =>                   00:05:51:03 =>                    00:05:36:11 =>
CLIP #: 116          CUT ..>>    CLIP #: 117          CUT ..>>    CLIP #: 118          CUT ..>>    CLIP #: 119          CUT ..>>

LEV  TRK1   0 dB  TRK2   0 dB    LEV  TRK1   0 dB  TRK2   0 dB    LEV  TRK1   0 dB  TRK2   0 dB    LEV  TRK1   0 dB  TRK2   0 dB

TAG: V59G/1 A                   TAG: S59E/3                     TAG: V59G/1 A                   TAG: S59H/4

SCRIPT:                         SCRIPT:                         SCRIPT:                         SCRIPT:
```

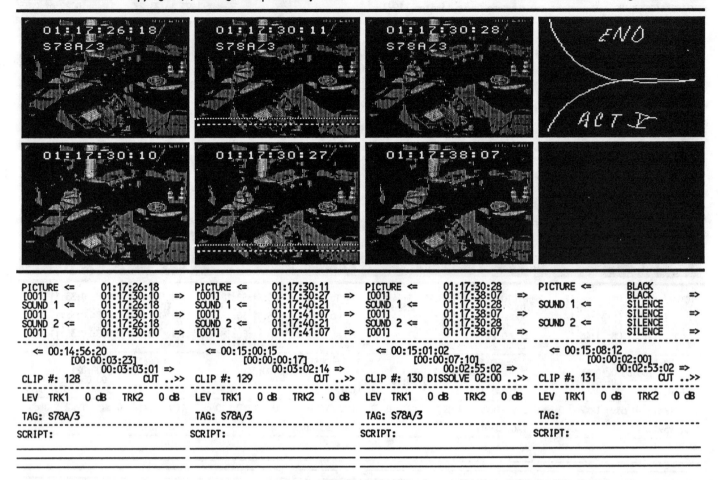

| PICTURE <= | 01:17:26:18 | PICTURE <= | 01:17:30:11 | PICTURE <= | 01:17:30:28 | PICTURE <= | BLACK |
| [001] | 01:17:30:10 => | [001] | 01:17:30:27 => | [001] | 01:17:38:07 => | | BLACK => |
| SOUND 1 <= | 01:17:26:18 | SOUND 1 <= | 01:17:40:21 | SOUND 1 <= | 01:17:30:28 | SOUND 1 <= | SILENCE |
| [001] | 01:17:30:10 => | [001] | 01:17:41:07 => | [001] | 01:17:38:07 => | | SILENCE => |
| SOUND 2 <= | 01:17:26:18 | SOUND 2 <= | 01:17:40:21 | SOUND 2 <= | 01:17:30:28 | SOUND 2 <= | SILENCE |
| [001] | 01:17:30:10 => | [001] | 01:17:41:07 => | [001] | 01:17:38:07 => | | SILENCE => |

|   <= 00:14:56:20   |   <= 00:15:00:15   |   <= 00:15:01:02   |   <= 00:15:08:12   |
|   [00:00:03:23]   |   [00:00:00:17]   |   [00:00:07:10]   |   [00:00:02:00]   |
|   00:03:03:01 =>   |   00:03:02:14 =>   |   00:02:55:02 =>   |   00:02:53:02 =>   |
| CLIP #: 128      CUT ..>> | CLIP #: 129      CUT ..>> | CLIP #: 130 DISSOLVE 02:00 ..>> | CLIP #: 131      CUT ..>> |
| LEV TRK1  0 dB  TRK2  0 dB | LEV TRK1  0 dB  TRK2  0 dB | LEV TRK1  0 dB  TRK2  0 dB | LEV TRK1  0 dB  TRK2  0 dB |
| TAG: S78A/3 | TAG: S78A/3 | TAG: S78A/3 | TAG: |
| SCRIPT: | SCRIPT: | SCRIPT: | SCRIPT: |

| PICTURE <= | BLACK | PICTURE <= | BLACK | PICTURE <= | BLACK | PICTURE <= | BLACK |
| | BLACK => | | BLACK => | | BLACK => | | BLACK => |
| SOUND 1 <= | SILENCE | SOUND 1 <= | SILENCE | SOUND 1 <= | SILENCE | SOUND 1 <= | SILENCE |
| | SILENCE => | | SILENCE => | | SILENCE => | | SILENCE => |
| SOUND 2 <= | SILENCE | SOUND 2 <= | SILENCE | SOUND 2 <= | SILENCE | SOUND 2 <= | SILENCE |
| | SILENCE => | | SILENCE => | | SILENCE => | | SILENCE => |

|   <= 00:15:10:12   |   <= 00:15:15:12   |   <= 00:16:00:14   |   <= 00:16:15:14   |
|   [00:00:05:00]   |   [00:00:45:00]   |   [00:00:15:00]   |   [00:00:03:00]   |
|   00:02:48:02 =>   |   00:02:03:02 =>   |   00:01:48:00 =>   |   00:01:45:00 =>   |
| CLIP #: 132      CUT ..>> | CLIP #: 133      CUT ..>> | CLIP #: 134      CUT ..>> | CLIP #: 135      CUT ..>> |
| LEV TRK1  0 dB  TRK2  0 dB | LEV TRK1  0 dB  TRK2  0 dB | LEV TRK1  0 dB  TRK2  0 dB | LEV TRK1  0 dB  TRK2  0 dB |
| TAG: BLK 5:00 | TAG: E.C. 45:00 | TAG: E.C. 15:00 | TAG: LOGO 3:00 |
| SCRIPT: | SCRIPT: | SCRIPT: | SCRIPT: |

final stages of postproduction in a manner similar to every other shot-on-film, network-quality series.

With the length of each scene precisely set, the composers score the episode according to the decisions made at the music-spotting meetings (see Chapter 5). A music recording session at the Paramount lot can complete the soundtrack for an episode in an afternoon.

Sound-effects editors go to work adding everything from footsteps to the sounds everyone else has been adding on the fly—phaser blasts, door whooshes, the clatter of a tray in the Replimat. If some dialogue doesn't come out clearly enough, actors "loop" their lines in a sound studio—in effect, dubbing themselves with their own voices. (The term loop comes from the days when actors would watch themselves on a film loop, rather than on a video monitor.)

In the meantime, office staff type up credit lists and circulate them to almost everyone involved in the production, checking for spelling, new job titles, and even new names.

For "Emissary," when it reached this stage, what had taken almost two hundred people more than five months in various production phases to complete had finally been distilled down to eighty-five minutes of videotape, plus credits, ready for airing the first week of January 1993.

And when that happened, for the first time, a STAR TREK series broke with tradition. Remember that review for *The Original Series* back in Chapter 2? Well, this is representative of how the world at large greeted *Deep Space Nine,* taken from Jeff Jarvis's review in *TV Guide,* February 13, 1993.

> **Brooks is a mighty presence; this could be his breakout role . . . Terry Farrell is cool and alluring as a wise old beast wearing a beautiful woman's body. Armin Shimerman has a wonderfully rodenty quality as Quark the casino owner, the Donald Trump of space. This cast is at least as strong as *The Next Generation*. But this series is far stronger, for it is more than just a spin-off—it's a wholly new show with its own vision and its own message for our new world.**

Wow.

If it had been a movie, everyone involved would have had a big party and gone on vacation.

But this was television.

All anyone involved with *Deep Space Nine* could do was go home and try to catch some sleep.

Because the next day they'd have to get up and feed the Machine by doing the whole thing over again.

For once, television is just like real life.

*The last line of the first season: "Then I guess we've made some progress after all." Fade to black.*

# SIXTEEN

# WHITHER

# DEEP SPACE NINE?

*STAR TREK . . . has given us a legacy—a message—man[1] can create a*
*future worth living for . . . a future that is full of optimism, hope,*
*excitement, and challenge. A future that proudly proclaims man's ability to*
*survive in peace and reach for the stars as his reward. Whither STAR TREK?*
*It really doesn't matter. We have its legacy . . . all we have to do is use it.*

—Stephen E. Whitfield

**W**ith those words, Stephen Whitfield brought *The Making of Star Trek* to a close.

His book was published in September of 1968, and Whitfield suspected that Star Trek could be facing cancellation by the next year.

Which is, of course, exactly what happened.

But what Whitfield never imagined, nor did anyone else connected with *The Original Series,* was the astounding afterlife that awaited the show. The cancellation of STAR TREK was not an end, but the first step in a brave new beginning, which is still going strong today.

For us now, in 1994, with STAR TREK such a powerful presence in popular culture, are there any projections for its future we can make that aren't self-evident?

Perhaps.

As a vehicle for storytelling, STAR TREK has such flexibility that there is little danger of its disappearing in the decade or two to come. By letting it evolve, by bringing in new story settings and new characters, Paramount has seen to it that there can be a STAR TREK for each generation—on television, in movies, in books and recordings and computer games, and, on the horizon, in virtual reality and interactive theme-park attractions. With that type of support, STAR TREK is most unlikely to grow moribund.

Will there be more series? Undoubtedly. Whether or not *Deep Space Nine* goes seven full seasons, there will be STAR TREK: VOYAGER. And perhaps when these

[1]Remember, this was written back when the STAR TREK preamble went, "To boldly go where no *man* has gone before."

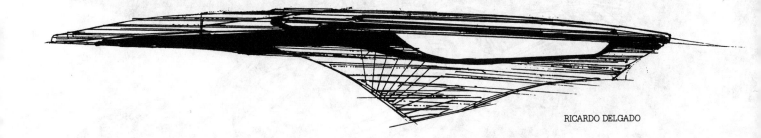

RICARDO DELGADO

An Enterprise *yet to be?*

two variations have reached the peak of their appeal, it might be time to return to another *Enterprise,* with an all-new crew.

But, more importantly as we look into the entertainment possibilities of the next century, we can see that just as *The Next Generation* helped usher in a new era for syndicated television in which the power of the traditional networks declined, a STAR TREK property might someday be perfectly poised to herald the five-hundred-channel universe.

In our first meeting with Rick Berman, we talked about the future of television and the possibilities of video on demand, and he agreed that sometime in the future, even the notion of an all-STAR TREK channel might not be out of the question.

Just as magazines are distributed today, subscribers would be able to download each new adventure of a future STAR TREK series as it was released. In between new adventures, all the other STAR TREK material would be available for review.

The ramifications of such interactive technology is what has led some futurists to proclaim even now that the five-hundred-channel universe is obsolete, destined to be replaced by the *single-channel* universe, where *everything* is available *on demand* to *everyone.*

Imagine, being able to speak to your television/computer hybrid and ask it for any information, any music, any visual presentation, at will.

Sound familiar?

It should. We've been watching exactly that type of technology at work for the past quarter century. On STAR TREK.

In 1966, STAR TREK was a dream shared by a few. Part of its appeal was based in science-fiction technology, but the heart of the dream lay in Gene Roddenberry's optimism for the future.

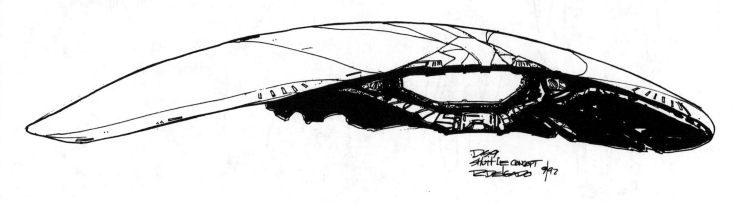

*There's still more to be explored with Deep Space Nine.*

Today, STAR TREK is an experience shared by millions. Its jargon has entered our vocabulary, its characters and technology are icons of the future throughout the world. It has, in some small sense, helped create our present by being part of the fabric of our society.

Let's hope that it has brought more to us than an appreciation of technology. Let's hope that a generation of children will grow up accepting without doubt that a man of color can command a space station and a woman can be his equal.

Let's hope those children know that what makes us human is not our differences on the outside, but all that is the same within us.

Whither *Deep Space Nine?*

That's not the question anymore. (Can't you hear Michael Piller asking, What makes it *personal?*)

The proper question is, Whither humanity?

Gene Roddenberry had an answer to that one, and almost thirty years later, we're still paying attention, every week, every episode.

Maybe that means he got it right.

## DS-9 AWAY SUIT
**STARFLEET PROTECTIVE UNIFORM**

BREATHING COLLAR OR "BREATHER"

ENVIRON-INDICATOR
MONITORS, WARNS USER

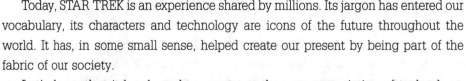

JIM MARTIN

# ROLL CREDITS

*Appendix 1*

*Round up the usual suspects.*

—Louis Renault

**C**redits for *Deep Space Nine* change from episode to episode as people change jobs, or simply because some crew members, such as editors and visual-effects supervisors, alternate the episodes they work on. That said, these are the credits for the first hour of the pilot episode, "Emissary, Part I," which, unfortunately, is by no means a complete listing of all the people who contributed to the show or the series.

## Main Title Credits

### STAR TREK
### DEEP SPACE NINE

*In the midst of a series that owes much of its visual flair to advances in computer imagery, visual-effects producer Dan Curry hand-inked this title logo. "I'm a master of low-tech and fifteenth-century technology," he says with a shrug.*

### Based upon
### "STAR TREK"
### Created by Gene Roddenberry

*Which means that not only is Roddenberry getting the credit due him, but his estate is receiving a creator's fee, plus a portion of the series' earnings.*

Starring
AVERY BROOKS
as Cmdr. Sisko

Also Starring
RENE AUBERJONOIS
as Odo

DISS

lyrical exploration
of D.S.9
DOWN ARM

SIDDIG EL FADIL
as Dr. Bashir

TERRY FARRELL
as Lt. Dax

DISS

from SECOND
RING TO O.P.S.
& PROMENADE

RICARDO DELGADO

CIRROC LOFTON
as Jake Sisko

COLM MEANY
as Chief O'Brien

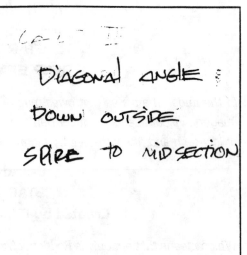

DIAGONAL ANGLE
DOWN OUTSIDE
SPIRE to MID SECTION

DISS

A preliminary storyboard for the
opening credits.

**Starring**
**AVERY BROOKS**
**as**
**Commander Sisko**

*Brooks's name comes first, with the other members of the ensemble appearing in alphabetical order. He is the commander, after all.*

**Also Starring**
**RENE AUBERJONOIS**
**as**
**Odo**

**SIDDIG EL FADIL**
**as**
**Doctor Bashir**

**TERRY FARRELL**
**as**
**Lieutenant Dax**

**CIRROC LOFTON**
**as**
**Jake Sisko**

*A good credit to have, since Lofton is not in every episode. It means he's considered part of the regular cast and not just a recurring character.*

**COLM MEANEY**
**as**
**Chief O'Brien**

**ARMIN SHIMERMAN**
**as**
**Quark**

**NANA VISITOR**
**as**
**Major Kira**

**Created By**
**RICK    &    MICHAEL**
**BERMAN       PILLER**

*And with that all-important credit, the opening title sequence fades to black . . . and after the commercial we resume with the following "supered"—as in superimposed —over the live action.*

# Opening Credits

## "EMISSARY"

### Special Guest Star
### PATRICK STEWART

*Lucky thing he was able to convince the producers of his other show to let him have some time off to do this one.*

### Guest Starring
### CAMILLE SAVIOLA

*. . . as the Kai Opaka.*

### FELECIA M. BELL

*. . . as Sisko's wife, Jennifer.*

### MARC ALAIMO

*. . . as DS9's previous commander, the Cardassian Gul Dukat. This is Alaimo's fifth STAR TREK role. His first role was as the Chief Delegate of the cannibalistic Antican contingent in the* Next Generation *first-season episode "Lonely Among Us." Also in the first season, he played Tebok, one of the first Romulans met by Picard and his crew, in "The Neutral Zone." That was followed by his first Cardassian role, Gul Macet, in "The Wounded," and, in what must have been a relief from all the appliances he had worn over the years, as the human gambler Frederick La Rouque, in the fifth-season* Next Generation *episode "Time's Arrow, Part I."*

### Music By
### DENNIS McCARTHY

*McCarthy wrote the Emmy-winning opening theme for the series, and because he also scored this episode, he receives sole music credit. Since individual episodes are scored by different composers, the music credit sometimes will read:* Music By [composer's name], Main Title Theme By DENNIS McCARTHY.

   *The music credit usually comes in the end credits, but for the two-hour version of the pilot, it appeared here.*

### Edited By
### ROBERT LEDERMAN

*Lederman is responsible for cutting together all the different shots into a coherent whole. Several editors' names will appear over the course of a season, because the length of time it takes to edit an episode means the producers must assign episodes to different editors on an alternating basis.*

   *Again, the editor's credit usually comes at the end of an episode.*

### Production Designer
### HERMAN ZIMMERMAN

Zimmerman is responsible for the visual appearance of everything onscreen. This credit is also usually found at the end of an episode.

### Director of Photography
### MARVIN RUSH

Rush is then responsible for capturing the visuals on film. Another credit that usually comes at the end of the show.

### Producer
### PETER LAURITSON

Lauritson's producer role gives him responsibility for the entire postproduction process. He filled the same role on The Next Generation.

### Supervising Producer
### DAVID LIVINGSTON

Livingston says his supervising producer role on Deep Space Nine is the equivalent of being a line producer on any other show. As such, he's responsible for the logistic and budgetary aspects of the production, as well as setting schedules. He is also an accomplished director and contributed the story for "The Nagus."

### Teleplay By
### MICHAEL PILLER

Screenplays are written for the movie screen, teleplays for television. This credit means Piller wrote the script, but that the story the script tells was written by someone else. If a writer, or team of writers, has written both the story and the teleplay, then the onscreen credit will read, "written by."

### Story By
### RICK BERMAN & MICHAEL PILLER

The unofficial style in screenwriting credits is that when two names are joined by an ampersand, it indicates that the writers have worked as a team. If the names are joined with the word "and," then it means the writers worked on the script independently of each other, usually with the last writer named being the last to work on it.

Credits are important not only for ego's sake, but because, under the Writers Guild agreement, they determine how the residuals for an episode are paid out. If a writer has sole "written by" credit, then that writer gets 100 percent of the residuals. Additional writers on a script reduce the residual payments proportionately, though the Guild does set minimum payments.

In order to insure that all writers are treated equally, the Guild has ruled that anytime a producer claims writing credit on a script written under the Guild's jurisdiction, that script must be subject to credit arbitration in which a panel of experienced writers reads all the different versions of a script and story in order to impartially arrive at a binding decision for how the credits must be shared.

## Directed By
## DAVID CARSON

*David Carson is a British director whose first American television assignment was for the third-season* Next Generation *episode "The Enemy." He came back later that same season to direct what is considered to be one of* The Next Generation's *best installments—"Yesterday's Enterprise."*

*The story then proceeds and the next credit doesn't appear until the final moments at the end of the last act, where it appears almost as a signature to all that has gone before. . . .*

## Executive Producers
## RICK   & MICHAEL
## BERMAN    PILLER

*The two people in charge of everything. On the creative side, they approve everything from each word of the script to the number of Bajoran extras on the Promenade. On the business side, they are responsible for approving senior staff and principal actors, and all financial matters related to the series' production.*

*Then, following the end of the episode, the last commercials, and the promo for next week's episode, come the final set of credits.*

# End Credits

## Associate Producer
## STEVE OSTER

*For the pilot episode, Oster's responsibilities were in postproduction, assisting Peter Lauritson. As of this writing, he is now a co-producer with additional responsibilities for postproduction, as Lauritson works on the* Next Generation *feature film.*

## Co-Stars
| | |
|---|---|
| **ARON EISENBERG** | **Nog** |
| **MAX GRODÉNCHIK** | **Ferengi Pit Boss** |
| **STEPHEN DAVIES** | **Tactical Officer** |

*Co-stars are those actors playing specific roles, whether or not they have lines. Extras, stand-ins, and stunt doubles do not usually receive onscreen credit.*

*Note Grodénchik's character designation—Rom had not been invented yet.*

| | |
|---|---|
| **LILY MARIYE** | **Ops Officer** |
| **CASSANDRA BYRAM** | **Conn Officer** |
| **JOHN NOAH HERTZLER** | **Vulcan Captain** |
| **PARKER WHITMAN** | **Cardassian Officer** |

*The first three actors all had double roles. They appeared in the teaser as part of the crew of the Saratoga, then later in the episode as wormhole entities.*

| WILLIAM POWELL-BLAIR | Cardassian Officer |
| FRANK OWEN SMITH | Curzon |
| LYNNDA FERGUSON | Doran |
| STEPHEN ROWE | Chanting Monk |

*In the script, Whitman's and Powell-Blair's roles were distinguished as Cardassian Officer #1 and Cardassian Officer #2. Each had one line. As Curzon, Frank Owen Smith had no lines, but is included here because he did play a specific character (seen in Jadzia Dax's flashback memory brought on by the Orb). The Chanting Monk was one of Piller's first ideas for the series, as noted in the pages from his notebook, reproduced earlier.*

| THOMAS HOBSON | Young Jake |
| DONALD HOTTON | Monk #1 |
| GENE ARMOR | Bajoran Bureaucrat |
| DIANA CIGNONI | Dabo Girl |
| JUDI DURAND | Computer Voice |

*Hobson's role was limited to being unconscious aboard the Saratoga. Majel Barrett has been performing STAR TREK's computer voices since the first series, but now often shares that role with Durand. (For the full two-hour version of "Emissary," which concludes with credits covering actors who appeared in both parts, Barrett is credited with the Computer Voice role along with Durand.)*

## Casting by
### JUNIE LOWRY-JOHNSON, C.S.A.
### RON SURMA

*Casting works both ways—suggesting actors who might be good for a role, and going after other actors on the suggestion of the producers. The C.S.A. after Lowry-Johnson's name stands for the Casting Society of America, a professional guild.*

## Unit Production Manager
### ROBERT della SANTINI

*"Bobby D," as he is affectionately known, handles the massive coordination of people and equipment necessary between what the first unit shoots and what everyone else needs. He also organizes the production meetings that allow all the departments to coordinate their efforts.*

## First Assistant Director
### VENITA OZOLS-GRAHAM

## Second Assistant Director
### ALISA MATLOVSKY

## 2nd Second Assistant Director
### MICHAEL BAXTER

The first assistant director (aka the first AD) is responsible for the set, including issuing call times, as well as directing background extras, and, almost incessantly, calling for "QUIET!" Ozols-Graham was always easy to pick out from the crowd because of the hands-free headset she wore to stay in constant communication with all parts of the production team. The other assistants cover everything from going to the actors' trailers to ask them to come to the set, to running errands for the director and the first AD.

## Costume Designer
## ROBERT BLACKMAN

Blackman heads a crew that includes other designers and costumers responsible for making, altering, and repairing everything worn on the series. A rule—of—thumb estimating cost—$1,000 per costume, and that's just for something as simple as Kira's uniform.

## Visual Effects Supervisor
## ROBERT LEGATO

For the first season, Legato oversaw and helped devise all the different visual effects used in the series, drawing on his extensive experience with The Next Generation. Legato left the series after the first season to become a visual-effects maven at James Cameron's Digital Domain. Legato's role on both STAR TREK series is now filled by visual-effects producer Dan Curry. The visual-effects workload is so great that he has two teams of specialists working for him—one team handles the even-numbered episodes, the other team handles the odd-numbered episodes.

## Make-Up Designed and Supervised by
## MICHAEL WESTMORE

Westmore heads the makeup department, as well as applying the makeup for some of the key actors. On the Paramount lot, a new makeup facility for Westmore is being constructed, which will be able to support four major productions at once, two of which will be Deep Space Nine and Voyager. The others will be used for features or other television series as needed.

## Scenic Art Supervisor/
## Technical Consultant
## MICHAEL OKUDA

## Senior Illustrator/
## Technical Consultant
## RICK STERNBACH

Scenic art is that which actually appears on the screen, such as computer graphics, signs, and equipment consoles. Illustrations are most often of props, vehicles, and sets—that is, things that will be constructed for which the illustration is a guide. See Chapters 9 and 11 for more detailed descriptions of Okuda's and Sternbach's many contributions to the look and the continuity of this series and The Next Generation.

*In the second season, Jim Martin joined the* Deep Space Nine *art department as the junior illustrator, and many of his imaginative designs are featured throughout this book.*

## Additional Visual Effects Supervision
## GARY HUTZEL

## Post Production Supervisor
## TERRI MARTINEZ

*Hutzel leads the odd-numbered visual-effects team. Terri Martinez (now credited as Terri Potts) keeps track of where all the elements of the show are as they wend their way through post-production.*

| | |
|---|---|
| Art Director | RANDY McILVAIN |
| Set Decorator | MICKEY S. MICHAELS |
| Set Designers | JOSEPH HODGES |
| | ALAN S. KAYE |
| | NATHAN CROWLEY |

*McIlvain works in Zimmerman's department, responsible for managing all the artwork generated for props, graphics, sets, and models.*

*Michaels was the person who found out about Mark Shepherd's paintings and used them to decorate Jake's bedroom as mentioned in Chapter 1.*

| | |
|---|---|
| Script Supervisor | JUDI BROWN |
| Special Effects | GARY MONAK |
| Property Master | JOE LONGO |
| Chief Lighting Technician | WILLIAM PEETS |
| First Company Grip | BOB SORDA |
| Wardrobe Supervisor | CAROL KUNZ |

*The script supervisor keeps track of continuity, all printed takes, and makes sure the dialogue is performed as written.*

*Special effects are practical—or mechanical—effects performed on the set. They include "pyros"—short for pyrotechnics—and "wire gags"—such as when a character or prop has to fly. Because special effects are often combined with visual effects—e.g. when a phaser beam burns a sparking hole through a door—a great deal of coordination between the two departments is required.*

*The property master is in charge of obtaining or building all the props that are required for a scene. A surprising number of props are purchased, such as glasses for Quark's bar and some of the decorations in various crew quarters. But most props are designed and built especially for the show, or pulled from storage and refurbished.*

*The chief lighting technician is the head gaffer, responsible for lighting the sets—a job that requires aesthetic knowledge of lighting as well as an electrician's skill.*

*Grips are responsible for camera positioning and movement. The first company grip positions and moves the camera used to film the principal actors under the director. The second unit, which shoots close-ups and inserts and other technical scenes, is not given a credit here, though it has its own technical crew, including grips and gaffers.*

*The wardrobe supervisor is part of Robert Blackman's team, responsible for making sure all the wardrobe requirements of the day are met.*

| | |
|---|---|
| **Hair Designer** | **CANDY NEAL** |
| **Make-Up Artist** | **JANNA PHILLIPS** |
| | **CRAIG REARDON** |
| | **JILL ROCKOW** |
| **Hair Stylist** | **RICHARD SABRE** |
| | **GERALD SOLOMON** |

*The hair designer works as part of Michael Westmore's team, creating hairstyles to complement Westmore's makeup designs.*

*The makeup artists apply makeup and appliances under Westmore's direction. Each of Westmore's team is also an experienced technician, capable of sculpting designs and pouring molds when not needed in the makeup trailer or on the set.*

*The hairstylists execute the hair designs, just as the makeup artists execute Westmore's makeup designs.*

| | |
|---|---|
| **Sound Mixer** | **BILL GOCKE** |
| **Camera Operator** | **JOE CHESS, S.O.C.** |
| **Key Costumers** | **MAURICE PALINSKI** |
| | **PHYLLIS CORCORAN-WOODS** |
| | **JERRY BONO** |
| | **PATTY BORGGREBE-TAYLOR** |

*The sound mixer operates the recording equipment used on the set.*

*The camera operator is the person who sits behind the camera, squinting through the lens, putting it through its paces under the direction of the director and the director of photography. The initials S.O.C. stand for the Society of Operating Cameramen, a union.*

| | |
|---|---|
| **Visual Effects Coordinators** | **MICHAEL BACKAUSKAS** |
| | **CARI THOMAS** |
| | **JUDY ELKINS** |
| | **MARI HOTAKI** |
| **Visual Effects Associate** | **LAURA LANG** |

*These people are part of the team that follows the production from the set to outside suppliers, insuring that visual-effects work is proceeding as planned.*

*After working on the pilot episode, Laura Lang, now Laura Lang-Matz, was hired back as a visual-effects coordinator. She says she seldom watches the show, but that her family never misses it, just so they can read her credit onscreen.*

| | |
|---|---|
| **Scenic Artists** | **DOUG DREXLER** |
| | **DENISE OKUDA** |

| Jr. Illustrator | RICARDO F. DELGADO |
| Video Playback Operator | JOE UNSINN |
| Video Consultant | LIZ RADLEY |

*For the most part, scenic artists create the artwork that actually appears onscreen, while illustrators create artwork for things that will be constructed.*

*The video playback operator works out of camera range to feed video signals to the live monitors on the Deep Space Nine sets. The video consultant helped plan the enormously complex system that permits the live video monitors on the set to be filmed without flicker or other interference. Mike Okuda says, "Liz is our hero."*

| Music Editor | STEPHEN M. ROWE |
| Supervising Sound Editor | BILL WISTROM |
| Supervising Sound Effects Editor | JIM WOLVINGTON |
| Re-Recording Mixers | CHRIS HAIRE, C.A.S. |
| | DOUG DAVEY |
| | RICHARD MORRISON, C.A.S. |

*The soundtrack of a Deep Space Nine episode consists of dialogue recorded on set, dialogue recorded in a studio (to correct improperly recorded lines, or for off-camera dialogue, such as the computer voice), music, and sound effects. The music editor is responsible for assembling the score of an episode, which can consist of from twenty to thirty individual recordings. The supervising sound-effects editor is responsible for insuring that every door hisses when it slides open, and that tricorders don't sound like phasers.*

*The re-recording mixers are the sound engineers who assemble all the separate sound elements into a complete soundtrack.*

| Production Coordinator | HEIDI JULIAN |
| Post Production Coordinator | DAWN HERNANDEZ |
| Assistant Editor | EUGENE WOOD |
| Visual Effects Assistant Editor | ED HOFFMEISTER |
| Pre-Production Associate | LOLITA FATJO |
| Production Associate | KIM FITZGERALD |

*The production coordinator, now Heidi Smothers, coordinates first-unit production.*

*The postproduction coordinator, now Dawn Velazquez, is Peter Lauritson's assistant.*

*The assistant editor works for the editor, keeping the tape machines loaded, transporting the computer disks with editing codes to the on-line editing facility, and generally assisting the editor with his work.*

*The visual-effects assistant editor is responsible for obtaining all the first-unit film required by visual effects, for example, footage of Sisko speaking from a runabout which has to appear on the main screen in Ops. He also supervises the transfer of dailies onto videotape for review, and is responsible for keeping track of all exposed film in storage.*

*The preproduction associate, script coordinator Lolita Fatjo, manages the writers' offices.*

*Production associate Kim Fitzgerald is Michael Piller's assistant. She can't read his handwriting either.*

| | |
|---|---|
| **Stunt Coordinator** | **DENNIS MADALONE** |
| **Construction Coordinator** | **RICHARD J. BAYARD** |
| **Transportation Coordinator** | **STEWART SATTERFIELD** |
| **Science Consultant** | **NAREN SHANKAR** |
| **Casting Executive** | **HELEN MOSSLER, C.S.A.** |

**Filmed with PANAVISION® Cameras and Lenses**

*The stunt coordinator is responsible for hiring stunt doubles, and planning stunts, which can be everything from a fall from a cliff to a fistfight to someone simply pushing through a crowd on the Promenade.*

*The construction coordinator insures that all required sets are built on time and on budget.*

*The transportation coordinator is responsible for everything from moving the entire first unit to a location site, to insuring that the proper models are shipped out for motion-control photography on time.*

*The science consultant reviews scripts and offers suggestions for keeping them consistent with what is known about present-day science, as well as what has been established for twenty-fourth-century science.*

*The casting executive handles the business functions of the casting department.*

*Most production facilities rent the camera equipment they need so they don't have to worry about maintenance and can always have access to the newest equipment. Panavision is owned by Paramount, so it usually provides all the equipment for Paramount productions.*

| | |
|---|---|
| **Motion Control Photography by** | **IMAGE G** |
| **Video Optical Effects By** | **DIGITAL MAGIC** |
| **Special Video Compositing** | **CIS HOLLYWOOD** |
| **Editing Facilities** | **UNITEL VIDEO** |
| **Post Production Sound By** | **MODERN SOUND** |
| | **HOLLYWOOD, CA** |

*These are the outside suppliers who provide specialized functions for the series.*

*Motion-control photography covers all model and miniature work. Video optical effects include phaser blasts and transporter effects. Video compositing is the process by which various visual-effects elements are combined into a single image, such as combining footage of a miniature science outpost with a matte painting of a barren planetary landscape as a runabout flies past. Editing facilities are where the final episode is assembled according to the off-line edit done on the lot.*

*Postproduction sound is the facility where all the sound elements are mixed to form a single, stereo, surround soundtrack.*

| | |
|---|---|
| **Main Title Design By** | **DAN CURRY** |
| **Matte Painting** | **ILLUSION ARTS** |

| | |
|---|---|
| Miniatures | **BRAZIL FABRICATION & DESIGN** |
| | **GREGORY JEIN INC.** |
| Computer Animation | **RHYTHM & HUES, INC.** |
| | **VISION ART DESIGN & ANIMATION** |

**Major League Baseball Trademarks Licensed by
MAJOR LEAGUE BASEBALL PROPERTIES, INC.**

*Visual-effects producer Dan Curry oversaw the design of the majestic opening title sequence seen at the beginning of each episode.*

*For the pilot episode, Illusion Arts produced the multi-plane matte painting of the Bajoran capital in ruins. For the last episode of the first season, footage of that painting was altered by computer graphics to show that the capital was being restored.*

*Tony Meininger, owner of Brazil Fabrication and Design, built the exquisitely detailed DS9 model. Greg Jein has been building spaceship models since the cult classic* Dark Star *and is a prolific builder of models for* STAR TREK *productions.*

*Rhythm & Hues created the Bajoran wormhole effects. Vision Art handles Odo's morphs.*

*A royalty was paid to Major League Baseball for the right to use the 1920 Cubs uniforms seen in Sisko's encounter with the Entities.*

*Translated into English, the legalese means:*

*—Paramount hopes it hasn't unintentionally libeled anyone (as if someone in Idaho named Gul Dukat is going to take offense at being portrayed as a member of a violent race of oppressors)—and if it did, it didn't mean to.*

*—Paramount owns all rights to the contents of this episode and if anyone attempts to derive a benefit from this episode without Paramount's permission, Paramount will use every legal means to stop that attempt, including having criminal charges pressed.*

*—Don't even think about using the words STAR TREK or Deep Space Nine in connection with anything, because Paramount owns them.*

*These warnings may sound ominous, but part of the responsibility of being a trademark owner is that should a copyright dispute ever arise, Paramount must be able to prove to a court that it took all possible steps to protect its ownership of STAR TREK. For the same reason, the Disney Company usually makes the news whenever it has to prosecute day-care centers for painting Disney characters on the wall. It's not that Disney lawyers don't like day-care centers or feel that their company is being deprived of earnings. But unless Disney goes after every unauthorized use of its copyrighted properties, it might undermine a later attempt to go after a large-scale pirate selling millions of dollars' worth of unauthorized Donald Duck T-shirts.*

*Likewise, Paramount must sometimes get tough with well-meaning fans who produce goods based on STAR TREK properties without intending to profit from them, in order to protect itself for major legal challenges to its ownership of STAR TREK.*

*I. A. T. S. E. is the International Alliance of Theatrical and Stage Employes, the union which represents virtually all technical job categories in film and television production. The presence of this logo on the screen shows that* Deep Space Nine *is union made.*

DOLBY SURROUND

Dolby and the ꚰ are trademarks of
Dolby Laboratories Licensing Corporation.

*The Paramount logo consists of the familiar mountain, partially ringed by stars. It was created around 1912-1913, by W. W. Hodkinson, an east coast film distributor. One day while doodling at his desk, he drew the first version of the mountain and beneath it wrote* Paramount, *the name of an apartment building on the way to work. The twenty-two stars were the final touch, added simply because they looked good.*

*The Dolby Surround logo indicates that the soundtrack for the episode has been recorded with the Dolby system surround-sound playback capability. Where available, of course.*

For the record, not counting actors or Berman and Piller, seventy-one people are listed in the credits for "Emissary"—less than half the number of people who actually contribute to its ongoing production as a series.

Not included in these credits are many of the producers' assistants, the writing staff, which had yet to be appointed, the alternate editing and visual-effects teams, and the staffs of the outside suppliers.

Though no one was able to give us an exact figure, most likely because it changes week to week, we estimate that for an average episode, close to 170 people are involved at some point in its production, not counting actors. Add a crowd scene of forty actors, with their attendant wardrobe and makeup people, and an episode's workforce could reach 230. (As of this writing, between the productions of *Deep Space Nine* and STAR TREK: GENERATIONS, along with the preproduction work on *Voyager,* about 500 people are employed by STAR TREK on the Paramount lot.)

Suddenly, those budget figures in Chapter 8 don't seem all that high after all, do they?

# FIRST AND *Appendix II*

# SECOND SEASON

# EPISODES

*This is where the adventure is. This is where heroes are made. Right here. In the wilderness.*

—Dr. Julian Bashir

*This wilderness is my home.*

—Major Kira Nerys

## First-Season Episodes

**Emissary**
Production #721 (As "Emissary, Part I" and "Emissary, Part II," the
two-hour pilot became Productions #401 and #402
Story by Rick Berman & Michael Piller
Teleplay by Michael Piller
Directed by David Carson
   *Series 2-Hour Premiere*
   After the Cardassians withdraw from Bajor, Sisko takes command of DS9, only to find he must leave his past behind if he is to face the future.

**A Man Alone**
Production #403
Story by Gerald Sanford & Michael Piller
Teleplay by Michael Piller
Directed by Paul Lynch
   Security Chief Odo's character is questioned when he is implicated in the murder of a shady Bajoran.

## Past Prologue

Production #404
Written by Kathryn Powers
Directed by Winrich Kolbe

A reunion with a member of the Bajoran underground forces Kira to choose between her people and her duty as a Federation officer.

## Babel

Production #405
Story by Sally Caves & Ira Steven Behr
Teleplay by Michael McGreevey & Naren Shankar
Directed by Paul Lynch

A mysterious epidemic sweeps over Deep Space Nine, and it is up to Kira to find an antidote.

## Captive Pursuit

Production #406
Story by Jill Sherman Donner
Teleplay by Jill Sherman Donner & Michael Piller
Directed by Corey Allen

Through a new friendship with a bizarre alien, Tosk, O'Brien and the rest of the officers of DS9 learn that other beings do not respect life as much as they do.

## Q-Less

Production #407
Story by Hannah Louise Shearer
Teleplay by Robert Hewitt Wolfe
Directed by Paul Lynch

Frequent *Enterprise* visitors Q and Vash introduce themselves to the crew of DS9, while the officers struggle to save the station from imminent destruction.

## Dax

Production #408
Story by Peter Allan Fields
Teleplay by D.C. Fontana & Peter Allan Fields
Directed by David Carson

Curzon Dax, Jadzia's former Trill identity, is accused of murder.

## The Passenger

Production #409
Story by Morgan Gendel
Teleplay by Morgan Gendel & Robert Hewitt Wolfe & Michael Piller
Directed by Paul Lynch

The crew's efforts to thwart a hijack scheme are complicated when a sinister alien criminal hides his consciousness within the brain of someone aboard the station.

## Move Along Home

Production #410
Story by Michael Piller
Teleplay by Frederick Rappaport and Lisa Rich & Jeanne Carrigan-Fauci
Directed by David Carson

Quark's attempt to deceive a newly encountered alien race places the space station's senior officers in a labyrinth of apparent danger.

## The Nagus

Production #411
Story by David Livingston
Teleplay by Ira Steven Behr
Directed by David Livingston

Quark is suddenly named leader of the Ferengi financial empire, and discovers that he's not only popular—he's now a target for death.

## Vortex

Production #412
Written by Sam Rolfe
Directed by Winrich Kolbe

An alien criminal from the other side of the wormhole tempts Odo by telling the shapeshifter he can put the changeling in contact with others like himself.

## Battle Lines

Production #413
Story by Hilary Bader
Teleplay by Richard Danus & Evan Carlos Somers
Directed by Paul Lynch

Sisko, Kira, and Bashir are stranded on a war-torn world where it is impossible for the combatants to die.

## The Storyteller

Production #414
Story by Kurt Michael Bensmiller
Teleplay by Kurt Michael Bensmiller & Ira Steven Behr
Directed by David Livingston

Against his will, O'Brien becomes a spiritual leader of a Bajoran village—and the only one who can save them from a destructive energy force.

## Progress

Production #415

Written by Peter Allan Fields

Directed by Les Landau

A stubborn old Bajoran farmer forces Kira to take a good look at how much she has changed since her alliance with the Federation.

## If Wishes Were Horses

Production #416

Story by Nell McCue Crawford & William L. Crawford

Teleplay by Nell McCue Crawford, William L. Crawford & Michael Piller

Directed by Robert Legato

When members of the station find their fantasies coming to life, it becomes the prelude to a very real danger which threatens everyone.

## The Forsaken

Production #417

Story by Jim Trombetta

Teleplay by Don Carlos Dunaway & Michael Piller

Directed by Les Landau

While an alien entity wreaks havoc with the station's computer, the irrepressible Lwaxana Troi sets her sights for romance—with Odo!

## Dramatis Personae

Production #418

Written by Joe Menosky

Directed by Cliff Bole

Odo is caught in the middle when an alien influence pits Kira against Sisko in a deadly struggle for control of the station.

## Duet

Production #419

Story by Lisa Rich & Jeanne Carrigan-Fauci

Teleplay by Peter Allan Fields

Directed by James L. Conway

Kira discovers that a Cardassian visiting the station could actually be a notorious war criminal.

## In the Hands of the Prophets

Production #420

Written by Robert Hewitt Wolfe

Directed by David Livingston

When a Bajoran spiritual leader objects to Keiko's secular teachings, she threatens to destroy the alliance between Bajor and the Federation.

# Second-Season Episodes

## The Homecoming

Production #421

Story by Jeri Taylor and Ira Steven Behr

Teleplay by Ira Steven Behr

Directed by Winrich Kolbe

Kira risks her life, and war with the Cardassians, to rescue a legendary Bajoran hero from a distant prison colony.

## The Circle

Production #422

Written by Peter Allan Fields

Directed by Corey Allen

Relieved of her post and sent back to Bajor, Kira helps to reveal the hidden force behind the Circle—and a greater secret that could destroy them all.

## The Siege

Production #423

Written by Michael Piller

Directed by Winrich Kolbe

While Sisko leads a daring last stand against the Bajoran takeover forces, Kira and Dax embark on a desperate mission to reveal the truth about the coup.

## Invasive Procedures

Production #424

Story by John Whelpley

Teleplay by John Whelpley and Robert Hewitt Wolfe

Directed by Les Landau

The crew must fight for Jadzia's life when a desperate Trill takes the group hostage and steals the Dax symbiont.

## Cardassians

Production #425

Story by Gene Wolande & John Wright

Teleplay by James Crocker

Directed by Cliff Bole

A young Cardassian, orphaned in the war and raised by Bajorans, causes turmoil on the station when his people attempt to reclaim him.

## Melora

Production #426

Story by Evan Carlos Somers

Teleplay by Evan Carlos Somers and Michael Piller & James Crocker

Directed by Winrich Kolbe

After falling in love with a woman whose species is unable to walk in "normal" gravity, Bashir develops a technology that could free her of her wheelchair forever.

## Rules of Acquisition
Production #427
Story by Hilary Bader
Teleplay by Ira Steven Behr
Directed by David Livingston

A Ferengi female who has defied the law and disguised herself as a male risks it all when she falls in love with Quark.

## Necessary Evil
Production #428
Written by Peter Allan Fields
Directed by James L. Conway

An attack on Quark's life brings Odo face-to-face with a five-year-old unsolved murder—for which Kira was a prime suspect.

## Second Sight
Production #429
Story by Mark Gerhred-O'Connell
Teleplay by Mark Gerhred-O'Connell and Ira Steven Behr & Robert Hewitt Wolfe
Directed by Alexander Singer

Sisko falls in love for the first time since his wife's death, but the object of his affections may not be all that she seems.

## Sanctuary
Production #430
Story by Gabe Essoe & Kelley Miles
Teleplay by Frederick Rappaport
Directed by Les Landau

Kira is torn when a displaced alien race arrives on Deep Space Nine and claims Bajor as its people's legendary homeland.

## Rivals
Production #431
Story by Jim Trombetta and Michael Piller
Teleplay by Joe Menosky
Directed by David Livingston

Quark feels threatened when a charming swindler arrives on Deep Space Nine and opens a competing bar.

## The Alternate
Production #432
Story by Jim Trombetta and Bill Dial
Teleplay by Bill Dial
Directed by David Carson

Odo's mentor arrives on Deep Space Nine intent on resuming his search for Odo's true origin.

## Armageddon Game
Production #433
*Story by Morgan Gendel
*Teleplay by Morgan Gendel and Ira Steven Behr & James Crocker
Directed by Winrich Kolbe

Bashir and O'Brien work to rid two alien races of deadly weapons, unaware that their hosts intend to sacrifice them as part of the peace process.

## Whispers
Production #434
Story by Paul Coyle
Teleplay by Paul Coyle and Michael Piller
Directed by Les Landau

O'Brien returns from a security mission to notice that the entire crew has seemingly turned against him.

## Paradise
Production #435
Story by Jim Trombetta and James Crocker
Teleplay by Jeff King and Richard Manning & Hans Beimler
Directed by Corey Allen

Sisko and O'Brien are stranded on a planet inhabited by a colony of humans who have rejected any form of technology.

## Shadowplay
Production #436
Written by Robert Hewitt Wolfe
Directed by Robert Scheerer

Odo and Dax try to solve the mystery of an alien planet whose inhabitants are disappearing without explanation.

## Playing God
Production #437
Story by Jim Trombetta
Teleplay by Jim Trombetta and Michael Piller
Directed by David Livingston

While hosting her first Trill initiate, Dax discovers a tiny, developing universe, which threatens to destroy the station as it expands.

## Profit and Loss

Production #438

Written by Flip Kobler & Cindy Marcus

Directed by Robert Wiemer

When Quark is reunited with the love of his life, a Cardassian who is now a fugitive, he is ready to sacrifice everything to win her back.

## Blood Oath

Production #439

Television story and Teleplay by Peter Allen Fields

Directed by Winrich Kolbe

Dax risks her life and her future with Starfleet to fulfill a blood oath made with three aged Klingons.

## The Maquis, Part I

Production #440

Story by Rick Berman & Michael Piller & Jeri Taylor and James Crocker

Teleplay by James Crocker

Directed by David Livingston

The Maquis, a group of renegade Federation colonists, violate the Cardassian peace treaty, risking interstellar war.

## The Maquis, Part II

Production #441

Story by Rick Berman & Michael Piller & Jeri Taylor and James Crocker

Teleplay by Ira Steven Behr

Directed by Corey Allen

An old friend of Commander Sisko's becomes an enemy when he leads an attack on a Cardassian colony.

## The Wire

Production #442

Written by Robert Hewitt Wolfe

Directed by Kim Friedman

Dr. Bashir must struggle to save the life of Garak, his Cardassian friend.

## Crossover

Production #443

Story by Peter Allan Fields

Teleplay by Peter Allan Fields and Michael Piller

Directed by David Livingston

A mishap in the wormhole sends Kira and Bashir into an alternate universe where Bajor is a tyrannical power and humans are slaves.

## The Collaborator

Production #444

Story by Gary Holland

Teleplay by Gary Holland and Ira Steven Behr & Robert Hewitt Wolfe

Directed by Cliff Bole

Kira is assigned to investigate a charge of treason against the man she loves.

## Tribunal

Production #445

Written by Bill Dial

Directed by Avery Brooks

O'Brien must face a Cardassian trial, with death the only possible verdict.

## The Jem'Hadar

Production #446

Written by Ira Steven Behr

Directed by Kim Friedman

A peace trip to the Gamma Quadrant pits the Federation against a powerful new enemy.

# HOW TO
# WRITE FOR
# DEEP SPACE NINE

*Instinct plus opportunity equals profit.*

—The 9th Rule of Acquisition

**D**eep Space Nine is one of the rare television series that is open to script submissions from *anyone,* not just experienced television writers. In fact, in the March 1994 issue of the Writers Guild of America, west, *Journal,* only two of the ninety-seven series included on the TV Market List specifically list a separate phone number for submissions by writers without agents—*Deep Space Nine* and *The Next Generation.* The Paramount hotline number to call to obtain information about submitting spec scripts to *Deep Space Nine* is 213-956-8301. A recorded announcement will give you all the details you need to know about requesting a release form and submission guidelines which will enable Paramount to accept and read your script. (And despite all the horror stories you might have heard about ideas being stolen in Hollywood, don't worry about signing a release form for a *Deep Space Nine* script. If the writing staff see an idea they like, they have the budget to buy it.)

Why are the STAR TREK series apparently so magnanimous in looking for contributions from first-time writers?

Because they are voracious consumers of stories.

Remember back to Chapter 3. There are 79 original series episodes, 6 original series movies, and, by the end of 1994, there will be 176 *Next Generation* episodes, one *Next Generation* movie, and at least 46 *Deep Space Nine* episodes. That's more than *300* STAR TREK stories. Yet, if *Deep Space Nine* and *Voyager* go on to match *The Next Generation's* success, then between now and 2001, Paramount's expecting to come up with 300 more!

That's not all. The 300 existing STAR TREK stories are only those stories that made it to script and then to production. Think of all the story ideas that were presented and turned down. Michael Piller conservatively estimates the stories pitched to *The Next Generation* alone at more than 4,000.

To further add to the story shortage, among television writers it's generally accepted that there are fewer than twenty basic story plots; some say fewer than ten.[1]

In other words, STAR TREK *needs* stories and will take them wherever it can find them.

Does this mean you should pick up the phone and book a pitch session with the writing staff right now? No. Not until you've read this Appendix and are willing to do some work.

Let's start with Michael Piller's own comments about what kind of story he's looking for.

## Developing a Story

"The only thing I can say to a new writer is that we need stories that are not about *things,* but about *people.* They have to be fresh in terms of their concept—we can't just repeat ourselves with things we've done before.

"The stories have to be about the main cast of characters and not about visitors to the space station. They can be stories that include visitors, but they must ultimately turn into catalysts for stories that we can tell about our own cast of characters.

"Premises that explore some nature of the human condition are the best shows. 'Duet,' which I find was probably the best show of the first season, was two characters in a room—very simple and very eloquent. It's one of my favorite kinds of shows.

"One of the things about *Deep Space Nine* that I've been very proud of in the second season is that it has a true social conscience. And the nature of the challenges that face the crew of *Deep Space Nine* is in some ways more difficult than the challenges that face the crew of *The Next Generation.* Because at the end of every hour of *The Next Generation,* they get on their horse and ride out of town. But the people who are on *Deep Space Nine* are stuck there to face the problems that are there week after week.

"If you want parallels to contemporary society and the problems that we live with, you will find that they are much easier to adapt to *Deep Space Nine* than they are to *Next Generation.* There are stories and subjects we wanted to do for years on *Next Generation* that we could never quite figure out how to do: the pollution show, or the AIDS show, or topics like that. The difficulty in doing those shows is because it's hard to come into somebody else's town or somebody else's planet and start fixing them and curing them and telling them what to do. It's not what STAR TREK is about.

"But when you deal with, say, the influx of refugees through the wormhole at *Deep Space Nine,* it's an immediate problem. It has to do with where we live, and where we're stationed, and the people who have different agendas coming together to argue about what's right and wrong, about telling the aliens that they can't stay

[1] *A Practical Manual of Screenplay Writing for Theatre and Television Films* by Lewis Herman reduces all possible plots to nine basic structures. In practice, these structures are usually interwoven as plots and subplots to create the dynamics of any given script.

Harris Yulin as Marritza and Nana Visitor as Kira in "Duet"—which Michael Piller feels was one of the best shows of the first season.

here. To me, there's a certain kind of heroism in facing a problem and sticking with it, and that's a hallmark of the characters of *Deep Space Nine,* something that we've discovered as we've gone along, that makes for interesting storytelling.

"So you can find ways of taking subjects out of contemporary life and out of your newspaper and turning them into *Deep Space Nine* stories more easily than you can for *Next Generation.* And, yet, there has to be enough distance between the reality and what you translate it into in Bajoran terms.

"The second-season two-parter called 'The Maquis' is very much based on situations that are going on in the West Bank and the Gaza Strip in the Mideast.[2] And we have managed to find a way to put it in Cardassian/Federation terms so that it becomes a story we can tell. It seems like it's perfectly part of the STAR TREK universe. It doesn't preach and it doesn't say anything specific about the Israeli situation, but you might get an understanding of the kind of conflicts that those people are dealing with, from this kind of story.

"We like character stories. We certainly like science-fiction stories. We take the people off the space station and through the wormhole more and more to go explore other areas of space. I just think the best advice I could give any potential writers is to make sure that *they're doing stories about our people.*"

[2]As of this writing, the Maquis are to play a part in STAR TREK: VOYAGER.

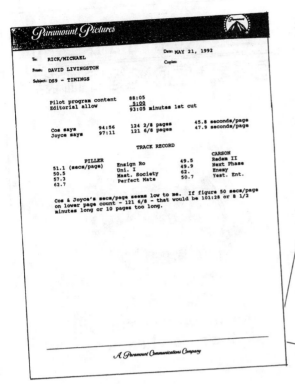

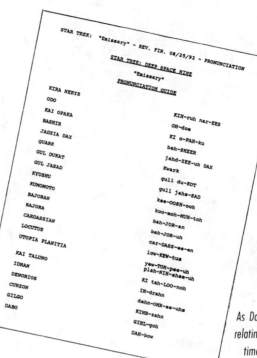

Left:

As David Livingston's arcane calculations relating script pages to seconds of screen time show, script length is of critical concern in planning the production of an episode.

Right:

Writers for Deep Space Nine have an extra duty to perform when they hand in their scripts.

## Selling a Story

So, you have an exciting story ripped from the headlines that fits perfectly into the STAR TREK universe and can be told in personal terms about the main characters of DS9. You also have read copies of *Deep Space Nine* scripts and know all about its teaser and five-act format so you know how to structure your story.[3] What do you do next? Come up with six or seven more stories. Now you might have something to sell. And there are basically two ways to do it.

The first is to write a spec script that's so good Michael Piller will buy it as soon as he reads it.[4] It's a long shot, but it's happened on *The Next Generation:* Ronald D. Moore's "The Bonding" and Melinda Snodgrass's "Measure of a Man" were both spec scripts, and both writers ended up with staff positions.

The second and more common method is to "pitch" a story to the writing staff that they will then want to buy. A pitch meeting involves the writer sitting down with one or more members of the writing staff and telling them several stories. It's not necessary for the stories to be fully worked out in act-by-act detail, but, ideally, they should have an intriguing beginning, some good character moments and plot twists, and a definite ending.

However, planning on pitching to the series doesn't relieve you of the need to write a spec script. Before Piller's office will book a pitch session with an unagented writer, someone on staff has to evaluate your work. The only way they can do that is to read your spec script.

Once your spec script has been evaluated—a process that can take between six and nine months—three outcomes are possible. The first is that Piller's office will return your script with a brief thank-you. The second is that your script will be

[3]Ideally, the teaser should be between 3 to 6 pages long, and each act should be about 10 to 11 pages long, to make a first-draft script of 55 to 56 pages. The script extracts reprinted in this book show the same indents and line lengths that the actual scripts must use, in a monospaced, 12-characters-per-inch font like Courier.

Understandably, Paramount is unable to mail copies of scripts to everyone who wants to submit stories to *Deep Space Nine.* Experienced television writers can obtain scripts from their agents.

[4]A spec script is a script written on the writer's own initiative, without an offer to buy it—hence, on speculation. No reputable production company asks writers to write on spec, but all companies usually need samples of a writer's work to evaluate before deciding whether or not to consider the writer for an assignment. When a writer is starting out and has no sales, one or two spec scripts work as a good introduction.

Does Piller actually read spec scripts? Only on the recommendation of someone on his staff. However, staff members do dutifully take scripts from the submissions pile every week to consider them. Good ones get passed around, then brought to Piller's attention for a final decision.

"In the Hands of the Prophets"

FINAL DRAFT
APRIL 2, 1993

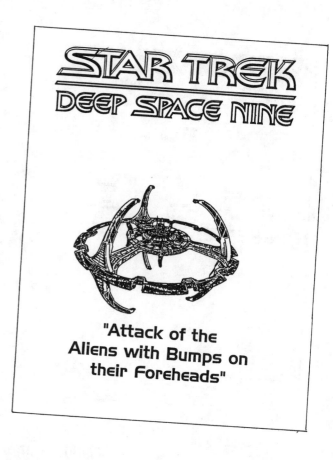

"Attack of the Aliens with Bumps on their Foreheads"

*Above left:*
*By the end of the first season, Deep Space Nine scripts had acquired a logo and a look of their own.*

*Above right:*
*Even though this script cover is displayed in the DS9 art department, we somehow doubt it will go into production anytime*

returned but you will be invited to pitch additional ideas. And the third is that Piller will want to buy your script—in which case it's fairly certain that you'll be invited to pitch as well. To date, no spec script submitted to *Deep Space Nine* has sold. But somebody has to be the first.

The concept that the series might reject a spec script but still want to consider new stories by the same writer isn't unusual. There are many reasons for rejecting a script that have nothing at all to do with how good the story is or how well it's written, the most common reason being that the script is close to something that is already being worked on. (We know a writing team who pitched a story to *Deep Space Nine* and were told it was so good it was being broadcast the next night! The writers had created a story that was virtually identical to an episode that had already been filmed but not aired. Given that an episodic-television story must fit a certain structure, and that all writers are working with the same character dynamics and setting, it's no surprise that so many similar stories are generated independently of each other. But because the writers had so obviously captured the style of the series, they were invited back.)

The fact that a writer has demonstrated his or her ability to write a 56-page script in the proper format, *without* spelling errors, concentrating on the main characters, and with dialogue in the characters' own voices, tells the writing staff that if the writer does pitch a good idea, then it won't be a complete waste of time and money to give that writer the script assignment.

Wasting time and money is a very real concern, because Paramount is bound by the rules of the Writers Guild of America, and the Guild clearly states that the money to be paid for a script is never contingent on the work being *acceptable*, it is contingent on the work being *turned in*. In other words, if you pitched a great story to the show and were assigned the script, and then turned in 100 pages of blank-verse dialogue that called for a $15 million visual-effects sequence, Paramount would still have to pay you for your completely unusable work. Thus, when the writing staff give out an assignment, they must be convinced that the person getting the assignment can actually complete it in a professional manner. Which is why the spec script is so important.

Presuming you write a spec script that earns you an invitation to pitch, what can you expect? First of all, a polite and enthusiastic audience. The writing staff need ideas and are under instructions not to break the flow of a writer's presentation.

On the writer's side, it's important not to take advantage of your audience. Have a quick version of each story as well as a long one. Tell the quick version first, giving the main premise in a minute or two, so the writing staff have an opportunity to skip over stories that are clearly not going to work. Then, if the basic premise is appealing and not already being developed, go into it in more detail. If the writing staff like the story, they will often ask questions or suggest alternate plot twists. Join in these conversations enthusiastically. Writing for *Deep Space Nine* is definitely a group experience and you're not only auditioning your ideas, you're auditioning yourself. After all, if the writing staff do want to buy one of your ideas, they're going to want to know if they can work with you. Let them know they can.[5]

Depending on the input from the writing staff, a pitch session can last anywhere from ten minutes to an hour, in which the writer might present six to eight stories, with perhaps half of them worked out in considerable detail, and half in broad strokes. Experienced television writers sometimes prepare a number of one-line ideas as well, to see if any concepts might intrigue the staff. But to pull this off, you have to be able to think on your feet about character interactions and story structure, which is why it's not recommended for beginning writers.

Even if your session has gone well, unless Michael Piller himself is in the room—unlikely for a first-time writer—you won't get a commitment. The decision to buy something always rests with Piller, who will listen to his staff report on likely stories. Sometimes, staff writers will indicate that they like a particular concept but feel the story hasn't been developed properly or in enough detail to convince them it could work as a script. In this case, they might suggest that *if* the writer were to work on the idea a bit more, they would be interested in hearing the idea pitched again. They must stress the "if" because if they outright asked you to work on it, that would be considered an assignment under Writers Guild rules and they'd have to pay you.

If you are invited back, by all means accept. Persistence and enthusiasm are two characteristics much appreciated at *Deep Space Nine*. And each time you talk with the writing staff, you will learn more about what they're looking for and how they think about stories already in progress. The next time you pitch, your stories should be even closer to what they're looking for.

[5] It is a matter of debate whether or not a writer should leave behind written "notes" after a pitch session. Under Guild rules, no studio can ask a writer to put words on paper without paying for the work. However, there is no rule that prevents a writer from volunteering to leave behind a few brief sentences for each story discussed. Many staff writers appreciate this courtesy, because they must prepare a written report of every pitch they hear.

If you do have notes to leave behind, be sure to tell the staff writers at the beginning of the session so they can adjust their note-taking accordingly.

# After a Sale

*Script details are often changed for production reasons. As originally written, this scene from "Dramatis Personae" called for Kira to haul Quark over the bar by his ears—which would have ripped Armin Shimerman's appliance off. Another change that occurred later in the script, because of this change, was that Quark appeared in a neck brace instead of ear bandages. Preproduction meetings are held to discover just these sorts of details.*

Let's be optimistic and assume that a few days after your pitch a staff writer gives you a call and says Michael Piller wants to buy your idea and would like you to come in and have a story meeting. You may or *may not* get the teleplay assignment—it isn't a given, particularly for a new writer.

People who aren't television writers generally have the idea that writing a script is like writing a novel: The writer (or writing team) sits down at a word processor, starts with FADE IN on page 1, and types through to THE END on page 56.

It isn't.

A novel is the creation of one (or two) people. It can safely be assumed that each word on the page is there because the writer(s) intended it to be there, and that the story is the sum total of those words, and nothing more. But as we've seen, a television script is simply a starting point for the creative contributions of dozens of people and for the technical skills of dozens more. And because so many people's time and efforts, and so much of Paramount's money, is riding on the successful completion of a *Deep Space Nine* script, it only stands to reason that each step is going to be monitored and adjusted before the next step can be taken. And that's exactly what happens.

The first step in the actual writing of a *Deep Space Nine* script has nothing at all to do with script format. It even has nothing at all to do with a script treatment broken into acts. It's simply the writing of a prose story, perhaps seven or eight pages long. The purpose of this exercise is to find the story's overall structure, and—most importantly—to put something down in writing to which the rest of the writing staff can respond.[6]

As an example, here's the original story written by Robert Hewitt Wolfe for the concluding episode of the first season, "In the Hands of the Prophets," dated February 18, 1993. It also serves as an illustration of the amount of detail that should be developed for a story pitch.[7]

### STAR TREK: DEEP SPACE NINE
#### "In the Hands of the Prophets"
#### Robert Hewitt Wolfe

   This story will explore the conflict between Federation values and Bajoran spiritualism.

   We open on Keiko teaching her students a course in DNA tracing . . . without being too on the nose, discussing the possible origin of life (amino acids? unicellular organisms? Bio-TECH help please). She is surprised when the Abbot of DS-9's Bajoran Temple visits her class. Keiko continues her lesson, nodding cordially to the Abbot, who does not acknowledge. After the lesson continues a while, the Abbot begins to interject questions—questions that challenge the scientific facts with spiritual assumptions taught by the Prophets, interpreted by the scholars, administered by centuries of Kais. Keiko explains the scientific theories

---

[6]Beginning writers often ask if the series will consider written spec stories instead of spec scripts. The answer is no.

[7]Because Wolfe was a staff writer at the time he wrote this script (he is now story editor for the series) he did not have to pitch the original concept. Instead, the starting point of the story—a controversy that begins when Keiko teaches a science topic at odds with Bajoran spiritual beliefs—was on an "idea board" in Michael Piller's office. On this board are written one-line descriptions of ideas around which Piller would like to see stories developed. Wolfe walked into Piller's office one day after finishing an assignment and asked if he could develop the science/spirituality conflict idea. Piller said yes, and Wolfe came up with what ultimately became the bookend to the pilot episode.

as best she can, but finally only infuriates the Abbot, who storms out, accusing Keiko of blasphemy.

Meanwhile, O'Brien has been called to Odo's office. One of Odo's security monitors is on the fritz. O'Brien assigned the repairs to his Bajoran apprentice, Anara, but she apparently never got around to it. O'Brien rolls up his sleeves and gets to work. Soon, however, he makes an upsetting discovery. One of his tools is missing . . . one he needs to complete the repairs. Odo suggests O'Brien misplaced it, but O'Brien is adamant . . . he doesn't misplace his tools. He asks the computer to locate the gizmo. There are several such tools on the station, so he orders the computer to run down the location of each.

Meanwhile, Keiko comes to Sisko and tells him about her confrontation with the Abbot. Sisko explains that since the loss of Kai Opaka, Traditionalist and Progressive factions have been vying for control of the Bajoran religious orders. The Traditionalists want to return Bajor to its antebellum traditions, with religion at the center of daily life. Sisko believes the Traditionalists are trying to exploit Keiko to force the issues. But Sisko promises to intercede on Keiko's behalf. As a Federation venture, her school must remain independent from the Bajoran government and separate from Bajoran religious conflicts.

Sisko tries to reason with the Abbot. No one is being forced to attend Keiko's school. Bajoran parents are free to withdraw their children if they wish. The Abbot doesn't see it that way. This is a Bajoran station and the school should abide by Bajoran traditions. Sisko quotes Prophecy to back up his point, but the Abbot remains unswayed. If Keiko doesn't recant her blasphemy and teach the Bajoran truth, the Abbot cannot be responsible for the consequences.

Sisko consults with Kira, who fears that, despite Sisko's best efforts, the situation will turn ugly.

As the story unfolds, we will find Kira's worst fears realized . . . egged on by the Abbot, a vocal minority among the Bajorans living on the station become increasingly hostile to the Federation personnel. Sisko takes all the logical steps to defuse the situation, but his efforts only seem to make things worse.

As Bajoran/Federation tensions rise, O'Brien finds himself confronted by a growing mystery. Not only is his TECH gizmo missing, so are a number of other tools. More importantly, Anara, O'Brien's Bajoran apprentice, has disappeared. Kira suspects Anara stole the tools and left, but O'Brien isn't so sure. Kira and O'Brien investigate. There is no record of the apprentice leaving the station. Eventually, they find Anara's combadge, but still no sign of the apprentice.

The situation on the station finally deteriorates to the point that Sisko goes to Bajor to consult with Bajoran spiritual leaders. But the Bajorans stonewall him. The only leader willing to talk to him is En-Kai Tyma Ran, a highly regarded Bajoran religious figure and a dark horse candidate to replace Kai Opaka. Tyma is a big, burly ex-terrorist, vigorous despite his years, who talks and dresses like the common people. As pacifist and a progressive, he is at odds with Traditionalist elements in the Bajoran Orders. Still, he is not without influence and promises to do what he can to help Sisko.

Back on the station, the Bajoran/Federation conflict is wearing on Kira and O'Brien's working relationship. Still, they conduct a second sensor sweep of the station, this time searching not for the tools, but for their component minerals (Federation tech like the tools and Cardassian tech like the station are easily distinguishable). This sweep turns up an inexplicable concentration of Federation building materials in one of the active power conduits. O'Brien takes the conduit off-line and checks it out. He and Kira find the melted remains of the tools, which have been destroyed almost beyond recognition. But that's not all. Along with the tools, they find a cellular residue of organic material . . . the scattered remains of a dead body.

Kira has Bashir examine the remains. The genetic material in the cells has been disrupted at a molecular level by exposure to the high intensity microwave radiation of the power conduit. Based on the level of disruption, Bashir dates the remains at three to four days old. Positive ID remains difficult, but Bashir is confident he will be able to reconstruct the DNA and ID the body. (Anara is obviously the most likely candidate.)

The situation on the station continues to worsen. Fringe elements of the Bajoran population, following the Abbot's lead, agitate against the Federation, intimidating the other Bajorans into cooperating. Children are withdrawn from Keiko's school . . . Bajoran supernumeraries fail to show up for work . . . the mood on the station gets uglier and uglier. Sisko goes to the Abbot and tries to work out the dispute, but the Abbot smugly insists that he is helpless to control his congregation's righteous outrage.

Back in the infirmary, Bashir makes an unsettling discovery. The cells Kira found were hit by a phaser blast, previous to their exposure to the microwave radiation of the conduit. Whoever the cells belonged to, their death was no accident.

Finally, the situation on the station becomes untenable. Keiko's life is threatened. Sabotage ruins a vital piece of station equipment. Sisko has no choice but to ask En-Kai Tyma to come to DS-9 . . .

Meanwhile, Bashir finally IDs the remains . . . the cells did belong to Anara . . . at least some of them did. There are two additional DNA groupings mixed in with Anara's. Three people were killed, not just one. And Bashir has no idea who the other two were.

En-Kay Tyma arrives on the station to mediate the dispute. Sisko stresses that this is a crucial test of Bajoran/Federation relations. If Bajor feels its culture and values are not respected, the Federation will not be welcome . . . but, likewise, if the Bajorans cannot learn tolerance, they will have no place in the Federation. Tyma and Sisko proceed to Quark's, where all sides will sit down to talk.

Soon after they leave, Bashir arrives in Ops. He has uncovered curious trace elements mixed in with the cellular residue . . . fibers of a type of course wool woven on Bajor . . . a fabric worn almost exclusively by Bajoran monks. Kira asks the computer if all the monks from the temple are accounted for. The computer responds the monks are all accounted for . . . they're on the Promenade, waiting to meet Tyma.

Cut to two of the monks . . . As Tyma approaches, they retrieve a pair of phasers that have been hidden on the Promenade . . . take aim at the En-Kai . . . and prepare to fire . . . just Kira as beams in. She alerts Sisko and the two of them stun the monk/assassins and save the En-Kai.

Unfortunately, neither assassin survives. They had taken a drug that caused the stun settings to be deadly. Still, things could have been much worse. If not for the careful work of the both the Bajoran and Federation personnel aboard the station, the En-Kai would have been killed.

Later, O'Brien and Kira report to Sisko and the Abbot. They confirm that the missing tools were used to deactivate the weapons detectors on the Promenade. Whether Anara cooperated willingly or was forced to help, they'll never know. The assassins killed her and the monks to cover their tracks. The Abbot expresses his thanks to Sisko and his crew for saving the En-Kai. The assassins had been surgically altered to be indistinguishable from the dead monks. It's a miracle they were detected at all. Sisko wonders aloud how the assassins knew the En-Kai would be on the station. Everything indicates that they prepared for days, even weeks in advance. What a coincidence that the Abbot chose this time to confront Keiko on her teachings. The Abbot agrees . . . an unfortunate coincidence.

The station soon returns to normal. More or less. Not all of the Bajoran students return to Keiko's school . . . there is still some underlying tension on the station . . . and in Quark's, Quark posts odds on who will be the new Kai. Tyma is now a four to one favorite.

There are many differences between the preceding story and the final episode, but the central structure is firmly in place. The changes came about as a result of a process similar in intent to the ongoing dialogue between Rick Berman and Michael Piller as they developed the story for the pilot. However, when Berman and Piller did so, they were the only writers involved and they had a relatively longer schedule. Now that the series is in full production, the back-and-forth creative input required to develop a story and script must take place at a faster and more efficient pace. Thus, instead of just two people being involved, the entire writing staff takes part in the process. And instead of squeezing in meetings over some "cheap chicken," the staff follows a more formal system of development.

First, after some initial feedback, the writer expands the story into a beat outline—each beat corresponding roughly to a scene. Here's Wolfe's original draft, dated February 23, 1993.

STAR TREK: DEEP SPACE NINE

"In the Hands of the Prophets"
Robert Hewitt Wolfe

2/23/93

TEASER

1. O'BRIEN'S QUARTERS

Miles and Keiko go through their morning routine. O'Brien's got a huge list of projects to work on. Keiko asks if his new Bajoran apprentice has been much help. Anara? She means well, but she's still learning. Keiko sends Miles off with a kiss and an admonishment not to eat any more glop-on-a-sticks. He's starting to put on a little weight.

2. PROMENADE

O'Brien passes the Kiosk on his way to work. He sees the glop-on-a-stick . . . tries to restrain himself . . . but finally gives in. "Maybe just one." As he buys a stick, a female Bajoran religious leader passes behind him, followed by a small retinue.

3. KEIKO'S SCHOOLROOM

Keiko teaches a class on the formation of amino acids (at a simplified level). Jake is present, Nog is not. As she begins her lesson, the father of one of her Bajoran students enters, followed closely by the female religious leader that passed O'Brien on the Promenade. The father introduces Pahr Winn and says the Pahr has come to observe the class. Keiko continues her lesson. Soon, however, Winn begins challenging her teachings. Keiko defends her lesson, but this only infuriates Winn, who accuses Keiko of blasphemy.

ACT ONE

1. SECURITY OFFICE

O'Brien works on Odo's security monitors, which are on the fritz. Anara was supposed to fix them, but she never got around to it. O'Brien discovers his favorite Phase Adjustment Wrench is missing. Odo suggests he misplaced it. "I don't 'misplace' my tools." O'Brien starts a computer search for the wrench.

2. SISKO'S OFFICE

Keiko comes to Sisko and tells him about her confrontation with Pahr Winn. Sisko recognizes Winn's name. Winn is an important Bajoran Traditionalist leader, roughly equivalent to an Archbishop. Sisko explains the Traditionalist-Progressive conflict. He promises to intercede on Keiko's behalf.

3. BAJORAN SHRINE

Sisko meets with Winn and tries to reason with her. No one is being forced to go to Keiko's school. Bajoran parents can withdraw their children if they wish. Winn: Not good enough. This is a Bajoran station and must abide by Bajoran traditions. If Keiko will not recant her blasphemy, Winn cannot be responsible for the consequences.

## ACT TWO

1. OPS

   Sisko consults with Kira, who speaks of Winn with admiration and gives a Bajoran perspective of the conflict.

1b. OPS

   O'Brien reports a problem to Kira. In addition to his wrench, a number of other tools from all over the station are unaccountably missing. As is Anara, O'Brien's apprentice.

2. SCHOOLROOM

   The father who brought Winn to the school withdraws his daughter from class. He is apologetic, defensive, maybe a little scared.

3. EXT. SPACE

   Log. Conflicts between the Bajoran and Federation individuals on the station are becoming more frequent.

4. OPS

   Many of the Bajoran supernumeraries haven't shown up for work, claiming to have "Gelerian Flu." Kira explains they are avoiding work either to show their support for Winn, or from fear of reprisals. Sisko decides to go down to Bajor.

4a. OPS

   O'Brien and Kira locate trace materials of the missing tools.

5. POWER CONDUIT

   Kira and O'Brien find the melted remains of the tools in an active power conduit. The tools have been destroyed almost beyond recognition. Along with the tools, they find a cellular residue of organic material . . . the scattered remains of a dead body.

## ACT THREE

1. KAI TEMPLE

   Sisko is stonewalled by a Bajoran monk. While he waits by the fountain, he meets Pahr Eniyo. A well respected progressive leader. He has heard about the situation on the station and is sympathetic to Sisko. They talk about Pahr Winn and Kai Opaka. After getting to know Sisko, Eniyo promises to see what he can do to help.

2. BASHIR'S LAB

   Kira and Bashir. A post-mortem of the remains shows the DNA to be disrupted on a molecular level by the power flow in the conduit. Might be Anara. Might not. Bashir is eager to investigate. Kira lacks confidence in him, but Bashir promises results.

3. O'BRIEN'S QUARTERS

O'Brien and Keiko talk about what's going on. Keiko hopes she's doing the right thing. O'Brien tells her he's never known her to do anything BUT the right thing. They share a tender moment. Keiko tells Miles she can tell he's been eating glop again. Miles confesses. "You see, I told you, you're always right."

4. OPS

Sisko returns.

5. COMMANDER'S OFFICE

Kira briefs Sisko on recent developments. Quark barges into the office. Confronts him about loss of business. Most of Quark's customers are Bajoran and they've been staying away in droves. Sisko says he's doing everything he can. Quark leaves. Kira strongly suspects outside agitators. Kira and Sisko discuss options, then Kira is called away to . . .

6. BASHIR'S OFFICE

Bashir hasn't managed to ID the body yet. Kira is about to chew him out, when Bashir reveals new info. The body was immolated in the power conduit after death. The victim was actually killed by phaser fire.

ACT FOUR

1. OPS

Conference with Sisko, Kira, O'Brien, Dax, Odo and Bashir. Who is Anara? Why was she murdered? Neither Odo nor Bashir have any clear answers. We're not even sure it was Anara's body. They're interrupted by news that some sort of sabotage (to be determined) has taken place.

2. CORRIDOR

Sisko, Kira and O'Brien examine the sabotage damage. If they hadn't been so lucky, someone could have gotten hurt or even killed. Kira identifies the triggering device as an old guerilla favorite.

3. BAJORAN SHRINE

Kira confronts Pahr Winn. The Pahr denies any knowledge of what has happened. Kira is furious. She used to look up to Winn, who was an important voice during the struggle for Bajoran independence. But the station is vital to Bajor. By damaging it, Winn is hurting her own people. Kira has lost all respect for Winn. Winn advises Kira to make sure she is on the right side of things in the days to come.

4. EXT. — SPACE

Time cut.

5. CORRIDOR

Miles walks Keiko to class. They talk about the wisdom of continuing the classes. Most of the children are gone, but Keiko is determined to continue. O'Brien leaves, and . . .

6. SCHOOLROOM

Keiko enters the classroom and orders the computer to turn on the lights, triggering a bomb.

ACT FIVE

1. <u>INFIRMARY</u>

   Bashir reports to Sisko and O'Brien that Keiko will be okay. Luckily, mostly superficial damage. O'Brien visits Keiko. Brings her a glop-on-a-stick.

2. <u>BAJORAN SHRINE</u>

   Sisko confronts Winn. Says this has got to stop. This is my station. This is my home. I will not stand for this any longer. Winn says it's none of her doing. This is between Sisko and the Bajoran people. Sisko disagrees. It's a Bajoran conflict. Sisko insists on a meeting between Kira and Winn to iron things out. Reach a working solution. Winn says she will only meet with an equal. Suggests Pahr Eniyo.

3. <u>AIRLOCK/PROMENADE</u>

   Pahr Eniyo arrives. He is confident this can all be worked out peacefully. He and Sisko proceed to the Shrine. Where they are greeted by Winn and the Abbot. Kira is called to the Infirmary.

4. <u>INFIRMARY</u>

   Bashir has almost got a lock on the victim's ID. As he reconstructs the DNA, however, he discovers TWO different genetic samples present. The first is indeed Anara. The second is the Abbot of the Shrine . . . the same Abbot Kira just saw on the Promenade. Bashir: "That's not possible. The Abbot has been dead for days."

5. <u>BAJORAN SHRINE</u>

   The conference begins. As Winn, Sisko and Eniyo begin negotiations, someone passes the fake Abbot a phaser . . .

6. <u>PROMENADE</u>

   Kira rushes through the crowd . . .

7. <u>BAJORAN SHRINE</u>

   The fake Abbot prepares to fire at Eniyo . . . and Kira rushes in at the last moment and saves Eniyo. She overpowers the fake Abbot, who commits suicide to avoid capture.

8. <u>OPS</u>

   O'Brien and Kira report to Sisko. They confirm that O'Brien's missing tools were used to deactivate the weapons detectors on the Promenade. Whether Anara cooperated willingly or was forced to help, they'll never know. The fake Abbot killed her and the real Abbot to cover his tracks. Pahr Winn enters and expresses her thanks to Sisko and his crew for saving Eniyo. The assassin had been surgically altered to be indistinguishable from the real Abbot. It's a miracle he was detected at all. Kira accuses Winn of being behind the whole plot. Winn lured Eniyo to the station, started the whole controversy to set up the assassination and do away with her rival. Pahr laughs. The charges will never stand. And lay one hand on her and there will be blood in the streets of Bajor. Kira and Sisko have no choice but to let Pahr Winn go free.

The forum in which the writing staff respond to an initial story is the infamous "story-breaking" session, in which the entire writing staff sit together and go through the outline, beat by beat, with the results of their efforts written on a large dry-erase board. Rick Berman receives all stories at the same time Michael Piller does. Though Berman does not attend the story-breaking sessions, he has already given his comments and suggestions to Piller, who then incorporates them into the session.

A typical story-breaking session can last more than ten hours, spread over two or three days—which helps explain why the staff prefer to buy stories from people with whom they can spend that much time and intense effort. Under Michael Piller's guidance, everyone involved with the writing of the series, from producers Ira Steven Behr and Peter Allan Fields to the WGA interns[8] to the writer of the episode, starts at the beginning of the story, discussing—sometimes arguing—about character development, plot points, dramatic developments, the Prime Directive, similar stories in other series and movies, production concerns—such as the number of sets or models required—and the ongoing presentation of Starfleet's mission in the Bajoran system and STAR TREK's multifaceted systems of alien motivations.

Snippets of dialogue will be suggested, the purpose of particular props will be discussed, the nature of character interactions explored, and—incessantly—hard questions will be asked. While the episode's writer is, in effect, in the hot seat, defending and making stronger his or her story structure, it is by no means a negative experience. Everyone in the room is there for the express purpose of crafting the best *Deep Space Nine* story he or she can. Everyone is free to make her or his own suggestions and to disagree with someone else's suggestions, but when the time comes for a judgment to be made, all eyes in the room turn to Michael Piller. Piller is open to every comment, generous with his praise and encouragement, but, in the end, each decision in the story-breaking session is made or approved by him, in his role as executive producer.[9]

At the end of the session, a final beat outline for the episode exists, covering teaser, act breaks, and all key plot points. Here's what Wolfe's outline for "In the Hands of the Prophets" became after it went through its story-breaking sessions.

[8]The Writers Guild of America, west, and its signatory companies, has established a voluntary training program for writers in "protected class" categories—female, ethnic minority, physically disabled, and forty years of age or older. Writers qualified under these categories must furthermore never have had any previous employment as a writer with, or have sold or optioned any piece of literary material to, any film or television production company.

Under this program, series that are in their second and subsequent years of production may hire qualified writers as interns for an initial period of six weeks, with an option to extend their term by an additional fourteen weeks at a current rate of about $520 a week. On *Deep Space Nine*, interns sit in on story meetings, write the story breakdowns on the board, read and report on spec scripts, and generally help the writing staff while absorbing incredible amounts of inside information, which usually helps in making a sale. (For example and for inspiration, intern writing team Jeanne Carrigan-Fauci and Lisa Rich worked evenings on "Move Along Home" and "Duet." Intern Evan Carlos Somers received story credit and shared teleplay credit on "Melora.")

See Appendix IV for the address of the Writers Guild to obtain more information, but remember that the Writers Guild does *not* administer this program. It's up to the aspiring writer to make contact with an interested series, generally by impressing the writing staff with a good spec script, good pitches, and enthusiasm. The STAR TREK series' support of this program is a mark of the sense of family that is so strong among the people who work on them, and Michael Piller's own commitment to helping beginning writers.

If you're good enough and willing to work and to learn, there are many starting points available in television scriptwriting.

[9]Rick Berman, of course, remains in the creative process through every stage of story and script development, before and after the story-breaking session.

STAR TREK: DEEP SPACE NINE

"In the Hands of the Prophets"

Revised Beat Outline

Robert Hewitt Wolfe

March 17, 1993


**TEASER**

1. PROMENADE

   Miles and Keiko walk to work. Keiko rides Miles a little about eating too
   many JUMJA STICKS, a Bajoran dessert. Miles admits that his new Bajoran
   apprentice NEELA has gotten him hooked on the stuff. Undercurrent of
   jealousy from Keiko.

2. KEIKO'S SCHOOLROOM

   Keiko teaches a class on the physics of the wormhole. A Bajoran monk,
   ABBESS WINN, observes the lesson, then starts asking Keiko questions
   about the wormhole based on Bajoran religious doctrine. Almost
   apologetically, Winn points out that Keiko's teachings are blasphemy and
   that she cannot be permitted to continue.


**ACT ONE**

1. SECURITY OFFICE

   O'Brien arrives to finish some work on an upgrade of Odo's Promenade
   Weapons Sensors, only to find that Neela has already finished the job. We
   see they have an excellent rapport, both on a professional and personal
   level. We can tell that if O'Brien wasn't married, he'd be very attracted to
   this woman. Neela starts to close the panel, but she's using the wrong tool.
   O'Brien reminds her that the panel accesses a security area and she needs a
   special tool, an EJ-7 Interlock, to open or close the panel. O'Brien goes to
   get his, but it's missing. Neela suggests he misplaced it. "I don't misplace
   my tools." Odo expresses his concern. With such a Probe, any number of
   sensitive systems could be accessed.

2. SISKO'S OFFICE

   Keiko comes to Sisko and tells him about her confrontation with Abbess
   Winn. Sisko was afraid something like this would happen sooner or later.
   He knows the situation may be much more complicated than Keiko thinks
   it is. It's the sort of issue that could dramatically effect the
   Federation/Bajoran relationship. Calls in Kira, who confirms his fear. Keiko
   and Sisko talk about how they will placate and/or defuse Winn. Kira shows
   them how grounded they are in the Federation perspective. She knows of
   and respects Winn. Points out that this isn't the sort of thing that you can
   just pave over.

3. BAJORAN SHRINE

Sisko meets with Winn and tries to reason with her. She avoids engagement in any meaningful dialogue. Sisko, on the attack, points out that Winn has no following on the station, that no one complained about the school before. Winn admits that her following is small, but says that does not obviate her relgious duty to defend the Bajoran faith. Nor does it change anything. Keiko has blasphemed the Prophets. If she doesn't recant, Winn cannot be responsible for the consequences.

ACT TWO

1. OPS

Dax, O'Brien and Neela track down the missing Interlock. Kira asks O'Brien about a missing crewman, Ensign AQUINO, who did not report for duty. O'Brien hasn't seen him since yesterday morning. They ask the computer, which reports that Aquino is not on the station.

2. SCHOOLROOM

The father of one of Keiko's students withdraws his daughter from class. He is apologetic, defensive, maybe a little scared.

3. PROMENADE

Odo starts search for Aquino. Notices and comments on arrival of Winn's monks from Bajor.

4. CORRIDOR

O'Brien and Neela track the missing Interlock to a Power conduit.

4a. POWER CONDUIT

O'Brien and Neela find the missing tool, half melted in the conduit. . . along with some charred organic material, and a melted combadge. Looks like they found Aquino. Will take to Bashir for analysis.

5. EXT. SPACE

Time cut.

6. PROMENADE

O'Brien talks to Keiko about his discovery. According to Aquino's log, Aquino went to check strange readings in the conduit. But something went wrong and he got killed. The O'Briens go to buy some Jumja sticks from the Kiosk, but the Bajoran merchant refuses to sell to them.

6a. PROMENADE - OUTSIDE THE SCHOOL

New Monks and Winn and children and parents outside school—Winn to Keiko, "Maybe I misunderstood. Please clarify for me and these people what you think about the wormhole." Shreds Keiko when she does so, but gives her an out. Just promise not to teach about the wormhole. Keiko refuses to be censored. Bajoran parents withdraw children from school. Keiko will continue teaching anyway—go off on Jake's worried expression.

## ACT THREE

1. OPS

   Crew puts clues together to figure out how Aquino died. Personal log, the tool, and a burned out safety circuit all point to an industrial accident. O'Brien has nagging doubts, doesn't believe Aquino would take his tool without asking. Jake arrives, Sisko asks what's wrong—they go into. . .

2. SISKO'S OFFICE

   Jake tells Sisko what happened, doesn't understand the Bajoran's problem with Keiko—Sisko explains Bajoran point of view. . . empties his pockets on how difficult the situation is. "What are you going to do?" says Jake.

3. EXT. BAJOR

   Matte shot.

4. INT. TEMPLE GARDEN

   Daar Bareil meets with Sisko. He is a very holy, very good man, a Ghandi like figure, and the clear favorite to be the next Kai. Winn is a loose cannon, but it would be inappropriate for Bareil to act as Kai before he is selected, and his selection is far from a done deal. Still he is sympathetic to Sisko and will do what he can.

5. OPS

   Sisko returns—finds out Winn's followers are arriving, and some of the Bajoran crewmembers are not reporting for duty. There continues to be tension with Kira who points out that the absent crewmembers may be symptomatic of an unworkable Federation/Bajoran relationship. Sisko asks to meet with Bajoran leaders.

6. INFIRMARY

   O'Brien asks Julian for a favor. He wants Bashir to check Aquino's remains. O'Brien strongly suspects murder. It makes O'Brien very uncomfortable to ask Bashir for help.

7. REPLIMAT

   Sisko and Kira meet with Bajoran leaders. Sisko, talking to the Bajorans, but really to Kira, reminds them of how far they've come. Interrupted by Winn, who turns up the heat. She knows Sisko has gone to Bareil for help. Says Bareil can't and won't do anything. Plays to Sisko's audience and neutralizes his success. Bajorans leave. Kira and Sisko have a moment together. Bashir and O'Brien arrive. They now have evidence that Aquino was murdered.


## ACT FOUR

1. COMMANDER'S OFFICE

   (All senior officers) Odo reports to Sisko on Aquino's day. Turbolift records do not agree with Aquino's log. Odo believes the turbolifts. Aquino was checking on the new Runabout, the Orinoco, not on the power conduit. O'Brien and Neela will investigate.

2. RUNABOUT PAD

O'Brien and Neela investigate. Once again we see their strong relationship. They are good friends and like working together. The investigation turns up nothing. No work was done on the Runabout. And none was required. Neela goes off duty. O'Brien lingers behind and looks at the closed panel. After some thought, he goes to the turbolift and asks it to take him to runabout pad two.

3. PROMENADE

Odo and Quark talk about the new arrivals from Bajor. Quark doesn't like them. They're not as good for business as they look. Odo uses the opening to grill Quark about Aquino's murder. O'Brien arrives. He didn't find anything at the Orinoco, but he decided to check the other runabouts. Someone did tamper with the Ganges. . . set up so it could be stolen at a future date. Odo looks accusingly at Quark, who denies all knowledge. O'Brien and Odo try to make sense of the situation, with Quark providing the criminal perspective. Why kill Aquino? Why set up a runabout to be stolen, but not do it? Because they intended to do something later, and needed a way to escape. What? It's got to be something. Before they reach a conclusion, there is a loud explosion.

4. PROMENDADE–OUTSIDE SCHOOL

School room on fire.


ACT FIVE

1. PROMENADE

Fire out—crowd gathers including Keiko, Jake. Sisko and crew survey damage—Sisko speaks with Abbess . . . promises that the school will be rebuilt. Federation will not give in to terrorist fringe. Winn denies any involvement, offers her followers to help with the clean up. Sisko gets a call from OPS. Bareil is calling from Bajor. Sisko leaves. As does Winn, but as she walks through the crowd, Winn gives Neela a look.

2. OPS

Sisko talks with Bareil. Bareil has decided things have gone far enough. He will come to the station to provide a calming influence. His presence will divert attention from Winn. Furthermore, he will meet with her and set her on the right path.

2a. OPS

O'Brien is still bothered by the attempt to steal the Ganges. Could it be related to the bomb? Doesn't make sense. Aquino was killed before Winn even arrived. School wasn't an issue yet. Must be something else. O'Brien uses the computer to track a series of security anomalies backwards. Various security force fields are set to be overridden. The Runabout lockouts were only the last domino in a chain. But where does it start?

3. BAJORAN SHRINE

Neela comes in—Abbess asks, "Why are you here?"—Neela says, "My escape route has been shut down."—Abbess: "The Prophet wills care for you."

4. EXT. SPACE

   Bareil's ship arrives.

5. AIRLOCK

   Sisko and senior officers greet Bareil—they begin to move forward.

6. OPS

   O'Brien traces the trail all the way back to the security office.

7. PROMENADE

   Sisko and Bareil and entourage emerge from airlock, greeted by large crowd—they move through with security officers guarding them—O'Brien arrives on turbolift, pushes his way through crowd to security office—we see Neela moving through crowd to school bus.

8. INT. SECURITY

   O'Brien alone uses tricorder to track down anomaly—realizes that the Promenade Weapon Sensors have been disabled. And that this was the trigger of the escape route . . . the first domino in the chain. The whole domino effect was set up through a specific system in Security . . . the same on Neela was working on earlier.

10. PROMENADE

    O'Brien fights his way through crowd—Neela's moving through on a collision course with the Daar—O'Brien uses his combadge to warn Sisko that Neela is up to something. Sisko tackles Neela just as she opens fire on the Daar—weapon discharges—Bareil is safe. Sisko is hero. Bareil is whisked away to safe location. Kira confronts Winn. It was all for Bareil, wasn't it. All the protests over the school. The Bomb. All just to bring Bareil to the station so he could be killed. Winn never really cared about the religious issues. Winn ignores her and walks away.

11. OPS

    Night shift. Sisko comes in to check on things, finds Kira working late. They talk about how much they've learned about each other. They've learned to respect and appreciate each other, despite their disagreements. We see that they've come a long way since they first met.

*Now* the writer is finally given the chance to go off and write a script. Two weeks is a standard schedule, though some scripts have been known to be banged out by the writing staff in a matter of days because of production demands.

After the agreed-upon time, the writer returns with a first-draft script, and, just as Berman and Piller then tore into Piller's script for "Emissary," the entire writing staff once again gathers for a script session in which the writer has to endure the dissection of her or his script, line by line and word by word.[10]

Though we don't have enough room to run through all the different revisions of "In the Hands of the Prophets," it is interesting to see how just the opening pages changed from the first draft to the final.

Here's the first-draft teaser, dated March 15, 1993.

[10]Novels and feature-film screenplays can be solitary pursuits, so it's possible to pursue them from any location in the world. However, because of television writing's collaborative nature, which requires many meetings for each assignment, it should be obvious why to make it as an episodic-television writer, it's almost always necessary to live in or near Los Angeles.

STAR TREK: DEEP SPACE NINE
"In the Hands of the Prophets"
TEASER

FADE IN:

1   INT. PROMENADE

O'BRIEN[11] and KEIKO, in mid-conversation, exit a
Turbolift onto the Promenade. O'Brien is animated,
enthusiastic.

> O'BRIEN
> Keiko, I'm telling you, Anara's a
> natural. The woman's got a feel
> for machinery that's almost
> instinctual.

Keiko doesn't want to hear about it.

> KEIKO
> Really.

O'Brien's talking more to himself than to Keiko and
doesn't notice the edge in her voice.

> O'BRIEN
> I mean, you should have seen the
> way she reconfigured that
> transporter pad. She'd never even
> seen one before and she did the
> job in half the time I expected.

> KEIKO
> How nice.

O'Brien finally picks up on Keiko's tone.

> O'BRIEN
> Something wrong?

Keiko covers up her feelings.

> KEIKO
> It's nothing.
> (changing subject)
> Have a good day at work.

She gives him a little kiss.

[11]The first time a character appears in a
script, his or her name is written in upper-
case.

> KEIKO
>
> And try to lay off the glop-on-a-
> stick. You know how it spoils
> your appetite.
>
> O'BRIEN
> (plays innocent)
> Glop-on-a-stick? Never touch the
> stuff.

Keiko smiles. Her bad mood (which O'Brien still
hasn't totally picked up on) dissipates. Keiko kisses
O'Brien and heads toward the schoolroom.

2    INT. KEIKO'S SCHOOLROOM

Keiko walks between the desks of her students and passes out sheets of
construction paper. As usual, most of her students are Bajoran, with a
handful of humans and other aliens. JAKE is present, but Nog is not.

> KEIKO
> (as she passes out
> paper)
> Okay, everybody, like we said
> yesterday, today we'll be learning
> about the wormhole.

------

During the script session for this episode, several comments and suggestions
were made about this opening. Michael Piller's main concern was that O'Brien's and
Keiko's dialogue was "too on the nose." That is, it went straight into setting up a plot
point instead of easing into the story by "having fun" with the characters.

Piller also commented that Keiko's phrase "lay off" was too colloquial for the
twenty-fourth century, and that though the term "glop-on-a-stick" was okay for
in-house use, if it was going to be mentioned in dialogue, the treat needed a Bajoran
name.

Here's how the teaser began in the final draft dated April 2, 1993.

------

STAR TREK: DEEP SPACE NINE
"In the Hands of the Prophets"
TEASER

FADE IN:

1   INT. PROMENADE

at the Kiosk—close on a glop on a stick in a
VENDOR's hand . . .

> KEIKO (O.C.)
>
> Too early for me . . .

Moving with the glop to reveal O'BRIEN who takes it . . .

> O'BRIEN
>
> You sure?

> KEIKO
>
> (makes a face)
>
> It's so sweet.

> O'BRIEN
>
> It's a natural sweetness from the
> sap of the jumja tree . . . more
> vitamin C than orange juice.
> Great way to start the morning.

He takes a lick. They move away from the Kiosk.

> KEIKO
>
> Since when did you become such an
> expert on jumja sticks?

> O'BRIEN
>
> Hmm? Oh, Neela told me.

The name Neela gets a subtle response from Keiko.

> KEIKO
>
> Did she . . .

> O'BRIEN
>
> Want a taste . . . ?

> KEIKO
>
> (firmer)
>
> I really don't like them.

O'Brien shrugs, suit yourself. A beat.

> KEIKO
>
> So. Is she working out any better
> than the last one?

O'BRIEN

Neela? She's terrific. She's
even taught *me* a few things.

KEIKO
(very dry)
I'm glad to hear her knowledge
doesn't end with jumja sticks . . .

O'BRIEN
(slow on the uptake)
Oh yeah, she's a good little
engin . . .
(now he realizes)
hold on . . .

KEIKO

What?

O'BRIEN

You're not thinking . . .

KEIKO

What are you being defensive?

O'BRIEN

Defensive . . . I'm not . . . <u>Keiko</u> . . .

She smiles, satisfied, secure in her marriage . . .

KEIKO
(teasing)
Just keeping you on your toes,
O'Brien.

O'BRIEN

Very funny, O'Brien.

She sticks her finger in the glop and sticks it gently
in his mouth . . .

KEIKO
(flirtatious)
Be careful who you share your
jumja sticks with . . .

Smiles sexily and walks away . . . off O'Brien's reaction . . .

2A OMITTED[12]

[12]In an earlier draft, a shot of the wormhole
opening near DS9 was to go here, but
when the script was revised to open on an
image of the wormhole in Keiko's classroom, the scene was unnecessary.

is standing in front of a large monitor/blackboard
with the wormhole displayed. As usual, most of
Keiko's students are Bajoran, with a handful of humans
and other aliens. JAKE is present, but Nog is not.
As she moves away from the monitor . . .

                    KEIKO
                 (continuing)
          Does anyone know what makes this
          wormhole so unusual?

---

See how the opening scene has become—what else—personal? Instead of Keiko's and O'Brien's conversation being about his Bajoran engineering assistant,[13] their interchange is about *them* and *their* relationship. Neela is part of it, of course, but, in the context of this scene, she's not the main purpose for their talk. That's important because of what happens when we see a scene in a television episode in which two characters start talking about a topic that seems forced, we immediately think, "This is going to be important to the story," thus spoiling whatever surprise the writer might have dreamed up.

But by writing a scene in which the focus misdirects us away from the expository material in it, the writer works like a magician—distracting us now so we'll be surprised later.

Notice also how the scene in the schoolroom starts with a visual bang, instead of with a realistic though uninteresting preamble by Keiko. An old rule of thumb for television writing is to start each scene near the end, which is exactly what happens now.

Stepping back to the first-draft stage, this is the point at which most first-time writers are cut off—assuming they made it this far to begin with.[14] Being cut off is not necessarily an indication that the script or the writer's writing ability is in any way deficient. Most often it is simply a question of efficiency. For example, it might take a three-hour script meeting to go through the revisions required for a second draft. That's a lot of time if you consider that the meeting is attended by the full staff. Then, after a weeklong delay during which the writer writes the second draft, more time is required on everyone's part to read the script, make notes, and then meet again. Faced with this possibility, sometimes it is much faster and easier for the writing staff to thank the writer and have one of the producers take three days to revise it without the necessity of scheduling lengthy meetings.

Now that we've been through the process of developing, pitching, selling, and writing a script, what are the odds of *you* succeeding in this endeavor?

Well, each season of *Deep Space Nine* is made up of twenty-six episodes. Of these, about ten to fifteen are written by the staff, including executive producers Berman and Piller, producers Behr and Fields, and story editor Wolfe. That leaves ten

[13]This is the long story about why "Anara" changed to "Neela."

One of the drawbacks of series television is that criminals almost always come out of the ranks of guest stars. For "In the Hands of the Prophets," the producers were worried that if O'Brien had a new assistant *and* an assassin was suspected on board in the same episode, viewers would immediately guess that the assistant was the assassin. To try and prevent that from happening too quickly in the story, Piller decided to write in O'Brien's assistant several episodes before the last of the season so that she would become familiar to regular viewers. Thus, Anara, a character who was created for "In the Hands of the Prophets," first turned up in episode 417, "The Forsaken."

Unfortunately, after that episode was filmed, the producers decided that the actor playing Anara wasn't the right type to play an assassin, and so decided on a different actor for episode 420. Since the name Anara had been used for the first actor's role, a new name, Neela, was created for the Anara replacement. Neela first appeared in episode 419, "Duet."

A leftover trace of Anara still remains in the episode, though. In Act Five, O'Brien and Dax break a computer code for which the key letters are A-N-A-R-A. If you have a still-frame VCR, you'll be able to read the code as it's being broken—and thanks to a mysterious programming virus originating in the *Deep Space Nine* art department, the intermediate codes that appear make it a very entertaining sequence.

[14]Under the Writers Guild Minimum Basic Agreement, the compensation for writing the story, first-draft, and final-draft teleplay for a one-hour, other than network, prime-time television episode is divided into three payments: 30% for the story, approximately 60% for the first draft, and the remaining 10% for the final. As of this writing, the payment for a story and teleplay is approximately $14,000. (For a one-hour, network, prime-time episode, the payment is approximately $22,000.)

Television scripts are most usually assigned on the basis of what is called a "step-deal," which means that once the production company has paid the writer for a specific stage in a contract, the company is not obligated to continue with that writer. If a writer turns in a story and the production company feels a staff writer is the better choice to write a script, then the original writer can be "cut off" at the story stage, paid for the story, but then have nothing more to do with the script. Likewise, writers can be cut off at the first draft, though most production companies make the final-draft payment out of courtesy. And even if an outside writer does turn in a final draft, it's really only a second draft, because it will continue to be polished by staff writers until the day it's put into production.

or eleven other scripts up for grabs. Some will be assigned scripts—that is, Behr calls writers whose work he knows, gives them a starting premise, and asks them to come in with a story. Others, perhaps five or six a season, will come about because of pitches or spec scripts.

If *Deep Space Nine* matches *The Next Generation*'s longevity, it has five more years to run, so there could be twenty-five to thirty script assignments open to first-time writers.

Someone's going to write them. Why shouldn't it be you?

# FURTHER

# INFORMATION

*Free advice is seldom cheap.*

—The 59th Rule of Acquisition

## Writing to the Cast and Crew

Any letters or packages sent to the cast and crew of the STAR TREK series at their home addresses are automatically returned or destroyed, unopened and unread.

To insure your letter will be read, the best choice is to send it in care of the studio:

Recipient's Name
c/o DEEP SPACE NINE
Paramount Pictures
5555 Melrose Avenue
Los Angeles, CA 90038, USA

Cards and letters are appreciated by everyone who works on the series, but because of the volume they receive, it's not possible for anyone, especially the actors, to reply to everything they receive. If you'd like to meet the cast or crew of *Deep Space Nine,* check out science-fiction media magazines or the official STAR TREK fan magazines for listings of STAR TREK conventions held in your area. Often the special guests will appear at an autographing table after their presentation, giving fans an opportunity to say hello and have a picture signed.

*Ferengi.*

Klingon.

*Just in case you ever make it to DS9, here's how to find your way around. Whoever thought the Cardassians would like bowling?*

*Vulcan.*

*Bajoran.*

*Federation Standard English.*

## 🌐 PROMENADE DIRECTORY

| | |
|---|---|
| O Amphitheatre 0l-005 | O Infirmary - Dr. Julian Bashir 02-682 |
| O Andorian Fast Food 0l-754 | O Jacobson's Used Photons 02-754 |
| O Bajoran Counsulate Office 0l-50l | O Jupiter Mining Corporation 02-842 |
| O Bajoran Customs Office 0l-484 | O Lodging and Accomodations 02-294 |
| O Banzai Institute 0l-088 | O Milliways 02-984 |
| O Berman's Dilithium Supply 0l-034 | O Pancho's Happy Bottom Riding Club 02-lll |
| O Bowling Alley 0l-854 | O Quark's Bar 02-854 |
| O Cargo Loading and Transfer 0l-l06 | O Replimat Cafe 02-395 |
| O Cavor's Gravity Devices 0l-332 | O Richarz' Accessories 02-734 |
| O Chief Engineer's Office 0l-409 | O Rush Dilithium Crystals 02-742 |
| O Curry's Martial Arts Training 0l-ll2 | O Schoolroom - Mrs. Keiko O'Brien 03-855 |
| O Del Floria's Taylor Shop 0l-383 | O Sirius Cybernetics Corporation 02-643 |
| O Diet Smith Corporation 0l-892 | O Spacecraft Resupply 02-992 |
| O Diva Droid Corporation 0l-874 | O Spacely Sprockets 02-023 |
| O Dock Master's Office 0l-843 | O Station Operations 03-658 |
| O Federation Consulate 02-375 | O Station Security 03-582 |
| O Forbin Project 02-874 | O Subspace Communications 03-584 |
| O Fredrickson's Squid Vendor 02-587 | O Tom Servo's Used Robots 03-585 |
| O Garak's Clothiers 02-485 | O Vince's Gymnasium |
| O Geological Assay Office 02-487 | O Vulcan Embassy 03-589 |
| O Gocke's House of Mirrors 02-875 | O Yoyodyne Propulsion Systems 03-853 |
| O Klingon Consulate 02-620 | O Chez Zimmerman 03-84l |
| O Import Protocol Office 02-583 | |

# Writers Guild Intern Program

For further information about the Writers Guild of America, west, and/or its intern training program, write to the Guild at 8955 Beverly Boulevard, West Hollywood, CA 90048-2456, USA.

# Publications of Interest

## Magazines

*The Official STAR TREK: DEEP SPACE NINE Magazine*
is published four times per season by the same company that publishes *Starlog* magazine. It's authorized by Paramount and contains interviews and articles about the series, plus lengthy synopses of episodes, all illustrated with extensive color photographs. Also, it carries numerous ads for *Deep Space Nine* merchandise and upcoming conventions.

If the magazine is not available locally, write to Starlog Press, 475 Park Avenue South, New York, NY 10016, to inquire about subscription rates.

*Star Trek: The Official Fan Club Magazine*
is published six times a year and covers the entire range of STAR TREK productions, including the upcoming *Voyager*.

For subscription information, write: The Official Fan Club, P.O. Box 111000, Aurora, CO 80042.

*The Journal of the Writers Guild of America, west*
is published eleven times a year as a forum for television and movie writers to discuss their craft. Each issue includes a TV market list of shows currently in production, and indicates which are open for submissions. For subscription information, write the WGA, west, at the address listed above under the entry for the Intern Program.

## Books

*The Making of Star Trek* by Stephen E. Whitfield and Gene Roddenberry.
A Del Rey Book published by Ballantine Books. Perhaps the best "making of" book ever written, plus it's about STAR TREK. A must read, still in print after twenty-six years.

*Star Trek Chronology: A History of the Future* by Michael Okuda and Denise Okuda. Pocket Books.
A comprehensive, illustrated account of the events of the STAR TREK universe, covering *The Original Series,* the movies, and *The Next Generation,* all in chronological order. Also includes an extensive index for cross-checking.

*Star Trek: The Next Generation Technical Manual* by Rick Sternbach and Michael Okuda, with a special introduction by Gene Roddenberry. Pocket Books.

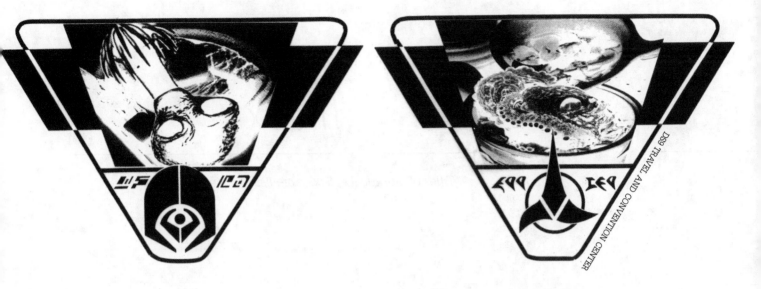

A wealth of information about the *Enterprise* 1701-D from the STAR TREK technical consultants, who have contributed so much to the consistency of the STAR TREK universe. A fascinating glimpse into STAR TREK's extensive back story.

*While on DS9, be sure to try these delicacies at the Replimat.*

*The Star Trek Encyclopedia: A Reference Guide to the Future* by Michael Okuda, Denise Okuda, and Debbie Mirek, with illustrations by Doug Drexler.
The ultimate STAR TREK reference book, detailing virtually every notable piece of information from *The Original Series,* the movies, *The Next Generation,* and the first season of *Deep Space Nine,* from A&A Officer to Zytchin III. Fully illustrated and impressive.

*Successful Scriptwriting* by Jurgen Wolff and Kerry Cox. Writer's Digest Books.
We've read dozens of books about how to write for television, and this is one of the clearest and most comprehensive. A solid starting point.

New books about the television industry are being published all the time. If the local bookstores in your area don't carry a wide selection, try going to the source. . . .

*Samuel French Theatre & Film Bookshops*
Worldwide mail order available from 7623 Sunset Boulevard, Hollywood, CA 90046, USA. Call 800-8-ACT-NOW in the United States, 800-7-ACT-NOW in Canada. Free catalogue of books available.

# Index

*Titles of individual episodes are listed under "episodes."*

## A

*Abyss, The* (film), 234
accuracy, attention to, 135
act(s) (television), 76n2
act-break structure, 76
action, 41
    character vs., 41–43
    *see also* live action
actors, xi, 9–10, 36, 47
    career commitments, 105
    characters belong to, 214
    crossover between TV and film, 186,
      193n*12*
    *Deep Space Nine*, 132, 172, 173–96
    dialogue and character relations,
      180–81
    difficulty of work days, 216–17
    elements brought to *Deep Space
      Nine*, 212, 213, 214
    missing lines, 219
    salaries, 29
    trailers for, 205–6
    *see also* extras; principal actors
advertisers, advertising, 33n*6*
    FCC restrictions on, 77n*2*
advertising time, sale of, 33
aero cow, 214n*15*, 245
aesthetics
    combined with technology, 224
airdate schedule, 246
Alaimo, Marc, 187n*8*, 262
Aldrin, Buzz, 23
alien
    meaning in *Star Trek*, 11n*4*
alien cultures/races, 145–46
    graphic elements used by, 122

aliens, 1, 9, 10, 11, 119
    in Bajoran wormhole, 83, 84
    characters in *Deep Space Nine*,
      9–10, 70–72, 108, 174
    encountered by Federation, 191
    Gamma Quadrant, 109–10
    the human in, 178
    motivations, 292
    relationship with humans, 114
    *see also* under specific group, e.g.,
      Bajorans
*Aliens* (film), 172
alien ships, 225
    models of, 234, 236
American Association for the
    Advancement of Science, 129
Amiga Video Toaster system, 235, 236
Amoros, Julian, 37
    character description in bible, 86
    renamed Bashir, 106
angle (camera instruction), 115n*15*
    *see also* camera angles/movements
Anglim, Philip, 187n*8*
antigrav technology, 108n*8*
appliance(s), 16, 18, 193, 262
    Ferengi, 192
    worn by Odo, 179
Arbitron (rating co.), 246n*1*
Armor, Gene, 265
Armstrong, Neil, 23
Arnaz, Desi, 23n*3*
art department, 170, 188n*9*, 236n*11*,
    267
art director credit, 267
artistic license, 233n*6*
Asimov, Isaac, 54n*13*

assistant director (AD), 185, 217, 218,
    219, 220, 245
assistant director credit, 265, 266
assistant editor credit, 269
associate producer credit, 264
"atmosphere"; *see* extras
Auberjonois, Rene, 106, 174, 178–79,
    185, 194n*14*, 217
    credits, 261
    in Odo morphing sequence, 239–40
    rehearsing, 214, 216
audience(s), 31, 42, 43
    measurement of, 246n*1*
    shift in expectations of, 24–25
audience (*Star Trek*), 19, 36
    inviting cast into living rooms, 174
    *Next Generation*, 75
    reaction to series, 33–34
    relating to crossover actors, 186
    syndicated series, 193n*12*

## B

*Babylon 5* (TV series), 72n*11*, 139n*1*,
    235, 236, 239, 241
Backauskas, Michael, 268
background plate(s), 239
background scenes, 172
back story(ies)
    of Bajor, 82
    J. Dax, 85
    *Deep Space Nine*, 103, 104
    Odo, 85–86
Bajor (planet), 37, 59, 75, 230
    capital city, 271

story development sessions, xi
story ideas, 279
    one-line, 283, 284n7
story line, 114
    high-concept, 42
    one-sentence premise, 82
story meetings, 284
story points
    dropped, in revised bible, 108–10
    pilot episode, *Deep Space Nine*, 74–75
story premises
    in bible, 76
story problems, techniques for, 114
story structure, 281, 282
storytelling
    and design, 161–62
    *Next Generation*, 55
    TV, 41–42, 43
Straczynski, J. Michael, 72n11
strap-ons, 234
stripping, 30, 33, 76
stunt coordinator credit, 270
stunt doubles, 206, 249, 270
style, 139
    in bible, 82
supervising producer credit, 263
supervising sound editor credit, 269
supervising sound effects editor credit, 269
Surma, Ron, 265
Symes, John, 44
syndicated series
    audience, 193n12
syndicated-television market, 23
syndicated television sales
    methods of, 30–32
syndication, 28, 31, 257
    *Next Generation*, 33n6, 36, 55
    number of episodes and, 76
    *Original Series*, 36
    *Star Trek*, 24

### T

takes, 211, 212n17, 248
    *see also* printed takes
Tartikoff, Brandon, 35, 44, 57–58, 68, 73
Taylor, Jeri, 119, 120–22
teaser(s), 76n2, 281
    final draft, 299–302
    first-draft, 297–99
Tebok, 262
TECH (script term), 108n6, 129
technical consultants, 119, 122, 126, 129–30
technical correctness, 135
technical matters
    described in bible, 76
Technical Primer(s), 7
technobabble, 184–85, 217

technology
    antigrav, 108n8
    combined with aesthetics, 224
    digital filming, 223
    enhancement, 242n16
    of M. Okuda, 122
    recognizable, 172
    science-fiction, 174, 257
    Starfleet, 139, 158
    *Star Trek*, 161–62, 243, 257
    television production, 161
    twenty-fourth century, 172
teleplay credit, 263
teleportation, 129
television
    collaborative enterprise, 142
    future of, 257
    magic of, 196
    logic of, 68
    as visual medium, 139
    *see also* episodic television
television industry, 39–40
television production, 16, 236, 240
    collaborative nature of, 120
television production technology, 161
television series
    as business, 29–30
    collaboration in, 1, 173
    creation of, x, 64
    development of, 75
    not renewed, 21n2
    pilot episodes, 74
    production of, xii, xiii
Terek Nor, 74
*Terminator* (film), 40–41
*Terminator 2* (film), 234, 239
Theiss, William Ware, 169
Thomas, Cari, 268
Thornton, Rob, 236
timing
    in editing, 250
title (*Deep Space Nine*), 73–74
Tony Award, 178–79
trademark, 272
trailers, 205–6
transportation coordinator credit, 270
transporter effects, transporters, 36, 242
treatment(s), 77
    changes in dramatic structure of, 108, 109–14
    *Deep Space Nine* pilot, 77, 88–101, 102
    "Ninth Orb," 127, 145
"Trek Starbursts" (stock images), 244
Trill (species), 85, 185
Troi, Deanna, 87, 182
Troi, Lwaxana, 44n4, 87
twenty-fourth century, 66, 224
    physics of, 122
    science of, 129

technology of, 172
*2001: A Space Odyssey* (film), 172, 228–30, 236

### U

uniforms, 36n9, 169–70, 214n23
United Federation of Planets, 46
United Nations
    documentaries, 46
Unitel (co.), 216
Unitel Video (co.), 242, 270
unit production manager credit, 265–66
Unsinn, Joe, 269
*U.S.S. Enterprise*, xi
    first, 21

### V

*Variety*, 21, 24, 28
Velazquez, Dawn, 269
Viacom, 31
video consultant credit, 269
video effects, 242n16
video on demand, 257
video monitors, 170, 171–72
video playback operator credit, 269
video optical effects credit, 270
videotape, 212n17, 248
    dailies transferred to, 269
    transferring film elements to, 242
Vision Art Design & Animation, 271
Vision Arts (co.), 240, 245
Visitor, Nana, 174, 193–96, 206n13, 216
    credits, 261
    rehearsal, 214
visual component of science, 220n30
visual effects, 35, 43, 132, 220, 221–45, 249
    approaches to, 241
    defined, 223
    description of, in bible, 82
    quality of, 139n1
    technique used, 224–25
visual effects assistant editor credit, 269
visual effects associate credit, 268
visual effects coordinator credits, 268
visual effects specialists, 224–25
visual effects supervisor credit, 266, 267
visual effects team, 250
visual elements, 241
    assembly of, 247–55
    creation of, 247
visual environments, 122
visual image, 169, 170
visual quality, 171, 234
*Voyager*, 1n2, 19, 37, 122, 266, 278
V-takes, 242
Vulcans, 11n4, 70, 158n1, 190